THE DISCOVERY OF THE ARTIFICIAL

T0189467

THE DISCOVERY
OF THE ARTIFICIAL

Behavior, Mind and Machines Before and Beyond Cybernetics

by

ROBERTO CORDESCHI

University of Salerno, Salerno, Italy

KLUWER ACADEMIC PUBLISHERS
DORDRECHT / BOSTON / LONDON

A C.I.P. Catalogue record for this book is available from the Library of Congress.

ISBN 978-90-481-6015-0

Published by Kluwer Academic Publishers,
P.O. Box 17, 3300 AA Dordrecht, The Netherlands.

Sold and distributed in North, Central and South America
by Kluwer Academic Publishers,
101 Philip Drive, Norwell, MA 02061, U.S.A.

In all other countries, sold and distributed
by Kluwer Academic Publishers,
P.O. Box 322, 3300 AH Dordrecht, The Netherlands.

Printed on acid-free paper

CONTENTS

ACKNOWLEDGEMENTS

The author and the publishers would like to thank the following for permissions to reprint figures:

Indiana University Press for permission to reprint Figure 143 from the 1962 edition of H.S. Jennings, *Behavior of the Lower Organisms*, originally published by Columbia University Press, New York, 1906.

San Francisco Press for permission to reprint Figure 9 from B.F. Miessner, *On the Early History of Radio Guidance*, San Francisco, 1964.

Chapman and Hall for permission to reprint Figure 7.5.1 from W. Ross Ashby, *Design for a Brain*, 2nd edition, Wiley, New York, 1960.

Dover Publications, Inc. for permission to reprint Figure 3 and Figure 4 from the 1950 unabridged edition of W. James, *The Principles of Psychology*, originally published by Holt, New York, 1890; Figure 69 from A.J. Lotka, *Elements of Mathematical Biology*, New York, 1956 (1st edition, with the title *Elements of Physical Biology*, William and Wilkins, Baltimore, 1925).

Oxford University Press for permission to reprint Figure 2 from W. McDougall, A contribution towards an improvement in psychological method. II, *Mind*, 1898, 7: 159-178; Figure 1 from W. McDougall, The physiological factors of the attention-process. I, *Mind*, 1902, 11: 316-351.

University of Illinois Press for permission to reprint Figure 1 from J.M. Stephens, A mechanical explanation of the law of effect, *American Journal of Psychology*, 1929, 41: 422-431; Figure 5 from G.K. Bennett and L.B. Ward, A model of the synthesis of conditioned reflexes, *American Journal of Psychology*, 1933, 45: 339-342. Copyright © 1929, 1933 by the Board of Trustees of the University of Illinois.

Helen Dwight Reid Educational Foundation for permission to reprint Figure 2 from H.D. Baernstein and C.L. Hull, A mechanical model of the conditioned reflex, *Journal of General Psychology*, 1931, 5: 99-106; Figure 1 from R.G. Krueger and C.L. Hull, An electro-chemical parallel to the conditioned reflex, *Journal of General Psychology*, 1931, 5: 262-269; Figure 14 from N. Rashevsky, Possible brain mechanisms and their physical models, *Journal of General Psychology*, 1931, 5: 368-406; Figure 1 from D.G. Ellson, A mechanical synthesis of trial-and-error learning, *Journal of General Psychology*, 1935, 13: 212-218; Figure 1 from H Bradner, A new mechanical 'learner', *Journal of General Psychology*, 1937, 17: 414-419. Published by Heldref Publications, Washington. Copyright © 1931, 1935, 1937

The American Psychological Association for permission to reprint Figures 5 and 6 from C.L. Hull, Goal attraction and directing ideas conceived as habit phenomena, *Psychological Review*, 1931, 38: 487-506; the Figure from T. Ross, The synthesis of intelligence. Its implications, *Psychological Review*, 1938, 45: 185-189.

Cambridge University Press for permission to reprint Figure 15.2 from P.N. Johnson-Laird, *Mental Models*, Cambridge, 1983. Copyright © 1983 by P.N. Johnson-Laird.

The British Psychological Society for permission to reprint Figure 2 from A. Tustin, Do modern mechanisms help us to understand the mind?, *British Journal of Psychology*, 1953, 44: 24-37; Figure 1 from J.A Deutsch, A new type of behaviour theory, *British Journal of Psychology*, 1953, 44: 304-317.

Gernsback Publications, Inc. for permission to reprint the cover of *Radio Electronics*, December 1951, and Figure 6 from E.C. Berkeley, Algebra in electronic design, *Radio Electronics*, February1952: 55-58.

New Scientist for permission to reprint Figure 3 from A.M. Andrew, Machines which learn, *New Scientist*, 1958, n. 4: 1388-1391.

HMS0 for permission to reprint Figure 2 from F. Rosenblatt, Two theorems of statistical separability in the Perceptron, *Proceedings of the Teddington Symposium on Mechanisation of Thought Processes*, vol. 1, London, 1959: 421-450; Figure 1 from A.J. Angyan, *Machina reproducatrix*. An analogue model to demonstrate some aspects of neural adaptation, *Proceedings of the Teddington Symposium on Mechanisation of Thought Processes*, vol. 2, London, 1959: 933-943.

IEEE for permission to reprint Figure 1 from W.S. McCulloch, A.G. Oettinger, N. Rochester and O. Schmitt, The design of machines to simulate the behavior of the human brain, *IRE Transactions on Electronic Computers*, December 1956: 240-255; Figure 1 from P.L. Simmons and R.F. Simmons, The simulation of cognitive processes. An annotated bibliography, *IRE Transactions on Electronic Computers*, September 1961: 462-483. Copyright © 1956, 1961 by IRE (now IEEE).

Pearson Education, Inc. for permission to reprint Figure 2.1 from A. Newell and H.A. Simon, *Human Problem Solving*, Prentice-Hall, Englewood Cliffs, N.J., 1972.

The McGraw-Hill Companies for permission to reprint Figure 1 from H.A. Simon, The control of mind by reality: human cognition and problem solving, in S.M. Farber and R.H.L. Wilson (eds.), *Man and Civilization*, New York, 1961.

Josiah Macy, Jr. Foundation for permission to reprint Figure 8 from H. von Foerster (ed.), *Cybernetics. Circular Causal Feedback Mechanisms in Biological and Social Sys-*

tems. Transactions of the Tenth Conference, New York, 1953.

Intellect Books for permission to reprint Table 3.2 from J.A. Barnden and J.B. Pollack (eds.), *High-Level Connectionism Models*, originally published by Ablex, Norwood, N.J., 1991.

MIT Press for permission to reprint Figure 2 from G. Tesauro, Neural models of classical conditioning: a theoretical viewpoint, in S.J. Hanson and C.R. Olson (eds.), *Connectionist Modeling and Brain Function*, Cambridge, Mass., 1990: 74-104; Figure 1 from J.-A. Meyer and A. Guillot, Four years of animat research, *From Animals to Animats 3*, Cambridge, Mass., 1994: 2-11.

The American Association for the Advancement of Science and the Authors for permission to reprint Figure 2, C_1-C_3 from R.D. Hawkins, T.W Abrams, T.J. Carew and E.R Kandel, A cellular mechanism of classical conditioning in *Aplysia*: activity-dependent amplification of presynaptic facilitation, *Science*, 1983, 219: 400-405. Copyright © 1983 by American Association for the Advancement of Science.

Plenum Publishers for permission to reprint Figure 5 from A. Gelperin, J.J. Hopfield and D.W. Tank, The logic of *Limax* learning, in A. Selverston (ed.), *Model Neural Networks and Behavior*, New York, 1985: 237-261.

The author and the publishers have made very effort to contact authors/copyright holders of the material reprinted in the present book. This has not been possible in all cases, and we would welcome correspondence from those individuals/companies we have been unable to trace.

ACKNOWLEDGMENTS

INTRODUCTION

The neurones concerned in the behavior of a single man probably exceed in number by a thousand-fold all the telephone lines in the world [...] Even if we knew the exact arrangement of each neuron in a man's brain it would take a model as large as St. Paul's Cathedral to make them visible to the naked eye (E.L. Thorndike, 1914; 1919).

To make a model which would reproduce all the behavior of a rat would require a mechanism probably as large as the Capitol in Washington (C.L. Hull, 1935).

A large building could not house a vacuum tube computer with as many relays as a man has in his head, and it would take Niagara Falls to supply the power and Niagara River to cool it. ENIAC with some 10000 tubes has no more relays than a flat worm (W.S. McCulloch, 1949).

The 'discovery' in the title of this book refers to the coming of age of a new concept of the machine. This concept is at the core of a methodology that profoundly influenced the sciences of the mind and behavior in the twentieth century. The main ambition of this methodology was to overcome, through that new concept of the machine, traditional oppositions between the inorganic and organic worlds, between the laws that govern the behavior of physical systems and those that govern the behavior of organisms, and between causal and teleological explanation.

The origins of this methodology are usually traced back to the middle of the 1940s, with the advent of cybernetics, which Norbert Wiener described, in his 1948 book, as the study of "control and communication in the animal and the machine." That is when the new machines, those equipped with automatic control and with forms, albeit primitive, of self-organization, seemed to suggest a way to escape those oppositions. Mechanical models were built to simulate adaptive behavior as well as various forms of learning of living organisms. The concepts of machine and teleology no longer seemed incompatible.

The fundamental insight of cybernetics, i.e. the proposal of a unified study of organisms and machines, was inherited, starting in the mid-1950s, by AI (Artificial Intelligence). However, AI proposed a different simulative methodology. To put it quite generally, this methodology used computer programs to reproduce performances which, if observed in human beings, would be regarded as intelligent. In the course of the quarter-century that followed, many cybernetics research programmes were cut back, if not altogether abandoned, in the face of the early successes of AI. This is recent history, and still more recent is the history of the revival of some cybernetic projects in the changed context of the 1980s. This revival brought about renewed interest in self-organizing systems, neural nets and connectionism, and influenced later developments in ALife (Artificial Life) and behavior-based and evolutionary robotics.

Some of the main points in this recent history are dealt with in Chapters 5 and 6 of the present book. One of my central claims is that certain basic features of the simulative methodology whose origins are usually put no further back than cybernetics, actually go back in significant ways to the early decades of the twentieth century. In the first four chapters of the book, while examining little-known, if not forgotten or unpublished, texts of the pre-cybernetic age, I investigate various projects involving artifacts that were considered to be mechanical models of organisms' behavior. I identify in those projects what Marvin Minsky called the "intellectual ancestors" of cybernetics, when he dated the latter's public emergence to the nearly simultaneous appearance, in 1943, of Rosenblueth, Wiener and Bigelow's paper on the teleological features of feedback machines, of McCulloch and Pitts' paper on neural nets, and of Craik's modeling approach in *The Nature of Explanation*. As a result of my investigation, the simulative approaches of the second half of the twentieth century should appear, in Chapters 5 and 6, in a light that should make it easier to grasp those elements, both of continuity and discontinuity, that they share with earlier stages in the discovery of the artificial.

In Chapter 1, taking my cue from the disagreement between Jacques Loeb and Herbert Jennings in the study of animal behavior at the beginning of the twentieth century, I bring to light some features of the discovery of the artificial. We shall see how, alongside the traditional opposition between reductionist and vitalist approaches in the study of organisms' behavior, another approach is adumbrated, in which the behavior of both "inorganic machines" and living organisms can be studied by referring to their functional organization. Furthermore, with the development of new technologies, it is suggested that a positive test for a behavioral theory is provided by building a machine that functions as the theory predicts. According to Loeb, the phototropic automaton (or "electric dog") built by John Hammond Jr. and Benjamin Miessner was precisely an "artificial machine" of this kind: it supported his own theory of phototropism in living organisms or "natural machines." As we shall see, Loeb's theory prompted the design or actual building of several phototropic robots: from Edward Tolman's "schematic sowbug" up to Walter Grey Walter's electronic "tortoises" and Valentino Braitenberg's "vehicles."

The heated disputes of Loeb's days about the opposition, in the study of animal behavior, between the world of intelligence and purpose on the one hand, and that of instincts and automatism on the other, now seem very distant. The same might be said of other more radical disputes, like that between vitalism and mechanism. And yet, various issues that were raised then with regard to both lower and higher animals were later raised with regard to machines. (After all, this is not by chance: had animals not been formerly considered as the true *automata*, lacking purposes and intentionality?) Think, for example, of issue of the legitimacy of describing animals in mentalistic or teleological terms or, if you like, of assuming towards them what Daniel Dennett calls the "intentional stance." As Jennings put it in 1906, "this [kind of description] is useful; it enables us practically to appreciate, foresee, and control [the] actions [of the animals] much more readily than we could otherwise do so."

Various issues recurring in those disputes are dealt with in Chapter 2. Early neurological and psychological associationism and connectionism (a term, it should be remembered, introduced by Edward Thorndike) is the framework for my analysis of early attempts to test hypotheses about the nature of memory, adaptation and learning through mechanical models. This kind of theory testing in the behavioral sciences appeared to the psychologist J.M. Stephens as a genuine *discovery*, when in 1929 he wrote about his "surprise" at finding the "startling possibilities" of building a working artifact embodying the hypotheses of his theory of learning. And the engineer S. Bent Russell, in discussing his mechanical model of simple forms of learning, had already pointed out that "as the cooperation of workers in different fields of knowledge is necessary in these days of specialists it may be argued that engineers can consistently join [with neurologists] in the consideration of a subject of such importance to man" as it is the study of nervous system. Bent Russell made this suggestion in 1913, about thirty years before the advent of cybernetics, and Wiener would have appreciated his words.

The "robot approach," promoted by Clark Hull in the context of behaviorism in the 1920s and 1930s, develops along the lines suggested by Bent Russell. The robot approach is the subject of Chapter 3. In this case, one is for the first time in the presence of a coherent research programme with an openly interdisciplinary calling, and of a fully aware simulative or modeling methodology, which raised the hope of progressively building 'intelligent' machines. Nicolas Rashevsky, who initially showed interest in Hull's approach, wrote in 1931 that a machine might be made that could not only express itself in a natural language and carry on a conversation but could also learn a language and even lie intentionally—even if the actual construction of such a machine would have taken "tremendous expense and labor."

In Chapter 4, I examine Kenneth Craik's position between Hull's robot approach and the new-born cybernetics, and discuss Craik's symbolic theory of thought. I also emphasize how various proposals for 'reconciling' natural science and teleology were discussed before the advent of cybernetics. These proposals appear to have been influenced by their author's acquaintance with some self-regulating artifacts, which were explicitly defined as *teleological* in the above-mentioned 1943 paper by Rosenblueth, Wiener and Bigelow.

I have already alluded to the content of Chapters 5 and 6, in which the notion of artificial as *computational* or *algorithmic*, not merely as *inorganic*, comes into focus with the advent of AI. Finally, in Chapter 7, while bringing out the main thread running through my entire investigation, I state some theses that I believe have characterized the different stages in the discovery of the artificial over the course of the twentieth century. I use these theses to identify the points of convergence and divergence between the different approaches and research trends discussed in my investigation, with the aim of understanding major critical points better. Furthermore, I try to identify in those theses the roots of certain conflicting positions that are still being debated today in much cognitive science and philosophy of mind, concerning, for example, functionalism, the role of representations, and intentional vocabulary.

The present book is not concerned with the history of those automata or robots that were built or imagined before the twentieth century. On the one hand, that history has already been told several times and from various points of view; on the other hand, the 'artificial' as understood in the present book is quite remote from the clockwork automata which were especially popular during the eighteenth century. Notwithstanding certain important intuitions of people like Jaques de Vaucanson, such automata could hardly be seen as pre-cybernetic machines endowed with actual sense organs, self-controlling or feedback devices and motor organs. They could not 'adjust' their responses to incoming stimuli. As for self-controlling automata, their early history was first carefully reconstructed by Otto Mayr. These machines are linked to the discovery of the artificial in so far as they exhibit some form of reactive behavior and, albeit in fairly elementary forms, some ability to change their internal organization when interacting with the environment on the basis of their previous 'history.' Hence, these machine exhibit different forms of adaptation, memory, and learning. However, machines of this kind, as well as other artifacts such as computer programs or contemporary mobile robots, are here chiefly analyzed as tools for theoretical investigations into intelligent behavior.

In fact, there are three stories, as it were, that are told in the present book. First, there is the story of building artifacts of different kinds and complexity whose behaviors, if exhibited by organisms, would be regarded as 'adapted,' 'learned,' 'intelligent,' and so forth. Second, there is the story of the attempts to build artifacts that could be considered as tools for building and testing theories about those behaviors. Third, there is the story of the gradually developing discussion about the implications of the first two stories for classical epistemological questions, the mind-body problem, the possibility of scientific theorizing about cognition, and the like. These three stories proceed in parallel, and I have tried to bring out salient conceptual connections between them.

Progress in electronics and computer science and technology allow current modeling approaches to obtain results that inevitably make pre-cybernetic machines, which play a leading role in much of the present book, seem rough and extravagant. These machines almost always are electrical circuits or electro-mechanical robots with fairly simple performances. Nonetheless, the wealth of interesting issues surrounding early stages of the discovery of the artificial is surprising. The present book shows how, with regard to different notions of the machine, many problems were raised which are still being dealt with by scientists and philosophers of mind currently working on organism's behavior and the human mind.

In fact, those pre-cybernetic machines, just like those of the cybernetic age and those in several current areas of research, were aimed at simulating *functions*, rather than at reproducing the *external appearances* of living organisms. The flight analogy argument ("if material is organized in a certain way, it will fly like an eagle; if it is organized in another way, it will fly like an airplane") was already stated by Hull, and would later recur in AI. Since many of those pre-cybernetic machines were built with the ambitious aim of testing hypotheses on organism behavior, they were designed to be working models embodying *theories*, whether psychological or neurological, about behavior. They neither surprise nor seduce us because of the fairly realistic appearance that characterized the automata of former centuries, which chiefly imitated the outward appearance of animals and human beings. On the contrary, their goal is an avowedly non-mimetic one. A behaviorist model of learning by conditioning does not have to salivate like Pavlov's dog; rather, it has to grasp some of the *essential features* of the learning phenomenon. As we shall see, this was the goal underlying the building of simulative models of behavior, a goal clearly stated from the outset: from the days of Hull and his early attempts to simulate conditioned reflex by means of electro-mechanical artifacts, continuing through the days of Grey Walter and his electronic tortoises, and up to much current AI and robotics.

Some of the pre-cybernetic machines described in the present book were rather carefully designed, as can be seen in the neat drawings by Bent Russell, or in the circuit diagrams by Norman Krim. Other machines are known to us through rough drawings, like those by Rashevsky, or through rather involved descriptions, like that of Hugh Bradner's mobile robot, or through informal descriptions, like that of Tolman's schematic sowbug. Still other machines were actually built, including those by Krim himself, by Hammond Jr. and Miessner, by H.D. Baernstein, and by Thomas Ross. Exhibited to the public, they were immediately dubbed "intelligent" or "thinking" machines.

The use of these mental terms in the case of machines that today seem so rudimentary stimulates reflections on their public impact and the exaggeration of their actual intelligent abilities—a phenomenon that occurred again and again until more recent times. A "thinking machine" was how William Ross Ashby's homeostat was called in the 1940s, and the very expression used for the first digital computers—"electronic brains"—speaks volumes in this regard. We can well imagine that, when Baernstein's electrical model of conditioned reflex was exhibited at the 1929 Convention of the Midwest Psychological Association, the impression it created was no less than the one created when Grey Walter's electronic tortoises were exhibited at the 1951 Festival of Britain, or when Arthur Samuel's computer program, which played successfully a game of checkers, was exhibited on the 1960 CBS television show *The Thinking Machine*—let alone the recent triumphs of chess-playing programs like Deep Blue, or the World Cup Robot Soccer competitions.

Quite different albeit related considerations could be made in the case of the new 'intelligent' war-machines from the very outset during the First World War. In 1915, for example, the radio-controlled torpedo embodying the simple self-orientation mechanism of Hammond Jr. and Miessner's electric dog was said "to inherit almost superhuman intelligence." The electric dog, initially a "scientific curiosity," Miessner remarked in 1916, "may within the very near future become in truth a real 'dog of war,' without fear, without heart, without the human element so often susceptible to trickery, with but one purpose: to overtake and slay whatever comes within range of its senses at the will of its master." Current development of 'intelligent' weapons make this observation fairly prophetic. And it reminds Wiener's worried judgment on those machines that, as far as their purposeful activity transcend the limitations of the human designer, "may be both effective and dangerous." As Wiener concluded in 1960, the designer could be unable to control a machine whose goal-seeking operation is so fast and irrevocable that, once he become aware that machine's final action has undesired consequences, he had not the time and the data to intervene before such an action is complete.

Various aspects of the discovery of the artificial that are emphasized in the present book have been mostly neglected in investigations on the sciences of the mind and behavior in the twentieth century. A number of authors who play leading roles in this book are not even mentioned or have only a small role in those investigations. Psychologists like Max Meyer or Stephens, let alone engineers or technicians such as Hammond Jr., Miessner, Bent Russell, or Ross, are cases in point. Other authors, who are usually presented as leading figures in the research of the period, are examined in this book in order to bring to light less-known aspects of their research, as in the case of Hull's robot approach or Jennings' views on "inorganic machines." Still other authors, who are towering figures, and justly so, in the usual investigations, are considered here chiefly in order to bring to light internal tensions in their views. The scanty hydraulic analogies of nervous conduction that William James inherited from Herbert Spencer and handed down to William McDougall are an appropriate case in point. Clearly, analogies have an important role in any scientific enterprise. Mechanical analogies for nervous functions, however, occupy a secondary position in the present book, compared to the, albeit naive, *working models* of such functions which were designed or physically realized. Those analogies are discussed in some sections of the present book because examining them allows one to clarify the context in which attempts to build those working models were made; furthermore, they constitute a neglected chapter in the history of psychology and neurology at the threshold of the twentieth century.

Working models or functioning artifacts, rather than scanty analogies, are at the core of the discovery of the artificial, and in two important ways. First, only such models, and not the analogies, can be viewed as tools for testing hypotheses on organism behavior. The way to establish the possibility that complex forms of behavior are not necessarily peculiar to living organisms is "to realize [this possibility] by actual trial," as Hull wrote in 1931 about his own models of learning. And Craik, in *The Nature of Explanation*, contrasted Hull's approach to mechanical models with former, vague "mechanistic views of life and behavior"; in the latter case, "on one hand there has been a tendency to *assert* a mechanistic theory rather than to regard it as a hypothesis which should, if followed out, indicate how and where it breaks down; and on the other hand, there has been little attempt to formulate a definite plan of a mechanism which would fulfill the requirements."

The second way in which working models, rather than analogies, are at the heart of the discovery of the artificial can also be introduced by means of Craik's words: "Any kind of working model of a process is, in a sense, an analogy. Being different it is bound somewhere to break down by showing properties not found in the process it imitates or by not possessing properties possessed by the process it imitates." This is a fundamental statement in the discovery of the artificial: behavioral models themselves can be *tested*. The same point was stated by Grey Walter: "If in the testing [models] fall short of expectation or reality, they do so without equivocation. The model hypothesis cannot bend of flow—it breaks with a loud crack—and from the pieces one can build a better model." And Donald MacKay stated that when a discrepancy between the behavioral model and empirical data is detected, one tries to modify the model in some respect, giving rise to a process of model testing and revision. Behavioral models, Herbert Simon has remarked, "are multicomponent creatures, and when our data don't fit the model, we are faced with a difficult diagnostic task to determine what to change—or whether to discard the entire model." As we shall see, a related and crucial issue is which *constraints*, and how severe, models should satisfy in order to be counted as explanatory tools. In Simon's words, "the important question is not whether we are imitating, but whether in fact the imitation *explains* the phenomenon."

The aim of the present book is not to provide a complete reconstruction of the various chapters in twentieth century neurology, psychology and philosophy of mind, but rather to identify some turning points marking the progressive, albeit discontinuous and

tortuous, discovery of the artificial. An effort will be made, however, to present these turning points in their actual contexts, not only to make them more comprehensible, but also to avoid slipping into anachronistic talk of anticipation. Otherwise, the discovery of
the artificial would boil down to a catalogue of elementary artifacts and robots: once sev-
ered from the context that influenced their construction or evaluation, these would not
seem credible bearers of new methodological proposals, distant as they are in time and
from current technology.

Even if these pitfalls are avoided, some readers might still remain dumbfounded by
the mentalistic interpretations that some designers put on the behavior of their pre-cybernetic machines. One of these machines is said to 'learn,' just because the resistance
changes in an electric connection; another is said to 'choose,' just because it automatically opens, or closes, a switch in a circuit. But to use Douglas Hofstadter's words, it is
hard to go back and imagine the feeling of those who first saw toothed wheels, hydraulic
valves or electrical circuits showing abilities that had been considered exclusive to living organisms. In addition to their being systematically overrated by the public, as already
mentioned, simulative methodologies seem bound to meet the following fate: mentalistic descriptions of the artifacts turn out not to be satisfying in the end, and what seems
'intelligent' behavior melts away as soon as it is reproduced in an artifact and becomes,
for that very reason, 'automatic.' Behaviorist models seemed trivially simple to those cyberneticians who were aware of them; cybernetic artifacts seemed intrinsically naive to
the builders of early intelligent computer programs; and the latter seemed stupid to some
of their successors in AI. "AI is whatever hasn't been done yet," was the paradoxical definition reported by Hofstadter.

The discovery of the artificial cannot readily be construed as a cumulative undertaking. At the start, it is the history of isolated efforts, with little contact among its leading
promoters. One exception is Hull's robot approach, but that was an experiment that
spanned a very short time and whose rapid eclipse, as we shall see, is perhaps exemplary. It is in the 1940s and 1950s that a real turning point comes about in the discovery of
the artificial, as a consequence of the rise of computer science and technology, and of automatic control. The diagram below, made by P.L. Simmons and R.F. Simmons in 1960,
shows the growth rate in a representative sample of 330 articles and books devoted to
behavioral models realized as mathematical simulations, electronic analogs or computer simulations between the end of the 1920s and 1959. In this diagram, the short initial
segment of the curve, up to the point corresponding to 1941, would include those isolated attempts at simulative modeling that took place at the outset of the discovery of the
artificial, and that are extensively dealt with in the present book (some of them are included in the sample). The publication of Wiener's *Cybernetics* in 1948 coincides with
an early peak in the curve, which increases exponentially after 1956, the year of the official birth of AI. In fact, it is beginning with these two dates that the modeling method
takes on recognized importance in the community of behavioral scientists, to the point
that one begins to speak of the "sciences of the artificial," as Simon put it in the title of
his 1969 book. And yet experimentation in the field of the artificial does not become cumulative for this reason. Rather, competing research programmes have coexisted or have

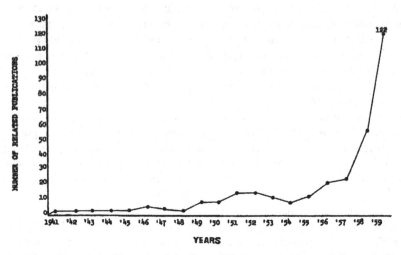

up to now alternated with each other: from different research trends in symbolic AI to current connectionism and neural net approaches and the '*nouvelle*' AI, which includes ALife and different trends in current robotics and synthetic modeling.

To sum up, the discovery of the artificial shares the model-building strategy that is pervasive in other provinces of science. The traditional sciences of the mind—psychology and neurology—addressed during the first half of the twentieth century issues concerning the experimental method and the building and testing of theories of organism behavior and mental life. The earliest behavioral models, designed as simple physical analogs, began to suggest that there might exist a *new* level for testing psychological and neurological hypotheses, one that might coexist alongside the investigations into overt behavior and the nervous system. This was the core idea of what Hull and Craik had already called the "synthetic method," the method of model building. This idea comes fully into focus with the advent of cybernetics, and especially when the pioneers of AI, who wanted to turn their discipline into a new science of the mind, found themselves coming to grips with the traditional sciences of the mind—psychology and neurology—and with their conflicting relationships. That event radically affected the customary taxonomies of the sciences of the mind. From that moment on, the question has explicitly been asked as to what the *right* level of abstraction for constructing explanatory models of mental life might be. Is it the level of 'symbols,' as proposed by classical AI, or that of 'neurons,' as proposed by new connectionism, or those of the genotype and evolutionary and developmental processes, as proposed by ALife, behavior-based and evolutionary robotics and synthetic modeling? And how well-founded are these distinctions?

Although our view of the machine has significantly changed, and is still changing before our eyes, every machine, once taken as a model, is inevitably a simplification of the simulated phenomenon, albeit in relation to the chosen level (or levels) of abstraction. "To what degree is the Rock of Gibraltar a model of the brain?," Ashby once wondered. And he answered, "It persists; so does the brain; they are isomorphic at the lowest level." In fact, the strategy of mental life models faces an unavoidable watershed. It can be maintained that these simplifications do not fatally impoverish the object being studied, once the right levels of abstraction have been found—that they are not "oversimplifications," as Craik put it. Or it can be held that the scientific study of mental life is bound to fail because of the very fact that it makes use of simplifications. In the latter case, hermeneutic or phenomenological intelligibility criteria might be preferred in the study of mind.

I believe that the latter position must face its own difficulties. The final test for models, however, is in the range of phenomena they actually contribute to explaining. The strategy of mental life modeling often raised hopes that it was unable to meet during its history. Nonetheless, this very history provides several lessons for contemporary research, and a wealth of experimental data has been made available that suggests how to establish novel links among the sciences concerned with mental life. The present book tries to document the hopes, defeats and successes in the midst of which the modeling strategy has its origin and growth.

Guides to the discovery of the artificial do exist, and I would like to mention them. Minsky's bibliography in *Computers and Thought*, the classic volume edited in 1963 by Edward Feigenbaum and Julian Feldman, is still extremely useful. The above-mentioned bibliography by P.L. Simmons and R.F. Simmons, "The Simulation of Cognitive Processes. An Annotated Bibliography," in *IRE Transactions on Electronic Computers*, 1961: 462-483; 1962: 535-552, is indispensable. Useful information is contained in various papers and books on cybernetics and the philosophy of psychology in the 1940s and 1950s, such as those by Edwin Boring, F.H. George, T.N. Nemes and Wladislaw Sluckin (these are all included in the list of references, as are other works and authors mentioned above). More than a guide is the set of four volumes edited by Ronald Chrisley, *Artificial Intelligence: Critical Concepts*, Routledge, London and New York, 2000, which collects a number of papers of interest for the discovery of the artificial and its development in the twentieth century.

Unlike other books, such as Martin Gardner's *Logic Machines and Diagrams*, which focuses on logic machines, the present book hardly mentions such machines, except in passing, being more interested in the psychological and neurological use of machines as behavioral models or as tools for understanding mental life. The very selection of the authors discussed here often shows the effects of that interest. As for the decades prior to the cybernetic age, those who tackled the subject of mechanical analogies and "inorganic machines" in the context of the synthetic method were, above all, behaviorist psychologists and neurologists or, before them, scientists and philosophers who had raised the issue of neuro-psychological mechanism.

To facilitate the reading of the book, I have confined to Plates the descriptions of how most machines work. To expedite their interpretation, I have occasionally provided simplified diagrams of some machines. The Plates are not necessary to an understanding of the text, and can be skipped by the reader who is not interested in the details of how those machines work. Most Plates on pre-cybernetic machines contain figures that have never been republished, unless in my earlier articles, or that have never been published at all, like those by Krim.

While writing various essays on the discovery of the artificial during past years, I have had the advantage of discussing the issues addressed in the book with several friends and colleagues, to whom I wish to express my gratitude. Vittorio Somenzi, together with pioneers such as Antonio Borsellino, Valentino Braitenberg, Eduardo Caianiello, Silvio Ceccato and Augusto Gamba, introduced several Italian researchers to cybernetics and AI, and to related philosophical problems in the study of mental life. He has profoundly influenced my training and my research. Giuseppe Trautteur has followed the writing of the book from its very beginning, giving a careful critical reading to its various versions. Ernesto Burattini and Marino Giannini helped me to achieve a better understanding of various points regarding some of the early machine models. Luigia Carlucci Aiello, Massimo Negrotti, Stefano Nolfi, Israel Rosenfield, Guglielmo Tamburrini and Achille Varzi were available on various occasions to read the manuscript and to discuss the issues dealt with in it. Pietro Corsi, Luciano Mecacci and Laurence Smith generously assisted me with their knowledge of the history of psychology and neuroscience. Different chapters of the book were read and usefully commented on by Luciano Floridi, Simone Gozzano, Marcello Frixione, Salvatore Guccione, Domenico Parisi, Silvano Tagliagambe, Settimo Termini and Graziella Tonfoni. Needless to say, none of these is responsible for any error or opinion, even though I have profited from their suggestions and criticism.

Last, but definitely not least, I am indebted to the late Herb Simon for carefully commenting on chapters of the book and for discussing points where our judgement differed. In discussions, he always forced you to go to the heart of a question. His scorn for philosophical disputes not grounded on a "solid body of fact" was only equal to that for idealized models in science that are unable to grasp the complexity of real phenomena.

To write this book has required no small number of visits to libraries around the world. These have been made possible by various grants made available by both the Italian Ministry of University and Scientific and Technological Research (MURST) and the National Research Council (CNR).

SERIES PREFACE

This series will include monographs and collections of studies devoted to the investigation and exploration of knowledge, information, and data processing systems of all kinds, no matter whether human, (other) animal, or machine. Its scope is intended to span the full range of interests from classical problems in the philosophy of mind and philosophical psychology through issues in cognitive psychology and sociobiology (concerning the mental capabilities of other species) to ideas related to artificial intelligence and to computer science. While primary emphasis will be placed upon theoretical, conceptual, and epistemological aspects of these problems and domains, empirical, experimental, and methodological studies will also appear from time to time.

The present volume offers a broad and imaginative approach to the study of the mind, which emphasizes several themes, namely: the importance of functional organization apart from the specific material by means of which it may be implemented; the use of modeling to simulate these functional processes and subject them to certain kinds of tests; the use of mentalistic language to describe and predict the behavior of artifacts; and the subsumption of processes of adaptation, learning, and intelligence by means of explanatory principles. The author has produced a rich and complex, lucid and readable discussion that clarifies and illuminates many of the most difficult problems arising within this difficult domain.

J.H.F.

SERIES PREFACE

CHAPTER 1

CHEMICAL MACHINES AND ACTION SYSTEMS

1. Introduction. Living organisms and machines

Jacques Loeb's investigations into the behavior of numerous lower organisms are justly famous. In particular, he carefully documented the way in which the orientation of bilaterally symmetrical lower animals depended on light, i.e. phototropism, a phenomenon that the botanist Julius Sachs had studied in plants. And Loeb's systematic monograph, *Comparative Physiology of the Brain and Comparative Psychology* published at the dawn of the twentieth century (Loeb, 1900), made his work popular with researchers in various fields.

The moth that infallibly flies towards a light source always brings to mind the explanation offered by Loeb: the muscles on the side of the animal struck by the light become more active than those on the opposite side. Hence the moth tends to orient its plane of symmetry in the direction of the light source and move towards it (a case of "positive heliotropism," see Figure 1.1). Thus the fact that the moth flies into the flame "turns out to be the same mechanical process as that by which the axis of the stem of a plant puts itself in the direction of the rays of light" (Loeb, 1905: 3). So Loeb concluded that organisms like this are nothing other than "chemical machines," and specifically "heliotropic natural machines."

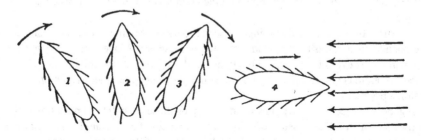

Fig. 1.1. Positive heliotropism (from Jennings, 1906).

Loeb soon generalized the results of his experimental studies in an attempt to establish a "mechanistic conception of life" that left no room for any explanation of the action of organisms, from the simplest all the way up to man, that was not expressed in "mechanical process" terms. This explanation could be as complicated as you wished, but would be qualitatively indistinguishable from explanation in physics and chemistry. Not only most animal instincts but also the "voluntary" actions of humans ought to be reducible to tropisms, and these in turn ought to be reducible to the physical and chemical properties of living protoplasm. Loeb realized that this was a long way to achieve a "complete" mechanistic view of life, i.e. one that could explain consciousness and free will in terms of physics and chemistry. Nonetheless, he reaffirmed his conviction that the study of simple organisms as heliotropic machines could lay the groundwork for understanding complex organisms (Loeb, 1912: 35).

In those same years the difficulties implicit in such a radical claim lent plausibility to very different approaches to the same problems. These approaches were developed not only by vitalist biologists such as Hans Driesch but also by who, without adopting extreme forms of reductionism, did not give up trying to find a mechanical explanation of the behavior of living organisms. Herbert Jennings was one of these. His ideas too gained popularity through a book, published a few years after Loeb's, *The Behavior of the Lower Organisms*, in which Jennings summed up his earlier investigations (Jennings, 1906). The simple organisms studied by Jennings, such as the *Paramecium* and the *Stentor*, are no less familiar to biologists and psychologists than Loeb's moth. But in Jenning's view, they display substantially different behavior.

It was Jennings who later radicalized the contrast with Loeb. Instead of the "synthetic" method inspired by radical reductionism that he ascribed to Loeb, Jennings proposed his "analytical" method, based on the study of the ways in which organism and environment, considered as a single system, interact. For Jennings this meant that the behavior of organisms cannot be reduced to tropisms or chains or hierarchies of tropisms. Even lower organisms could not always be studied directly as chemical machines reacting passively to the external environment. Instead, there were general laws regulating the behavior of organisms that could be discovered by observing how organisms are influenced by the environment and how they in turn influence the environment by following different adaptive strategies, depending on the complexity of the action system at their disposal.

The rift between Loeb and Jennings arose in the area of the study of lower organisms. Although interest in this kind of study soon flagged, the issues faced were among those that marked the evolution of influential trends in the sciences of the mind and behavior in the twentieth century, especially with the emergence and then the dissolution of behaviorist psychology.

A goodly number of these issues stand out among those we will be considering in the following chapters. These issues will come up from a less familiar angle in the present chapter, where they will be considered in relation to the different machine models that Loeb and Jennings proposed in their investigations of lower animals. Alongside the reductionist stance in the study of organism behavior, there is another stance, for which the behavior of "inorganic" machines and that of living organisms as well can be studied by referring to their functional organization.

Consistent with this stance is the thesis that in the control and prediction of the behavior of living organisms, starting with the lower animals, it is impossible to do without a teleological and mentalistic vocabulary, one that uses the terms 'meaning,' 'purpose,' 'choice,' 'intelligence,' and so on. The question arises whether this language can legitimately be used outside the world of living organisms, namely, in the world of inorganic nature and machines, a question which will arise again and again in the following chapters and which has been a much-debated issue among philosophers of mind. Actually, the possibility that the same regulatory principles that find their most complex realization in the behavior of living organisms are also at work in the world of the inorganic lays the groundwork for a reconciliation of the teleological and the causal explanation.

2. Loeb and the orientation mechanisms of Hammond: "natural" and "artificial" machines

In the years round 1915 it was not unusual to read in American newspapers and popular science magazines alike the description of a machine that looked like little more than a toy but attracted much attention for its unprecedented features as an "orientation mechanism." It was designed in 1912 by John Hammond Jr. and Benjamin Miessner and constructed by the latter, who introduced it two years later in the *Purdue Engineering Review* under the name by which it became popularly known, the "electric dog." It is worth looking at how Miessner described the behavior of such a machine in his book *Radiodynamics: The Wireless Control of Torpedoes and Other Mechanisms.*

This orientation mechanism in its present form consists of a rectangular box about three feet long, one and a half feet wide, and one foot high. This box contains all the instruments and mechanism, and is mounted on three wheels, two of which are geared to a driving motor, and the third, on the rear end, is so mounted that its bearings can be turned by electromagnets in a horizontal plane. Two five-inch condensing lenses on the forward end appear very much like large eyes. If a portable electric light be turned on in front of the machine it will immediately begin to move toward the light, and, moreover, will follow that light all around the room in many complex manoeuvers at a speed of about three feet per second. The smallest circle in which it will turn is of about ten feet diameter; this is due to the limiting motion of the steering wheel, moving so long as the light reaches the condensing lenses in sufficient intensity. Upon shading or switching off the light the dog can be stopped immediately, but it will resume its course behind the moving light so long as the light reaches the condensing lenses in sufficient intensity (Miessner, 1916: 194-196).

Figure 1.2 shows what this phototropic robot looked like, and Plate 1.1 describes the way the orientation mechanism worked. The explanation of its working, Miessner stressed, was "very similar to that given by Jacques Loeb, the biologist, of reasons re-

Fig. 1.2. Hammond and Miessner's phototropic robot. Left, the robot follows a flashlight beam; right, the inside of the robot (from Miessner, 1916; also published in *Electrical Experimenter*, 1915).

Plate 1.1

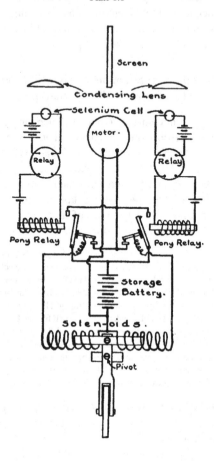

The orientation mechanism of Hammond's "electric dog" possesses two selenium cells, which, when influenced by light, effect the control of two sensitive relays. These relays in turn control two electromagnetic switches which effect the following operations: when one cell or both are illuminated, the current is switched onto the driving motor; when one cell alone is illuminated, an electromagnet is energized and effects the turning of the rear steering wheel. In this case, the resultant turning of the machine will be such as to bring the shaded cell into the light. As soon and as long as both cells are equally illuminated in sufficient intensity, the machine moves in a straight line towards the light source. By throwing a switch, which reverses the driving motor's connections, the machine can be made to back away from the light. When the intensity of the illumination is so decreased by the increasing distance from the light source that the resistances of the cells approach their dark resistance, the sensitive relays break their respective circuits, and the machine stops. (From Miessner, 1916)

sponsible for the flight of moths into a flame." In particular the lenses corresponded to "the two sensitive organs of the moth" (p. 196). Miessner explained the main reason for interest in this automatic device: Hammond's dirigible torpedo "is fitted with apparatus similar to that of the electric dog, so that if the enemy turns their search light on it, it will immediately be guided toward that enemy automatically" (p. 198).

This use as war material should not come as a surprise. At the time Europe was engulfed in the war that would come to be known as the First World War. Hammond and Miessner pioneered the study of radio-controlled mechanisms and then target-seeking automatic systems. Several of their patents made a fortune during both world wars. At the time Hammond was already famous for the dirigible torpedo described by Miessner, which, in effect, was a remote control radio-directed boat. The *Electrical Experimenter* gave an enthusiastic description of the device in 1915 and pointed out its possible military uses as an "intelligent" weapon (it seems to have "almost superhuman intelligence"), finding it one of the more "hair-raising inventions" so far employed "in the present titanic struggle for the supremacy of Europe."[1]

Efforts had already been made to construct wireless controlled systems, partly for military use. Miessner himself had reconstructed and reported that story for *Scientific American*, and the latest advances in technology seemed about to make their construction a reality (Miessner, 1912). Since 1910 Hammond had been running a research laboratory in Gloucester, Massachusetts, where, attracting increasing attention from the military, he was perfecting his radio-controlled torpedoes. Miessner was one of his main collaborators in the years 1911 and 1912 and wrote a long description of these devices for *Radiodynamics*, in which he also referred to earlier work, in particular the so-called "teleautomata" or "self-acting automata" built in New York between 1892 and 1897 by Nikola Tesla, another pioneer of radio-controlled systems.

But the collaborative efforts of Hammond and Miessner were short-lived. Miessner was convinced that his work in Gloucester had not received the recognition it deserved, and the two men quarrelled over the priority of various patents and inventions. Miessner gave his version of this story in a book published decades later, *On the Early History of Radio Guidance* (Miessner, 1964).[2] He said that "Hammond tried desperately to stop its [*Radiodynamics*] publication, by intimidating the publisher and myself, and by appealing to the War Department on grounds of security" (p. 42). One of the bones of contention was priority in the invention of the electric dog. Miessner claimed that his contribution was decisive for the actual design and construction and mentioned some of his earlier insights as well as a sketch Hammond drew in 1912 (Figure 1.3). Miessner also remarked that "Hammond had been much taken with the writings of Jacques Loeb" (p. 36).

Miessner considered the automatic orientation mechanism he designed for the elec-

---

[1] The magazine reported the interest of both American and Japanese governments in acquiring the patent (*Electrical Experimenter*, September 1915: 211). The June 1915 issue of the magazine described the public exhibition of "Seleno," as the electric dog was called (p. 43).

[2] Miessner died in 1967 at the age of eighty-six and outlived Hammond (1888-1965). He was an electrical engineer, and as an inventor no less eclectic than Hammond (although their lives were quite different). At the time Miessner published his 1964 book, radio-controlled systems were no longer his main field of interest, and he was mainly concerned with building electronic musical instruments.

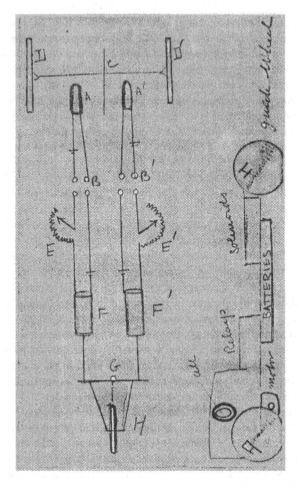

Fig. 1.3. Hammond's 1912 sketch of the "electric dog" (from Miessner, 1964).

tric dog an important advance over earlier devices, because it made Hammond's torpedo self-directing. And recent experience in anti-submarine defense showed that this capacity could be further perfected. "The electric dog, which now is but an uncanny scientific curiosity," Miessner concluded, "may within the very near future become in truth
a real 'dog of war,' without fear, without heart, without the human element so often susceptible to trickery, with but one purpose: to overtake and slay whatever comes within
range of its senses at the will of its master" (Miessner, 1916: 199).

    This forecast was fully realized with the arrival less than thirty years later of automatic
control systems that really lacked the "human element" Miessner spoke of. It was another
conflict, the Second World War, that was to be "the deciding factor," as Norbert Wiener
stressed, for those systems in cybernetics, this time based on mathematics developed by

Wiener himself and on the newborn technology of computing machinery (Wiener, 1948/1961: 25).

But the self-direction capacity of Hammond and Miessner's automaton was of sufficient interest for "the famed Rockefeller Institute biologist, who had proposed various theories explaining many kinds of tropism," which was how Miessner referred to Loeb. Loeb reprinted almost the whole of Miessner's description of the automaton in one of his most famous works, *Forced Movements, Tropisms, and Animal Conduct*, which came out during the same period (Loeb, 1918: 68-69).

Loeb had been working for thirty years on the tropisms of simple living organisms, "natural heliotropic machines" like the moth. Now with the orientation mechanism of Hammond and Miessner he had before him an "artificial heliotropic machine," as he called it. His interest was justified. To artificially simulate or reproduce the heliotropic behavior of the organisms he studied required a machine that was altogether different from the automata of the earlier mechanistic tradition, which was based on the concept of clockwork mechanisms and therefore incapable of exchanging information with the external environment. In short, what was needed was a machine with sense organs, a negative-feedback control device, and motor organs.[3] Hammond and Miessner's automaton was just such a machine: it could automatically adapt its behavior to the changing conditions of the external environment and adjust its movements by means of a negative-feedback control device (the rear steering wheel always brought the machine back in the direction of the light the moment it went too far off course).[4] This is the lesson Loeb learned:

It seems to the writer that *the actual construction of a heliotropic machine not only supports the mechanistic conceptions of the volitional and instinctive actions of animals but also the writer's theory of heliotropism, since this theory served as the basis in the construction of the machine.* We may feel safe in stating that there is no more reason to ascribe the heliotropic reactions of lower animals to any form of sensation, e.g., of brightness or color or pleasure or curiosity, than it is to ascribe the heliotropic reactions of Mr. Hammond's machine to such sensations (Loeb, 1918: 69, my italics).

This passage explicitly states an idea that was to enjoy increasing favour in the explanation of animal and human behavior. The idea is that the construction of a machine that behaves like the living organism studied by a theory constitutes a test of that theory's plausibility. For an idea of how important Loeb considered the Hammond and Miessner machine, suffice it to consider the basic assumption of the "mechanistic conception of the volitional and instinctive actions of animals" he referred to in the passage quoted above.

In general form, this conception assumes that "living organisms may be called chemical machines," marked first of all by a capacity for automatic development, self-preser-

---

[3] As it will be clear later on, it is this "chain" of elements that characterizes some of the newer communication machines popular during the cybernetic age (see, for example, Wiener, 1950, Chapter 1, and p. 142 below).

[4] Rossi (1970) traced the philosophical background of the early mechanistic tradition. Mayr (1970) provides a reconstruction of the very beginnings of the concept of feedback. The builders of later and more evolved electronic animals, like Walter Grey Walter's "tortoises," usually referred to Loeb's investigations on tropisms (see Chapter 5 below).

vation and reproduction. The question immediately arises what if any difference there is between these chemical machines and other, "artificial" machines. Here is Loeb's answer:

The fact that the machines which can be created by man do not possess the power of automatic development, self-preservation, and reproduction constitutes for the present a fundamental difference between living machines and artificial machines. We must, however, admit that nothing contradicts the possibility that the artificial production of living matter may one day be accomplished (Loeb, 1906: 1).

That is what Loeb had to say before the construction of the Hammond and Miessner machine. Now since he classified most of the unconscious instincts of animals (which he interpreted as automatic tropisms) as self-preservation mechanisms, he must surely have considered the machine a step on the road to the elimination of the fundamental difference between natural (living or "chemical") machines and artificial (inanimate or "inorganic") machines. By simulating a living organism's heliotropic behavior, the Hammond and Miessner machine suggested that the same principles that sufficed to explain the machine's behavior—those of physics—also sufficed to explain the behavior of lower animals and plants and that there was no need to look elsewhere. In particular, the correct way to study animal behavior was not by introspective psychology but by the objective and quantitative method of physics. As Loeb had already stated, "the same method and heuristic principles" of physics were valid for researchers in animal behavior, i.e. "to illustrate the mechanism of complicated machines by the comparison with simpler or older machines of the same kind" (Loeb, 1900: 240). The causes allowing the control and prediction of the allegedly voluntary movements of these animals are always mechanical in nature. "By the help of these causes it is possible to control 'voluntary' movements of a living animal just as securely and unequivocally as the engineer has been able to control the movements in inanimate nature" (Loeb, 1905: 107).[5]

Therefore the instincts, as tropisms, are no less automatic nor more conscious than simple reflexes. Stating his position in what was then a very lively debate, Loeb argued that the only difference between instincts and reflexes was that the reflexes involved a single organ or group of organs, while instincts marked the response of an animal in its entirety. The elimination of introspective ("speculative" or "metaphysical," as Loeb called it) psychology from the sciences of animal behavior seemed consistent with Loeb's refusal, in *Forced Movements, Tropisms, and Animal Conduct*, to ascribe mentality to the lower animals, since it had been demonstrated that they reacted to stimuli in a fully automatic and unconscious way. The moth did not fly towards the flame out of "curiosity," nor was it "attracted" by or "fond of" the light. It was simply "oriented" by the action of the light, just like the Hammond and Miessner machine. And it was through Loeb's description in *Forced Movements, Tropisms, and Animal Conduct* that the machine came to the attention of philosophers and biologists. The philosopher Julian Huxley, for example, quoted Loeb's account of the electric dog as one of the arguments to keep one on guard against the "dangers of anthropomorphizing the animals" (Huxley, 1927: 339). And the biologist George Crile argued that the complex organic phenomena of perception and action, such as acti-

---

[5] Pauly (1987) emphasized the importance in Loeb of the idea of the control of behavior. His book provides an insightful account of Loeb's scientific work not considered here.

vation of distance receptors and variations in the intensity and speed of responses, might be less difficult to understand if one considered the workings of such man-made machines as the Hammond and Miessner electric dog and wireless torpedoes. Crile shared Loeb's antivitalist conclusion that some organic phenomena "are no less demonstrable and operate no less by physical laws than does the man-made device" (Crile, 1921: 203).

But while Miessner appealed to the authority of Loeb to explain why his electric dog functioned comparably to the way the moth behaved, he showed that he did not understand the conclusions Loeb drew from his experiments. It may be no accident that when Loeb mentioned Miessner's account of his own machine in *Forced Movements, Tropism, and Animal Conduct,* he omitted the following passage in which Miessner attributed to him an anthropomorphic interpretation of the moth's behavior:

> According to Mr. Loeb's conclusion, which is based on his researches, the moth possesses two minute cells, one on each side of the body. These cells are sensitive to light, and when one alone is illuminated a sensation similar to our sensation of pain is experienced by the moth; when both are equally illuminated, no unpleasant sensation is felt. The insect therefore keeps its body in such a position, by some manner of reflex action, as will insure no pains (Miessner, 1916: 196).

Of course such an anthropomorphic interpretation of reflex action, and the corresponding description of the behavior of a machine that reproduced that action, was altogether foreign to Loeb's intentions. His main concern was to keep his distance from such contemporary scientists as Alfred Binet, Francis Darwin, Ernest Haeckel, and George Romanes, who in varying degrees used anthropomorphic language in explaining the behavior of lower animals.[6] All this helps to clarify the nature of Loeb's constant suspicion of evolution, for such evolutionists as Haeckel and Francis Darwin went so far as to find psychic life in all living organisms (even plants, in the case of Francis Darwin). Moreover, Loeb found evolutionary terminology infected with anthropomorphism, at least in what he considered its extreme version: why, for example, say that an animal acts for "its best end" or that it is "better suited" to light, say, when "I have never observed a 'selection' of a suitable intensity of light?" (Loeb, 1912: 53). Aside from interpreting the end of any adaptive behavior, the apparently purposeful nature of animal instincts cannot be set against reflexes. Hence Loeb's ultimate conclusion: "the analysis of animal conduct only becomes scientific insofar as it drops the question of purpose" (Loeb, 1918: 18). But this conclusion does not entail elimination of the category of purpose, voluntary action, intelligence, in short consciousness, from physiology generally. On the contrary, Loeb considered the question of pursuing and finding the mechanisms underlying psychic or conscious phenomena "the most important problem in physiology" (Loeb, 1900: 258).

For Loeb the fundamental or elementary process that unequivocally pointed to the existence of psychic life in the world of living organisms was associative memory. It consisted basically in the particular capacity of *certain* living organisms to learn by way of

---

[6] Boakes (1984) provides an introduction to the premises and developments of discussion of the behavior of lower and higher animals. In the years we are considering there were very different positions on the matter (especially about the origin of consciousness), and preliminary surveys were already being written. Frost's is worth reading (Frost, 1912). The use of anthropomorphic language on the part of an engineer like Miessner is an example of ascribing 'mental' attributes to machines, a subject we will consider later on.

associations of elementary sensations. While he opposed the continuist interpretation of psychic life typical of "many Darwinists," Loeb recognized different degrees of associative memory in the animal world, which, however, he thought could be interpreted as sudden changes on the phylogenetic scale. On the contrary, it is the difference in distribution of associative memory that provides the basis for "comparative psychology," which Loeb thought worthy of a place among the behavioral sciences.

Basically what was involved were differences in the ability to make different associations and the facility with which they were produced by individuals belonging to different animal species at a certain level of their ontogenetic development. Ability and ease of association found their fullest achievement in the adult human being, especially in gifted individuals. Nevertheless, it was not a matter of features that are qualitatively different than those of other living organisms. Indeed, when the presence of those features was experimentally observed, Loeb did not hesitate to use anthropomorphic or mentalistic language in describing the behavior of certain animals, and he used terms such as "attempt," "memories," "visual images of memory" (p. 272).[7] At the same time he scorned the disputes about animal intelligence, which were quite heated at the time. His aim continued to be the pursuit of the physical and chemical conditions that made associative memory possible, and he refrained from tracing mental or psychic life where it was absent or where there was no need to assume it existed. Otherwise, if we were consistent we could no longer set a limit to the existence of psychic life among the different species of the organic world, nor between the organic world and the world of the inorganic and artificial:

> Plants must therefore have a psychic life, and, following the argument, *we must ascribe it to machines also*, for the tropisms depend only on *simple mechanical arrangements*. In the last analysis, then, we would arrive at molecules and atoms endowed with mental qualities (Loeb, 1900: 13, my italics).

Machines too would have a psychic life then, something which is manifestly absurd. Loeb's conclusion is consistent with his subsequent enthusiasm for the Hammond and Miessner machine. It artificially reproduced a living organism's *automatic* behavior with a simple negative-feedback device. The machine's performance, like that of a living organism, did not change because of learning, and hence there was no trace of associative memory. It is in this sense that the machine lends support to the theory of tropisms. How can one ascribe intelligence to a living organism if it behaves *like a machine*? That would be the same as ascribing intelligence to a machine! For Loeb here, a machine is something automatic that displays *no variety or spontaneity in interaction with the external environment*; automatic action is synonymous with *uniform and unvarying action*. One might well ask what problems this idea of the machine raised in the light of Loeb's ideas about mechanism.

---

[7] To take an example that was recurrent at the time in the debate over animal intelligence, Loeb acknowledged associative memory even in invertebrates such as certain wasps and argued that such an opponent of the anthropomorphic trend in the study of animal instinct as Alfred Bethe went "too far" in denying its existence (Loeb, 1900: 265). It was a very rudimentary associative memory, involving at most associations intimately linked with animal instincts (for example, memory of where the nest was), and as such a mark of slight intelligence (p. 273). Such a memory was comparable indeed to that of human beings who, because of some brain damage, are unable to make versatile associations (p. 345).

3. The dispute over automata after Huxley.
"Automatic" and "plastic" regulation of behavior

The opposition between automatism (or machine-like behavior) and intelligence (or spontaneous behavior) was not new. It seemed to radicalize what was then a common opposition among researchers in animal behavior, that between reflex and instinct (tropism in the case of Loeb) on the one side and memory, learning, will, and consciousness on the other.

Without going farther back in time, in Loeb's day the concept of automatism in the study of animal behavior was firmly bound to the notion of reflex action.[8] The man who made that the fundamental unit of an evolutionary explanation of behavior was Herbert Spencer. In the 1885 edition of the *Principles of Psychology*, Spencer introduced the idea of automatism, when he described as "purely automatic" the behavior sequence of an organism when it takes the form of reciprocal, immediate and univocally defined coordination of single adaptive actions. We shall see in the next chapter that behind this idea lies the picture of nervous current as a flux along paths connecting the sensory or afferent system with the motor or efferent system. What is worth noting here is that in Spencer's description the two systems, afferent and efferent, are connected by a loop. For example, the sequence of actions in animal motion is described with explicit reference to an automatic control device, the one used in the steam-engine governor, where "the arrival of the piston at a certain point itself brings about the opening of a valve serving to admit the steam which will drive the piston in the reverse direction" (Spencer, 1855: 536).

An organism's automatic behavior thus, as in Loeb's case, suggests that of a machine equipped with a self-regulatory device. Again the comparison to a machine suggests that the action involved is "totally unconscious." Reflex action and instinct considered as compound reflex actions, namely as organized chains of reflexes, may be substantially different in terms of complexity, but the distinction is "simply one of degree, and not of kind" (p. 553). According to Spencer, while the simplest forms of adaptation may be achieved by automatic processes, complex forms require that the organism develops a capacity that has nothing automatic about it, the ability to make associations, to acquire new habits, and to learn—in short, to act on the basis of memory. How it was possible that such a *non-automatic* associative capacity could emerge from a previous activity consisting of *automatic* reflexes and organized chains of reflexes, and by what modifications in the nerve paths between the sensory system and the motor system that might happen, was not a problem that Spencer set at that point. He was to deal with such a problem in later editions of the *Principles of Psychology*, and for the moment we shall not pursue it further, postponing analysis of Spencer's position on these matters until the next chapter.

In Loeb's day, instead, there was still lively debate arising from Thomas Huxley's essay "On the Hypothesis That Animals Are Automata" (Huxley, 1874), in which he went

---

[8] Fearing (1930) gives a classical historical reconstruction of this notion in physiology. But Chapters 4 and 5 of Boakes (1984) and some of the essays in Corsi (1994) are worth looking at.

back to discuss Descartes' classic claims on animal automatism[9], and argued that animals might be considered *conscious automata*: in fact, their nervous system had developed a special physical apparatus as a "collateral product," as Huxley put it, which case by case we call memory, will, consciousness and so on.

In more recent times, at first against the background of Spencerian evolutionist claims, William James challenged Huxley's idea of consciousness as a passive epiphenomenon. James' thesis in "Are We Automata?" starts out from a radical opposition between *automatism* and *unpredictability* (James, 1879).[10] On the one hand there is what James called "determinateness," which is equally typical of the actions of lower animals and of those actions of the higher animals that do not involve brain centers, namely reflex and instinctive actions. These are characterized by a "machine-like" regularity of response. On the other side is the "incalculableness" typical of actions produced by the brain centers, in particular in humans, which are characterized by an extremely large variety of modes of adaptive response. Hypothetically, the advantages and disadvantages of the two types of response were described by James through what he called the "dilemma" between two extreme but equally inefficient cases:

> We may construct [a nervous system] which will react infallibly and certainly, but it will then be capable of reacting to very few changes in the environment—it will fail to be adapted to all the rest. We may, on the other hand, construct a nervous system potentially adapted to respond to an infinite variety of minute features in the situation; but its fallibility will then be as great as its elaboration. We can never be sure that its equilibrium will be upset in the appropriate direction (James, 1879: 5).

Now from a physical point of view (considering the brain a "physical machine pure and simple," as James put it), we may imagine the former hypothetical nervous system as a machine capable of self-regulation in a very specialized way in interaction with the environment, while we must consider the latter system, if we are to consider it as a machine at all, as a machine the functioning of which is "random and capricious" (p. 14): "It is as likely to do the crazy as the sane thing at any given moment [...]. The performances of a high brain [like the latter above] are like the dice thrown forever on the table. Unless they be loaded, what chance is there that the highest number will turn up oftener than the lowest?" (p. 5). Such a poorly organized hypothetical higher nervous system would work extremely inefficiently. The problem might be set then in the following terms: how could the dice be *loaded*? Obviously by introducing into this hypothetical nervous system a principle of selection between the many possible alternative responses, a principle that would foster successful adaptive responses. As we shall see in the next chapter, for James this principle was ultimately teleological in nature, and hence neither physical nor mechanical. It was the principle of conscious experience. But to make this system "efficient" (neither rigidly automatic nor totally causal), it has, so to speak, *to stop being considered a machine*. The teleological explanation conflicts with the causal explanation, because it concerns the functions of consciousness: the notions that concern it (choice, purpose and so) have absolutely unique features (pp. 7-16).

---

[9] See Rossi (1970).

[10] A modified version of this paper became a chapter of the *Principles of Psychology* (James, 1890).

James' criticism of Huxley was meant to show that, from an evolutionary standpoint as well, consciousness critically increased the efficiency of a complex nervous system and was not merely a passive adjunct. But Charles Lloyd Morgan in "Animal Automatism and Consciousness" (Morgan, 1896) attacked Huxley's claim in more general terms. According to Morgan, Huxley defined "automaton" and "automatic" so broadly that the terms became useless. So Morgan proposed a restricted definition. Setting aside the details, he connected the subject of the automaton with regulation and control more explicitly than others and exemplified a claim we shall have occasion to mention again.

Morgan distinguishes two kinds of regulative processes. One is adaptation to the external environment marked by the rigidity and invariability of the organism's response, as in the case of reflex and instinct. The other is adaptation to the external environment characterized by the plasticity and modifiability of the organism's response, as in the case of intelligent, learned, or voluntary behavior, which can be characterized by "a choice, based on previous individual experience and dependent upon the association of impressions and ideas." The term "automatic" is appropriate only to the former regulative process. It is not applicable to the latter process, which implies conscious guidance or control of action based on "choice" and a developed associative ability, for "an intelligent automaton [...] is a contradiction in terms" (Morgan, 1896: 10-12).

So it is when one observes behavior varied or modified by experience that one must assume the separate existence of "centers of intelligent or conscious control," which stand "above the level of automatism" (p. 11). The kind of organization Morgan described is actually hierarchical and is rather reminiscent of descriptions proposed later in terms of the exchange of information between different systems: the various levels of the hierarchy act and react reciprocally in order to optimize the self-equilibration capacities of the system as a whole. The lower levels do not always have access to the higher levels, those of consciousness. As Morgan pointed out in *Animal Behavior*, consciousness "probably receives information of the net results of the progress of behavior, and not of the minute and separate details of muscular contraction" (Morgan, 1900: 105). Morgan seems to reach the same conclusion mentioned in the foregoing, namely that the lower centers of automatic control can be described as a machine, but *not* the higher centers. Significantly, in the analogy with the hierarchical system, the higher centers correspond to the human element that optimizes choices in a complex situation, for example, to "the person who sits in a central office and guides the working of some organized system in accordance with the information he is constantly receiving, who sends messages to check activity in certain directions and to render it more efficient and vigorous in others" (p. 118).

As to the actual nature of these higher or conscious control centers, Morgan offers an hypothesis of his own which he calls "monistic" in contrast to Huxley's "epiphenomenistic" one. For Morgan a conscious state is *concomitant* to a nervous state without any causal relationship between them. Rather it is two ways of looking at a single phenomenon. Therefore the subjective or mentalistic language used by the psychologist is just another way of expressing what the physiologist would say (pp. 309-310).

We will have more than one occasion to deal with this set of problems, which run from

the relationship between automatism and plasticity of behavior to the reduction of instincts to chains of automatic reflexes, the different solutions to the mind-body problem,
and the kind of language appropriate for describing organisms and machines. The reason for mentioning here some of the hypotheses regarding the nature of automatism that
were discussed in Loeb's day was to focus on the specific questions of Loeb's reductionist
and mechanistic claims.

To begin with, Loeb was distant from Spencer, James and Morgan because of their
shared evolutionary stance regarding the way conscious activity rises out of increasingly less "automatic" processes. And what in particular distanced Loeb from James was the
idea of teleological explanation that could not be reduced to a physical or causal explanation.[11] Nevertheless several features of Loeb's claim about the distribution of associative memory refer to a very sharp distinction between unconscious automatism (reflex,
instinct, tropism) and intelligent, conscious choice (based on associative memory), a distinction that in many ways echoes those considered in the foregoing. So is an *intelligent
automaton* a contradiction in terms for Loeb too?

Now Loeb always defines instincts, reduced to tropisms, as "automatic mechanisms"
(Loeb, 1906: 5), and "automatic mechanisms" indicate the absence of associative memory, the low level of which thus renders the reactions of some animals "similar to automatisms and less intelligent" (Loeb,1900: 267 and 347). Nevertheless, in keeping with
his reductionist and mechanistic conception, Loeb did not consider associative memory,
however developed, an organizational principle that is qualitatively different than "simple mechanical arrangements," which are at the root of the automatic responses of lower organisms (tropisms). Associative memory was still a "mechanical arrangement" (Loeb
used the same expression) found in certain organisms when their nervous systems, in particular, had reached a given degree of phylogenetic and ontogenetic development. Intelligence, learning capacity, consciousness and will are nothing but functions of this particular "mechanical arrangement," i.e. associative memory (p. 303). At this point Loeb
states that he is following in the steps of Ernst Mach and argues that since these functions find their full realization in a rich and complex associative capacity, they have nothing to do with the "self-consciousness" of philosophers or "metaphysicians," as he rather
disdainfully calls them. Elsewhere Loeb is even more explicit: associative memory is
nothing more than the "source" of more tropisms, which may make instinctive behavior
more complex in such a way, for example, that an animal might be induced to return to
a place that corresponded to a visual memory image.[12] For Loeb, this case is not qualitatively different from that familiar to psychiatrists of a patient's fixation on an object of
which he has a memory image (Loeb, 1918: 171).

What Loeb suggested here was the possibility of the future extension of the tropism

[11] Loeb's reference to agreement with James on this point (Loeb, 1900: 261) does not seem pertinent, especially in light of James' reservations (James, 1890, vol. 2: 516).

[12] Instructive in this regard is the way in which Loeb interpreted Pavlov's conditioned reflex (which we will
consider in the next chapter). Loeb considered conditioning to be a process of habit formation, and conditioned
reflexes as the equivalent of images in associative memory. As such, conditioned reflexes "can vary and multiply the number of possible tropistic reactions," and "what we call a memory image of a 'conditioned reflex'
is not a 'spiritual' but a physical agency" (Loeb, 1918: 167).

theory to the study of the behavior of the higher animals including man, in line with his mechanistic conception. Indeed, as William Crozier, a student of Loeb, pointed out a few years after his teacher's death (in 1924), "Loeb's approach to the problem of individual organic behavior was initially and primarily philosophic, in the sense that through recognition of the elements of action and the modes of their control he looked to find an answer to the puzzles of free will and determinism" (Crozier, 1928: 213).[13]

Now the very possibility of extending the theory of tropism to human conduct necessarily requires that both unconscious automatisms and conscious or voluntary actions share the same elementary functional unity: the tropism, the cornerstone on which both rest. The higher processes of associative memory require the existence of evolved nerve centers that not all organisms possess. Nevertheless these higher nerve centers are responsible only for an increase in the *complication* of reactions that are basically always and only tropistic in nature.

The question that arises at this point is: what is the nature of this complication? In other words, how is it possible that such "simple mechanical arrangements" as tropisms and reflexes can become a "mechanical arrangement" endowed with such peculiar features as to give rise to spontaneous modification of behavior, in a word, to learning. Passing reference was made to the problem in regard to Spencer, and it will be considered at greater length later on. Now let us return to the specific questions raised by Loeb's reductionism, and in particular to some aporias regarding his concept of consciousness as associative memory, which, not coincidentally, became a subject of debate for his contemporaries. Thus we can introduce some problems, first amog them the role of mentalistic vocabulary in the description of behavior, that we will have occasion to come back to more than once in the following chapters.

For Loeb, voluntary conscious action does not entail an appeal to complexity in the evolutionary sense (consciousness gradually arising from automatisms) or in the dualist sense (consciousness as a peculiar teleological function). The control of behavior is entrusted to a *single* physico-chemical or tropistic mechanism that can be perfectly detected in simple cases (hence their interest), but less easily in other cases, given our generally incomplete understanding of the physico-chemical mechanisms underlying associative memory. In the latter cases, to use Loeb's words, the organisms "'seem' to possess freedom of will" (note Loeb's continual use of quotation marks when talking about will). Actually, "the tropistic effects of memory images and the modification and inhibition of tropisms by memory images make the number of possible reactions so great that *prediction becomes almost impossible*, and it is this impossibility chiefly which gives rise to the doctrine of free will" (Loeb, 1918: 171, my italics).

This conclusion might be summarized as follows for the problem that interests us here: when organisms display simple tropistic behavior, their actions are "machine-like" (p. 171) and are therefore completely predictable. If additional factors are responsible for the behavior of organisms (associative memory being the most important but, as we shall see, not the only factor), it becomes complicated, our understanding remains inevitably

---

[13] The criticism of that philosophic claim is as old as its formulation by Loeb. On developments of Loeb's mechanistic conception of life, see Pauly (1987), especially Chapter 7.

incomplete, and since, as observers, we fail to control and predict the behavior of those organisms, we are inclined to attribute various degrees of free will and consciousness to them. Is this the point, one might ask, at which *we cease considering living organisms as machines*—as machines whose performance might be comparable to that of "inorganic machines?" It is hard to find a clear answer in Loeb. Indeed, his stance towards so-called "inorganic machines" exposes the problems left open by the reduction of consciousness to associative memory.

Let us suppose we give an explicitly affirmative reply to the last question: the living organisms which we are inclined to credit with different degrees of free will and consciousness must be considered exclusively as organic or chemical machines, whose behavior has nothing to do with that of inorganic or artificial machines. Consciousness is thus a function of some particular "mechanical arrangements" that, when not directly observed, can be hypothesized from the overt behavior of those organic machines, and suggest the presence of associative memory. One might ask just what these mechanical arrangements are and what their peculiar nature is. Actually Loeb is ready to acknowledge that there is one essential feature of an organism's memory that can be simulated by some inorganic machines: the (passive) ability to reproduce impressions in the same chronological order but in different circumstances than the original, a feature that is typical, for example, of an ordinary phonograph (Loeb, 1900: 257; 1906: 6). But Loeb is not equally ready to acknowledge another feature, which is surely no less essential: the (active) ability to make associations (for example, between the smell of a rose and the visual memory image of that flower). At the time, Loeb seemed to exclude the possibility of inorganic or artificial machines endowed with that ability, i.e. the ability to make associations and to learn. The only machines able to do so were *certain* organic or chemical machines endowed (at least) with particular "mechanical arrrangements" constituting the physico-chemical mechanism of associative memory.

But stressing this feature of associative memory as peculiar to (certain) organisms raises some problems. Let us go back to the Hammond and Miessner machine we started out with. According to Loeb, the machine showed that if an inorganic machine can be built that displays the behavior typical of a living organism, the behavior of that living organism is automatic. Thus there is no trace in it of intelligence or will or psychic life, and it is superfluous to describe it in anthropomorphic or mentalistic terms. But, as we know, even the apparently *voluntary* behavior of certain living organisms is actually the result of a complex network of tropistic reactions and hence is also *automatic*. And yet the description of that behavior in psychological or mentalistic language—that is to say, in terms of consciousness, will, intelligence, and so on—is in this case legitimate for Loeb. We have already seen why: because of the observer's incomplete understanding of the specific "mechanical arrangements" deputed to associative memory, which *complicate* an otherwise predictable response. But then these mechanical arrangements actually determine the behavior of the living organisms that embody them with a determinateness comparable to that of *any* automatism. One might therefore raise the objection to Loeb that while the observer in these cases makes legitimate use of psychological and mentalistic language, it would be equally legitimate *not* to do so.

And what is more, is it not true that the observer chooses to use psychological and mentalistic language in studying the behavior of very simple organisms that actually lack associative memory, but whose control mechanism is as yet unknown to him? And does-n't Loeb admit as much when he points out that some behavior "seems" to be free and voluntary when we fail to reduce it to tropisms, even in the case of simple unicellular organisms? In this case, as in that of complex organisms and human beings, "as a matter of fact, the action of each individual is again determined by something, but *we do not know what it is*"(Loeb, 1918: 172, my italics).

If this is so, the conclusion is that the unpredictability of behavior is essentially due not to the objective presence of a complex control mechanism in the living organism we observe but rather to our ignorance, as observers, of the control mechanism *as it actually is* (even if it is tropistic). Before considering some other consequences of this conclusion, it would be worthwhile to study a different position than Loeb's on the nature of intelligence and consciousness and the appropriate vocabulary for describing the behavior of organisms.

4. Jennings and the action system

In the same period Herbert Jennings was pursuing his own line of study on lower organisms, and published an important essay in 1910, "Diverse Ideals and Divergent Conclusions in the Study of Behavior in Lower Organisms," in which he set forth his methodological credo regarding the then prevailing trends in the study of animal behavior.[14] Jennings called Loeb's method "synthetic," because the units of work were physico-chemical components and principles on the basis of which Loeb tried to explain the behavior of the living organism. In opposition to the synthetic method he ascribed to Loeb, Jennings offered his own "analytic method," which he said he shared with organicist researchers in animal behavior, especially Jakob von Uexküll.[15] In the analytic method the unit of work is the living organism as a whole; and the variability of its behavior under the action of the external environment is studied together with the change produced in

[14] There is no completely satisfactory reconstruction of Jennings' thought. There are references to his conflict with Loeb in Pauly (1987, Chapter 6).

[15] Note that Loeb considered his own method an "analytic procedure," because he proposed using physiologically simple components (reflexes, tropisms) to track such complex phenomena as the central nervous system (Loeb, 1900: 1). Elsewhere Loeb also described his scientific aim "to derive the more complex phenomena from simpler components" (Loeb, 1912: 58). And this ideal was widely shared by the tradition of physiological study, which ultimately acknowledged the two methods, analytic and synthetic, as complementary. If anything, the analytic method was preferred as synonymous with "experimental analysis," as in the case of Claude Bernard, one of the physiologists most concerned about methodology in the biological sciences at the time. To establish physiology as a science, said Bernard, "the living organism has to be taken apart piece by piece, so to speak, like a machine when you want to study and understand all its workings [...]. The study of biological phenomena must therefore be analytical and gradual and conducted with the same experimental method that the physicist and chemist use in analyzing the phenomena of inanimate bodies [...]. Through this [experimental] analysis complex phenomena are gradually broken down into increasingly simple phenomena [...]. First these [complex] phenomena must be taken apart [...] and then the organism *in toto* must be ideally reassembled by synthesis" (Bernard, 1865: 88-89).

the environment by the action of the organism, a change that in turn provokes a reaction on the part of the organism (Jennings, 1910: 352-354). This two-way organism-environment action had been at the heart of Jennings' most important book, *The Behavior of the Lower Organisms*, published a few years earlier, with its detailed study of adaptation and self-regulation in a host of lower organisms. In Jennings' words:

> In most cases the change which induces a reaction [of the organism] is brought about by the organism's own movements. These cause a change in the relation of the organism to the environment; to these changes the organism reacts. The whole behavior of free-moving organisms is based on the principle that it is the movements of the organism that have brought about stimulation; the regulatory character of the reaction induced is intelligible only on this basis (Jennings, 1906: 293).

It is no accident that a few decades later this passage from Jennings and others of the same tenor attracted the attention of the cybernetician William Ross Ashby. He referred to this idea and to the "function circles" that von Uexküll used to describe the indissoluble interaction between organism and environment as exemplary contributions to the study of the processes of equilibration between organism and environment as a single system.[16]

This idea of the relationship between organism and environment is the basis of what Jennings called the "action system." It depends on the internal structure and organization of the organism and can be defined as the set of the organism's actions or movements that provoke all regulative behavior, from "negative reactions" away from unfavorable stimuli to "positive reactions" to favorable stimuli by way of trial-and-error. As a result the organism changes its behavior and enters a state of adaptation to the external environment. The action system can actually effect only a certain number of adaptive movements, those which its internal structure allows (Jennings, 1906: 345). That is to say, there are *limits* to the adaptation of an organism, be it higher or lower, and hence "choice [as a result of adaptive or regulative behavior] is not perfect" (p. 330).

Jennings' notion of an action system is very general, so much so that he uses it to describe the regulative behavior of all organisms, lower and higher, including man. The work of Morgan and Edward Thorndike on the behavior of higher animals, to mention only those Jennings refers to in *Behavior of the Lower Organisms*, provided many important concepts that went into the definition of action system (for example, that of trial-and-error learning), just as the speculations of Spencer and James Mark Baldwin could suggest the general laws regulating the way an action system works. But it is legitimate to say that the major innovation of Jennings' approach was to consider the identification of an organism's action system as the most important step in the study of regulative behavior (p. 107).

Now what distinguishes higher organisms, and man in particular, from lower organisms is the enormous complexity of their action system. Yet it is a difference in degree: what makes comparison between them possible is the regulative nature of the behavior that makes up their respective action systems.

[16] Ashby (1940; 1952/1960). The text quoted by Ashby is von Uexküll (1920). Ashby's claim and the notion of equilibration are considered in Chapter 4 below. Jennings implicitly referred to the notion of function circles, as will become clear later. (On von Uexküll see Chapter 2, section 7.)

An example from *Behavior of the Lower Organisms* may shed preliminary light on the matter and will be helpful later as well. One of the lower animals Jennings studied most closely (his analyses are still classics) is a unicellular organism classed as a Protozoon, the *Stentor*. This organism has a very limited action system consisting of some five different reactions to external stimuli that interfere negatively with its normal state of being (for example, it changes position, contracts, or moves away from the disturbing agent). Jennings considers such a rudimentary action system sufficient to conclude that we are not in the presence of reflexive or tropistic behavior (same response to same stimulus) but fairly ductile and varied behavior. When *Stentor* is threatened by a disturbing agent, it tries out the different aforementioned movements that make up its action system and selects the one adapted to restoring its normal state of being. This, in short, is Jennings' version of the "law of selection of varied movements," which he traces to the evolutionist tradition running from Spencer to Baldwin (p. 302).

What is more, *Stentor*'s action system makes it possible to explain how *Stentor*'s response to the same stimulus (for example, the same disturbing agent) may change in the course of time. Actually, according to Jennings, since the stimulus does not change, and since no structural changes can be observed in the organism, it must be concluded that it is the *internal state* of the organism which changes and which causes a change in the response (p. 178). In other words, in different internal states the organism reacts differently to the same stimulus.

The observed change in response to the same stimulus suggests that the state of an organism at a given moment may depend on its past "history," i.e. on stimuli received in the past and on earlier responses to those stimuli. Jennings extends this "dynamic" character of internal states, which Baldwin, among others, observed in higher organisms, to lower animals in the form of the second principle that regulates the working of an action system: the "law of the readier resolution of physiological states" (p. 291), which is the basis for forming new habits, or learning, even in such simple organisms as *Stentor*. If we try to imagine, then, that *Stentor*'s action system includes different observable reactions to internal or "physiological" states A, B, C, D, E, then in the presence of a given external stimulus S that disturbs it, one may predict, on the basis of the law of selection, that the animal will react by *trying out* the different reactions and *select* the successful one, that corresponding, say, to state D. The law of readier resolution then makes it possible to predict that if *Stentor* is subjected several times to the same stimulus S, it will respond directly with the reaction corresponding to D, without repeating the earlier reactions corresponding to states A, B, C, and *fixing* on D as the adaptive reaction. One can say that the other states are resolved more readily in state D.

Thus the action systems of simple organisms display equally simple forms of individual "history" and "experience," so that *Stentor*'s behavior depends not only on its anatomic structure or the physico-chemical nature of the external stimulus but first of all on its different internal physiological states. Jennings concludes that in order to explain the variability of the organism's different regulative behaviors, "we are compelled to assume" the existence of different internal states (p. 251). We can express the matter in these terms: the transition from one behavior to another in an action system is the result of the organism's transition from one internal state to another. There is every evidence that at the time Jennings thought these internal physiological states were authentic hypothetical entities. The task awaiting future physiological research was to identify their actual features, and this seems to be the subsequent step of the analytical method he fostered.

The way Jennings traces it, the difference between the synthetic and the analytic methods might be much better appreciated by looking at the different models of machine advanced by Loeb and Jennings. This may clarify their different stance both towards the criteria for the control and prediction of the behavior of organisms and, ultimately, towards reductionism. So we shall now turn to these researchers' different models and defer till later in the chapter an analysis of their position on the nature of explanation and reductionism.

Loeb's machine model in the study of lower animals was what we might now call a negative-feedback automaton. Its control system does not entail learned modifications of behavior, which is to say that it includes *only one invariable decision rule*. On the contrary, Jennings fostered a different model even in the study of lower animals, a machine capable of displaying selective behavior, i.e. capable of adapting itself actively (by trial-and-error) to the environment. This machine control system is "plastic" in Morgan's sense and could be viewed as the machine action system. We might describe this as a control system that does not generally include a single invariable decision rule but *a whole set of decision rules*, which account for changes in internal states and the corresponding behavior.

Jennings' idea of a machine with the plastic features of an action system was far from being a contradiction in terms, as Morgan alleged. Jennings did not think it harked back to any principles of regulation that were qualitatively different from those of the world of physics and chemistry and inorganic matter. Hence the analytic method does not entail introducing into biology any principles of explanation that are incompatible with those of physics and chemistry. Jennings came back to this point several times, surely in part to resist fatal embrace of vitalists such as Hans Driesch and William McDougall, who had immediately accepted his criticism of the theory of tropisms and his insistence on the complexity of the living being.[17] Jennings stated that he did not share von Uexküll's vitalism, because it was incompatible with the method of verification, the only method admissible in studying the behavior of living organisms. And at the same time he declared his total "admiration" of the consistency with which Loeb had pursued his experimental work.[18]

---

[17] Driesch's *Philosophie des Organischen*, published in 1909, enjoyed great popularity in those days, and might be considered the synthesis of the vitalist philosophy that Driesch had derived from his earlier experimental investigations (Driesch, 1909). McDougall took up Driesch's ideas in more systematic form in his *Body and Mind* and mentioned Jennings' work as support of vitalism (McDougall, 1911). There will be more than one occasion to consider McDougall, the great foe of any kind of mechanistic explanation of the behavior of living organisms.

[18] Quoted by D.D. Jensen in the introduction to the 1962 edition of Jennings' *Behavior*. Jensen also quotes extensively from Jennings response to criticism of *Behavior*, including Loeb's review (see Jennings, 1908). Some aspects of von Uexküll's vitalism are considered in Chapter 2 regarding his use of mechanical analogies, as well as Jennings' dissent from the method of "intuition" that von Uexküll proposed as a peculiar methodological principle for biology.

Clarifying his position regarding von Uexküll, Jennings pointed out that he based the organism's activity on arrangements that did not fall into the category of passive automatism, because they were not conceived as "fixed and final" machines but as machines that "are continually changed by the environment and by the action of the organism itself." But he went on to say that he was convinced that "even these changes occur in an essentially machine-like way" (Jennings, 1909a: 332). Even without mentioning it explicitly, he was referring to the action system, a machine that was "not fixed and final" that would account for an organism's ability to regulate its own behavior in a varied and spontaneous way in interaction with the environment, without necessitating any appeal to vitalism.

Jennings granted that observation of the behavior of organisms, including lower organisms, provided a clearer perception of the two principles governing the action system, that of selection and that of readier resolution. Indeed, behavior is "the prototype for regulatory action," and "regulation constitutes perhaps the greatest problem of life," he said, picking up Spencer's view (Jennings, 1906: 338). Nevertheless, Jennings thought that other examples of action systems, no less significant than that of the behavior of organisms, could be described even in the world of inorganic nature. It is clear that this idea, if consistently accounted for, might make possible an altogether new way of looking at the problems of choice, learning, and purposeful action that Loeb raised in terms of associative memory. The presence of action systems *outside the world of living organisms* would be one possible way of showing its truly mechanical character.

Actually Jennings observes, first of all, that the mechanisms of *individual* selection are no different than those of *natural* selection. In this regard he goes back to an idea of Baldwin's, that of organic selection. Just as the individual chooses and then (through the law of readier resolution) fixes the tendentially best adaptive move in his action system, so nature chooses and then (through a mechanism that is similar in principle) retains the most adaptive variations. The individual makes its choice from among the individual's different responses (consider *Stentor*'s action system), while nature makes its selection from among the different responses of different individuals: "the thing selected is the same in each case—namely the adaptive reaction" (p. 325).

Secondly, according to Jennings there is a similar regulatory or adaptive mechanism in the organism's *internal* processes, the ones that regulate the organism's response, for example, to changes in temperature. These phenomena were beginning to be studied carefully, phenomena that had led Claude Bernard to describe the organism as a complex of systems tending to keep its internal environment constant. But Jennings described all this in terms of his own. He thought that internal organs also had "something corresponding to the 'action system'" (p. 347); they had a fairly limited number of possible chemical changes to select and retain, depending on the two general regulation laws.

Finally, the *inorganic* world also displayed something similar to the law of readier resolution. Jennings makes several explicit references to the case of the hysteresis of colloids (the substances that make up living protoplasm), in which he saw a manifestation of associative memory in its most elementary form.

Loeb also referred to the phenomenon of the hysteresis of colloids in connection with associative memory. In the additions to the 1907 Italian edition of *Comparative Physiology*, Loeb specified that he considered memory phenomena in a "merely physical" sense as "belonging to the category of those aftereffects that physicists call hysteresis," and went so far as to suggest the possibility of replacing the term "associative memory" by the term "associative hysteresis" (Loeb, 1900: 367 and 376 of the Italian edition). The examples he gave were elastic hysteresis and the hysteresis of colloids. An elastic body that undergoes the action of force or weight displays the phenomenon of hysteresis. When the action of the force is removed, the body never returns to its original length, and its structure remains altered. Then it is said that the effect of the force has left a trace in the body, and that the body has changed in regard to its previous "history" or "experience." Likewise, in the case of colloids, "their qualities often depend in the clearest way upon the former history of the colloid, its age, its previous temperature, and the time this continued: in short, on the way it has reached its present condition." Jennings quoted this passage from a contemporary chemistry book to show that from a mechanistic viewpoint associative memory was not a grounded criterion for ascribing consciousness, since there was an elementary form of it even among inorganic colloids (Jennings, 1906: 317 and 334). Jennings quotes neither Loeb nor others like him who argued that consciousness was a function of associative memory. But it is clear that right here can be found the origin of Jennings' different concept of the role of consciousness in adaptive behavior.

Loeb identified consciousness with associative memory but had to restrict the range of the latter in order not to find consciousness everywhere (perhaps even in molecules and atoms). And his choice of the term "associative hysteresis" instead of "associative memory" did not make things any clearer, since he could not have interpreted physical hysteresis as a form of *true* associative memory (the latter found only in *certain* living organisms). For the same reason, i.e. to keep from finding consciousness everywhere, Jennings tried a completely different strategy.

He made a distinction between phenomena of true consciousness and those displaying forms of memory, ability to make associations, choice, purposeful activity, and so on (see Jennings, 1906, Chapters 20 and 21). The former can be endorsed only by the *subjective* experience each one of us has; while the others, without sufficient criteria or evidence of self-awareness, can be ascertained as *objective* facts first in the behavior of animals, lower and higher alike, and then, albeit in a form that is not always obvious or easily detectable, in a host of natural and even inorganic phenomena. Actually Jennings does not delve very deep into the different questions that might arise at this point, for example, what might be called the question of other minds, or the role of introspection in endorsing the alleged subjective states of consciousness and their features. For Jennings, the teleological or intentional features of such states, for example, are not sufficient to conclude that those states elude causal explanation. The matter was given very cursory attention in Jennings' writings of the time and the conclusion was that there was "no basis for theories of vitalism" (p. 244).[19] For Jennings it would seem that this conclusion

---

[19] We will not pursue the evolution of Jennings' thought, nor that of others such as Morgan, along increasingly marked emergentist lines, partly in connection with studies that followed Jennings' work on lower organisms. On emergentism see, for example, Jennings (1927).

can be documented in the objective study of the behavior of lower and higher animals. Such behavior suggests no "reasoning by analogy" to support the attribution to animals of consciousness as a subjective experience. In other words, we cannot tell if the internal physiological states of adaptation and learning of non human animals are accompanied by conscious states like those we are willing to attribute to human beings.

5. Machines and functional organization

According to Jennings' conclusions, 'intelligence' becomes synonymous with adaptive and self-regulatory behavior, albeit with extremely different degrees of efficacy, and this behavior can be observed through experimental study of the different action systems along the entire scale of the biological and physico-chemical worlds alike. Differences in individual action systems are large and striking but they do not indicate any difference in regulative principles. Jennings was led to recognize in the inorganic, as well as the organic world, the feature of the action system by which the vitalists most specifically distinguished the living being: the ability variously to select a regulative or adaptive response in terms of *purpose*.[20]

Given Jennings' ease in contemplating action systems *outside the world of living organisms*, one might wonder if it were legitimate to hypothesize something like an action system in machines as well, in those "inorganic" or "artificial" machines which Loeb explictly denied had any ability to change their internal organization.

Jennings spoke at least once, in the aforementioned 1910 essay, of "inorganic combinations [or arrangements] that we call machines." He did not explicitly mention action systems on that occasion. But "relations that are extremely perplexing," which he thought could "be illustrated from inorganic arrangements [machines] as well as from organic ones [lower and higher organisms]" (Jennings, 1910: 361), are the very ones that in *Behavior of the Lower Organisms* he considered typical of a living organism's action system, namely, the ability to react in the same way to different stimuli and in different ways to the same stimulus (the case of *Stentor*). Nonetheless, looking at the inorganic arrangements or machines that Jennings considered actually capable of these "extremely perplexing" relations, the array of examples turns out to be inadequate.

According to Jennings, an ordinary typewriter is an "inorganic arrangement" that displays the same capacity as a living organism such as *Stentor* to take on different states to respond differently to the same stimulus: the typewriter prints upper-case letters in one key state and lower-case letters in another. An inorganic arrangement capable of making the same response to different kinds of stimuli is the electric circuit in which the switch that makes the bell ring can be closed by a higher or lower contact depending on whether

[20] Driesch claimed that regulation was teleological in character, and the idea was picked up soon after by McDougall in the aforementioned *Body and Mind* (1911). More than once Jennings challenged Driesch's need to explain regulative processes in terms of the Aristotelian notion of "final cause" (in agreement with Loeb), precisely because Jennings did not believe that the reference to the future (purpose as *future cause* of action) was an exclusive feature of the behavior of living organisms (Jennings, 1910: 367). Chapter 4 is dedicated to the issue of reference to the future in the teleological explanation.

the connection to the switch is lengthened or shortened. To make the contact in the two different cases, it suffices to heat or cool the connection (two very different "stimuli").

These would be what Jennings considered "parallel conditions" between machines and living organisms. And this would also exemplify in artifacts the principle that explains the "inconstant" nature of behavioral responses typical of living organisms, "the principle of the *shift* in the arrangement" or in the state (p. 362). Anyone can see that such artifacts do not have action systems except in the sense of having distinct states (somehow comparable to the physiological states of simple organisms) and the ability to shift from one state to another, and of changing or retaining the response. Nevertheless, the ability of these machines to change state and give rise to "inconstant" responses is not the result of an adaptive or regulative selection under the influence of the environment, much less the fixation of a selected response. On the contrary, these machines clearly lack the spontaneity that characterizes the self-regulative reaction of the action system of living organisms.

It is hardly worth mentioning that machines with this feature simply did not exist in Jennings' day. And his insistence on the "inconstant" behavior he improperly attributed to the machines he mentioned points rather to a claim still debated, namely the analogy of a living organism to a machine that has the ability to change its internal organization spontaneously. Nevertheless, it soon became clear (as we shall see in later chapters) that to reproduce something like an action system in an artifact would require machines endowed with this ability, however rough and limited it could be.

There is, however, one aspect of Jennings' claim about "parallel conditions" between organisms and machines that, despite the scanty examples he proposed, deserves attention. It might be expressed in these terms: the behavior of inorganic arrangements or machines and that of living organisms alike can be explained by referring to their *functional organization* rather than to their respective physical and physico-chemical properties. Here the similarity between organism and machine suggested to Jennings a more precise formulation of his objection to Loeb's extreme reductionism, and at the same time it suggested a better way to defend mechanism against the criticism of vitalist biologists and psychologists.

Indeed, the reason Jennings rejected the idea of considering lower organisms as "mere masses" of some kind of material, the physico-chemical study of which would by itself reveal the laws of behavior, was because he already considered these organisms as material "arrangements" or "structures," the organization of which made them comparable to complex machines (Jennings, 1910: 360). The complexity of these machines comes from the aforementioned "perplexing properties" of living organisms that Jennings thought he had documented experimentally in *Behavior of the Lower Organisms*. In the 1910 essay he states this complexity through the "principle of the shift in the arrangement," a principle it seems correct to call *functional*, since it concerns the organization of an action system and not its material composition. Actually, in *Behavior* Jennings said that the behavior of living organisms "is not determined by the permanent properties of colloidal substance;" and more explicitly, "we cannot predict how an animal will react to a given condition unless we know the state of its internal physiological processes" (Jennings, 1906: 258 and 231). In the 1910 essay we are told that in analyzing the behavior of organisms as "complex machines," once given the principle of the shift in the arrangement, "what we find out is *how certain machines work*, rather than the direct physical and chemical properties of certain substances" (Jennings, 1910: 360, my italics).

The functional nature of that principle, independent of the specific material composition of an action system, is made clear through analogy with *inorganic* machines. The following passage from Jennings, which has not been taken into consideration, deserves special attention. It shows that the same function can be performed in different ways in machines, that this is no small matter as far as criteria of *prediction* of their behavior are concerned, and that this conclusion is also true of living organisms.

> From the same mass of substance we can make many different arrangements or machines, acting in entirely different ways, so that we could never predict the reactions of the machines from a knowledge of the chemical and physical properties of the unarranged substance [...]. We could, moreover, make the same machines, showing the same reactions, from a different kind of material, with different properties. We could then never predict the reactions of these by knowing merely the chemical and physical properties of the material of which they are composed. The specific action of each depends on the specific arrangement of its material. This is exactly what we find in organisms, including the lowest as well as the highest (Jennings, 1910: 361).

Hence organisms and machines can be studied through their *functional organization*, and it is this idea that chiefly underlies the complexity of which Jennings speaks. His analytic method is a way of studying behavior that we might well call *top-down*. What makes this method legitimate for Jennings is that first of all we still do not have a complete reduction of concepts and relations at the level of overt behavior to the sciences of chemistry and physics. But were we to succeed in that enterprise, Jennings would still not abandon description of the organism at *that* level, in short, at the level of the action system. Thus, for Jennings the idea of action system had authentic explanatory primacy; in other words, there are concepts, relations, and generalizations at the action system level that cannot be directly formulated in the vocabulary of the lower level (they "cannot now be expressed in the terminology of physics and chemistry," he says). Again, this applies not only to living organisms but also to machines. As Jennings put it, what good would it do to describe a (inorganic) machine "in terms of the movements of electrons or ions?" (*ibid.*) So we may conclude that in studying what he calls the "natural history" of behavior (p. 356), the analytic method is justified, so to speak, by its predictive success. When dealing with systems, be they natural or artificial, that are endowed with a complex organization of behavior, explanation in terms of chemistry and physics can tell only part of the story.

The functional interpretation of action systems suggested here is wholly consistent with the properties that make it a plastic system and not a "slave" to stimuli from the external environment. The passage from Jennings quoted at the beginning of the preceding section, which caught Ashby's attention, leads to the conclusion that the cause or stimulus that sets the action system in motion is not a *separate* phase from the movement or reaction. More generally the action is circular, two-way, as Ashby remarked in the first edition of *Design for a Brain*, noting that "the behavior of *Stentor* [as described by Jennings] bears a close resemblance to the behavior of an ultrastable system" (Ashby, 1952: 103).

Ashby defines a system as "stable" when it can adjust or regulate its behavior on the basis of a simple negative feedback device, *a single decision rule*. One example of that system is the Hammond and Miessner automaton itself. A system is "ultrastable" when it is also able to change its internal organization in order to react appropriately to outside disturbance. An ultrastable system *has a set of decision rules* that allow it to display selective behavior, in other words, an action system that can make choice *automatically*.

A diagram from the second edition of *Design for a Brain* (Figure 1.4) shows that Ashby's observation is likewise fully justified from the standpoint of our functional interpretation of the Jennings action system. The figure shows what Ashby called "a little ultrastable system" (Ashby, 1952/1960). Here the external environment and R (the reacting part of the organism) are linked through two feedback loops, indicated by the arrows. R is defined only functionally; its physical or anatomical composition is not known. This is sufficient to describe the different ways the organism functions, both the adaptive ways with successful reactions, and the non adaptive with other reactions. Ashby's diagram can be used as a schematic representation of *Stentor*'s action system when it reacts to a disturbance from the environment (according to the law of selection of varied movements mentioned in section 4 above).

Let us suppose that initially none of the organism's vital functions is threatened, or in Ashby's terminology, that no "essential variables" take on values beyond the normal physiological limits. This is indicated in the diagram by a dial with strokes, which mark those limits. *Stentor*, then, is in a physiological state corresponding to stable behavior that can be predicted from among those kinds of behavior in its action system. In Ashby's terminology, we can say that the essential variables vary within the norm and act on certain parameters S that may finally give rise to adaptive behavior that can be observed through R. When an external agent threatens of disturbs some vital function of *Stentor*'s, the essential variables are pushed over the limits, and the parameters S take on different values. In other words, the organism tries out one of the possible movements in its action system, corresponding to one of its internal states, in order to bring the variables back within the norm. Thus one observes a change of behavior in R. If the attempt fails, the feedback loop dealing with the essential variables is activated again, in hopes of bringing them with the limits of tolerance.

We shall see the development of Ashby's ideas on the threshold of the cybernetic age.

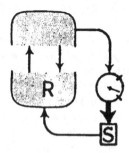

Fig. 1.4. A little ultrastable system, from (Ashby, 1952/1960).

But we can already say that a need Jennings began to sense when he stressed the famous "parallel conditions" between organisms and machines became perfectly explicit with Ashby, a need for a theory of which organisms and machines, given the common functional organization of their respective action systems, were in some ways different instances.

6. Men, animals and machines. Reductionism and mentalistic language

It should be pointed out that for Jennings the fact that behavior was modifiable did not mean that it was completely indeterminate and thus evaded causal explanation. In the years he studied lower animals, he shared Loeb's idea of a causal and mechanistic explanation of behavior. And he continued to do so, but with an important caveat: "the causes [of behavior] lie partly within the animal; each phase of the movement aids in determining the succeeding phase" (Jennings, 1906: 251). This caveat suggests the degree to which Jennings dissented from Loeb. And it was no small dissent.

It is true that for Loeb, unlike Jennings, knowledge of the physico-chemical stimulus and the anatomical structure of an simple organism was sufficient to control and predict its behavior interpreted as a tropism, and the consideration of what Loeb called "vague" internal physiological states was superfluous if not misleading (Loeb, 1918: 17). Consider the chemical effect of light on an animal with bilateral symmetry, such as the moth (Loeb's favorite example): the organism's reaction to light is always the same. We could say that its action system consists of a single movement or active behavior, and the corresponding physiological state is wholly dependent on an external stimulus. Failing this, that behavior is blocked; the organism, as it were, has no 'history.'

Nevertheless, others have strained Jennings' criticism of the tropism theory to the point of setting up Jennings as the theoretician of organisms' complexity against a Loeb maniacally seduced by the automatism of tropism.[21] Without going into great detail, it is worth nothing first Loeb's own protest that, starting with his first work in 1889, he had always stressed that in most cases the heliotropic reactions of a lower animal were influenced by the different (internal) physiological conditions it might be in, namely, by hormonal conditions and metabolism (a hungry animal may react to light differently than one that is not, and "this latter fact has been overlooked by several writers," Loeb, 1912: 47). Jennings would have agreed: "the study of animal heliotropism revealed the fact that one and the same animal may react differently toward the light during different periods of its existence," corresponding, for example, to different states of its metabolism (Loeb, 1905: 112). In short, not all heliotropic machines behave in the simply predictable way the moth does. So what is the real source of disagreement between Jennings and Loeb?

To begin with, notwithstanding that it was not always possible to show clearly that all behavior could be interpreted as a tropism, Loeb still believed that tropism had general explanatory validity as a model to which other cases could be reduced. These cases would prove to be what they actually were, namely cases that differed in the quantity but not in the quality of the factors involved in tropistic response. We have already seen that

---

[21] Such interpretations of Loeb as that by Griffin (1976) are unusable in this sense.

this applied to associative memory as the main source of *complications*, and what problems that involved. In this case, "the question is, which peculiarities of the colloidal substance can make the phenomenon of associative memory possible?" (Loeb, 1900: 17). The same is even truer for other factors: metabolism, hormonal factors, and what Loeb called "differential sensibility," a simple heliotropic organism's sensibility to sudden changes in light. This may well "complicate and entirely obscure the heliotropic phenomena," which must be kept in mind along with other factors, if "we wish to trace all animal reaction back to phsyico-chemical laws" (Loeb, 1912: 55). But none of this made any difference for Loeb, while Jennings (1909b) protested that differential sensibility did. So Loeb concluded (with implicit reference to Jennings) that if we speak of "adaptation" instead of "orientation," or use such terms as "trial-and-error," or "selection of varied movements," we are indulging in anthropomorphic speculations that "cannot even be expressed in the language of the physicist" (Loeb, 1918: 16). And he warned "those who are familiar with current controversy concerning heliotropism" that the Hammond and Miessner machine did "not support theory of 'trial-and-error'" (Loeb, 1915: 781).

What Jennings ascribed to Loeb as synthetic method might be defined as a *bottom-up* method. For Loeb it was a matter of studying organisms as chemical machines, marked, that is, by a precise physico-chemical microstructure, and this study would reveal the laws of behavior. The mentalistic language ("choice," "trial-and-error," and so on) should be used only where phenomena of associative memory were found, but in principle it could be eliminated, and at the very least it was subordinate to the language of physics. And this was the language of tropisms.

Jennings' adoption of a *single* mentalistic language in the study of the behavior of animals, be they higher or lower, may instead be interpreted as part of the strategy of the analytic method. The action system is not influenced solely by internal processes such as the hormonal and by metabolism but also by changes in physiological state which depend on the organism's past "history" (for example, past stimuli and past reactions to those stimuli), the very ones that Loeb presumably considered too "vague" to be used in the study of lower animals. This is the sense, then, of Jennings' caveat concerning causal explanation. It is through the understanding of an organism's history that its behavior can be predicted. It is the regulative principles of the action system that make behavior predictable at the level of *rational* response, so to speak. Since the response is regulative, it cannot be "haphazard," as he put it (Jennings, 1906: 179). Rather, given the complexity of the behavior of organisms generally, conclusions from experimental study are *statistical* by nature (Jennings, 1908: 710).

To summarize, for Jennings, this strategy is not a preference for introspective psychology or metaphysics, as Loeb put it, but is justified by the *continuity* Jennings believed could be objectively observed in manifestations of intelligent behavior ("choice," "trial-and-error," "attention," "discrimination," and so on) from the lowest to the highest levels of the evolutionary scale. Even the lowest organisms, in the great majority of cases, elude purely tropistic description. What is involved instead is a well-defined level of control and prediction of behavior, the level of the action system running "from amoeba to man," as Jennings put it, which can be described in terms of self-regulation. Thus mentalistic language is the language of the analytic method, and it is justified by this fundamentally *objective* feature of behavior, not by the underlying physiological and ultimately physical referents.[22]

But what is to be said about the *subjective* states that mark conscious activity? Jennings thought the problem of whether or not non human minds, the minds of animals, had consciousness was insoluble. Since there is no way of justifying it by analogy with our subjective experience, the attribution of subjective or conscious states to animals is merely a choice on the part of the observer. This is a choice that may be justified by criteria of utility and predictive power. Whether animals *really* have such subjective states is not a problem that concerns consideration of animals by the analytic method. This is one of Jennings' important conclusions:

> We do not usually attribute consciousness to a stone, because this would not assist us in understanding or controlling the behavior of the stone. Practically indeed it would lead us much astray in dealing with such an object. On the other hand, we usually do attribute consciousness to the dog, because this is useful; it enables us practically to appreciate, foresee, and control its actions much more readily than we could otherwise do so. If amoeba were so large as to come within our everyday life, I believe beyond question that we should find similar attribution to it of certain states of consciousness a practical assistance in foreseeing and controlling its behavior [...]. In a small way this is still true for the investigator who wishes to appreciate and predict the behavior of amoeba under microscope (Jennings, 1906: 337).

Without raising the problem of the consciousness of lower animals, a philosopher as concerned with the problem of non human minds as Daniel Dennett thought that spatial scale had a powerful built-in bias against attributing some kind of 'mind' to certain living systems. "If gnats were the size of seagulls, more people would be sure they had minds, and if we had to look through microscopes to see the antics of otters, we would be less confident that they were fun-loving" (Dennett, 1996: 73). Dennett would consider the lower animals Jennings studied as genuine "intentional systems," systems about which it is hard not to assume what he calls the "intentional stance": in order to control and predict the behavior of these systems, we decide to use mentalistic language *as if* they were rational agents which, in interaction with the environment, pursue a purpose and make 'choices' on the basis of 'beliefs' and 'desires,' and so on (Dennett, 1978). So a stone is not an intentional system, but plants are and some artifacts as well, and, again, we ascribe mental properties to them.

We are a long way from the artifacts that Dennett is inclined to consider intentional systems, and in the following chapters we shall cover some little-explored ground on that track. But to stay with Jennings, his proposal of a, so to speak, pragmatic criterion for at-

[22] Elsewhere Jennings was more specific about his position, reconfirming that it was one thing to disagree on the relative liberality of the use of mentalistic terms endowed with an objective experimental counterpart and another thing to disagree about the very legitimacy of using mentalistic terms in experimental work. The former might be a simple "divergence in practical details," and he seemed to believe that was what actually separated him from Loeb. As Jennings concluded, it was clearly "impossible to avoid [mental] words completely," for even Loeb did so in speaking of "associative memory." Jennings noted that for Loeb associative memory was an objective phenomenon, but it was no less objective than "trial-and-error" was for him (Jennings, 1908: 709). However, it seems to have become clear to Jennings (1910) too that the difference between the two positions was whether or not there was an objectively verifiable sudden change in the evolutionary scale.

tributing consciousness to animals can be viewed as a possible reply to the aporias concerning Loeb's reduction of consciousness to associative memory.

We saw that for Loeb mentalistic language was legitimized only by the objective counterpart of associative memory in living organisms, which was absent in lower animals, plants and machines alike. The observer (especially the scientific observer or investigator) had to attribute associative memory, through the use of mentalistic language, only to those organisms in which it could be objectively observed. But we saw that, since the explanation of the mechanism of associative memory consisted in complete reduction to tropisms, mentalistic language could always be eliminated when that reduction was made. Yet the use of that language might always be due to the observer's inability to effect the reduction. Indeed, it was not impossible that an observer might improperly attribute associative memory to an organism if he were not able to distinguish the tropistic feature of its behavior. Hence Loeb's claim to an objective criterion of consciousness seems incompatible with the fact that the decisive factor in attributing consciousness is the observer's subjective ignorance of how the behavior control mechanisms of an organism work.

Jennings did not equate consciousness with the ability to remember, make choices, learn, act purposefully, and so on, so the attribution of conscious states to animals could be more consistently interpreted as a choice of the observer (of the scientific observer in the case of the amoeba). In general, we do or may treat animals *as if* they were conscious, without worrying about whether they *really* are, and we do so to control and predict their behavior. And aside from the case of the moths that turn towards the light, "even those who claim that animals are automata do not treat them as such," is how the biologist Robert Yerkes put it in his appreciation of the "reaction [of Jennings and other biologists] against extreme objectivism" (Yerkes, 1906: 383).

The disagreement between Loeb and Jennings about consciousness seems to be echoed a few years later in the writings of John Watson, which marked the official birth of behaviorism (Watson, 1913). One is tempted to say that the aporias in Loeb's view of consciousness paved the way for a radical solution to the problem in the form of a psychology that did *without consciousness*. Actually Watson defined psychology as "a purely objective experimental branch of natural science," and its programme, the "prediction and control of behavior," seemed to be a reformulation of Loeb's programme; but at the same time he decreed his celebrated expulsion of consciousness from psychology on the basis of criticism of claims that Loeb shared about associative memory.[23] Watson considered them a failed attempt to state "a set of objective, structural and functional criteria" of psychic phenomena, and he concluded that "one can assume either the presence or the absence of consciousness anywhere in the phylogenetic scale without affecting the problems of behavior by one jot or one tittle; and without influencing in any way the mode of experimental attack upon them" (Watson, 1913: 199).

[23] It was Pauly (1987: 172-173) who pointed out the revival of Loeb's idea of the control of behavior in Watson's manifesto of behaviorism. Watson studied with Loeb in Chicago in the early years of the twentieth century (O'Donnell, 1985) and soon shared some of his ideas. But what seemed to separate him from Loeb was the conception of mental life. Jensen reconstructs Watson's relationship to Loeb and to Jennings in the aforementioned introduction to Jennings (1906).

CHAPTER 2

NERVOUS CONDUCTION:
EARLY CONNECTIONISM, PHYSICAL ANALOGIES AND MACHINES

1. Introduction. Neurological hypotheses and machines

In the previous chapter we saw that for Loeb associative memory was a mark of intelligence and learning capacity. His thesis was that the lower organisms did not have associative memory, a thesis that seemed to be corroborated by a machine that was actually built by an engineer, Benjamin Miessner. The machine displayed behavior that was indistinguishable from that of a lower organism, and since it was a machine, and since it was automatic, it was by definition without associative memory or the ability to learn.

At the time, another engineer, S. Bent Russell, was discussing the possibility of a machine endowed with memory that could simulate the working of a nervous system capable of rudimentary forms of learning. Paradoxically he appealed to the authority of Loeb, in part to explain the importance of his own machine (had it not been Loeb who considered the function of associative memory the "great discovery" to be made in physiology and psychology?) and in part to identify the ability to learn as the criterion for showing that the machine itself had associative memory (had it not been Loeb who said that "if an animal [...] can learn, it possesses associative memory"?) (Russell, 1913: 20 and 35). With a misunderstanding not unlike that of Miessner, who credited Loeb with an anthropomorphic explanation of reflex action, Russell interpreted in terms of *inorganic* machines associative memory, which Loeb considered a proper subject for physiology, not engineering, a feature of some organisms but never of machines.

Russell saw no particular difficulty in the physical explanation of the nervous discharge that occurs in simple reflex action, where a given stimulus always evokes the same response. So he proposed to simulate with his mechanical device some phenomena of conductivity in the nervous system that he called "perplexing": they were phenomena in which the same stimulus could evoke different responses or in which different stimuli evoked the same response, namely phenomena displayed by organisms capable of learning.

The following is Russell's simulation method, as expounded in his 1913 paper in the *Journal of Animal Behavior*. He first summarized the hypotheses on nervous conduction that seemed to be generally accepted by psychologists, then described a hydraulic machine that he said "embodied" these hypotheses, and proceeded to "compare the results obtained with the machine with those given by live nervous connections." This comparison made him think it possible that a mechanical device could simulate the "essential elements" that, according to the most widely accepted neurological hypotheses, accompanied inhibition, habit formation and other forms of learning. He concluded with a study of the differences between machine behavior and that of the nervous system, expressing the hope that "with some modification" the machine would be able to simulate more complex forms of learning.

It was a method that seems quite sophisticated for the period in which it was proposed, exactly thirty years before 1943, the year which is usually considered to mark the birth of cybernetics. With its potential and its limitations this method marked an important point in the history of the sciences of the mind and behavior. In the present chapter and the next two we shall follow some of the germinal phases only hinted at in Chapter 1.

But which hypotheses on nervous conduction inspired Russell when he designed his machine? The authors he mentioned were Herbert Spencer, Max F. Meyer, and Edward L. Thorndike. These are fairly disparate and heterogeneous figures, but they all shared the associationist slant and the idea that the variability of behavior observed in habit formation and learning might be explained as the result of some modification of nerve tissue. Anyway, the authors Russell mentioned disagreed on the exact nature of that modification. In the wake of Spencer and Meyer, there emerged several versions of the so-called "drainage theory" of nervous conduction, a theory that James picked up from Spencer and that was refined by McDougall. The analogy that inspired the theory was that of nervous current as continuous fluid flowing through a network of natural channels or pipes connected by one-directional valves. These valves were later made to correspond to synapses. The deviation of a nervous current from one direction to another, which would explain learning phenomena, occurred through a physical process comparable to that of a liquid or fluid being drained. As for Thorndike, he had proposed a theory of nervous conduction as an impulse transmitted by a complex system of "connections" or "bonds" between stimulus and response (S-R). These connections could be strengthened or weakened depending on the effect produced by the response, which could subsequently modify the direction of the nervous current and give rise to learning. For some traits at least, this system was compared to a telephone network of countless units, corresponding to neurons, that allowed the nerve message to be routed through an enormous multiplicity of conduction lines.

In the present chapter we shall first examine the different concepts of learning that go back to these two theories of nervous conduction. Thus we can make clear which neurological hypotheses Russell embodied in his machine and, most of all, what was new in his approach as compared with the mechanical analogies used not only by mechanistic psychologists like Meyer but also by vitalist psychologists and biologists like McDougall and von Uexküll. Russell's machine was designed as a working mechanical model of some "perplexing" phenomena of the nervous system and worked according to certain neurological hypotheses embodied in it, but the hydraulic analogies for the nervous system, based on drainage, came down to partial and forced images of fluid dynamics not infrequently bolstered by ad hoc explanations. Furthermore, the use of these analogies depended on whether or not a purely physical explanation of learning and mental life seemed sufficient, and this gave rise to the conflict between "Automaton Theories" and "Ghost Theories," which is how McDougall and Meyer, respectively, polemically characterized those theories that refused to introduce a non-physical cause or agency into the explanation of learning and mental life and those theories that instead considered it indispensable. We shall mention the later evolution of Russell's neurological thinking, which led him to support hypotheses about nervous conduction that seemed equally distant from drainage theory and from Thorndike's theory and altogether closer to certain of Watson's claims. We shall end the chapter by describing a simulative methodology even more explicit and resolute than Russell's, proposed by the psychologist J. M. Stephens. He tried to embody in a simple electro-mechanical device the law of effect, the most important of the laws of what Thorndike called the "connectionist" theory of learning.

However rudimentary Russell's machine and Stephens' were, they are a novelty in the field of the study of organism behavior when they are compared with the aforementioned scanty mechanical analogies. Notwithstanding, we shall dwell on these analogies at length in this chapter. On the one hand, they constitute a little-known issue in the history of psychology and neurology and stimulated the rise of a connectionist view of nervous activity. On the other hand, the very intricate difficulties in which those analogies were involved show up the actual novelty of a modeling approach, which lies in building working artifacts that embody explanatory hypotheses on behavior, and as such is at the core of the discovery of the artificial.

2. Nervous conduction as drainage: Spencer, James and McDougall

Aside from vague references by British empiricists, David Hartley in particular, it was Spencer who explicitly connected the formation of mental associations with the formation of nervous connections.[1] In the following, almost forgotten passage of the first edition of his *Principles of Psychology*, Spencer formulated a law of formation and "consolidation," as he put it, of the connections between parts or nervous states of the organism, a law with which modern neurological associationism made its debut in the wake of psychological associationism.

> The law in virtue of which all physical states that occur together tend to cohere, and cohere the more the more they are repeated together, until they become indissoluble [...] is the law in virtue of which nervous connections are formed. When a change in one part of an organism is habitually followed by change in another; and when the electrical disturbance thus produced is habitually followed by a change in another; the frequent restoration of electrical equilibrium between these two parts, being always effected through the same route, may tend to establish a permanent line of conduction—a nerve (Spencer, 1855: 544 n.).

So what Spencer called the "general law of intelligence," which explained the association of ideas, was the same law that should explain the formation of new nerve connections. These gave rise not to "perfectly automatic" responses, like those aroused by reflex activity and instinct, but to unpredictable and initially "irregular" responses, as Spencer put it, which showed that memory must be present. And this was what made it possible for the organism to adapt to the environment in a not wholly passive way, that is to say, to acquire new habits in the form of *new* automatisms and to learn.[2]

The description of the hypothetical physical mechanism of the *formation* of nerve connections underlying association was very vague, and that continued to be the case in sub-

---

[1] James (1890) mentioned these antecedents, and the story was subsequently reconstructed by McDougall (1911, Chapter 8).

[2] See above, p. 11.

sequent editions of the *Principles*, which were extensively rethought and expanded. Although this hypothetical mechanism was later described in different terms, Spencer continued to think of an organism's nervous system as a system of forces in equilibrium. In general, every sensory stimulus from the external environment was treated as an alteration of that equilibrium, which could be followed by its restoration. According to Spencer, when the organism was stimulated from outside, it was as if a force were added or liberated at a particular point A of its nervous system, which force, being resisted by smaller forces around, gave rise to a motion towards other points in the nervous system. Suppose that there was a point B elsewhere in the organism at which a force was being expended. In this case motion would arise between A and B, and thus in the nervous system a "line of least resistance" would have been forced, like a drainage channel, between point A, at which excess energy was liberated and point B, where it could be absorbed. In this way equilibrium would be restored in the nervous system (Spencer, 1855/1890, vol. 1: 511-512). This, for example, is the way the phenomenon of a stimulus in a specific part of the organism habitually followed by a contraction in some other specific part was treated.

Figure 2.1a shows Spencer's "network of lines of least resistance" in a nervous system where one of the "afferent fibers" A runs from point *a* to all points *e* of the "efferent fibers" E. If tension is established between point *a* and all points *e*, it must be susceptible to suppression by flows through the connections between point *a* and points *e* for the system to return to equilibrium.

Spencer distinguished the formation of new connections between different points or centers of the nervous system from the *facilitation* or *fixation* of connections once they are formed. Facilitation consisted in the gradual increase of permeability of the connections, and it was repeated use that turned a "vague course," the newly formed connection, into a "definite channel" with a lower resistance, in which the passage of the nervous impulse could gradually be made easier (p. 515). In this way a "permanent line of conduction" is fixed according to the above-mentioned general law of intelligence, and thus the organism acquires the ability to make a new association; actually he becomes able to change his response and to learn.

A similar description of the formation and fixation of nerve connections can be found in Bain's *Mind and Body*.[3] Bain's neurological statement of the law of association is as follows:

In consequence of two [nervous circuits] being independently made active at the same moment, [...] a strengthened connection or diminished obstruction would arise between these two, by a change wrought in the intervening cell-substance (Bain, 1873: 119).

Figure 2.1a shows Bain's "hypothetical scheme" of nervous connections (p. 111). The unequal intensity of stimulation of fibres *a*, *b*, *c* causes nervous currents of different intensity, and this difference of intensity ends in a difference in the nervous circuits converging in cells *X, Y, Z*, which are supposed to be the commencement of motor fibres, each concluding in a distinctive movement or response. Once new connections or nervous cir-

---

[3] I am indebted to Carmela Morabito for drawing my attention to this point.

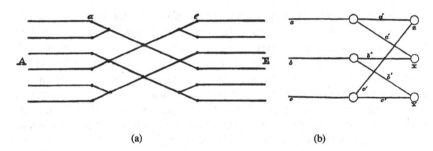

(a)   (b)

Fig. 2.1. Networks of nervous connections: (a) from Spencer (1855/1890); (a) from Bain (1873).

cuits are formed, they are to become fixed, in order to have "the physical bond underlying memory, recollection, or the retentive power of the mind", as Bain put it (p. 116)

Bain's and Spencer's descriptions of the formation and fixation of a nervous connection are rather obscure. Bain quite briefly used the analogy of electrical induction in order to give an idea of the diffusion of nervous current. As to Spencer, he recurred to the aforementioned analogy of drainage, but it is not sufficiently clear how drainage actually works when different cortical centers are repeatedly stimulated in immediate succession, the physical correlate of the association of ideas. Among psychologists, it was James in his *Principles of Psychology* who tried to formulate more detailed hypotheses about the nature of this phenomenon.[4]

James thought that, generally speaking, for any physical system to form new habits and maintain them through the course of time, it must be capable of changing its internal structure or organization as well as putting up some "resistance" to the cause for change. Only in this way could a physical system achieve a new internal structure or organization without so to speak disintegrating, i.e. it would be capable of reaching a new state of equilibrium. This kind of system must necessarily be *plastic*. "Plasticity [...] in the wide sense of the word," James wrote, "means the possession of a structure weak enough to yield to an influence, but strong enough not to yield all at once. Each relatively stable phase of equilibrium in such a structure is marked by what we may call a new set of habits" (James, 1890, vol. 1: 105).

There has always been interest in the existence in the physical world—the world of "dead matter," as James called it—of this kind of plasticity, whereby a system's behavior can be influenced by its previous history. We have already run into the observations of Loeb and Jennings about 'memory' found in the inorganic world in the form of different kinds of hysteresis, and Spencer also commented on the physical analogies that might be made with some phenomena of organic memory. James too was rather attracted by the superficial aspect of these analogies, so much so as to make comparisons between water flow and nerve currents, between a natural channel's resistance to water and that of nerve paths: "wa-

[4] The literature on James' *Principles* is vast. Suffice it to mention the collection of essays edited by Johnson and Henley (1990) on the centenary of the book's publication. Walker (1990) deals with James (and Spencer) in the history of connectionism (see Chapter 6 below).

ter, in flowing, hollows out for itself a channel, which grows broader and deeper; and after having ceased to flow, it resumes, when it flows again, the path traced by itself before."[5]

While this kind of plasticity already existed in dead matter, it was in "organic matter" and nerve tissue in particular that it appeared in its most spectacular form and the form hardest to explain by these vague physical analogies. In the previous chapter we emphasized James' "dilemma" between a rigid and completely determined or "automatic" nervous system and a ductile and completely undetermined or "casual" nervous system. Neither of these nervous systems is capable of achieving the fairly stable new states of equilibrium James spoke of, i.e. of forming new habits. The former, rigid system offers too much resistance to change, in the sense that the currents aroused by sense organs would always flow along pre-existing paths. The latter, ductile system offers too little resistance, since those currents could flow with the same casualness along equally permeable paths. To resolve the dilemma we should imagine a different kind of nervous system in which the paths formed by the currents have modifiable resistance, but only when certain conditions are present, and in which the modifications can be saved and consolidated, or at least do not disappear at once. In other words, we have to imagine a *plastic* nervous system.

The currents, once in, must find a way out. The only thing they can do, in short, is *to deepen old paths or to make new ones*; and the whole plasticity of the brain sums itself up in two words when we call it an organ in which currents pouring in from sense organs make with extreme facility paths which do not easily disappear (James, 1890, vol. 1: 107, my italics).

Like Spencer, James seems to distinguish the *consolidation* of a pre-existing nervous path from its *formation*. Both processes are made possible by the plasticity of the nervous system, but for James the formation of new paths is the truly "difficult mechanical problem" (vol. 1, p. 108). As we shall see, the problem of consolidation or fixation of already formed paths is no less difficult a problem in so-called "mechanical" terms. But for James, it is the formation of new paths that seems the central problem. It does not of course concern the paths of the nervous system that are responsible for reflexes and instincts, and as such innate, but concerns the paths that develop as a result of the interaction of the organism's nervous system with the outside world: the latter are the paths that concern habit formation and learning.

Indeed this is a problem that James set, as did all those before and after him who imagined the nervous system as a complex hierarchy of sensory-motor reflex arcs and then had to explain how a system made up of such rigid connections, the basis of determined behavior, could acquire *new* connections, the basis of observed variability of behavior. After all, this was the problem that Loeb tossed out in the various dilemmas about the relationship between tropism and associative memory, between automatic response and learned or voluntary response.

[5] Quoted by James (1890, vol. 1: 106). James had already quoted this passage from a contemporary writer in an article on habit formation published in 1887 in *Popular Science Monthly*, which was then absorbed in the chapter on habits in *Principles of Psychology*. Delboeuf had objected to the use of these analogies: "As for me, these channels hollowed out by flowing water [...] communicate nothing clear to my mind [...]. I know *Popular Science* well, but isn't it a bit too popular?" (quoted in Perry, 1935, vol. 2: 92). Most of these analogies do not appear in James' *Briefer Course* published in 1892.

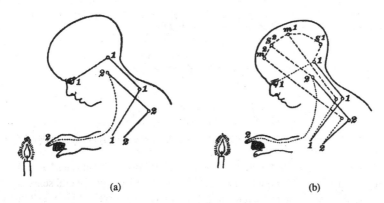

(a)   (b)

Fig. 2.2. A child learns not to get burned, according to James (1890)

To clarify the nature of this difficulty, let us take an example that we will come to in the course of this chapter, so popular was it in James' day and long afterwards, the example of the child who learns not to burn itself.[6] In this regard James discussed two hypothetical nervous systems. In one case (Figure 2.2a), he imagined a nervous system consisting of only two sensory-motor reflex arcs, which were assumed to be innate. One connected the eye to the muscles controlling the arm's forward motion in the direction of the flame, and the other connected the hand to the muscle controlling the withdrawal motion of the hand. (The nerve paths of the reflex arcs are indicated as '1' and '2'; dotted lines for afferent paths and unbroken lines for efferent ones.) With a nervous system reduced to these two sensory-motor paths the child's behavior would be the same on any occasion. The stimulation of the retina would always call forth the arm's movement forward, and the burn would cause the hand to pull back, and the child would never learn to avoid fire. To explain why this does not happen in reality, why such inflexibly stereotyped behavior is not usually seen, and why totally casual behavior is not seen either, James complicated the plan of the nerve paths by introducing others that reached the centers of the cerebral cortex (Figure 2.2b).

According to one neurological hypothesis at the time, one adopted by James, a sensory stimulus that moves down (towards the lower centers) and gives rise to a reflex response tends also to involve higher brain centers, making possible the formation of new paths, which initially offer higher resistance to the nervous current than that offered by

[6] James (1890, vol. 1: 24-27). The example is particularly famous in its Cartesian version, which illustrated the reflex arc, based on the hydraulic analogy of nerve paths as pipes connected by valves and traversed by water. Descartes got the idea from the automata of the fountains in the St. Germain gardens (see Fearing, 1930, and Boakes, 1984). As for James, he referred particularly to the description given by the Austrian neurologist Theordor Meynert, which was based on a clear distinction between the lower centers of the nervous system, which James considered *"en masse* as machine," i.e. "automatic," and the hemispheres, capable of "spontaneous" response. But James tended to blur this distinction, in part because he seemed to see at least "a degree of spontaneity and choice" (vol. 1: 72-78) in lower animals as well, which he described in words not unlike those Jennings used against Loeb. It is not our purpose here, however, to consider James' neurological sources (which he carefully cites, especially in the first three chapters of the *Principles*), interesting as they are.

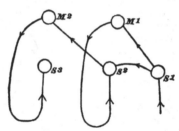

Fig. 2.3. Formation of a new nervous path during learning, according to James (1890).

the paths constituting the reflex arcs.[7] Thus longer circuits or "loop lines" are added to the "direct" sensory-motor circuits, *new* paths that come from peripheral sensory areas and go to higher sensory areas before going down to the motor areas. In Figure 2.2b these loop-lines are indicated by broken lines, in particular loop-line s1-m1-s2-m2, which starts out from the projection of the visual stimulus of the flame towards the cerebral hemispheres (where James said it was deposited in s1 as "image" or "idea") and ends with the propagation of nervous current down from m2 in the final gesture of withdrawing the hand. This is why on a subsequent occasion the sight of the flame arouses in the child the image or idea of the pain caused by the burn *before* he again instinctively reaches out for the flame. It is new behavior of clear adaptive value based on the acquisition of a *new* association (of flame with pain) and the *inhibition* of harmful behavior.[8]

While this description mixes the language of the new-born neurophysiology with the traditional psychological idiom, it clarifies the nature of the "difficult mechanical problem" of how new associative paths are formed. What has to be explained, given that nervous current is like a flux, is why this current does not continue to flow along well-defined channels with lower resistance, such as the reflex ones, but instead heads for much more indistinct paths with higher resistance, such as those that run through the cerebral hemispheres, and finally overcomes that resistance.

At this point, James recognized that these were very vague hypotheses but explicitly picked up the Spencerian account of the nervous system as a system whose parts, constantly kept in states of different tension, are just as constantly tending to equalize their states through drainage channels that are indistinct at first and then increasingly definite (vol. 1: p. 109). Figure 2.3 shows how it might be possible to explain in the very elusive idiom of the analogy with drainage the *physical* process of the formation of a new nerve path that lets the child learn not to get burned (vol. 2: 591).

Here, arc S1 is the visual cortical center that discharges by a reflex path to center M1, which gives rise to the instinctive movement of reaching for the flame, and S2 is the cortical center stimulated by the subsequent sensation of pain evoked by the burn, which gives rise to another instinctive movement caused by center M2 and consisting in withdrawing the hand (S3 is any third center stimulated as a consequence). While the two in-

[7] James quoted the description of the phenomenon given by the psychologist James McKeen Cattell (James, 1890, vol. 1: 92 n.).

[8] This is not the place to consider the possibility long entertained by James of the mechanical justification of the *anticipatory* feature of a response (a behavior) *caused* by an idea (see especially Chapter 4 below).

stinctive sensory-motor connections should be considered innate, James believed that during the first experience a new path is formed between the two cortical centers S1 and S2 by a process that can be summarized as follows. Since S2 is stimulated immediately after S1, it *drains* the latter, according to the general hypothesis, which James said he derived from Spencer, that drainage always starts from a nerve center that *has just been discharging* and is thus in the best condition to be drained (the case of S1) in the direction of a nerve center that *is now discharging*, which therefore exercises the strongest draining power (the case of S2). Once the new path S1-S2 has been formed in this way, a subsequent stimulation of center S1 alone will discharge into S2 *before* S2 is stimulated by M1, and this is the physiological or physical cause of the *inhibition* of M1. With the same stimulus the organism now offers a different response: in this case, when the child sees the flame he will not extend his hand to reach for it.

As James admitted in a similar case (vol. 2: 589), "one does not immediately see" why on *subsequent* stimulation of S1 *alone* (the cortical center of sight), the drainage power exercised by S2 (the cortical center of pain) over S1 is greater than that originally exercised by M1 (the center that regulates the arm's movement towards the flame). James then had to postulate that once a new path was formed between two cortical centers (like that between S1 and S2), the nervous current or tension aroused by the stimulation of the one *henceforth tends to be drained by the other*. And this is how the new path would be *consolidated* or *fixed*.

Yet this consolidation of a nervous path does not seem fully accounted for by the analogy with drainage. In James' description, the analogy may be invoked only in the case of (at least) *two immediately successive stimuli* that excite (at least) two cortical centers, one of which, as we have seen, is thus able to drain the other by a new path. Now in order for the drained current that has followed the path once to follow it again upon repetition of a *single stimulus*, it is necessary that *some trace remain* of the previous passage of current (and the corresponding lowering of the path's resistance). It is the nervous system's plasticity that allows this, for the new paths, as we saw, "do not easily disappear." But what accounts for it is not the analogy of drainage, which works when there is *double* stimulation of separate cortical centers, but the analogy we mentioned first, that between the nervous paths and natural modifiable channels. By referring to the latter analogy, one might conclude that the nervous paths, like modifiable channels, become increasingly permeable with the passage of flow. But at this point, there are *two* analogies at work, and they are superposed without being integrated in an attempt to describe the formation of a new habit in purely physical or physiological terms. James himself did not seem satisfied by these "already too protracted physiological speculations" (vol. 2: 591), and for now we shall not pursue them further. But he was sure that once a path was formed by drainage, it became increasingly efficient through repetition or use, and hence the new path between S1 and S2 eventually became consolidated or fixed.

The hypothesis of nervous conduction as drainage is the basis of James' "law of habits," which is close to the laws stated by Spencer and Bain:

> When two elementary brain-processes have been active together or in immediate succession, one of them, on reoccurring, tends to propagate its excitement into the other (James, 1890, vol. 1: 566).

McDougall was one of the first to reconsider James' law of habits. His opinion was that the law did not explain the "difficult mechanical problem" that James set himself: how new connections are made between two cortical "processes" or centers stimulated in immediate succession. According to McDougall, to say that center B *drains* A did not seem sufficient, because once a center A has been excited, it propagates or irradiates its excitement to many centers, so what still remains to be explained is why A ultimately establishes a new connection with B *in particular* and not with any of the other centers that are excited at the same time as A or immediately thereafter. Why does the burned child learn to associate the sight of fire with a sensation of pain? Why does a child who *sees* a dog and at the same time or right after *hears* the word 'dog' learn to associate these two different stimuli, when the sight of the dog may well be accompanied by many other visual and auditory stimuli? The mere succession in time of stimuli does not seem to explain why a new connection is formed between them. The child who learns not to burn himself or to associate the animal dog with the word 'dog' and not with any other of the many contiguous stimuli does so because at that moment his *attention* is attracted exclusively by the two stimuli in question and not by others that also activate different centers of his nervous system. Attention *shifts* from one (the sight of the dog, say) to the other (hearing the word 'dog') and vice versa, one after the other.

McDougall's conclusion in his *Primer of Physiological Psychology* was that James' law of habits could explain in physical terms only *the second part of habit formation*, namely, how "in reappearing again," through use or repetition, paths that have *already been formed* and traversed by nervous current could be consolidated. But the law said nothing about *the first part of habit formation*, namely about what made the impulse first take *that particular path* among the many possible ones and thus lower the resistance of that path.

McDougall explained this by the "law of the attraction of the impulse," which he believed solved the problem James left open, and which he called "a crucial problem for physiological psychology" (McDougall, 1905: 126). McDougall's law was intended to establish the physiological correlate of attention. The law proposed a physical mechanism underlying the selection that led the subject *to associate* one stimulus with another specific one among the many that immediately followed. This process of selection was also what explained why the activity of a cortical center like B could *inhibit* the activity of another cortical center like A, and why the more intense B's excitation the stronger the inhibition it exercised: association and inhibition were but "two effects of one process," the selective process of attention (McDougall, 1906: 354).

This is why McDougall interpreted the same example treated by James in Figure 2.3 on the basis of *two* neurological laws: his own law of attraction and James' law of habits.[9] For our purposes let us take Figure 2.4, in which the two pre-existing reflex arcs S-H-K-M and S0-W-Z-M0 stand for seeing and reaching for the flame and burning and withdrawing the hand, respectively. According to the hypothesis that James also pointed out, the activation one after the other of the two reflex arcs in Figure 2.4 ends with their respective responses, but it also helps stimulate the two higher cortical centers S1 and S2 via direct paths upwards.

---

[9] See McDougall (1898: 164-168; 1905: 131-133; 1906: 352-354).

McDougall thought he could better develop James' physical analogy of drainage to explain why a specific connection is established between S1 and S2, one *selected* among many possibilities. In his version, when S2, the pain area, is excited immediately after S1, the visual area, S2 by virtue of its particularly intense excitation *attracts* the nervous current liberated in several other cortical centers. Nevertheless, S2 attracts the current liberated in S1 *to a greater degree* because, according to McDougall, S1 was excited immediately before and has more of its just-discharged nervous current ready to disperse towards S2, which has just been discharging. The *formation* of a new association, between reaching for fire and feeling pain, along the path from S1 to S2, is thus matched by the *inhibition* of a center like S1, which has the effect of suppressing the response that involves reaching for the flame.

Thus, the law of the attraction of the impulse says that the greater flow from one cortical area to another, stimulated one after the other, is directed along a privileged channel, the "associative path," which in the present example goes from center S1 to center S2. For McDougall this was the only plausible physical explanation of the selective process of attention. It was only at this point that James' law of habit came into play: the *new* associative path was consolidated by use or repetition, and the subsequent stimulation of S alone tended to discharge towards S1, S2 instead of towards M.

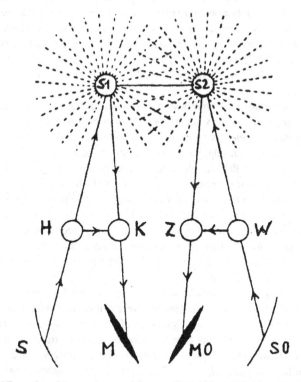

Fig. 2.4 Formation of a new nervous path between S1 and S2, modified from McDougall (1898).

For McDougall, as for James, there seemed to be no problem in the fact that if the analogy with drainage were taken seriously this last assertion would not be accounted for. McDougall adopted only the hypothesis that once the nerve paths were formed, they *preserved a trace of the passage of current*. In this way a kind of automatized habit would be fixed, that involved the formation of neural paths of a higher order or level, the "loop-lines" James spoke of.

On closer inspection, however, McDougall's interpretation of James' law of habits as a mere law of use is fairly reductive. James too referred to earlier speculation, especially Spencer's, and distinguished between the process of forming new paths and the process of nervous facilitation *once given paths were formed*. And his law of habits was intended to explain both phenomena. Suffice it to reread the statement of such a law mentioned above. True, as McDougall pointed out, it refers to a path *already formed*, since it speaks of one "brain-process" that is discharged into another "in coming back again." But James' law also states clearly *how the path was formed* and how one of the two processes was discharged into the other at the earliest occasion: since the two processes "have been active together or in immediate succession," the second *drained* the first, *attracted* nervous current to itself, and *formed* what James elsewhere also called a new "associative path." James is actually vague about the specific selective physical mechanism of attention, but he too sketches out an explanation that closely resembles the one subsequently advocated by McDougall in terms that were no less vague. The associative paths of which James too speaks are all the paths that might be formed between S2 and other cortical centers, "the deepest paths" (James, 1890, vol. 2: 585), and *inhibition* is a "partial neutralization of the brain-energy" (vol. 1: 451), in our case of the energy of the cortical center S1.

Thus James too envisaged the hypothesis of inhibition through drainage, which would offer a physical explanation of the selective process of attention. Actually, James' *Principles* and McDougall's *Primer* are separated by a short space of time: short but crucial, marked as it is by important turning points in the history of neurology. At least two dates are worth remembering. In 1891 Wilhelm Waldeyer recapitulated the experience of neurophysiology of the time in the neuron theory, and in 1897 Michael Foster and Charles Sherrington formulated the hypothesis of synapses as connecting points between anatomically distinct neurons. The two ideas, of neuron and synapse, laid the groundwork for a clear and unified idiom with which to formulate neurological hypotheses in psychology and replace the vague and fluctuating neurological statements of Spencer, Bain and James, which were all based on "nervous states," "vibrating tracts," "elementary brain-processes," "points of the organism."

McDougall, for example, used the new idiom in his description of the nervous system to give systematic order to several ideas that were still unclear at the time of James' *Principles*. Figure 2.5 shows McDougall's schema of the nervous system as a hierarchy of conduction paths between afferent or sensory neurons S and efferent or motor neurons M. A neuron is represented by a line joining two terminal strokes, and a synapse by a pair of these strokes (McDougall, 1902: 333). The conduction paths consist of a chain of neurons, which are innate and rigidly structured at the lower layer (layer I of simple reflexes), less structured at the next level up (level II of fairly complex instincts), and highly modifiable or not yet organized at the higher levels (levels III and IV of associative areas of the hemispheres).The more evolutionarily complex and ontogenetically developed the nervous system, the more of these latter conduction paths there are. Unlike the lower level paths (which are "automatic" at origin), the higher level paths are marked by varying degrees of attention, will, or consciousness and tend to be organized in support of acquired habits (and, as such, in support of new automatisms).

In McDougall's description of the nervous system, the degree of organization of conduction paths depends on the degree of specific resistance offered by the synapses to the passage of nervous current or energy. In the figure, the greater the length of the terminal strokes representing the synapses the lower the threshold of resistance, which must be

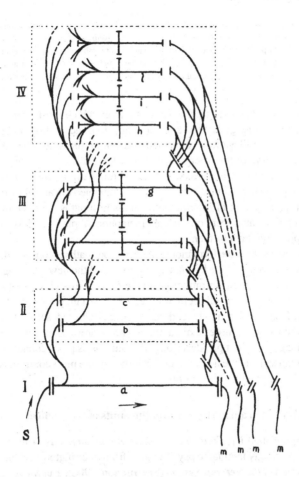

Fig. 2.5. Levels of connections between synapses in the nervous system, from McDougall (1902).

equated or exceeded for current to get through. But this value may be lowered by repeated passage of the current at short time intervals, which weakens the resistance. This lowering may also be temporary, in the sense that the original threshold value tends to be restored, though not immediately, and the new associations or habits tend to disappear if they are not sufficiently consolidated. Thus it is the synapse that constitutes the variable element of any conduction path as well as *the seat of memory of the nervous system*, since it preserves a trace of the passage of the impulse.

And the higher the level in the hierarchy, the less organized the links, the higher the resistance of the corresponding synapses, and the greater the possibility of changing the threshold value and preserving the modification, the very *plasticity* of which James spoke. This is how the laws of Spencer, Bain and James that we have considered appear in the new language of neurology:

> An association of two groups of neurons means a change at the synapses which constitute the physiological boundary and points of contact between the neurons of one group and those of the other (i.e. physiological contact, not necessarily physical contact); a change of such a nature that thereafter any excitation can spread more readily across the synapses from one group to the other. Such a change, such a diminution of the resistance at the synapses, seems to be the normal result of the passage of the excitation process across them (McDougall, 1901: 607).

McDougall hypothesized that the nervous energy which must overcome the resistance of the synapses, energy that he called "neurin," must accumulate in the afferent part of the nervous system like a fluid subjected to a certain pressure. The afferent neurons constituted the reserve of this energy, which was kept at a given "tonus" (McDougall, 1903). The amount of energy released by the afferent neurons was in proportion to the intensity of the peripheral stimulation, and it was channeled towards the efferent neurons along the complex system of intermediate conduction paths we have mentioned. His speculations on the matter were on a purely metaphorical plane, and for our purposes it is not worth pursuing them further.

In conclusion, as far as the formation of new nervous paths is concerned, it was chiefly advances in knowledge and the hypothesis formation of the new neurology that marked a difference between James' formulations in the *Principles* and those of McDougall in the *Primer*. McDougall himself seemed to realize at certain points that his own law of the attraction of the impulse merely rendered more explicit an idea that James had already had. What he added was a more detailed, though no clearer version, of the physical analogy with drainage (for example, describing the neurons as pipes connected by one-way valves, the synapses) and the neurin hypothesis, two of the most controversial aspects of the neurological associationist tradition.

3. Meyer's drainage theory and the limits of mechanical analogy

When Meyer published *The Fundamental Laws of Human Behavior* in 1911, the theory of synapses was already familiar to psychologists from Sherrington's celebrated book *The Integrative Action of the Nervous System* (Sherrington, 1906). But Meyer never used the term 'synapse' in his book, because, as we shall see, he considered it compromised by a "mythological explanation" of adaptive and intelligent behavior. He described the functions of synapses, however, with the image of a "meeting point of two or more neurons" (Meyer, 1911: 42). His idea of nervous plasticity was also inspired by the drainage analogy, and what he was later to call "the law of double stimulation" (Meyer, 1934) was used to explain the same phenomena that McDougall thought could be clarified with his law of the attraction of the impulse, such phenomena as the formation of new associations and inhibition.[10]

The hydraulic analogy had its apotheosis in Meyer's book. All the main manifestations of the nervous system, including reflexes, instincts, habit formation and various kinds of learning were explained in terms suggested by the analogy. Meyer made an effort not to use it in the vague way his predecessors had. Not unlike McDougall, he compared the functional properties of a neuron system to those of a system of pipes filled with a fluid, liquid or gas, connected by one-way valves—the "meeting points" between neurons, in other words, the synapses. One end of the system, corresponding to the sense apparatus, is initially closed, and the other end, corresponding to the motor apparatus, is subject to negative pressure or suction, which tends to draw the fluid in its direction. A stimulus may have greater or lesser intensity, and that determines how much the sensory end of the system, closed at the outset, will open up, which determines how strong or weak the flow is towards the other end, i.e. the motor apparatus. It must be assumed that the fluid that flows away is always replaced when the system is not subject to stimulation (i.e. when the sense apparatus end of the system is closed).

For Meyer too the hydraulic analogy was intended to give plausibility to a physical explanation of the formation of a new nervous connection, or to use his terminology, a "variation of the nervous path" underlying a "variation of response." Figure 2.6 shows the same example used by James and McDougall to describe in a single scheme the *formation* of an association and its "negative aspect," as Meyer called *inhibition* (p. 91). The figure shows a pipe system in which each pipe corresponds to a neuron (each neuron has the shape of an arrow-like line indicating direction of flow). Briefly, imagine that the initially closed end S_b of the pipe system is opened immediately after and wider than S_a (which would correspond in the analogy to the fact that the stimulus causing the burning pain is stronger than the visual stimulus that precedes it). In this case the stronger flux from S_b attracts the weaker flux from S_a and conveys it towards output M_b instead of M_a (pp. 92-93). This is the process that Meyer called "deflection," which is the effect of the suction of a fluid by a jet pump used for drainage or for air exhaust, and for him it simulated the *attraction* of a weaker nervous current by a stronger one. The deflection occurs because of the common pipe $S2_{ab}$, $M2_{ab}$, corresponding to the usual "associative" or "connecting" neuron, as Meyer too called it, which is shared by the two reflex arcs corresponding to S_a, S'_a, M'_a, M_a and S_b, S'_b, M'_b, M_b. This makes it possible to inhibit a response but also to form a new sensory-motor path from S_a to M_b (indicated in the figure by a wavy line). As

[10] Meyer's interests were not limited to the theory of learning discussed here. During his long life (1873-1967) he dealt with many subjects, mainly acoustics and hearing, especially in regard to music. At the turn of the nineteenth century he moved from Germany to America, where he was always an outsider on the fringes of influential academic life. There is a biography by Esper (1966; 1967).

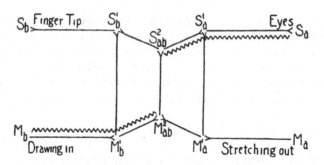

Fig. 2.6. Variation of the nervous path in a child who sees the flame (S_a), reaches for it at first (M_a), feels pain (S_b), and then avoids it (M_b), from Meyer (1911).

with McDougall, the stronger nervous flux has a particularly lively mental state, attention, as its physiological correlate. The strongest flux corresponds to the state that dominates the mind at a certain point: attention consists in the capacity of that flux to deviate (or to "attract," as Meyer put it) weaker flows and neutralize their effect.[11]

Strictly speaking, the *formation* of a new nervous path ought to consist in the veritable *growth* of a new associative connection, a structural modification of the nervous system in response to stimulation from the external environment, which would justify the appearance of a new habit. But the drainage analogy, especially when it is depicted by a system of tubes connected by one-way valves, as in the case of McDougall and Meyer, suggests a weaker interpretation of the formation of nervous paths. Since drainage can occur solely along existing channels, even if those channels have never before been used to carry a fluid, it would seem that the nervous current cannot but follow those unused already existing paths, so they are *new* only in the sense of not being used. From Spencer to Meyer everyone was aware, within the limits of neurophysiological knowledge at the time, that nervous tissue might have a capacity for growth. Spencer devoted several pages to the subject full of speculation, which James judged for what they were—obscure and contradictory (James, 1890, vol. 1: 109 n.). When James spoke of the passages we have cited above he generally interpreted the formation of new paths in the sense of a "potentiality" displayed by some nervous fibers that "are not originally pervious" (vol. 2: 584). With the neuron theory McDougall was able to revive the precise hypotheses advanced by neurophysiologists at the time concerning the various phenomena of synaptic growth (McDougall, 1901), but it is not always clear how far this was involved in learning and, more important, what relation it had with the drainage analogy. Meyer instead

---

[11] This is the substance of Meyer's aforementioned law of double stimulation (see also Meyer 1908a; 1908b; 1909). He subsequently offered a polemical reminder that this law, which he published in 1908, was none other than Pavlov's conditioning law, of which he was unaware at the time (Meyer, 1934: 181-182). The double stimulation shown in Figure 2.6 might well be interpreted as the substitution of stimulus S_b by stimulus S_a in evoking the conditioned response M_b, according to the popular version Watson gave of Pavlov's theory. Meyer seems to have distanced himself from Watson's version, dismissing as trivial the frequentist concept of learning of which Watson was the principle exponent (see section 6 of the present chapter).

took the drainage analogy more literally and believed explicitly that the growth of neurons was required to explain some phenomena of learning that could not be described in terms of deflection (Meyer, 1911: 100-106).[12]

Nevertheless, for Meyer deflection remained the chief mechanism that explained the variation of response that followed upon learning. Meyer's image of the nervous system, one with which we are already familiar, was a hierarchy of neural arcs of increasing resistance as you ascend from reflex arcs to higher cerebral centers (p. 49). McDougall could have accepted this image of the nervous system (except that it did not include synapses) and the deflection analogy alike. The drainage hypothesis inspired Meyer's law of deflection by double stimulation and McDougall's law of attraction, and both laws tried to suggest the same physical mechanism to account for a nervous current channeled along a "less permeable" path with greater resistance towards a higher center rather than along a well marked path of lower resistance directed to a motor center. As McDougall concluded in the *Primer*, only in the event that the neural mechanism suggested by the law of attraction failed to give a satisfactory explanation of that phenomenon would its origin inevitably have to be sought in "psychical energy or 'mind'" (McDougall, 1905: 128). In that case attention as an autonomous mental state would be the *cause* of the attraction of one nervous current by another and of the consequent change in response.

But this was the problem. Could learning (and attention, will, consciousness, and so on) be satisfactorily explained in terms of neural mechanisms *alone*? Although McDougall and Meyer both accepted the drainage analogy, their positions were far apart concerning the nature of explanation and the role of neurology in psychological investigations.

The same year that Meyer's *Fundamental Laws of Human Behavior* appeared, McDougall published *Body and Mind* (McDougall, 1911). In the new book McDougall did not reject the explanation of mental process in neurological terms he had advanced in the *Primer*, but that explanation was now described as "speculative" and insufficient to account for the *subjective* component of mental life. McDougall now concentrated on aspects of his thinking that had stayed in the background for some years: the autonomy of mental life and the impossibility of sharply dividing the study of psychological and neurological factors in explaining the behavior of living organisms. It was not that he had failed, in the years before *Body and Mind*, to focus on interactions between the psychological and physiological side of behavior. He had dealt with the problem of relationships between neurology and psychology with the so-called "method of residues." According to this method, neurophysiological considerations were the first basis of the study of organisms, but whatever could not be completely clarified by that approach would be a *residue* that could be explained only by assuming genuinely autonomous mental activity. The direction of attention, for example, would have a different cause than that offered by the purely physiological and mechanical factors described by the drainage analogy.

---

[12] Consider the gradual automatization of manual skills once acquired (like writing or playing a musical instrument). This entailed more than a deviation of nervous flux along high resistance paths never used before, rather a veritable shortening of those paths by a "short-circuiting" process that Meyer considered a veritable growth of an associative neuron, using a different analogy than deflection. We shall make future reference to other stances on the problem of nerve growth in connection with Thorndike's dissent from Watson (see below, p. 64).

Nevertheless, in those years McDougall seems to have believed that the existence of this residue or "inexplicable factor" could neither be excluded nor conclusively affirmed. So it made sense to postpone consideration of the residue until the development of neurological study made it necessary, meanwhile "keeping our minds open to the possibility of its reality" (McDougall, 1902: 318).

While the interaction between the psychological and the neurophysiological remained part of the method of residues for the time being, a position described as "dualist-interactionist", as well as "animist", was openly maintained in *Body and Mind*. Body and mind and are two different things, and it is the action of the mind in its entirety (as will, consciousness, intention and so on) that *causes* the processes of organization of the nervous system at its highest level, the level of modifiable paths. In practice the mind "forces" a nervous current along an initially more resistant path rather than along one with lower resistance (McDougall, 1911: 278-280). McDougall vigorously took up a hypothesis he had advanced in the past (McDougall, 1901) and considered the synapse the site at which interaction between mental and physical phenomena took place. Thus the synapse was not simply a point of variable resistance of the nervous system, but the place in which mind or soul performed its role as "guide" to nervous current.

The main object of McDougall's polemic in *Body and Mind* were some of the authors we have already considered, people he described as supporters of "Automaton Theories," which is to say "anti-animist" solutions to the mind-body problem. These included Huxley and the epiphenomenists, for whom mental life had no independent reality of its own but was the direct result of physico-chemical reactions in the brain. They also included the proponents of parallelism, for whom mental and brain processes merely accompanied each other in time, without there being any necessary causal relation between the two, which might be seen as two different orders of reality whose relation was one of simple *concomitance*. McDougall considered Lloyd Morgan, among others, a proponent of parallelism, but the same idea could also be ascribed to Meyer.

According to Meyer, the physical mechanism of deflection, however "hypothetical"[13] it might be, was sufficient to explain all the notions of introspective psychology, including association of ideas, attention, will, and consciousness. Nevertheless, while none of these notions might, strictly speaking, be considered the cause of a nervous phenomenon, they were not caused by a nervous phenomenon either. Instead, nervous and mental processes were "more probably [...] strictly simultaneous" (Meyer, 1911: 229). It could be said that Meyer never had to turn to the subjective, mental or psychic as the *cause* of a variation in response, but when something like that seemed to be present, it was always *accompanied* by some change involving the nervous paths (at the level of the higher centers). This conclusion, as we shall see more clearly in section 7 below, was the on-

---

[13] The choice of words also reflects the different stances of the two men: what was "hypothetical" for Meyer was "highly speculative" for McDougall (1923a: 179). McDougall said with a touch of self-criticism (almost echoing James) that he had "indulged in a good deal of physiological speculation" (p. 37 n.). This at a time when he was explaining his hydraulic analogies of instincts seen as "springs of energy," which became very popular and widely discussed, although they had been offered offhandedly to "those who like mechanical analogies" (p. 109).

ly one Meyer believed could be drawn from the very incomplete knowledge of the nervous system at the time.

Thus, the difference between Meyer and McDougall is not a small one. For Meyer
deflection was sufficient to explain variability of behavior, but for McDougall the analogous mechanism of attraction was not sufficient, while plasticity of the brain hemispheres was the physical feature necessary for this variability to appear. "Mechanistic explanation" was such that "a sufficient knowledge of the structure and physico-chemical
constitution of the nervous system would enable us to describe completely in terms of
physical and chemical changes the causal sequence of events that issues in any action,
no matter how much deliberation, choice, and effort may seem to be involved in its preparation and resolution" (McDougall, 1911: 112).

Actually, when McDougall opened hostilities against "Automaton Theories" in *Body
and Mind*, he seemed to be explicitly reviving an area of discussion already familiar to
James, who used the same expression to refer to theories that denied the mind a causal
role of its own and an independent existence of its own (Huxley's epiphenomenism was
the recurrent example). Like McDougall in the *Primer*, James in the *Principles* was always concerned with finding a physical explanation of variability of behavior, but every
proposal left him unsatisfied, because it always seemed to go back more or less to some
form of Automaton Theory, in which the mechanical analogy became pervasive and was
taken too seriously, so to speak. Reasoning thus turned into "an argument from analogy,
drawn from rivers, reflex action and other material phenomena where no consciousness
appears to exist at all, and extended to cases where consciousness seems the phenomenon's essential feature" (James, 1890, vol. 1: 454).

These words show James' underlying dissatisfaction with the whole apparatus of
physical analogies which he had introduced or utilized. And the reader of the *Principles*
may sometimes have the feeling that James takes away with one hand what he has given
with the other. Long neurological explanations of various psychological processes, like
those we have already considered, unfailingly alternate with statements that reduce or
question their import. Thus James said he suspected that the "radically physical point of
view" of associative processes, according to which they are always explicable in mechanical terms, was "an unreal abstraction" (vol. 1: 24 n.). And in the many pages he
wrote about the analogy between nervous conduction and drainage he would let fall the
following kind of remark: "However it be with other drainage currents and discharges,
the drainage currents and discharges of the brain are not purely physical facts. [...] I shall
therefore never hesitate to invoke the efficacy of the conscious comment, where no strictly mechanical reason appears why a current escaping from a cell should take one path
rather than another" (vol. 2: 583-584). We mentioned above James' difficulty in explaining in mechanical terms how a new response was *fixed* once it had been formed through
the drainage of nervous current: he admitted that "one does not immediately see" how.
Well, to overcome this difficulty he said at once that in this case the physical process of
drainage had a "psychical side" and that a certain intention or feeling in the pursuit of an
action "may be the reason why certain [nervous currents] are instantly inhibited and others helped to flow" and, in fixing a response, the reason why a certain drainage channel

is temporarily opened wider (vol. 2: 589). "Physiological speculations" was how James described the attempts to explain variability of behavior always in exclusively physical or mechanical terms. And McDougall came to the same conclusion in *Body and Mind*.

Meyer certainly could not share this opinion, because he took very seriously the possibility of a physical explanation of learning. His problem was the one James set, which can be summarized in the following question: once it was seen that the drainage analogy could explain why, in the case of double stimulation, "variation of response" was caused by the deflection of a weaker nervous current by a stronger one, could the same analogy be used to account in physical terms for the subsequent *fixation* of variation which was demonstrative of learning? In other words, could the physical analogy of drainage explain the observed fact that after (perhaps repeated) double stimulations of S_a and S_b in Figure 2.6, stimulus S_a alone could deflect nervous current towards M_b, through the associative neuron $S2_{ab}$, $M2_{ab}$, instead of towards M_a through the original reflex link, "so that the finger is withdrawn as soon as the flame becomes simply visible?" (Meyer, 1911: 94).

What needed explaining in physical terms was actually an important feature of the plasticity of the nervous system to which we have already referred on more than one occasion, that of having a form of 'memory,' i.e. being able to preserve at least for a while the trace of the acquired capacity to deviate nervous current from one path to another. To account for this feature, Meyer assumed that every neuron had its own *susceptibility*. When nervous current went through the neuron system, it was met by resistance that, according to Meyer, lessened in proportion to the intensity and duration of the current. Now the lessening of a neuron's resistance, resulting from the passage of nervous current, does not disappear at once but endures for a while, and this endurance is its susceptibility.[14] To make the explanation "biologically plausible," Meyer linked susceptibility with an idea that was widespread in neurology at the time, the idea of associative higher neurons, the ones connecting neurons at various levels, starting with the reflex arcs (pp. 114-115).

Meyer thought susceptibility was the solution to the problem of the fixation of new responses. During the phase of *variation* of response through dual stimulation of S_a and S_b mentioned above (Figure 2.6), the initially high resistance of associative neuron $S2_{ab}M2_{ab}$ was substantially lessened, because deflection sent a particularly strong nervous current through it in the direction of M_b. And resistance *remained low for a time*, so that after repeated stimulation of S_a and S_b, at a certain point stimulus S_a *alone* was sufficient to drive the nervous current through the associative neuron in the direction of M_b and thus *fix* the changed response.

In general, then, the nervous current aroused by a stimulus smoothes the way, so to speak, for the nervous current aroused by its repetition, if the repeated stimulus *comes soon after*. Each time the current meets less resistance, which would not be the case if there were a long interval between a stimulus and its repetition. Resistance starts to increase again the longer the interval between stimuli. This explains why an experience is fixed or 'remembered,' and fixed better and better through repetition and use, and it also explains how experience is lost or 'forgotten,' and more and more so through non-rep-

[14] Meyer certainly took the term from the theory of electromagnetism and also included a reference to hysteresis.

etition and disuse (which Meyer refers to as "negative susceptibility"). Thus susceptibility denotes a particular kind of hysteresis of nervous tissue, a kind of 'memory' of the neurons: their ability to keep and then gradually lose lessened resistance.

But despite Meyer's intentions, it was once again at this point that the physical analogy of nervous conduction with drainage and the neuron as a pipe with a one-way valve proved to be deficient. Unlike the system of neurons endowed with susceptibility, the hydraulic system of Meyer's analogy *does not by itself suggest the presence of any kind of 'memory.'* To find an equivalent for susceptibility in the hydraulic analogy, one would have to imagine that the tubes had a resistance that could somehow be modified by the intensity of the flux through them and that in the course of time this would leave a trace. It is here that Meyer revived a fairly *different* hydraulic analogy, that between nervous paths and modifiable channels, to which James too had recourse (p. 87). Susceptibility, established by intensity and duration of nervous flow, would by analogy seem to suggest a feature of a natural channel traversed by a rushing flow of water: the channel offers reduced resistance to the passage of a second flow and less and less resistance to following flows. And this happens only if the time interval between the different flows is not long. Otherwise the channel would naturally tend to close again (pp. 105-106).

In the end, Meyer made use of two analogies. The more specific of the two was between deflection and a jet pump, which was intended to account for the *formation* of a conduction path with low resistance (and a resulting new response). The other analogy was a vague one and referred to the usual natural, modifiable channels, which was intended to account for the *fixation* of that path (of that response). The latter analogy, the one that might suggest the presence of some physical form of memory, joined with the former no less clumsily in Meyer than in his predecessors.[15] Indeed, from Spencer onwards, the analogy of modifiable channels was taken for granted in any explanation of the fixation of a new nervous path in the various versions of nervous conduction as drainage, and referred to a form of hysteresis. In terms of the neuron theory accepted by Meyer, the analogy ought always to explain the following neurological hypotheses: 1) every passage of nervous current lessens the resistance of a neuron; 2) the neuron maintains each reduction of resistance for a length of time; 3) the capacity to maintain resistance reduction (susceptibility) is a primary feature of higher associative neurons.

But Meyer did not use susceptibility solely to explain response fixation. On closer inspection, change in response, as the result of the formation of a new path through deflection, was possible only when two stimuli were simultaneous or nearly so. In order for drainage to take place between two nervous processes, in order that the weaker process could be *attracted* by the stronger process, the latter had to become active before the other had completely ceased being active (p. 120). And Meyer wondered what was the nerv-

[15] The idea that the jet pump pipes have to be modifiable to preserve a trace of the change in resistance appeared in earlier articles (Meyer, 1908a: 301; 1908b: 363-364) but not in his 1911 book *Fundamental Laws of Human Behavior*, where resistance to flow varies only as a function of the length and not the section of the tubes and is modified by the intensity and duration of flow passage. In the earlier articles Meyer used the two analogies as evidence of the usefulness of mechanical analogies for the nervous system without raising the problem of integrating them in the explanation of nervous conduction phenomena.

ous correlate of learning by the association of two stimuli that were not *simultaneous* but *successive* one to the other. He added another mechanism of response variation to answer the question, a mechanism in which the crucial role was played not by deflection but by the summation of two successive stimuli on neurons endowed with susceptibility.[16]

Following Meyer, if the two stimuli are successive rather than simultaneous, the outline of new response formation shown in Figure 2.6 should be read in the following terms. While most of the nervous flow aroused by stimulus S_a produces response M_a, another part of it reaches associative neuron $S2_{ab}M2_{ab}$ at the same time and weakens its resistance. When in rapid succession stimulus S_b is evoked, most of its flow produces response M_b, but part of it also reaches associative neuron $S2_{ab}M2_{ab}$ at the same time; and according to the hypothesis of susceptibility, the already lessened resistance of the associative neuron is lessened further still. As successive stimuli accumulate, provided they are not too far apart in time, they so weaken the resistance of associative neuron $S2_{ab}M2_{ab}$ that a new conduction path is ultimately formed. It is clear that in this case too neuron susceptibility plays a central role: a trace of weakened resistance must have been maintained, because the accumulation of stimuli has produced the desired effect, and this cannot be explained by the mechanism of deflection through drainage.

In sum, Meyer seems, not always consistently, to contemplate *two mechanisms of response variation*: deflection of a weaker nervous flow by an almost simultaneous stronger one, an offshoot of the drainage analogy; and repetition or summation of stimuli at fairly rapid intervals of time, which recalls the vague analogy of natural modifiable channels. This latter mechanism crucially presupposes the hypothesis of susceptibility, a hypothesis that always has to be added to explain the *fixation* of a response once it has changed.

At this point one might ask if the hypothesis of susceptibility doesn't make the drainage analogy superfluous. The summation of stimuli and its effect over time ought to suffice to explain how a new response is formed as well as fixed. So there would be no need to use two different mechanisms as Meyer is forced to do. And this is a path that was actually pursued. Before turning to it (in section 6), we shall consider another different mechanism of response formation.

4. Thorndike and the origins of connectionism

Despite Thorndike's indebtedness to such of his predecessors as Spencer, Lloyd Morgan, Baldwin, and James, the importance and influence of his associationism are due chiefly to his commitment for more than fifty years to experimental research, which was always the testing ground for hypotheses regarding his main interest, learning processes.[17]

---

[16] Meyer certainly is not clear on the role this second mechanism plays in his theory. Sometimes it seems it has nothing to do with deflection (Meyer, 1911: 87 and 128) and consists in mere repetition of stimuli close in time. At other times it is considered as the deflection of a stimulus "by any directly preceding one" (p. 234). In any case, it is clear that the repetition of two stimuli over a length of time is such that the effect produced by the second stimulus is influenced by the first, and this leaves the neuron at a level of subliminal excitation.

[17] See Jonçich (1968) for Thorndike's education, his intellectual debts, and his role in several fields of psychological research. On the present occasion we shall describe only some of Thorndike's ideas from what is considered the first stage of his connectionism, from 1898 to ca 1930 (see Hilgard, 1956, Chapter 2).

In particular, in *Animal Behavior*, published in 1911, Thorndike considered the "connection system" the core of these processes. An organism's ability to learn depends on the complexity of its connection system. And this system consists of "connections" or "bonds" between stimuli coming from the external environment, and collected by a "receptor system", and motor responses. Motor responses in turn are the set of reactions with which an organism interacts with the environment in an adaptive way, its "action system," as Thorndike calls it, referring back to Jennings (Thorndike, 1911: 248 and 274). Thorndike claimed that in general much less was known about the connection system than about the action system and the receptor system. It was up to experimental work to shed light on the structure and functional organization of the connection system, while ontogenetic and philogenetic evolutionary study was still to shed light on how it changed and developed. There were different degrees of complexity in connection systems, going from organisms in which the connection system consisted essentially of reflex and instinct connections all the way through to organisms in which the connections were relatively modifiable by experience and thus gave rise to increasingly varied behavior. The neurons that made these connection systems were the root of nervous plasticity; they were the "associative" or "connecting" neurons typical of higher nervous centers, to use the terminology Thorndike shared with others (Thorndike, 1919: 148).

At the time of his earliest published writing about animal intelligence, Thorndike said he was pursuing James' neurological hypotheses (Thorndike, 1898: 81). Indeed, as McDougall developed the part of James' thought which insisted that human mental processes could not be reduced to specific neurophysiological processes, Thorndike started out by developing the mechanistic aspect apparent in James' neurological speculations, in the conviction that "behavior is predictable without recourse to magical agencies." For him, the laws of formation and modification of the manifold S-R connections that make up the human nervous system were not qualitatively different than the laws governing the functioning of the connection system of other animals (Thorndike, 1911: 241). Moreover the human connection system, in its endless complexity, was sufficient basis for mental life: "If we had perfect knowledge of the entire history of a man's brain, if we could from second to second see just what is going on in it, we should find in its actions and consequent changes the parallel of his life of thought and action" (Thorndike, 1919: 168).

It was James who compared the functioning of the brain's hemispheres to that of the switchboard at a telephone exchange, when he presented what he called a "radically physical point of view" of habit formation, the concept we have already seen, according to which the higher nervous centers establish associative paths between already existing reflex arches. To compare the brain to a system of telephone lines suggested it might be possible to multiply contacts between basic elements (James, vol. 1: 26).[18] Thorndike picked up the analogy on several occasions and on occasion went so far as to call associative neurons "switchboard neurons." But he noted that this analogy captured only some features

[18] The analogy between brain and automatic telephone exchange was already widely known and became very popular. Meyer (1911) suggested it as a vague image of nervous transmission but he dropped it at once in favour of the jet pump analogy, which he believed illustrated in detail the transmission of nervous current.

of nervous connections, including the reception and transmission of nervous messages but not the capacity of such connections for modification through experience.

> Neurons learn, so to speak, to form, break and modify their interconnections [...]. But of course no mere machine has such a power to modify its working, to make or break connections in accordance with the frequency of their use and the desirability or discomfort of the results to which they lead (Thorndike, 1919: 147).

This passage might indicate the causes behind a problem which is left open by all the vague mechanical analogies we have been reviewing and which always seems to be the same. These analogies never give a convincing account of the form of nervous system 'memory' underlying variability of behavior, habit formation, and learning. In Thorndike's case, to explain how nervous connections were formed and modified was paramount to establishing laws of learning, hence laws that the connection system was subject to. The last part of the passage cited alludes to these two laws.

What Thorndike always considered the primary law of learning involved a radical reformulation of the traditional law of habits, different versions of which we have considered, from Spencer to McDougall. In the consolidated idiom of neuron theory, it goes like this:

> When any neuron or neuron group is stimulated and transmits to or discharges into or connects with a second neuron group, it will, when later stimulated again in the same way, have an increased tendency to transmit to the second neuron group as before, *provided the act that resulted in the first instance brought a pleasant or at least indifferent mental state. If, on the contrary, the result in the first case was discomfort, the tendency to such transmission will be lessened* (Thorndike, 1919: 165-166, my italics).

The italicized passage is the characteristic feature of Thorndike's formulation of his law of habits and the nucleus of the much-discussed "law of effect" that gave him his altogether special place in the history of associationism. Such a law set forth the idea that association is not the result of the mere temporal contiguity of two stimuli but is an effect of the response. This effect takes the form of a state of satisfaction (desirability, pleasantness) or discomfort (annoyance, trouble) of the organism, as a result of which the connections between the neurons involved are strengthened and "stamped in" or weakened and "stamped out."[19] Thus learning consists in varying the strength of R-S connections, and more specifically in facilitating or inhibiting synaptic conduction. This is how the hungry cat in Thorndike's famous experiments learned to get out of the cage (the puzzle box, as it came to be known) in which it was shut up. By various random trials the animal finally selected the movement that opened the cage and let it reach the food. In successive learning cycles, the connection between that movement and the stimulus which provoked it was strengthened, while all the others, which did not lead to success, were progressively weakened and finally eliminated. This is the way the child learned not to get burned: the effect of touching the flame and the sensation of pain weakened the connection between the visual stimulus and the original motor response until it was finally eliminated.

---

[19] Postman (1947) is still an indispensable account of the history of the law of effect, in which it is clear that Thorndike was influenced by thinkers who had already treated the role of pleasure and pain in adaptation and learning, including Bain, Spencer, and James.

In this form of selective or trial-and-error learning, frequent stimulation of a connection always improved final performance. So Thorndike assigned frequency a role in another law, the "law of exercise," in which he summarized the traditional doctrine that connections which are strengthened are those most frequently stimulated ("law of use"), while connections which are weakened are those less frequently stimulated ("law of disuse").

According to Thorndike, nervous current is not conveyed through a complex system of connections by a hypothetical mental agency active at the synapse level, according to the "mythological explanation" Meyer so hated, but neither is it conveyed by a hypothetical mechanism of drainage. Thorndike's explanation goes back to the selectionist line of thought in psychology and neurology, a line that still thrives today: connections are selected by a process like that of Darwinian natural selection, which is the neurophysiological side of learning. Thorndike's formulation is quite explicit.

On its physiological side behavior in the higher animals is a struggle for existence amongst neuron connections. The formation of a habit means the survival of one connection, the elimination of a futile response to a given situation means the death of another (Thorndike, 1908: 591).

Since learning is a result of selection, it occurs when the organism *does* something. It is a sort of learning by doing based not on simple repetition of a response but rather on the fact that response must occur in order to be facilitated or inhibited. Subsequent experimental evidence led Thorndike to reconsider the importance of the law of use: mere repetition, "practice without zeal," as he put it, was not alone sufficient to account for learning. The law of effect continued to play a central role in Thorndike's account of learning, although later experimental work persuaded him to reconsider its role (for example, while reward always strengthens a connection, punishment does not always or necessarily weaken it).[20]

Reducing the role of mere practice, then, the selective mechanism of connection formation was entrusted chiefly to a motivational component, the satisfying effect of response. In an attempt to be consistent with his mechanistic stance, Thorndike avoided using mentalistic terms to describe a satisfying state and an discomforting state, and offered what he considered objective definitions. A satisfying state was what "the animal does nothing to avoid, often doing such things as attain or preserve it," and a discomforting state was one that "the animal commonly avoids and abandons" (Thorndike, 1911: 245). He realized, however, that these definitions in terms of "gross behavior" might be dismissed as circular, since they were based on what they were meant to define (namely a satisfying state and a discomforting one). So he tried to find a definition that referred to the language of neurophysiology, and suggested a possible "physiological parallel" for these states (Thorndike, 1908: 594). He formulated an accessory law, the "law of readiness," which was meant to specify the working of the physiological mechanism underlying the law of effect. According to this law, for example, a satisfying state corresponded to a connection that was *readier* than any other to conduct nervous current.

[20] See the aforementioned chapter in Hilgard (1956) regarding Thorndike's experiments and the development of his thought about the laws of effect and use.

This formulation, which was rather vague, was meant to explain, for example, why the child was attracted to the flame: the stimulation of the neurons in the visual area prepared a specific "behavior series" consisting in turning to the flame, extending the arm and so on (Thorndike, 1914: 53).

At the beginning Thorndike thought that discovering the exact nature of the readiness mechanism was "one of the notable tasks of the sciences of human behavior" (p. 56), but later he became more cautious about the possibility of defining the "conduction units" at the source of motivation in terms of neurons. "The connectionist indeed realizes the difficulties of explaining human nature as a system of connections between neurons" (Thorndike, 1931: 7). Hobart Mowrer quoted this remark of Thorndike's and thought the suggestion was that the psychologist's attention ought to be centered mainly on studying an organism's gross behavior rather than on what Thorndike called "the internal behavior of neurons" (Mowrer, 1960a: 218). This point raises the question of the levels at which living organisms can be studied, a subject to which we shall return.

5. Inorganic nervous systems: Bent Russell's machine

The two theories of nervous conduction discussed in this chapter, drainage and connectionism, were reinterpreted and revised several times in the years that followed and were subjected to criticism of various kinds.[21] In the years in which Russell was designing the machine we considered at the beginning of the chapter, the two theories were in a fairly advanced stage of development.

Russell thought he could infer two ideas from Spencer, Meyer and Thorndike, the authors he explicitly cited as his inspiration: (1) that frequent stimulation of neurons at short time intervals results in a strengthening of the connections between neurons and an increase of their conductivity (or in a decrease of their resistance), and that a trace of that increase would remain in the form of an increase of conductivity (or a decrease of their resistance), which might be temporary or permanent; and (2) that stimulation of neurons followed by a period of rest results in a weakening of the connections and in a decrease of their conductivity (or an increase of their resistance), and the longer the period of rest the greater the decrease in conductivity (or the increase in resistance).

These two statements summarize the main features of Russell's picture of the neurological knowledge of his time, in the form he derived from the authors whose positions we have described in the foregoing sections (Russell, 1913: 16-17).[22] Briefly, we shall refer to these statements as the Standard Theory of nervous conduction. Russell did not seem to be aware of the different slant of the two theories of which those authors were

---

[21] Karl Lashley and Gestalt psychologists were the harshest critics of the two theories, albeit from different standpoints (see Lashley, 1924). Another issue was the compatibility of the drainage theory with what was known at the time about the chemical nature of the transmission of nerve impulse, an issue considered by physiologists such as K. Lucas and M. Verworn (see the discussion in Dodge, 1926).

[22] Russell quoted Spencer's *Principles of Psychology* (1894 edition), Thorndike's *Animal Intelligence*, and Meyer's *Fundamental Laws of Human Behavior*, which he said particularly inspired him. In fact Russell's machine looks like an attempt to closely simulate various forms of learning described in *Fundamental Laws*, even when Meyer is not specifically mentioned.

proponents, the drainage theory and the connectionist theory, or at least he was uninterested, so that the features of the two theories he highlighted are ultimately the vaguer ones.

To see that this is true, let us briefly review the course of our reconstruction thus far. The idea that the frequent repetition of stimuli at short time intervals played a part in the explanation of the nervous correlate of learning went back to Spencer, at least in the form that was most popular among psychologists at the time. Although it was equally accepted as a necessary law in Meyer's drainage theory and in Thorndike's connectionist theory, it was not the law that best characterized the two theories. Thorndike considered mere repetition insufficient at least when, including it in the law of use, he remarked that the S-R connections are formed chiefly because they are followed by reward or in any case by a satisfying state for the organism, according to the law of effect, which he considered more fundamental and not reducible to the law of use. The situation in Meyer is a bit more complicated. He ultimately rejected the law of repetition as trivial in favor of the law of double stimulation, in which he said he had always seen the key postulate of learning. Nevertheless, he envisaged a *second* mechanism of learning, this one based on the repetition of stimuli at short intervals, which presupposed the hypothesis of neuron susceptibility. In general, however, both Thorndike and Meyer, like their predecessors, from Spencer to James and McDougall, acknowledged that repetition, or use, had an important function in *consolidating* nervous paths or connections once they were formed (depending on the postulates of the different theories). All excluded the possibility that repetition alone could always explain how new nervous paths or connections were *formed*, or rather how the change came about in nervous flow to originally "vague" (to use Spencer's term) paths or connections or those with higher resistance.

So despite Russell's appeal to the psychology authorities of the day, the Standard Theory was rather outside the frame of reference of the two theories of nervous conduction then prevalent. In any case, it seems that Russell was aiming at the building of an artifact that embodied neither the law of attraction or deflection of impulse that characterized the drainage theories, nor the connectionist law of effect. Rather, he was aiming at the building of an artifact that demonstrated the role of time and stimulus repetition in various forms of learning. In particular, his machine simulated the result of frequent and rapid succession of two nervous processes, i.e. a phenomenon quite similar to that of susceptibility, rather than the result of the deflection of one nervous process by another, stronger one. Susceptibility, it will be remembered, was introduced by Meyer to explain the nervous correlate of learning by the association of two stimuli that were not simultaneous but followed one after the other. It is no accident that Russell's references to Meyer's *Fundamental Laws* concerned the points at which Meyer developed the idea of neuron susceptibility, an idea that Russell explicitly placed at the heart of his machine simulation, while his references to Thorndike's *Animal Intelligence*, at least his explicit references, concern the law of use rather than the law of effect.

It is interesting to look at the way Russell's machine was meant to simulate the nervous system features described by the Standard Theory. We do this, first to notice how original some features of his mechanical analogies were in comparison with other confused and conventional analogies, including the hydraulic kind based on drainage; and second, to evaluate subsequent refinements that Russell made to the Standard Theory. These led him to embrace a wholly frequentist explanation of the nervous correlate of learning, one quite similar to that Watson was to propose soon after, as we shall see in the next section.

What might be called the fundamental unit of Russell's machine is the "transmitter" shown in Plate 2.1. The transmitter is actually a valve, the maximum opening of which changes in the course of time as a result of being repeatedly activated, and this changes the intensity of the flow of water or compressed air that passes through it. The proponents of the hydraulic analogies we have examined always needed a physical mechanism that was sensitive to time and intensity of flow in order to account for a nervous path's capacity to change its resistance in the course of time and to preserve the trace. Meyer, for example, had to translate neuron susceptibility into the analogy of natural modifiable channels, since the jet pump analogy alone was unable to explain this kind of memory. Thorndike seemed to reject the idea that something analogous to the nervous system such as a network of *inorganic* connections could display memory and learning. But Russell's transmitter was designed as a working artifact and endowed with a simple form of 'memory,' since the transmitter's behavior was influenced by its previous history. The time interval between one stroke and another of the spur valve of the transmitter, described in Plate 2.1, was the machine version of the time interval that established the change in a nervous connection's conduction as predicted by the Standard Theory, according to which nervous conduction increased with repeated stimulation at brief intervals of time and decreased in the opposite case.

But the analogy between the functioning of the nervous system and that of the machine did not end here. According to the Standard Theory, certain initially low-conductivity nervous connections could be "forced," as Mayer put it, through frequent and rapid stimulation, to transmit the nervous signal and so become high conductivity connections. In the machine an effect of this kind could be simulated by the combined action of several transmitters working in different combinations. Russell called the device that controlled the working of several connected transmitters a "coupling gang." It was the machine's functional equivalent of the network of nervous connections of high and low conductivity. Burt rather than describe the device, let us see how Russell used it in simulating the nervous correlate of inhibition.

In our Figure 2.7 three transmitters are connected in a network (shown schematically as T1, T2 and T3) with their respective outlet pipes, through which the fluxes discharge into two sides, as shown by the arrow-like lines coming from T1 on one side and T2 and T3 on the other (for the sake of simplicity, the inlet pipe is not shown in the figure). These fluxes must be imagined as giving rise to two antagonistic movements or responses R1 and R2.[23] The transmitters are connected in different ways via two sensory terminals S1 and S2, which correspond to receptors or sense organs. When a sensory terminal is struck, some transmitters are activated while others are not (because if a sensory terminal is

---

[23] Actually the activation of the different transmitters in Russell's device channels the fluxes in two counterpoised pipes in a "stream meter." The stream meter controls the movement of a piston rod in a cylinder in opposite directions (the two antagonistic movements) but is controlled in turn by the transmitters that govern the fluxes (Russell, 1913: 24-26).

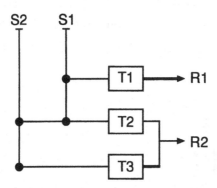

Fig. 2.7. Russell's transmitter network simulating the effect of time and repetition in modifying nervous connections in the child who learns not to get burned.

struck, it pushes against and works the spur valves of certain transmitters in the manner shown in Plate 2.1). For example, striking S1 activates T1 and T2 at the same time but not T3. The pipes corresponding to initially high conductivity nervous paths are indicated by a solid line. This means that striking S1 causes a much greater flux towards R1 than towards R2 and evokes response R1, while striking S2 evokes R2. But let us suppose that S1 and S2 are both struck frequently and in rapid succession. As the figure shows, both act on transmitter T2, which is thus subjected to frequent activation at short intervals of time and conveys an increasing flux towards R2, greater in any case than the flux that would result from striking S1 and S2 separately. After a 'training' period consisting of rapidly repeated striking of S1 and S2, it is sufficient to strike S1 alone to get response R2, the latter prevailing over R1 since the two responses are antagonistic.

Russell thought that this transmitter network simulated the inhibition of a response, R1 in this case. He also took the example of the child who sees a flame (S1), reaches for it (R1), gets burned (S2) and withdraws its hand (R2) (Russell, 1913: 18-19). It could be said that the machine gives an approximate simulation of Meyer's law of double stimulation, according to which stimulus S1 replaces stimulus S2 in evoking response R2.[24] In Meyer's terminology, inhibition is the "negative aspect" of the variation in response and its fixation. The machine seems to behave in accord with the hypothesis that a single nervous mechanism accounts for the two phenomena of variation and inhibition of response, just as so many others thought, from McDougall to Meyer.

This completes the analogy of the machine's workings with that of nervous connections according to the Standard Theory: the initially low conductivity hydraulic channel that is activated by S1 and evokes response R2 has been 'forced' to become highly conductive after repeated stimulation at short intervals of time. At this point, it is clear that the novelty

[24] Approximate simulation because Russell's transmitter networks do not really *replace* one stimulus with another, but rather one response *prevails* over another. This, it would seem, depends on the role played by the transmitter's lag valve (valve 12), which when shifted as in Plate 1 remains open and always lets some amount of fluid through.

Plate 2.1

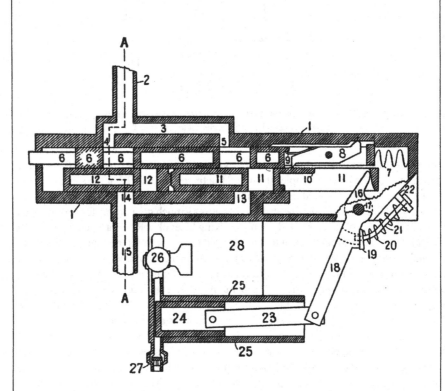

Bent Russell's hydraulic transmitter consists of three valves so arranged that the spur valve 6 slides over the other two valves 11, the ratchet valve, and 12, the lag valve. The combined sliding movement of the three valves closes and opens ports 4 and 5 and ports 14 and 13, to a variable degree, to the flux, which is assumed to remain constant, coming from the inlet pressure pipe 2. The flux is thus transmitted through the ports to the outlet meter pipe 15.

In the figure (from Russell, 1913), the transmitter is shown with the spur valve 6 at the extreme end of its inward (i.e. rightward) stroke, as in receiving a stimulus. The spring 7 is thus compressed. This is the fully activated position. In this position, ports 4 and 5 are open to flux coming from the inlet pipe 2. Ports are closed when valve 6 is permitted to return to its outward (i.e. leftward) position, because it is pushed back by the spring 7. This corresponds to the absence of stimulus. In this position, there is no discharge through the transmitter. Also the racket valve 11 and the lag valve 12 are shown at the right end of their strokes in the figure.

Valve 11 is connected to valve 6 by means of pawl 8 which, attached to valve 6, is held down on ratchet 10 by the pawl spring 9 so as to engage it. When valve 6 begins its leftward stroke, by means of the pawl it pushes valve 11 for a certain distance, i.e. until the pawl is tripped, by striking the lug on its top against a shoulder in the transmitter case 1. At this point, the lever spring 20, by means of the rocking finger 16, forces back valve 11 (as to plunger 24, briefly its function is to retard the return stroke of valve 11). In its forward stroke, valve 11 pushes valve 12 leftward. As the latter is independent of the former, valve 12 does not follow valve 11 in its subsequent return stroke.

Briefly, owing to the way the valves are connected, we see that the greater the frequency of the successive strokes on spur valve 6, the further the ratchet valve 11 is pushed forward, the wider port 13 is opened to the flow coming from port 5. Moreover, the further the ratchet valve 11 is pushed forward, the greater the leftward shift of the lag valve 12, and the wider port 14 is opened to the flow coming from port 4. If the time interval between one stroke and another of valve 6 increases, valve 11, pulled back by lever spring 20, will tend to return to its position at the extreme right. Issue port 13 will consequently automatically and gradually tend to close its own opening, so reducing the flow, while port 14 will not open further, since valve 12 will no longer be pushed forward.

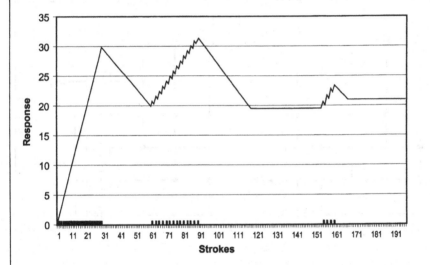

We show the performance of a hypothetical transmitter in this curve (once given certain values for the velocity of the sliding valves and the opening of the ports). A rapid succession of strokes by spur valve 6 causes, as a response, an increased opening of the transmitter and thus a cumulative increase in the flux discharged through outlet pipe 15. When the strokes are spaced out there is a reduction in the area of the opening, owing to the fact that valve 11 gradually closes port 13, and thus there is a reduction in the flux discharged. Because valve 12 does not came back from the position to which valve 11 pushed it forward, it does not reduce the opening of port 14. Thus the flux becomes stable. If the frequency of the strokes increases, there is again an increase in the flux discharged.

Bent Russell thought he embodied in the transmitter the distinction between the "*temporary* increase" of neuron susceptibility, which is simulated through the functioning of valve 11 (a kind of short-term memory), and the "*permanent* increase," which is simulated through the functioning of valve 12 (a kind of long-term memory). In this way the transmitter does not completely 'forget' its previous performance.

of this still rudimentary device is that the analogy it proposes is not the vague and worn-out one between nervous current and hydraulic flux but between, on the one hand, nervous connections that are forced to respond to certain recurrent stimulations and in the course of time induced to respond more promptly, and, on the other hand, hydraulic channels 'forced' to respond by the combined action of transmitters that vary the intensity of outflow over a period of time. Indeed, the transmitters embody at least some essential elements of Meyer's neuron susceptibility, and their diminished resistance through frequent stimulation seems sufficient to explain both the formation and fixation of a new response.

Russell described various examples of transmitter nets. Some of them consisted of more simple networks. All networks simulated forms of learning of different complexity, not always with sufficient realism but always through frequent and rapid repetition of stimuli. Plate 2.2 gives an outline description of two: network (a) simulates an elementary nervous system learning how to make a choice, for example, an animal's choice

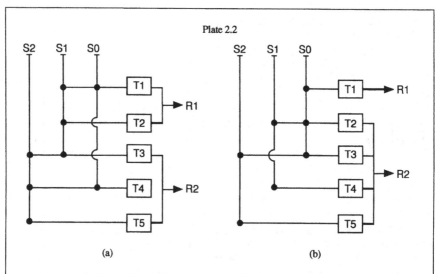

Plate 2.2

(a)   (b)

In the network of transmitters (a), let us suppose that S0 is the sensory terminal that is stimulated from the environment, R1 is a movement to the right and R2 a movement to the left. It is to be supposed that the stimulation of S0 alone does not cause movement in either direction, while, for example, the stimulation of sensory terminals S0 and S2 evokes response R2, a movement to the left. Now, if we repeatedly and rapidly stimulate S0 and S2, transmitter T4 will as a result discharge an increasing flux; and at a certain point the flux will be greater than that discharged by any other single transmitter. After a 'training' period consisting of repeated rapid stimulation of S0 and S2, the machine will respond with R2 (movement to the left) when S0 alone is stimulated. In the same way the machine can be 'trained' to respond to S0 alone with R1 (movement to the right) after rapid and repeated stimulation of S0 and S1.

In network (b), the response R2 is evoked by the rapid repeated stimulation of S0 and S1, and subsequent to that response sensory terminal S2 is stimulated. In this way the two transmitters T2 and T3 further increase the discharged flux that evokes the response R2 when S0 is stimulated, and 'reinforce' that response.

when it learns to avoid an obstacle; network (b) simulates what Russell called the physiological "correlatus of satisfaction." The term is typical of Thorndike, and his was the terminology that Russell seemed to use, without citing Thorndike, to describe that particular form of association of ideas in which the connections are "reinforced or stamped in" by the positive effect of a response (Russell, 1913: 33). Russell described this effect as a pleasant stimulus for the organism, for example, a kinesthetic or proprioceptive stimulus produced by a response acts backwards as a "counter-signal," as he called it, to further strengthen the corresponding S-R connection.

Actually, the machine seems to simulate roughly a sort of supervised learning, for (as seen in the details of Plate 2.2) the pleasant stimulus reinforcing the machine's response is not produced as a counter-signal by the machine's response itself. It is the operator who provides the pleasant stimulus from outside by activating a hitherto inactive transmitter. This gives rise to the usual frequent and rapid repetition which does reinforce the response. Further elaboration of this network might be used to simulate, albeit superficially, what Russell called the "selection of responses by satisfaction," again without naming Thorndike. In any case the use of Thorndike's terminology seems to be a mere descriptive convenience, since it is clear that Russell's transmitter firstly works according to the law of use or repetition.

6. Other ideas about nervous conduction

Although Meyer's 1911 *Fundamental Laws of Human Behavior* paved the way for behaviorism, Watson is considered its official founder because of the article already mentioned, which appeared in the same year that Russell published the description of his machine (Watson, 1913).[25]

Watson's picture of the nervous system is the one that was popular in the days of Spencer and James, Loeb and Jennings. And Watson's interpretation is rigorously mechanistic, which puts him close to Loeb in many respects. The unit of behavior is the reflex arc. Chains of reflexes constitute an instinct if their organization is innate or a habit if acquired. Watson did not, however, get into the trouble that Loeb had with associative memory, and nervous plasticity was less of a problem since for him the traditional "difficult mechanical problem" of the formation of new nervous paths was a false problem. In Watson's first systematic effort, *Behavior* (Watson, 1914), he criticized all hypotheses about the formation of nervous paths, be they the connectionists' "neurological mechanism" of learning or the drainage analogies he never liked.[26] For him there was no need

[25] According to the psychologist Walter Pillsbury, Meyer, in his *Fundamental Laws of Human Behavior*, "propounded all the essentials of the doctrine [of behaviorism] a year or more before Watson adopted his position" (quoted by O'Donnell, 1985: 215). For the development of Watson's investigations, see Buckley (1989) as well as sections of O'Donnell's book.

[26] Elsewhere Watson wrote that "in the past we have been too content with making brain pictures and mechanical neural schema to always look carefully enough at our behavior facts. We need in psychology all of the available facts that the *neurologists* can give us, but we can very well leave out of consideration those ingenious puzzle pictures that compare the action of the central nervous system with a series of pipes and vales, sponges, electric switchboards and the like" (Watson, 1919: 19).

to speak of forming a *new* nervous path, except in the particularly weak sense of a path not yet traversed by nervous current. For behavior to be modifiable it was sufficient that there be a weakening of the resistance on pre-formed paths, or chains of reflex arcs, through the summation of different stimuli, be they heteroceptive, coming from the outside environment, or proprioceptive, caused by movement within the organism. In reviewing *Behavior*, Thorndike concluded that Watson's claim required imagining a brain that was fairly unmodifiable from birth, whereas what was known about the growth, degeneration and regeneration of nerve tissue seemed to support the opposite hypothesis, namely the possibility that truly new nervous connections could be formed (Thorndike, 1915: 464). But Watson stuck to the thesis he had advanced in *Behavior*.

When a stimulus arises in a receptor there is just as orderly a progression of events then as later when the habit is formed, viz., the stimulus is carried off along preformed and definite arcs to the effector in the order in which the arcs offer the least resistance to the passage of the current. This order may vary with variations in the sum of intra- and extra-organic stimulation. *There is no formation of new pathways* (Watson, 1914: 259, my italics).[27]

It is worth noting that the same stimulus may give rise not to just a single reflex response, as stressed by the traditional version of the reflex arc, but, under the right conditions, to a whole succession of reflex responses, depending on the sum of stimuli coming from different sources, within and without the organism. These stimuli weaken the resistance of some chains of reflex arcs instead of others, and the responses are formed and fixed as a result of the repeated use of these chains, or, as Watson puts it in vaguely neurological terminology, depending on the "condition of tension in the conductors." In other words, there is no drainage, nor the satisfying effect of a response.

Watson gave an exemplary interpretation of the behavior of a hungry animal learning to get out of a puzzle box, which Thorndike explained by the law of effect (Watson, 1914: 259-260; 1919: 294). According to Watson, the stimulus represented by the environment (the puzzle box), together with the (internal) proprioceptive stimuli prevalent at a given moment aroused a host of random responses or movements in the animal in a series of behavior cycles during which it learned to get out of the puzzle box. In each cycle some movements, the successful ones, were fixed, while the others, the "useless" movements (the ones not needed in opening the puzzle box) were eliminated. Since both successful and useless movements were random to begin with, Watson's answer to the question of what mechanism eliminated the useless ones could only be probabilistic. In the first behavior cycle, a random series of movements, corresponding to the activation of a chain of reflex arcs, was interrupted by the successful movement. In a subsequent cycle, another equally random series of movements, corresponding to the activation of another chain of reflex arcs, was also interrupted when the same movement recurred, and so on until the organism responded to the original stimulus directly and solely with the successful movement. This turned out to be the most frequently exercised movement

[27] Returning to the subject, Watson explained that in his opinion the enormous number of nervous paths in the brain at birth, which could be inferred by observing the behavior of even a very small child, was sufficient to hypothesize that the nervous paths could join up in different combinations to give rise to the formation of habits of different complexity (Watson, 1919: 272).

(the only one that always appeared in each trial series) and the most recently exercised (the last before another subsequent trial series begins), so it was the most likely to be repeated, other things being equal. Hence learning was not due to the formation and strengthening of connections or bonds corresponding to situations that were satisfying to the organism, but *only* an automatic modification of pre-formed chains of reflex arcs after repeated stimulation. Watson rejected Thorndike's first law, the law of effect, the motivationist formulation of which he particularly disliked, but he accepted Thorndike's second law, that of use, which he formulated as the "law of frequency and recency."

In *Behavior* Watson explained that this law could give rise to habit formation through the process of "substitution of the stimulus." This process actually summarized his interpretation of Pavlov's conditioning and was wholly equivalent to what Meyer described in his law of double stimulation: a stimulus is conditioned when it replaces an immediately following unconditioned stimulus to evoke the same response. Watson rejected all the paraphernalia of the draining analogy, and what he saw in stimulus substitution was not a process due to the deflection of one nervous current by another stronger one but a process due to the weakening of the resistance of nervous paths as a result of repeated summation of immediately following stimuli.

Jennings was unaware of Pavlov's experimental work but, following the learning principles formulated by Spencer and Bain, he had already described in the language of the "law of the readier resolution of physiological states" a form of learning in which one stimulus evoked a response that was previously evoked by another.[28] This was a process based on associative memory for which "the response at first given to one stimulus comes, after a time, to be transferred to another one" (Jennings, 1906: 334). Watson (1914: 260) rejected Jennings' vague physiological terminology. For him, in the case of organisms having a nervous system, a physiological state was a "summation" of internal and external stimuli that activated certain reflex arcs. An organism's state changed when other reflex arcs were activated. However, Watson described the mechanism of stimulus substitution by appealing directly to Jennings' law of readier resolution. Figure 2.8 shows the chain of two reflex arcs—A, S and B, R—involved in conditioning as stimulus substitution according to Watson. Here Pavlov's dog is subjected to a conditioned stimulus (the sound of bell, A), which is followed by the neutral or unconditioned stimulus (food, B), and that gives rise to the response to be conditioned (salivation, R). The sequence of events A, B, R—which occur close in time—is replaced by sequence A, R after conditioning. In other words, B is no longer needed. The explanation is that stimulus A cannot evoke response R until B has evoked it. At the same time, stimulus A is added to B in weakening the resistance of the effector trait Y in the B, R arc to the point that it can by itself evoke response R. In this case too, as in selective learning, the resistance of a connection is overcome by frequent repetition or use.[29]

In Thorndike's aforementioned review of *Behavior*, he charged Watson, as he had Jennings and such psychologists as Stevenson Smith, over the insufficiency of the principle

[28] See above, p. 19.

[29] We shall not here consider how faithful Watson's interpretation of conditioning was to Pavlov's stance, but see Mecacci (1979) on the question.

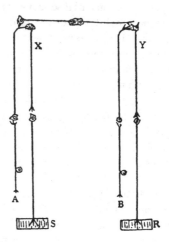

Fig. 2.8. Stimulus substitution in evoking a conditioned response, from Watson (1914).

of readier resolution or that of frequency and recency to account for the general dynamics of learning (Thorndike, 1915: 464-465). The fact that a response recurs more frequently and recently in each learning cycle is not enough for it to be selected. For in every cycle several different responses (the aforementioned useless movements) may appear more frequently that the response that is ultimately successful. And if this is successful, it is because of the final *effect*, not because it occurred more frequently and recently.

When Russell published his mechanical model of nervous conduction in 1913 his ideas on the matter were somewhat eclectic. Several later articles, especially those published in 1916 and 1917, were much clearer.[30] Russell no longer quoted the authors he had referred to in formulating the Standard Theory on which he based the design of his machine (except for Spencer, though not regarding the laws of learning). On the other hand, while the substance of the theory was unchanged, it took on a more consistent, albeit not particularly original, form. It was now summarized in the principle Watson had considered the basis of any kind of learning, the law of frequency and recency. Russell no longer called upon his mechanical model of 1913 in support of the theory. Instead he described a hypothetical neurological mechanism that would explain the selective distribution of impulses in networks of neuron connections and in general the strengthening of some connections rather than others, which was at the basis of various kinds of associative memory and learning.

The hypothesis Russell advanced was that of a "dual common path" shared by several receptors or sensors, in other words, an associative or connecting neuron that might be stimulated by a combination of sensory neurons, including proprioceptive ones. Rus-

[30] Russell (1916; 1917a; 1917b), but see also Russell (1915; 1918; 1920; 1921). These writings do not seem to have been widely read by psychologists and biologists. As an engineer who turned to psychology Russell remained a shadowy figure. He appears in an occasional bibliography by way of the article in which Meyer (1913) described the machine built by Bent Russell, "an engineer of St. Louis," as he put it.

sell thought that this hypothesis, which was certainly not new, could account for habit formation as the result of lowered resistance at the synaptic level, which would suggest the existence of "different possible paths of [nervous] transmission," as he put it when quoting Pillsbury (1911).[31] Thus the nervous impulse might be distributed along these paths in such a way as to discharge most along the path where the synapse offered lower resistance and least along the path where at the time the synapse offered higher resistance, with the final effect that after "repeated small discharges [...] the resistance was decreased" in the second path as well (Russell, 1916: 232). For example, in Watson's diagram in Figure 2.8, associative neuron Y ought to be the common path of A and B.

Following Watson, Russell argued that the dual common path hypothesis could explain the stimulus substitution in Pavlov's conditioning (Russell, 1917a: 66). Looking at Russell's machine, we might retrospectively suggest that a hypothesis very like the common path seems to be incorporated in the transmitter network in Figure 2.7. In this case, transmitter T2 would reproduce the corresponding associative mechanism. But it would do so in a very approximate way, since the simulation of stimulus substitution is not very faithful. Since the activation of S1 ultimately evoked response R2 in this transmitter network, it looks as if Russell was at that point trying to simulate stimulus substitution, albeit without fully succeeding, in evoking a response by frequent and rapid stimulation, as per the interpretation he knew from Meyer's *Fundamental Laws*.[32] It was an interpretation similar to the one Watson proposed immediately thereafter. As we have seen, however, for Meyer this was but one of *two* mechanisms for forming a nervous path, due to neuron susceptibility. The other and more important mechanism was deflection. But for Watson frequent and rapid repetition was the sole mechanism that explained how a new response wa formed as well as fixed, and he considered any hypothesis of deflection or drainage of nervous currents superfluous.

7. Engineers' machines and biologists' machines

Russell did not offer an antivitalist interpretation of his machine as a confutation of the thesis of the radical irreconcilability of organic and mechanical laws and processes. He simply made a general observation that, being formulated in 1913, thirty years before the birth of cybernetics, sounds highly prophetic to the modern reader.

It is thought that the engineering profession has not contributed greatly to the study of the nervous system, at least since Herbert Spencer, an engineer, wrote his book on psychology. As the cooperation of workers in different fields of knowledge is necessary in these days of specialists it may be argued that engineers can consistently join in the consideration of a subject of such importance to man (Russell, 1913: 21).

[31] A version of the dual common path principle was stressed by Sherrington (1906, Chapter 4), who distinguished "private" paths belonging to single receptors from "common" ones, where paths from different receptors or from a different order of private paths converged. The distinction seems to echo Russell's (1916), but that expression was used by several authors. Meyer (1911), for example, used it to refer to the associative neuron. He subsequently criticized the idea that a common nervous path could be described in the "mythological" terms of a motivationist connectionism, which looks like an allusion to Thorndike (Meyer, 1925).

[32] It is possible that Russell abandoned his simulative device in these subsequent papers partly because he was aware of the machine's limitations in simulating the stimulus substitution (see especially Russell, 1917b: 421).

This was probably the first time it was suggested that the new discipline of engineering might work alongside physiology and psychology at the difficult task of deciphering the "perplexing" phenomena of the nervous system underlying intelligent behavior. The readers Russell was addressing as a "member of the engineering profession" would not have been accustomed to such proposals. And the appeal to the authority of Spencer seems to have been intended to justify such an unusual suggestion, which, by the way, was one that Russell never repeated in his subsequent writings.

It was Meyer who drew an antivitalist conclusion from Russell's machine in a 1913 article that followed an early attack on McDougall in "The Present Status of the Problem of the Relation between Mind and Body" (Meyer, 1912). We saw that the publication in 1911 of McDougall's *Body and Mind* was the start of that author's battle on behalf of vitalism or "animism" against any kind of mechanism. Following the direction indicated by Driesch, this battle increasingly heightened the contrast between the two opposing positions. Meyer's immediate reaction to McDougall's book was exemplary. In his 1912 article, he presented McDougall as the man who championed the "Ghost Theory" of animal behavior (Meyer, 1912: 365-366). Meyer objected that all that was needed to explain learning—which McDougall considered an ability exclusive to living organisms—were neurological hypotheses accounted for by the physical analogy of deflection described in his *Fundamental Laws of Human Behavior*, which was also published in 1911. In particular, he rejected the synapse theory, which he thought McDougall compromised by bringing back into neurology such "mythological" mental entities as consciousness, will and so on. Here was another "ghost" to turn the nervous current in the direction of one path rather than another, as "a switchman [who] turns the switch in the railway road," as Meyer put it. His attack went back to James and forward to James' followers (including Thorndike, or so it would seem) in the following passage, which is interesting as a forerunner of the polemical objective of the new-born behaviorism:

> It was among European psychologists chiefly that the physiological doctrine of the synapse reintroduced the ghost into the explanation of animal behavior. In America the ghost became popular through the great influence of one man, James, whose followers assign to one kind of mental states which does not seem to have any proper business, to the feelings, the job of stamping and stamping out complete paths of nervous conduction. But they never state any definite law of explaining how the proper feeling itself, with its stamping power turned in the proper *direction*, comes into existence at the proper time (Meyer, 1912: 369).

So the radicalization of the two positions at the time took the form of contrasting slogans. For McDougall mechanism or parallelism was an "Automaton Theory," and for Meyer animism or interactionism was a "Ghost Theory." But Meyer did not consider the choice between the two positions a metaphysical one, as McDougall presented it in *Body and Mind*, but rather "a question which can be answered only by appealing to observation," in other words to future progress in science. Only then would it be known if there was a causal relationship between mental and nervous processes, the hypothesis of interactionism, or a relationship of simultaneity, the hypothesis of parallelism. Given the incompleteness of neurological knowledge at that time, declaring oneself interactionist was the result of a philosophical impatience that led psychologists to "fill in the gap with a ghost"; while declaring oneself parallelist was a choice compatible with the development of neurological science (pp. 366 and 369). In short, parallelism was closer to the spirit of scientific research, because it was a kind of application of Ockham's razor: a subjective factor should not be invoked as the cause of the behavior of living organisms if one can do without it.

While a "purely objective science of animal behavior," as Meyer put it, was the ideal at which to aim, one consequence of its achievement might be the disappearance one day of subjective and mentalist vocabulary from psychology. Meyer thought this vocabulary had an important role to play then in sectors of psychological research in which neurological knowledge was far from complete, because of the results obtained in treating various kinds of mental pathology in analyses in which primarily subjective terminology was used (coming from Europe, Meyer mentions that of Freudian psychiatry). But the psychologist's task always remained that of fostering the translation of subjective terms into the objective terms of neurology, with the constant aim of establishing "definite nervous correlates for all the specific mental states and functions [...]. I venture to predict," Meyer wrote, "that those terms of mental function, for which no nervous correlate can be found, are the very ones which are superfluous, can be spared from our descriptions of mental life in man and animals" (p. 371).

McDougall too, in presenting his method of residues, spoke of the need to try to translate subjective psychological terms into the language of neurology. But this translation did not mean that psychological or subjective language should ever be eliminated, since it was justified by the inevitable appearance of an inexplicable "residue," inexplicable because *untranslatable* (McDougall, 1902: 327). Thus the contrast between parallelists and interactionists highlights the conflict between two different concepts of scientific vocabulary for studying the mind, a conflict that revived some of the themes that had divided Loeb and Jennings a few years earlier. In the field of the science of the mind in the twentieth century, the position that rejected introspective and mentalist vocabulary prefigured the imminent arrival of behaviorism and some claims to eliminate the vocabulary of psychology in favour of that of neurology, while the other position defended the introspective method and mentalism.[33]

But Meyer's dispute did not end there. In *Body and Mind* McDougall had also rejected the possibility of a machine that could change its behavior over the course of time in order to achieve some purpose or end by trying appropriate means, in the way that an animal does, when faced with an obstacle, "in virtue of some obscure, directive power" (McDougall, 1911: 242-243). In his aforementioned 1913 article, "The Comparative Value of Various Conceptions of Nervous Function Based on Mechanical Analogies," Meyer rebutted this with Russell's machine, which was capable of displaying some of the forms of learning he had described in *Fundamental Laws*, a machine "which obeys no ghost whatsoever, but only the laws of mechanics" (Meyer, 1913: 559). As interpreted by Russell himself, the machine could also simulate the nervous connections of an animal learning a path around an obstacle (see Plate 2.2), the very case that McDougall had mentioned

---

[33] McDougall later remarked that it was he in 1905 in his *Primer* who defined psychology as the "positive science of conduct or behavior," although he was not in sympathy with the unexpected subsequent extremism of the "behaviorists" (McDougall, 1923a: 38 n.).

to demonstrate some of the insuperable limits of machines. This led Meyer to an antivitalist conclusion: "If it is proved that a *mechanical organism* can learn and forget without the interaction of a ghost, we have no right to assert that a *biological organism* can not" (*ibid.*, my italics).

Meyer's claim in this article was that the anti-mechanists were behind the times, since machines did not seem to be as *rigid* as they used to be considered. Nevertheless, while Meyer recognized the usefulness of Russell's machine as an antivitalist argument, he hastened to qualify its importance as an aid in explaining a behavioral phenomenon. Actually, Meyer displayed a conventional approach to mechanical analogies in the study of behavior. The mechanical analogies that interested him were the ones that he considered "easily translatable" in neurological terms. He saw them as teaching aids in neurological explanation. Thus his analogies were meant to be simple and direct, with an apparatus based mainly on hydraulic transmission and described with the indispensable minimum of non-neurological terms. As we have seen, these terms did not go much beyond the traditional vocabulary of drainage theories. Hence his ultimate dissatisfaction with Russell's machine, which with transmitters, valves, coupling gangs and all the rest seemed too complicated to be useful for the mainly *didactic* purposes of the neurologist and psychologist.

Meyer seemed to grant the usefulness of analogies in the incomplete state of neurophysiological knowledge at the time. He maintained, for example, that "for the very reason that the chemistry of the neurons is a thing of the future, we may picture to our own imagination the processes going on in the neurons in terms not necessarily chemical," but in terms of hydraulic flux, pressure, resistance, and so on (Meyer, 1911: 58). At the same time "there is no justification for the remark not infrequently heard, that psychology can make no further theoretical progress, that we have to wait until the anatomy and physiology of the nervous system have made a long step in advance" (Meyer, 1908b: 372). But for him mechanical analogies remained essentially teaching aids. If "a teacher of psychology wants to give his students more than a mere classification of mental states," if "he wants to show them how the laws of mental life can be understood as a part of the natural laws governing a highly developed organic being," then—since we do not possess a detailed physiological knowledge of nervous activity—mechanical analogies help to understand how the quantitative properties and relations of neurons and the comparable quantitative changes in those properties and relations are generally sufficient to explain such phenomena as habit formation, without having to invoke the usually "ghostlike" or "mythological" entities (pp. 360-361).

Nevertheless, Meyer failed to realize that by restricting himself to drainage theory analogies, simple and "easily translatable" in neurological terms but irreparably deficient as analogies of nervous conduction, he could never resolve the difficulty he had created for himself: the hydraulic system that inspired his analogies did not embody the kind of neural memory he called "susceptibility."[34] But it was the very fact that a *working device* could simulate, albeit incompletely and in simple cases, what was considered one of the essential features for any physical explanation of learning, i.e. memory, that

[34] I shall not here consider the fact that Meyer (1913: 561) thought Russell gave an incorrect interpretation of the definition of susceptibility in *Fundamental Laws*.

made Russell's machine so innovative. What we might call Meyer's pedagogical stance in evaluating mechanical analogies led him to the error of considering Russell's machine on a par with the imaginary machines that von Uexküll had proposed in the years immediately preceding.

When commenting on Russell's machine in his 1913 article on the value of mechanical analogies, Meyer mentioned the mechanical analogies of von Uexküll, who by this time was gradually approaching vitalism from an anti-Darwinian stance. Von Uexküll was convinced, as he had written in 1908, that "Driesch had succeeded in demonstrating there was no trace of any machine-structure in the germ cell, and that it consisted rather of equivalent parts. This explodes the dogma that the organism is only a machine" (von Uexküll, 1908: 9).[35] Nevertheless, von Uexküll considered it possible and useful as well to compare organisms to machines of varying complexity. But to what end? Not, for example, with the same purpose as a reductionist à la Loeb, who went so far as to consider living organisms "chemical machines." Von Uexküll openly contrasted the *causal explanation* ascribed to physiology, which concerns the physico-chemical material "structure" of the living organism, with the *teleological explanation* ascribed to biology, which concerns the "plan" according to which that structure is achieved. That plan could not be explained by the method of verification, but it could be grasped or illustrated by *intuition*, for "biology is in its essence 'intuition' (*Anschauung*)" (von Uexküll, 1908: 16). And intuition was the core of the analogy between organism and machine. That analogy is not meant to *test* or *verify* anything; rather, to *show* how the machine works makes it possible to grasp how the organism works. Intuition and evidence, *Anschaulichkeit* in his terminology, are the main principles of biology.

So it was not a matter of building working machines as a test of a behavioral theory, as Loeb considered Hammond and Miessner's automaton, or machines whose performance could be compared with that of an organism, as Bent Russell suggested. Indeed, von Uexküll did not think of functioning machines that embodied the principles of a behavioral theory but rather of abstract machines, "fictitious schemata" as he called them (von Uexküll, 1903: 291). And in general "the schema [...] is not a theory at all, but merely a sign language by means of which it is possible to express new results in a clear (*Anschaulich*) way."[36]

There are several concepts of the hydraulic analogy of drainage theory behind von Uexküll's "schemata." One example is "tone," a form of energy conceived as a fluid or liquid that spreads evenly through the nerves as if they were pipes. So one imagines

[35] Von Uexküll did pioneering work on lower organisms and proved more intransigent than Loeb in opposing the use of mentalistic terms in the study of animal behavior. From the beginning he was openly hostile to psychological description in physiology and declared himself against the idea of "animal psychology" because it was impossible to find any sure evidence of mental life at any level of the philogenetic ladder. In 1899 he signed an essay together with the physiologist Albrecht Bethe and Theodor Beer in which a new objective terminology was proposed for the study of animal behavior, an essay that no one then concerned with the subject could ignore (see, for example, the aforementioned review by Frost, 1912). Von Uexküll's ideas played an important part in the revival of holistic philosophical themes, as shown by the case of Ludwig von Bertalanffy (see von Bertalanffy, 1968). See Harrington (1989) in this regard.

[36] Quoted in Jennings (1909a: 327), which is still an interesting review of von Uexküll's early work.

valves and containers of different capacity that regulate, collect and distribute the flux of tone. Again, what von Uexküll was most concerned with stressing was the mnemonic and pedagogical import of these avowedly fictitious mechanical schemata: "what is important is [...] that the schema allows us to put together experimental data in a clear way, and to impress them in our memory as fictitious relations" (p. 289). In particular, the concept of tone "cannot be submitted to physical analysis, nor is it possible to give a mathematical statement of it: it is a purely biological concept, a mere schema (*ein blosses Schema*), through which the experimental data can be put together in a clear way" (p. 287).[37] The reference to the "purely biological" character of the idea of tone and to the "fictitious" nature of the schema thus go back to *Anschaulichkeit* as the *non-quantitative* method proper to biology.

The ambiguities in Meyer's comparative evaluation of the different mechanical analogies of the time are clear at this point. His reference to the pedagogical import of his own mechanical analogies "for the sake of '*Anschaulichkeit*,' to use Uexküll's phrase," as he put it (Meyer, 1913: 562), is misleading in itself. For while Meyer quoted von Uexküll, at the same time he defended the *quantitative* feature of his own mechanical analogies (p. 555), in distinct conflict with the method espoused by von Uexküll. Meyer did not realize the different attitudes that von Uexküll and Russell had towards machines. Let us go into further detail on this point, which is at the core of what we call the discovery of the artificial.

We can take a very simple case: let us summarize von Uexküll's hypotheses about the relationship between nerve, muscle and what he called the "representant" (*Repräsentant*), and we shall see his description of a mechanical analogy that would make it possible to achieve the *Anschaulichkeit* of that relationship (von Uexküll, 1903).

Von Uexküll describes the representant as the mediator between muscle and the central nervous system, so that each muscle is connected to that system by its own representant. The function of the representat is to regulate through the nerve the pressure of tone on the muscle. So when the pressure of nervous tone is increased, there is a corresponding increase in muscle tension. And if muscle tension proves insufficient to resist, let us say, an external traction force, the representant acts on the muscle by increasing the pressure of nervous tone. Figure 2.9 shows the mechanical analogue of this physiological process according to the *Anschaulichkeit*. Here the nervous tone can be 'seen': it has to reach and act on the muscle, spread from the central nervous system (the "intercentral connecting pipe") to the representant (R.p.), whose accordion shape suggests its modifiability. From here tone goes through pipe N (nerve), which is closed at the end by a membrane M, which indicates that the nerve can act on the muscle only in the form of changing the pressure of nervous tone. And it is a change in pressure that pushes forward the membrane into what von Uexküll calls the "bound-tonus room" (*Raum G.T.*). The pressure may be stronger or weaker and hence the forward push of the membrane will be stronger or weaker. The effect will be the conversion of more or less bound-tonus into free tonus, which by a fairly complicated play of opening and closing valve K will fill the "free-tonus room" (*Raum F.T.*). From here the free tonus at last spreads through valve

---

[37] Loeb expressed significant reservations about von Uexküll's metaphor of tone from the point of view of his own *quantitative* analyses of lower organisms in terms of chemical reactions (Loeb, 1918: 21 n.).

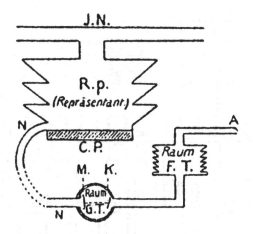

Fig. 2.9. The "representant" in the hydraulic analogy of von Uexküll (1903).

A to muscle with more or less pressure and causes a corresponding greater or lesser increase in the tension of the muscle, which is now capable of exerting resistance to an external traction force. The free-tonus room is accordion-shaped, which shows its variable capacity, depending on the length of the muscle. The different nerve-muscle-representant units, like the one described here, are 'seen' as connected to each other in a very elaborate way, in order to regulate the distribution of tonus to the various muscles of the organism. The result is a machine schema that looks surprisingly complex, with pipes, valves, storage tanks: what is shown in Figure 2.10 represents the diagram of part of the nervous system of a simple organism.[38]

Jennings had this to say about this complicated diagram:

It seems [to me] that, even for practical purposes, [von Uexküll] has overestimated the value of a rather gross *Anschaulichkeit*. The bringing in of machine-like structures—tubes, valves, etc.—that confessedly do not exist, seems rather to confuse than to aid the mind. It is not possible to conclude directly from the properties of the assumed machines as to what physiological properties one will find, for the parallelism is far from complete, so one must try to keep the system of machinery separate from the system of physiological facts: there are two systems to grasp in place of one (Jennings, 1909a: 330-331).

As Jennings rightly observed, von Uexküll's analogies were based on machine-like structures that "do not even profess to be verifiable." He rejected von Uexküll's opposition between the method of verification ascribed to physiology and that of the *Anschaulichkeit* appertaining to biology as the science dealing with the construction of the "plan" of organic structures. For Jennings the method of verification could not be excluded from any discipline that took the living organism as its object of study.[39] Thus biology and physiology were "peacefully in union" under the same method of verification:

[38] *Spinunculus*, a worm whose behavior von Uexküll studied in depth.
[39] See above, p. 20.

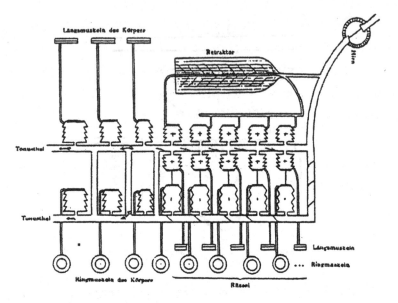

Fig. 2.10. The nervous system of *Spinunculus* in the hydraulic analogy of von Uexküll (1903).

"we shall be interested in the plan of the organism," wrote Jennings, "so far as it is *verifiable*, and to work out the verifiable plan we shall be forced to consider the actual forces, materials and arrangements, not fictitious ones" (Jennings, 1909a: 335).

Meyer made this very criticism of von Uexküll, mentioning Jennings' above statement, but he thought it applied to Russell as well (Meyer, 1913: 559). He rejected von Uexküll's analogies because they were too complicated as compared with his own in *Fundamental Laws*, and at this point he compared von Uexküll's analogies to Russell's 'complicated' hydraulic machine. Is this a correct conclusion? Of course, the "forces, materials and arrangements" Russell considered were also not the actual, i.e. organic, ones: Russell was designing an *artifact* that could simulate them. But little more need be said to realize the different attitudes that von Uexküll and Russell had towards their machines.

Russell's aim was to make some neurological hypotheses more convincing by way of what he called a "practical device" that could simulate them. This could be interpreted in a weak sense (using a device to show that some hypotheses were *evident* or *Anschaulic*) or in a strong one (using a device as a *test* to argue in favor of some hypotheses). We shall see that the latter soon became the prevailing sense: actually, it is the core of the modeling method in behavioral sciences. Both senses were probably involved in Russell's claims, but when Meyer likened Russell's machine to von Uexküll's because they shared what he considered a distracting complexity, he missed Russell's modeling aim. The machines that came out of von Uexküll's imagination were never intended to *work* according to a psycho-physiological theory, notwithstanding the flood of terms he borrowed from mechanics and hydraulics to describe them. The complexity of Russell's machine was that of a device designed to work, but if von Uexküll's machines had any complexity, it was primarily because they were, as von Uexküll himself put it, "fictitious."

For Russell there was no question of wondering whether or not the hydraulic devices given as analogues of certain neural functions were *translatable* in neurological terms for pedagogical purposes, or "for the sake of '*Anschaulichkeit*'." Russell indeed stressed the possibility of performing the *same functions* with a machine *physically different* than the one he described, a machine working not by hydraulic pressure or compressed air but with electric control, i.e. by electrical transmitters, and equipped with electromagnets to control other components (Russell, 1913: 26-27). Actually, Russell's main aim seems to have been not to suggest vague analogies but to build a machine that embodied certain neurological hypotheses, and could work effectively in simulating some of the organism's functions. The only way to make this possible was to use physical (hydraulic or electrical) devices of the required complexity, as far as the technology of the time would allow. Hence Russell's appeal, "as a member of the engineering profession," for multi-disciplinary collaboration in the study of the nervous system, but the appeal was so ahead of its time that Meyer was not ready to pick it up: he let it drop.

8. Stephens' connectionist machine

As already mentioned, Thorndike's motivationist terminology was unsatisfactory to many behaviorist psychologists. Notwithstanding Thorndike's specifications, the role of satisfaction and discomfort in choosing successful responses and eliminating unsuccessful ones was considered paradoxical: psychic causes intervened in giving rise to physical effects.[40]

This is the context of J. M. Stephens' proposal. He suggested giving Thorndike's claim a "strictly mechanistic interpretation" and eliminating such subjective psychological terms as satisfaction and discomfort from the formulation of the law of effect, all to the good of the neurological definitions Thorndike himself had advanced. According to Stephens, when Thorndike stated such definitions he did "not seem to regard the neural condition in itself as the determiner" of learning (Stephens, 1929: 429-430).[41]

The mechanistic interpretation of the law of effect that Stephens advanced was based on the data recorded by Thorndike: with the same stimulus an organism (the cat in the puzzle box, for example) reacts initially with random responses, then selects the successful response, and from that point on tends constantly to respond the same way. Stephens stressed that the agency selecting the successful response was not a mental state of satisfaction but the *effect* of the response, which by "retroaction," as he put it, activated a specific neural mechanism consisting in the possible variation of the resistance

[40] Actually, for non-mechanistic psychologists *this* was the very problem that needed explanation. McDougall made it the basis of his criticism of the mechanistic interpretations of Thorndike's connectionism as well as of Watson's frequentist view. According to McDougall, success and failure in behavior are impossible without the "discriminative guidance of action" by pleasure and pain respectively (see McDougall, 1925, Chapter 6).

[41] See Postman (1947) for the place of Stephens' views in the context of the different interpretations of the law of effect. Several years later, Stephens mentioned his unchanged conviction that Thorndike's law of effect could explain every form of learning, and that even the Pavlovian conditioning could be reduced to the law of effect (see the preface to Stephens, 1967).

of the connection responsible for that response.[42] Generally speaking, one effect might increase the resistance of the connection, another not. As usual, the problem was the exact nature of this neural mechanism, in which the subjective terminology of satisfaction and discomfort was translated into objective terms: which hypothesis to choose among the many that proposed to explain how the resistance of nervous connections changed?

The way Stephens looked at this question is an interesting sample of the simulative method in its germinal phase. He started from the observation that many theories had handled learning in terms of "elements of conduction bodies, connections and variable resistance," all things that can be analyzed "independently of protoplasm." Without referring explicitly to those theories, Stephens advanced his own proposal for achieving a mechanical synthesis of these inorganic elements in such a way as to realize a kind of "nonprotoplasmatic learning," which would be a genuine "synthetic test" of neurological hypotheses, in this case the hypotheses that were meant to explain the change in resistance of nervous connections. A "learning machine," he concluded, could represent, if not a proof, at least an "argument in favour" of a learning theory.

It is worth looking at the following passage, in which the pioneering writer shows surprise that an idea was making headway via the suggestion of a mechanistic metaphor, the idea of a new view of the relationship between neurology and psychology and a new chance to test a psychological theory—an idea that we shall come back to more than once.

The above conception occurred to me as a means of evaluating those expositions of learning couched in neurological terms. This test of possible synthesis had, at first, only theoretical interest. To my surprise, however, I found that some of the analyses presented startling possibilities of mechanical synthesis [...]. I have given the description of the machine first and then tried to point out the principles of its operation [...]. I have then tried to indicate the theories from which the present conception was generated, through the medium of synthetic verification, and to point out the modifications [...]. I have tried to use no explanation of animate learning which could not be considered to work in a machine. I have considered protoplasmatic organisms as very complicated machines and nothing further (Stephens, 1929: 422 and 423).

Very complicated machines then, but *what kind*? For there to be learning according to Stephens' interpretation of the law of effect, two devices are required. The first must be capable of discriminating between (at least) two conditions, the second must keep on changing S-R connections until one rather than the other of those conditions appears, and cease to do so when the successful connection is selected. Might it be possible to build

[42] Stephens actually introduced the term "retroaction" in a later article in which he picked up the psychologist Leonard T. Troland's idea of "retroflex action" and agreed with Troland's idea of the greater "adaptive value" and "biological utility" of the successful response chosen by the organism (Stephens, 1931). On that occasion Stephens introduced some modifications of his original hypothesis, and described another machine that would synthesize it. Although Troland's viewpoint was different, he thought of "translating" Thorndike's motivationist terminology into neurological language, in an attempt to discover a selective response mechanism at a neural level that could make the idea of the "adaptive value" of the successful response interpretable in objective terms. Troland (1928) used different terms for a new version of Meyer's idea that a mental state of pleasure or pain could be interpreted in terms of an increase or decrease in nervous current. Retroflex action and related loop notions used by psychologists and physiologists have been considered suggestive of the notion of feedback (see Miller, Galanter and Pribram, 1960: 43-44, and also Mowrer, 1960a: 320). The same could be said of other notions we are discussing, such as Stephens' retroaction and Russell's counter-signal.

a working machine that would realize, so to speak, this kind of selective-learning mechanism? In Stephens' words, could the "essential elements" of this conception of learning be "synthesized into a machine which modifies its own responses to achieve a given end?" This was the question with which we left Jennings in Chapter 1, when the artifacts that he thought could display an organism's "perplexing" ability to modify its behavior, did not actually have even a rudimentary form of such an ability.[43]

The machine Stephens designed in response to this question took the form of the electrical circuit in Plate 2.3. It looks as complicated as it does odd. This rudimentary machine was designed to 'learn' to drive away a disturbance from the external environment, the disturbance being a finger touch. Every time the response fails to drive off the finger, it changes. When a response is "selected" that drives the finger away, that response is kept.

Stephens' machine might be described as a device that realizes some of the simpler features of the "little ultrastable system" described by Ashby (see Figure 1.4). When the essential variables are within the norm (i.e. when the moving bar B in Plate 2.3 is in the center) the machine is in a state of equilibrium. As soon as the essential variables are driven out of the norm by the finger touch, the machine responds by 'trying' to restore the state of equilibrium. Actually, the machine changes its internal organization (thanks to the possibility of positioning needle switch J in Plate 2.3 in two ways when stimulated from outside) and 'tries' the two different behaviors of which it is capable. When one of these behaviors does not bring success, i.e. when the variables do not return within the norm, the state of equilibrium is not restored. Then the machine 'tries' the other behavior, in accordance with what Ashby made a general rule in the second edition of *Design for a Brain*: if the attempt fails, change the way of behaving; when and only when the attempt is successful, maintain this way of behaving.[44] The performance of Stephens' machine was actually very poor: it was able to respond to an input stimulus having potential connection with only two different responses. Stephens believed this limitation (as well as others he discussed) could be overcome, for in principle a machine could be built with a number of responses corresponding to a number of possible stimuli. Nevertheless, this limitation also makes the machine a particularly trivial instance of 'ultrastability.'

The machine had the two devices that Stephens considered necessary to explain learning according to the law of effect: that of discriminating between different conditions, and that of changing connections until a condition was reached that was successful or had "survival value," and then keeping the corresponding connection. The neurological hypothesis that Stephens considered the basis of the law of effect was embodied or synthesized in the machine: if a given response failed to have the successful effect, the resistance of the connection that gave rise to that response was increased, but if the response were successful that did not happen.

[43] See above, pp. 23-24.

[44] Ashby (1952/1960). In the first edition of *Design for a Brain* Ashby, in giving an example of an organism behaving as an ultrastable system, referred to the action system of *Stentor* as described by Jennings. In the second edition of the book he referred to the experiments in trial-and-error learning conducted by Thorndike and other psychologists. Ashby's definition of ultrastability was meant to distinguish between *change in behavior* and *change in state* within the same behavior, a distinction we shall return to in the last section of Chapter 4.

Plate 2.3

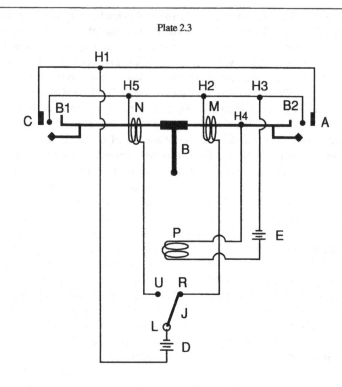

Stephens' machine is presented here in a simplified diagram. The letters correspond to those in Stephens' original circuit (from Stephens, 1929), also shown below.

The machine was designed to 'learn' by trial-and-error to drive off anyone who touched it. Let us suppose we press a finger on A and thus close the electrical circuit that runs through H1 and passes through battery D to L, where it finds needle switch J on contact R and thence through magnet M closes in A. The passage of the current activates magnet M, which attracts movable bar B. This causes rod B2 to move to the right and its point strikes the finger that is still pressing on A. Under these conditions the machine's internal organization does not change. If we put our finger on A again, the machine will continue to drive it off with the same reaction.

Now let us suppose that we put our finger on C. Since needle switch J is always in the same position (as in the figure), the current will go along the same circuit as before to H2 but this time close in C. Magnet M is again activated and again shifts rod B2 to the right. This time, however, it does not find the obstacle of the finger on A and, when it finishes its run to the right, it closes another circuit, the one that goes from B2 through H3 to battery E and magnet P, and then B2 by way of H4. While current goes through magnet P, the magnet attracts the needle switch J towards J's zenith, breaks the contact with R and (via a device designed by Stephens) closes in U. Now one must imagine a rapid sequence of events. While the finger is still pressing C, the contact between J and R is broken and another contact is established between J and U, with the result that current from C now goes from L to U and activates magnet N and closes through H5. At this point, N attracts rod B1, and its point strikes the finger, which is still on C. The presence of the finger prevents contact being established between B1 and C, which would again activate magnet P and thus break the contact just established between J and U.

Now, as long as this contact is maintained, the current, which passes through C as through A, will always activate magnet N. So if we continue to press our finger on C, the machine will always react with the same response, i.e. shifting rod B1 to the left and driving away the finger. If instead we go back and press A, the machine will at first react by shifting rod B1 to the left, but since it meets no obstacle, it will close a different circuit, the one going from C through H5, H2, and H3 to reach battery E and activate magnet P, and thus re-establish contact between J and R (as in the figure), and when A is stimulated again, it will evoke the reaction we already know, i.e. it will drive the finger away from A.

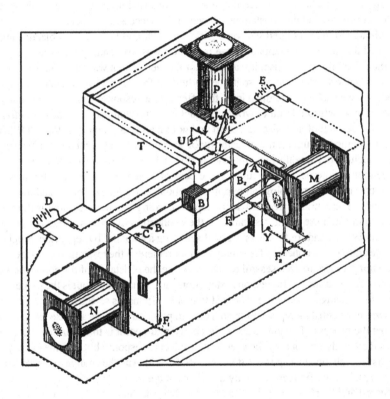

Stephens remarked that the resistance of connection L-R and that of connection L-U changes depending on whether needle switch J rests on R or U. Once the machine has been 'stimulated' by finger touch, if the resistance between L and R is less than that of the other connection, the response will take place through R and M. If that response drives off the finger (the response is thus successful), the resistance of the connection will not be increased. If instead that response does not drive off the finger (the response is a failure), the resistance will be increased.

Reassured by what he called an "argument in favour" of his neurological hypotheses, i.e. having synthesized them in a machine, Stephens thought he could reject rival hypotheses, including the drainage and frequentist hypotheses, and what he called the "traditional" hypothesis, i.e. the idea that was widely shared, by Thorndike just as much as by Watson, according to which, if a nervous current flowed towards one connection rather than another, it was because the resistance of the first was somehow lowered (because the threshold of the corresponding synapse was lessened). In particular, Stephens (1929: 429) rejected the idea that nervous current flowed because of a difference in potential, in line with the electrical or hydraulic analogy for which a great decrease in the resistance of any one connection drained most of the energy from other connections. On the contrary, the working of the machine suggested that learning consisted in the increased resistance of failed connections and the constant resistance of the successful connection.[45]

Although Stephens shared Watson's criticism of Thorndike's use of subjective terms, he argued that use or frequent and close repetition was a secondary factor as compared with the effect of the response: it was this, not frequency, that was the selective agency. Indeed, he inverted the role of use in the traditional frequentist interpretation: only if a connection were *already* stamped in by the effect of the response could it be further consolidated by repetition. In other words, the fact of being stamped in is the *condition* for frequent repetition of an S-R connection and not vice versa (Stephens, 1931: 149). The machine seemed to suggest the plausibility of Thorndike's argument against Watson.

In conclusion, Russell's machine and Stephens' both achieved rudimentary forms of change in their internal organization on the base of their previous history, but they embodied two different neurological hypotheses about learning. Russell's machine seems to embody an essentially frequentist concept, according to which learning is due to the reduction through use of the resistance of the connection that gives rise to a successful response. What stands out is the process of selecting a response by repetition. Stephens' machine embodies a concept of learning as an increment in the resistance of connections that do *not* give rise to a successful response, while the resistance of the connection that does give rise to a successful response stays constant. What stands out is the process that gives rise to change in response. The fact that one response is selected and fixed, which is shown by its constant repetition from a certain point onwards, is a consequence of the fact that the process of change ceases. Stephens' main point is that learning can be understood by studying not only the agency that selects a response but also the agency that gives rise to a change in response (Stephens, 1929: 428). And the change in response cannot be explained by frequency, but by the effect of the response itself.

Russell and Stephens were both aware that their machines could simulate only simple kinds of learning. Yet they both hoped that more complex kinds of learning could be simulated as progress was made in the construction of simulative machines. And in any case, the very existence of those machines offered at least a preliminary argument in favour of the *sufficiency* of the physical principles involved: "no new principle" need be

---

[45] Dunlap (1928) summarized the empirical evidence that led Stephens (1929: 429 n. 2) to consider this hypothesis more biologically plausible than others.

called upon, according to Stephens, and hence learning might not be a distinctive (i.e. non-physical) feature of living organisms.

At the beginning of connectionism, with Russell and much more explicitly with Stephens, the following idea made headway: an "inorganic" or "non-protoplasmatic" machine that behaves as predicted by the behavioral theory whose "essential elements" (as both Russell an Stephens put it) it embodies is an argument in favour of that theory. As we saw, this was also Loeb's conclusion in regard to Hammond and Miessner's machine. But the difference was not insignificant. For Loeb the mere existence of that machine, of that automatism, suggested that learning was an exclusive feature of certain organisms considered as *organic* machines. The new idea was that learning was a particular form of automatism, that choice could be made automatic, and that even *inorganic* machines could learn: 'new' artifacts suggested a way of bridging the gap between the organic and the inorganic.

CHAPTER 3

THE ROBOT APPROACH

1. Introduction. Forms of learning

More than once we have had occasion to note that a form of learning which might be described in terms of Pavlov's conditioned reflex was quite familiar to modern psychological and neurological associationism. When the West, especially the United States, learned of Pavlov's work, psychologists posed the question of how conditioning might fit into the framework of the different forms of learning that had already been studied.[1] In Watson's version, conditioning, understood as stimulus substitution, could be explained by the temporal contiguity of the conditioned stimulus to the unconditioned stimulus and to the response to be conditioned, i.e. the response that was evoked initially by the unconditioned stimulus. Watson pointed to temporal contiguity of stimulus and response to explain other forms of learning as well, including selective or trial-and-error learning, which according to Thorndike was based on the law of effect. Thorndike did not ascribe much importance to conditioning as stimulus substitution (or "associative shifting," as he put it). He considered conditioning a very limited form in comparison with selective learning and, in any case, a form based on other principles. From his point of view, if learning by conditioning could result from simple contiguity, more complex forms such as selective learning could be explained only by the strengthening of certain S-R connections as set forth by the law of effect.

The dichotomy that Thorndike saw between his principles of learning and those of Pavlov led to various classifications based on the differences between the two forms of learning, not to mention attempts to proceed in a direction other than the reduction of both to simple temporal contiguity, as Watson proposed. According to Stephens, for example, learning by conditioning could be fully explained by, and hence reduced to, the law of effect, which remained the sole law of learning. Stephens found confirmation in the functioning of his mechanical model, where every response of Pavlov's dog to a stimulus to be conditioned that did not have the appropriate effect, namely greater adaptive value (such as the response that prepared for the intake of food, namely salivation), did not become a conditioned response, and the corresponding S-R connection was stamped out.

Clark Hull suggested that the two forms of learning, selective and by conditioning, were particular cases of a single principle, that of primary reinforcement, by which it is

---

[1] Classic accounts of the development of different learning theories, before and after Pavlov's ideas came to the West, are given in Hilgard and Marquis (1940), Postman (1947), and Spence (1951). Western psychologists first became familiar with Pavlov's work in 1906, when *Science* published the text of one of his lectures, and R.M. Yerkes and S. Morgulis described his experiments in an article in 1909. But it was Watson who familiarized the West with the principle of the conditioned reflex in the study of learning, which he wrote about in *Behavior* in 1914. When Pavlov's book was translated (Pavlov, 1927), his work became well known to American behaviorists. For an introduction to the subject, see Mecacci (1979).

always and only the S-R connection that is strengthened, and this leads to the reduction or elimination of an organism's drive. The hungry cat in the Thorndike box selects and fixes one response among several evoked at random: the one that is followed by primary reinforcement in the form of food intake. Such a response leads to a reduction in the drive and has the maximum adaptive value for the animal. The case of Pavlov's dog is more complicated but does not entail a different principle, because in conditioning too the learned response leads to the reduction of a pre-existing drive. What changes is the situation in which the principle is applied. Actually, in conditioning it is not one of the animal's several possible responses that is followed by primary reinforcement but a single response; and what is more, this response is not one the animal selects but one that is induced by the experimenter, namely salivation. Since salivation has always been in close temporal contiguity with food intake (or primary reinforcement), it acquires its own so-called "secondary" reinforcement capacity.

Hull, like Stephens, wanted to interpret the law of effect in objective terms: reformulating the law in terms of the organism's drive reduction meant freeing such a law from Thorndike's controversial references to pleasure and discomfort. When reviewing Thorndike's *Fundamentals of Learning*, Hull said that he referred initially to such an objective law in his own investigations and interpreted it as the law of conditioning (Hull, 1935a: 821). What in this case was central to the explanation of learning was reinforcement in the presence of a drive and not the subjective component of motivation. It is sufficient to reconsider the formulation of the principle of primary reinforcement to see that Hull shared Thorndike's neurological hypotheses of connectionism, namely, that learning always occurs through the strengthening of some neural connections or bonds and the weakening of others. But Hull was never particularly interested in the neurological details of connectionism. His writings only occasionally make reference to results from neurology and do not contain the frequent drawings of the nervous system taken from neurological texts of the time which Thorndike usually included in his writings. Hull picked up a distinction that Edward Tolman had made and maintained the study of the laws of learning at a markedly "molar" level, i.e. he thought that the laws should be drawn chiefly from the study of the overt behavior of organisms, given our scant understanding of the laws at the neurophysiological or "molecular" level.

Thus, Hull claimed that he had started out by objectively interpreting the law of effect as conditioning with reinforcement, and that in this way he was able to eliminate Thorndike's motivational references from the explanation of learning and adaptation. Hull also thought he had made explicit an aspect neglected by Pavlov, namely that reinforcement is always connected to the reduction of a drive of the organism. For Hull, though reinforcement was the basis of adaptation and learning, it was a wholly "automatic" mechanism: it regulates the organism's dynamic relations with the external environment, and it is solely because of its greater complexity that it differs from simple reflexes or the many mechanisms that regulate the organism's internal environment (the ones Walter Cannon termed "homeostatic"). Hull's made continuing efforts in his theoretical and experimental investigations to explain this complexity on the basis of the principles of associationism and connectionism. In one of the first articles he wrote on the subject, he described the conditioned reflex as "an automatic trial-and-error mechanism which mediates, blindly but beautifully, the adjustment of the organism to a complex environment" (Hull, 1929: 498). This marked the first step towards integrating two forms of learning in a single set of assumptions. At the same time, Hull insisted that in so far as it could be explained or "deduced" (the term he preferred) from the principles of associationism and connectionism, *every* form of learning, however complex, was a purely physical process that involved increasingly complex degrees of automatism.

Hull explained that he used "blind" in the sense that where learning or reinforcement of neural connections is concerned, "it is not assumed that there is available for its guidance and control any disembodied soul or spirit," not in the sense that these processes work without "recognized principles" (Hull 1930a: 250). No Ghost Theory could take the place of the search for the molar principles of learning. Hull dealt with the problem that we have been looking at since Chapter 1 in terms of the contrast between automatic and plastic control of behavior. He did so by opposing the Gestalt psychologists, who claimed that the different forms of learning could not be explained by the principles of associationism and connectionism. Nonetheless, Hull did not base his defense of those principles on the bare hypotheses advanced by such behaviorists as Watson, for whom the automatism of the nervous system was reduced to the possibility of activating different pre-existing chains of reflex arches. As we shall see, Hull tried, instead, to do justice to certain ideas of the Gestalt psychologists.

In his later work too, Hull continued to defend the hypothesis of the automatic nature of all forms of learning. But in the late 1920s and mid-1930s, he urged that the hypothesis could be corroborated by results from a new kind of investigation conducted alongside experimental psychology. The point was to start building machines that could simulate the simplest learning processes in order ultimately to build others, which Hull called "ultra-automatic" or "psychic" machines, with a hitherto unexplored degree of automatism that could simulate the most complex kinds of learning typical of higher organisms and humans. In the course of our investigation into the discovery of the artificial we have already seen some proposals along the lines of this simulative methodology, including the machine as a test of a psychological theory, the functional comparison of machine and organism, the idea that successful simulation of the most *elementary* forms of learning would ultimately make possible the simulation of *complex* forms, and the interpretation of simulation itself in an anti-vitalist vein. In the case of Hull and some of his followers, this method took the form of a particularly explicit and consistent proposal, even in light of the evolution it underwent beginning a decade later, in the cybernetic age.

The present chapter will describe the development of the simulative methodology of Hull and other researchers from a different background, which hark back to the idea of the automatic and mechanical nature of mental processes. The electromechanical devices and robots they built, primitive forebears of the synthetic animals of cybernetics, were meant to embody some of the principles that inspired Hull's theoretical and experimental investigations of learning. We shall be looking at least at those aspects of such investigations which help to clarify the aims of those researchers. We shall conclude the chapter with a consideration of the reasons why Hull abandoned his simulative approach.

2. Simulating learning processes.

Hull was a psychologist who had studied logic and engineering. He also designed a machine for automatically producing syllogistic conclusions. But according to his *Idea Books*, the diary he kept regularly all his life, at least as early as 1927 he was thinking of an altogether different machine that could simulate the processes of learning by conditioning in living organisms.[2] It seems that Hull publicly launched the idea of this kind of machine in 1928, almost as a challenge to those attending one of his weekly University seminars, at which theoretical problems in psychology and the laws of learning were discussed (Hull later said that "my suggestion [was] that a model might be made to test the theory"). The following week, three devices were brought to him that reproduced the conditioned reflex: two were arrangements of very crude wooden levers, but one, designed by H. D. Baernstein, a chemist who had been at the earlier seminar, was particularly ingenious. It was displayed in May 1929 at the Midwest Psychological Association Conference in Urbana, Illinois. Baernstein's device attracted wide interest, and the press referred to it as a "mysterious mechanical brain," the forefather of a whole generation of "thinking machines."[3] The aim of Hull's challenge was explained in an article he and Baernstein published in July of the same year in *Science*. They situated their project within the "mechanistic tendency of modern psychology" and described it in the following terms:

If it were possible to construct non-living devices—perhaps even of inorganic materials—which would perform the essential functions of the conditioned reflex, we should be able to organize these units into systems which would show true trial-and-error learning with intelligent selection and the elimination of errors, as well as other behavior ordinarily classed as psychic. [...] Learning and thought are here conceived as by no means necessarily a function of living protoplasm any more than is aerial locomotion (Hull and Baernstein, 1929: 15).

Hull later remarked that "there was a time when the properties of aerial locomotion were associated only with organic life," but now it was clear that "if material is organized in a certain way, it will fly like an eagle; if it is organized in another way, it will fly like an airplane." In general, "it is only a question how the material is organized that determines how it will behave" (quoted by Gray, 1935-36b: 413).

[2] The description of the syllogistic conclusion machine, which was also mentioned by Martin Gardner (Gardner, 1982) was never published, and Hull referred to it only occasionally. In Hull's autobiography he said that it was made of "concentric sheet-metal plates" (Hull, 1952: 146)—a kind of Lullian machine. But Hull had already distinguished between a logical machine and a "psychic" one (as he called it) and made it clear that the former had nothing to do with his hopes for the latter, which were to simulate the versatile and adaptive behavior of a living organism. "When, and if, this takes place the thinking mechanism will surely be a far more subtle and complete character than a mere logic machine consisting of sliding disks. [...] Fertility, originality, invention, insight, the spontaneous use of implements or tools—these things, clearly, do not lie in the syllogism" (Hull, 1935b: 220 and 219 n.). Another of Hull's automatic machines, this one for calculating statistics (a newspaper report was headlined "Machine does year's work in a day"), is in the Smithsonian Institution and dates to 1925 (C. Eames and R. Eames, 1990: 89). Hull died in 1952 and his *Idea Books* (Hull, 1962) were published posthumously, selected and edited by his secretary, Ruth Hays. The present chapter refers to Hull's work from the late 1920s to around the mid-1930s. For the evolution of Hull's thinking, see the excellent analysis of Smith (1986).

[3] This information comes from "Thinking Machines," an article that appeared in the popular journal *Harper's Magazine* in 1936 (Gray, 1935-36b).

Certain ideas were clearly in the air, and Hull and Baernstein's proposal was fully ac-
cordant with the approach Stephens independently proposed that very year, i.e. the "synthetic approach" to the study of learning apart from the features of living protoplasm.[4]
Both Hull and Stephens were thinking about "non-living devices" that had a specific capacity which traditional machines did not have, that of changing their internal organization in response to an outside stimulus and varying behavior as predicted by a learning
theory. "In designing a learning machine," Hull wrote in his *Idea Books* in 1927, "I felt
the necessity of providing a device to vary the reactions so that trial-and-error could take
place effectively" (Hull, 1962: 823). Hull's project looked like the first realization of the
hope Bent Russell expressed in 1913 that psychologists, neurologists, and engineers
might work together in the study of the principles of learning—a genuine "robot approach," to use Hull's own expression.[5] Hull was referring to Russell when, in introducing another device—that built by Robert G. Krueger, an electro-technical engineer interested in psychology—he wrote that this was "not the first time that a model intended
to parallel adaptive behavior has been designed" (Krueger and Hull, 1931: 262).

Baernstein's and Kreuger's devices were intended to simulate several features of conditioned reflex learning. These devices might be considered as the "units" about which
Hull and Baernstein spoke in the *Science* article: when organized in more complex systems, these would display several forms of behavior typical of higher organisms. Actually, what is typical of the robot approach is the idea that successful simulation of elementary learning processes is the premise for simulating higher mental processes.

To get an idea of how these devices worked, it suffices to look at the simplest one,
built by Krueger. As the figure in Plate 3.1 shows, the device consisted of a set of electric circuits. A charged battery E is inserted in the first circuit and uncharged batteries E_1,
..., E_5 in the others. When switch S_u is pressed, lamp L lights because battery E is charged.
This reproduces the simple or unconditioned reflex, where S_u is the unconditioned stimulus (food in the case of Pavlov's dog) which always evokes the same reflex response
(salivation at the sight of food), and this corresponds to the lamp going on. Since the other batteries are uncharged, lamp L does not light if any other switch S_1, ..., S_5 is pressed.
These may be considered as neutral stimuli to be conditioned (a sound, a light and so on).
The simulation of conditioning in its simplest form takes place if one imagines pressing
switch S_u and one of the others, say S_1, simultaneously. In this case the current from battery E flows through the lamp and battery E_1 as well, and charges the latter. This operation simulates double stimulation during conditioning and gives sufficient charge to battery E_1 that when switch S_1 alone is pressed, the lamp glows, although faintly. In other

[4] The description of another electric machine simulating some features of conditioning was published in 1930
but "for purposes of demonstration in introductory psychology," as the author put it (Walton, 1930: 110), rather
than to test a psychological theory, which was the explicit aim of Hull and Stephens. It should be noted, however, that some researchers' altogether *pedagogical* interest in machines (Meyer was considered in the previous chapter in this connection) sometimes rears its head in other authors who seem more interested in using
machines in connection with a *theory* of behavior.

[5] As we shall see (in section 7 below), Hull adopted the expression "robot approach" several years later in
his *Principles of Behavior* (Hull, 1943: 29-30). Notwithstanding, we use this expression here because it captures the spirit of the simulative approach Hull adopted from the late 1920s to the mid-1930s.

words, S_1 has acquired the ability to evoke a response that previously was evoked by S_u, which is what happens in simple conditioned reflex learning. If the action were repeated several times, there would be a progressive increase in the glow of the lamp, which would be roughly comparable to a learning curve. As the authors remarked, in this model, learning consists of an accumulation of energy in some strategic points rather than "a synaptic change at strategic points capable of releasing energy from a general reservoir," from a viewpoint like the drainage hypothesis we discussed in the previous chapter (Krueger and Hull, 1931: 263).

Krueger's device (again see Plate 3.1) seemed to provide a fairly simple simulation of certain phenomena predicted in Pavlov's theory, for example, experimental extinction (gradual disappearance of the conditioned response if not followed by the unconditioned

Plate 3.1

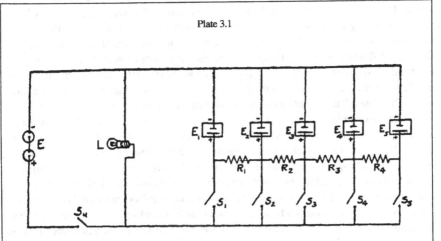

Krueger's device (from Krueger and Hull, 1931) simulated some features of conditioning (the circuit in the Figure functions as long as battery E remains sufficiently charged).

For example, *experimental extinction* corresponds to the fact that once the electrical circuit has been 'conditioned,' as described in the text, if switch S_1 alone is pressed repeatedly, then battery E_1 gradually runs out and lamp L no longer lights. But if S_1 is pressed again some time after E_1 is exhausted, the lamp, because of a phenomenon of regeneration, will light again, albeit briefly and weakly, the process recalling *spontaneous recovery*.

Moreover, the circuit is constructed so that if S_u and S_1 are pressed simultaneously in order to 'condition' the latter, the current flows not only through E_1 but through E_2 and all the other batteries as well in a progressively reduced way because of resistances $R_1, ..., R_5$. If S_1 and S_u are pressed frequently, the batteries will gradually recharge until the lamp lights if any switch after S_1 is pressed, albeit with a progressively weaker glow, a phenomenon that recalls *irradiation*.

To simulate *redintegration* a whole set of other switches, for example, S_1, S_2, S_3 must be pressed repeatedly at the same time as S_u, and the 'conditioning' must be stopped only when the lamp has reached the maximal glow. At this point, the lamp will light if any one of the three switches is pressed, but the glow will be weaker than it would be if the whole set of switches were pressed.

stimulus or reinforcement), spontaneous recovery (later reappearance of the conditioned response after a period of extinction), irradiation (weaker conditioned response to increasingly different stimuli of the same class as the conditioning stimulus, for example acoustic stimuli), and redintegration. Redintegration means that the unconditioned stimulus is associated not with a single stimulus to be conditioned, as in ordinary conditioning, but with several different stimuli (or to use Hull's terminology, a whole "redintegrative stimulus complex"), each of which can evoke a response by itself. For example, if the Pavlovian dog sees a colored light every time the bell rings and it is fed, eventually the colored light alone will evoke salivation.

Baernstein's device is a more complicated electrical circuit than Krueger's, with heat-regulators in the form of 'U'-shaped glass tubes containing toluene and mercury (Baernstein and Hull, 1931). Figure 3.1 shows one of these tubes, the. "conditioner." Briefly, imagine that the chamber with toluene, a liquid that expands rapidly when heated, is surrounded by a heating wire. When the toluene is heated it expands and the mercury level rises. In this way wires of different length in the right side of the tube close the circuits that help 'condition' the lighting of a lamp at different times. According to the authors, the lamp is the responding system, while the heat-regulators correspond to the synapses. Actually, the tubes are time-lag relays that make Baernstein's device a discrete-state machine, at least as compared with Krueger's, which is a completely analogical machine.[6] In Plate 3.2 a simpler electrical circuit than Baernstein's original is described.

Hull considered redintegration particularly important and argued that it made possible a fuller account of learning and adaptation processes than did ordinary conditioning (Hull, 1929: 498). He considered redintegration no less automatic a mechanism than ordinary conditioning, although redintegration was the basis for more complex forms of learning. For example, Hull believed that, in a redintegrative organism, one might "deduce" the existence of a mechanism of "divergent excitation" or "intraserial competition" between different responses which is the basis for forms of selective or trial-and-error learning, not all of them within the reach of lower organisms. In the years when he was increasingly committed to the robot approach, Hull offered his 'deductions' in a fairly qualitative way but later had recourse to other descriptive criteria. The following reconstruction is useful for our purposes.[7]

In the mechanism of divergent excitation or intraserial competition a constant or persistent stimulus is connected to mutually incompatible responses with different strengths. For example, this stimulus may be thought of as persistent hunger pangs. In selective learning like that in Thorndike's box, these alternative responses form a sequence of single acts, the random acts of the hungry animal trying to get out of the box. Hull called this kind of learning by trial-and-error "simple," because just one of the possible acts is

---

[6] The difference in the memory cells affects the degree of realism of some of the simulations of the two different machines. For details, see Cordeschi (1991).

[7] See Hull (1929, 1930a, 1930b, 1931). The idea of deducing principles explaining behavior from other, more basic assumptions was typical of Hull's stance generally, especially when compared with that of other behaviorists such as Burrhus Skinner. Nevertheless, as time went by Hull gave increasing importance to rigorous formalization and systematization of the fundamental principles of psychological theory. On this matter (which is referred to again in section 7 below) and on Hull and Skinner, see Smith (1986).

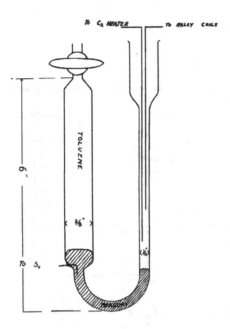

Fig. 3.1. Baernstein's conditioner relay (from Baernstein and Hull, 1931).

required for success and drive reduction. Some robot-approach simulation-models were based on the mechanism of divergent excitation, so it is worth looking at the way Hull 'deduced' this mechanism from the presence of a constant or persistent stimulus in a redintegrative organism.

Suppose that S_1, S_2, S_3 are unconditioned stimuli coming from the environment, for example the puzzle box in which a hungry animal is kept, and R_1, R_2, R_3 the animal's different 'simple' acts or mutually incompatible responses to these stimuli (Figure 3.2a). Actually, there are also proprioceptive (internal) stimuli s_1, s_2 aroused in the organism by those responses, but we shall not consider them for the moment. Now, every redintegrative stimulus complex, corresponding to the dotted rectangles in the figure, includes stimuli like S_i and s_i, which change from complex to complex, but it also includes one stimulus *that is always present in every complex.* It is the internal stimulus S_D, evoked by the drive arising from the need for food of the hungry animal closed in the puzzle box. Hull assumes that this stimulus is initially neutral but can get conditioned to all the responses in the sequence (Figure 3.2b). Suppose that only one response, say R_3, is followed by reinforcement, because it is the one and only response that lets the animal escape the box and get to the food (actually, it is the one and only response that is biologically successful). And suppose that initially the connections $S_D \rightarrow R_1$ and $S_D \rightarrow R_2$ have greater strength or power of excitation. The lack of subsequent reinforcement will progressively weaken those connections (experimental extinction), while reinforcement in $S_D \rightarrow R_3$ will pro-

Plate 3.2

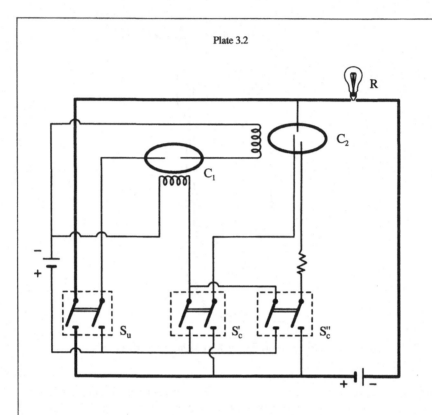

This circuit (a simplified version of Baernstein's) applies the properties of the U-valves, represented here by C_1 and C_2. The circuit includes push buttons S_u, S'_c, S''_c. When S_u is pressed the lamp R lights, and this reproduces the unconditioned reflex. But the lamp does not light when S'_c or S''_c is pressed, the stimuli to be conditioned.

If button S'_c is pressed for a few seconds, the closure of the first pair of contacts sends the current through the heating wire surrounding the valve C_1. This way, the toluene in the valve expands, the mercury rises, and the circuit closes. After this has taken place, press S_u: its first pair of contacts closes the main circuit and, as before, this causes lamp R to light. At the same time, the second pair of contacts, via C_1, closes the circuit that sends the current through the heating wire surrounding C_2, the conditioner shown in Figure 3.1 in the text. Two wires lead to C_2. The longer one comes from S'_c, and the shorter one from S''_c. The toluene heats up and makes the mercury rise in C_2 until it reaches the first and longer of the two wires and closes the circuit. Now, before C_2 cools off and the circuit is reopened, if we press S'_c, its second pair of contacts closes the circuit to R, which now lights. The circuit reproduces the stimulus substitution typical of conditioning.

Push button S''_c can be used to reproduce other forms of conditioning in the circuit involving a *second* stimulus to be conditioned.

gressively strengthen the latter. To the extent that the drive stimulus S_D can get conditioned to every response, it can evoke all of them, depending on the different strength of the corresponding connections. This is precisely the mechanism of divergent excitation, which establishes intraserial competition between the different responses in a sequence. Such a mechanism can be recognized because of what Hull called a "single dynamic core," the persistent stimulus S_D, in the redintegrative stimulus complexes that cause a sequence of responses.

In a 1930 article, "Simple Trial-and-Error Learning," Hull examined in detail the mechanism of divergent excitation in what he called a "high-class redintegrative" organism. He analyzed the theoretical strength of the S-R connections and the theoretical values of reinforcement, experimental extinction, and spontaneous rediscovery in the different behavior cycles in the light of the organism's "previous history," in short the strength of the various S-R connections in successive behavior cycles. Hull summarized the changes in the organism's performance in a table showing that the number of errors decreased from one cycle to the next, with the result that learning tended to become readier in successive cycles. And in the last cycle the organism reacted with the successful response at its first attempt (Hull, 1930a: 247).

Hull emphasized that the behavior of this hypothetical redintegrative organism displayed "persistence of effort at solution by means of varied response" (p. 255). This was a behavior that vitalist thinkers and psychologists usually ascribed to what they called "intelligent" or "purposive" organisms, in order to distinguish it as "psychic" in contrast to the behavior of "ordinary automatic machines" (this, for example, was McDougall's claim in *Body and Mind*). Hull concluded his article by pointing out that if his explanation or 'deduction' of simple selective learning was correct, it showed that this kind of intelligent or purposive behavior could be deduced from the principles of associationism and connectionism. So there was no need to turn to other hypotheses and introduce principles foreign to a purely mechanistic explanation. If this were true, it should not have been hard to construct a machine displaying this and even more complex kinds of behavior (p. 256).

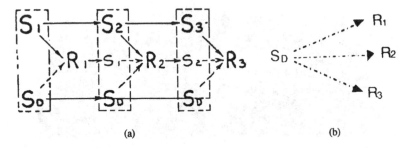

(a)   (b)

Fig. 3.2. (a) Stimuli S_1, S_2, S_3 from the outer world evoke different responses R_1, R_2, R_3 in a redintegrative organism. Proprioceptive (internal) stimuli s_1, s_2 are in turn evoked by responses. (b) Stimulus S_D is conditioned at every response (broken arrows) by the mechanism of divergent excitation (modified from Hull, 1931).

One can imagine Hull's satisfaction when two electromechanical models embody-ing the principle of divergent excitation were built in line with his 1930 article on "Sim-ple Trial-and-Error Learning." The first model was built at Yale University by George Bennett and Lewis Ward, and Hull followed the realization of the project. Figure 3.3 shows a photograph of the model, which the authors believed worked in a more biolog-ically plausible way (i.e. a way closer to synapse theory) than the Baernstein and Krueger models, because electrochemical cells of variable resistance were used in it as physical analogues of neurons. The device reproduced the mechanism of divergent excitation for only two antagonistic responses. It was a particularly simplified simulation of selective learning, but the designers' hope, as well as Hull's, was that future versions of the mod-el would be able to simulate more complex cases of divergent responses (Bennett and Ward, 1933: 342).

A student at the University of Miami, Douglas G. Ellson built the second divergent excitation model with a different aim. He wanted to reproduce in greater detail the be-havior of a hypothetical organism that learns the correct response through the "simple" trial-and-error procedure Hull described in his 1930 article. Thus the model had to sim-ulate the changes in an organism's performance in successive behavior cycles and the time it took, so that it would be possible to *predict* the responses of such an organism. Ellson entered the data on the machine's learning performance in a table, showing that they cor-responded closely to the data on an organism's learning performance reported by Hull. This may be the first time an attempt was made to make a detailed comparison between the intelligent performance of an organism and the 'intelligent' performance of an arti-ficial model, a case in which the model reproduced not only the ultimate performance but also the *limits* of the organism (regarding memory, for example) and the timing of its reactions.

As Plate 3.3 shows, the machine behaved in a way that Ellson said he had not pre-dicted. As it was initially set up, the machine was unable to choose between two differ-ent responses: it seemed to develop a kind of "experimental neurosis," as Ellson put it. Actually this phenomenon ought to have been easy to predict in such a simple machine.

Fig. 3.3. The Bennett and Ward (1933) learning model. To simulate the antagonistic nature of the two re-sponses, the lights indicated by numbers 5 and 6 never go on at the same time after pressing switches 1-4, which correspond to two pairs of stimuli, one conditioned and the other unconditioned.

Plate 3.3

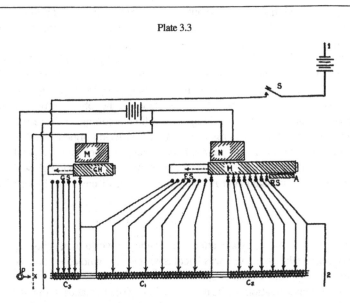

The following is a simplified description of Ellson's machine, shown above (from Ellson, 1935). The machine includes three electromagnets with different initial strengths, namely 100, 70 and 30 units. The electromagnets were connected to devices that could be increased or diminished in strength by varying the number of turns in their respective windings (see C_1, C_2, and C_3 in the figure). These devices let the machine simulate the modifiability of the strength of the S-R connections of a hypothetical organism learning by trial-and-error.

To simplify, think of the electromagnets as arranged radially around a central spring-suspended soft-iron pendulum. When the circuit activating the magnets was closed, the pendulum was attracted by the magnet that was initially the strongest, the one with 100 units, let us call it x. To reproduce the situation Hull described, the pendulum had to 'learn' by trial-and-error to move in the direction of another magnet, the one which represented the correct response but was initially the weakest, the one with 30 units, let us call it z. When the magnets were activated and the pendulum went to x, this response was weakened. The machine was set in such a way that when the pendulum came in contact with magnet x, it closed the circuit that operated a device to reduce the number of turns in the magnet's windings by more than 30. The strength of attraction of magnet x, initially 100, was reduced to less than that of magnet y. Since the machine remained active (thus simulating the persisting stimulus S_D, i.e. the need for food in the case of the hypothetical organism described by Hull), the pendulum was attracted by magnet y, which was stronger at that moment. Then the device was activated to reduce its strength by 30 units. After several subsequent contacts with magnets x and y, always followed by a 30-unit diminution of strength, the pendulum was finally attracted by magnet z, and this time the device increased its strength by 10 units, thus simulating the reinforcement that follows correct response. Subsequent 'learning cycles' reached a point at which the pendulum was always attracted by magnet z.

As the machine was originally set up, the strength of magnet x, which attracted the pendulum, decreased from 100 to 70 units after the first trial, so that magnets x and y both had 70-unit strength. At this point, the pendulum began to swing back and forth in circles without touching either of the two magnets (while the third magnet, z, had 30-unit strength). In these conditions the machine seemed unable to respond, so to avoid this it was necessary to make magnet x at least a bit stronger.

Ellson acknowledged that this was so but insisted that "the important point is that it had not been predicted," and from this he drew a more general conclusion. He claimed that with later machines or models, "purposely used as 'mechanical hypotheses,' it is quite possible that psychologically unexplained phenomena may be duplicated and probable explanations suggested analogous to physical explanations" (Ellson, 1935: 217). This was a further confirmation that there was no need for non-physical principles to explain organism behavior, according to the anti-vitalist stance of the robot approach. Ellson considered mechanical models valid as long as they did not contradict the results of the experimental research that psychologists conducted on living organisms. These models were not a substitute for research but might be a spur to further psychological investigations. Thus, Ellson touched on several issues in simulative methodology which we will have occasion to emphasize in our investigation into the discovery of the artificial.

3. Rashevsky's physics of mind

The robot approach attracted some attention outside the world of psychologists as well. One of the first to take an interest was Nicolas Rashevsky, who corresponded with Hull and Baernstein regarding the latter's machine.[8]

Rashevsky's investigations in the new discipline of mathematical biophysics centered on the unified study of the properties of physical and biological systems, a field that in the early decades of the nineteenth century attracted the attention of several researchers interested in the application of mathematics to the biological sciences. D'Arcy W. Thompson was immediately recognized as a precursor, since his 1917 book, *On Growth and Form*, looked at growth through the eyes of classical mathematics. Later Alfred Lotka and Vito Volterra constructed their famous mathematical models of the interaction between populations of living organisms. In 1925 the *Elements of Physical Biology* was published, the book in which Lotka suggested a generalized thermodynamics of living systems (Lotka, 1925/1956). At about the same time the biologist Ludwig von Bertalanffy was beginning the investigations that would lead to his formulation of general system theory.

Rashevsky's aim was to bridge the gap between the study of physical systems and that of living systems, a project which had also stirred Ellson's enthusiasm. In fact, Ellson considered such a project consistent with Hull's approach, and it seemed to him to fulfil the hope (common among certain psychologists) of a scientific method in psychology, borrowed from such a mature science as physics ("physics, one of the most concrete of sciences, and psychology, one of the most intangible, are finally discovering that they appear to have a common source," Ellson, 1935: 216). Rashevsky tried to

[8] Rashevsky received the then unpublished manuscripts of Hull and Baernstein (1929) and Hull (1930b). See Rashevsky (1931b: 403). Hull refers to his contact with Rashevsky in a note of July 2, 1930 in his *Idea Books*. (I am indebted to Laurence Smith for informing me that the man mentioned by Hull is actually Rashevsky.) On that occasion Hull said he was doubtful about letting Rashevsky have access in the future to his manuscripts on simulation machines, because Rashevsky was at a research department that he considered with suspicion. It was a pity, Hull concluded, "because I think that we could do each other a lot of good and could cooperate effectively in the advancement of science" (see Hull, 1962: 839). On Rashevsky's life and his role in the history of neural nets prior to McCulloch and Pitts (1943), see Aizawa (1996) and Abraham (forthcoming).

demonstrate that there were physical systems with certain features typical of mental processes, such as rudimentary forms of memory and variable behavior (Rashevsky, 1931a). He tried to discover which features of learning exhibited by physical systems might be "more likely to be actually realized in the brain of higher animals" and outlined a genuine "physical theory of mental processes" (Rashevsky, 1931b: 368).

Rashevsky interpreted learning in physical or physico-chemical systems as a form of hysteresis. At a given moment, the properties and reactions of the system are determined not only by conditions in the external environment at a that moment (such external parameters as temperature, pressure or whatever else influenced the system) but also by the way the environment has changed in the past, by the system's previous 'history' or 'experience.' The idea certainly was not new. As we have seen, hysteresis had been invoked on several occasions to give plausibility to the physical explanation of certain kinds of memory. Moreover, electromechanical models based on the robot approach were being built in those same years, using the hysteresis properties of different kinds of memory cells. But Rashevsky was interested in a particular kind of hysteresis that seemed capable of reproducing at least some simple features of the conditioned reflex. This form of hysteresis was displayed by complex systems with not one but several states of equilibrium.

Let us consider Rashevsky's example. Imagine a system S composed of thermodynamic systems that possess two states of equilibrium, for example, a particular colloidal solution composed of individual particles of different sizes, or more generally, of different kinds. It can be shown that this system, when subject to a variation in the environment, behaves in the following manner. Initially the system does not change its state when either a or b is varied alone. But if a is varied in such a way as to assume a definite value a_i and then b is varied, and if this procedure is repeated several times, then the system will acquire the property of changing its state when a is varied alone and assumes the value a_i. All this vaguely recalls the formation of a conditioned response in a living organism, in which the neutral stimulus (a is varied and assumes a definite value) must precede the unconditioned stimulus (b is varied). It also recalls experimental extinction, because in the long run, unless b is varied as 'reinforcement,' it is impossible to obtain a 'conditioned' response consisting in the transition of system S from one state to another simply by varying a alone so that it assumes a definite value (Rashevsky, 1931a: 219-220).

Rashevsky explained the behavior of S-like systems with examples of hysteresis in colloidals, but these examples were only theoretical. The properties of S-like systems were deduced from thermodynamic considerations of complex systems with several states of equilibrium, but, while the phenomena referred to did not conflict with ideas in physiology, there was no empirical evidence for them. Perhaps this is why Rashevsky suggested later on that the starting-point be an assumption "based not *a priori* on physical considerations but suggested by neurological facts," and that these facts be combined with "the results of a physico-mathematical, thermodynamic study of cellular dynamics" (Rashevsky, 1935: 83 and 84).[9] At that moment, however, systems with S-like theoretical

[9] In the third edition of *Mathematical Biophysics,* Rashevsky reviewed his approach in the early 1930s to distinguish it from the approach in his own book, which in its various editions saw the development of automata theory and computer science (Rashevsky, 1938/1960, vol. 2, Chapter 1).

properties seemed to be of great general interest, and Rashevsky tried to refine his approach so that S-like physical systems with two states of equilibrium would also display such other features of conditioning as spontaneous recovery. In addition, by duly connecting systems of this type, Rashevsky thought he could also reproduce a reaction similar to a conditioned response to specific patterns of stimuli, or *Gestalten* of stimuli, as he put it.

Hull had hoped that a machine might be built that could display this kind of behavior, i.e. a machine that could be 'conditioned' not to a simple stimulus or, as in the case of redintegration, to a stimulus complex but to certain *particular* combinations of stimuli in a given complex (Krueger and Hull, 1931: 268). This machine would have had to discriminate between different patterns of stimuli and respond to one pattern and not to the others, in the way that an organism does when it duly reacts, say, to a specific combination of acoustic stimuli, such as one sequence of musical notes and not any other. Following Hull, Rashevsky described how a hypothetical physico-chemical system that could display this kind of response would work, and he also described a machine that could simulate it. His machine looked like a way of giving concrete form to the idea, advanced by Hull and Baernstein (1929), of organizing mechanical devices that reproduced simple conditioning as "units" of a machine that could display more complex mental behavior, such as, in this case, stimulus-pattern recognition and pattern discrimination. In Rashevsky's machine design, the units that reproduced simple conditioning were actually Baernstein circuits (see Plate 3.4).

Rashevsky described other electromechanical machines, more or less directly inspired by Hull's approach. He seemed to share to some degree the anti-vitalist assumption and the idea of the machine as a way of testing a psychological theory that characterized the robot approach. Hull ended his article describing Krueger's model with the hope that progress in the robot approach would offer a new way to overcome what he called the "permanent impasse" created by the abstract conflict between mechanists and vitalists, an impasse which could be exemplified by the old contrast between Automata Theories and Ghost Theories. In fact Hull believed that mechanists would win out in the "practically virgin field" of building simulation machines and would show that it was truly possible to explain the behavior of higher organisms without using concepts that he believed to be without explanatory power, mere "names of disembodied functions (ghosts)" such as "nous, entelechy, soul, spirit, ego, mind, consciousness, or *Einsicht*" (Krueger and Hull, 1931: 267).

Rashevsky tended to take a more cautious stance than Hull regarding the philosophical disputes over vitalism and mechanicism, but he declared himself "rather mechanistically inclined" and believed that his interpretation of learning as a property of a physical system raised serious problems for vitalists (Rashevsky, 1931b: 386). And picking up from the position of one of the most authoritative proponents of vitalism, Hans Driesch, Rashevsky prophesied that the day would come when a machine could not only express itself in a natural language and carry on a conversation but could also *learn* a language and even *lie* intentionally. In principle it was not impossible to construct such machines, but it would have taken "tremendous expense and labor" (p. 403).

Rashevsky seems to have shared the functionalist claim that machines and living or-

Plate 3.4

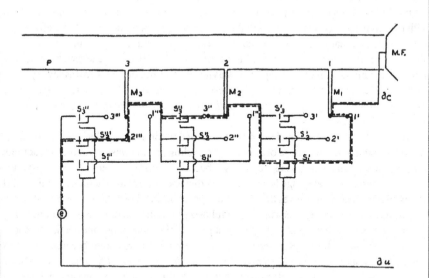

Rashevsky used this rather vague diagram (reproduced here, with a correction, from Rashevsky, 1931b) to describe the working of a machine that could simulate conditioning to a stimulus pattern. The machine consists of nine circuits that reproduce simple conditioning arranged as the *s* are in the diagram. Such circuits correspond to nine Baernstein circuits (see Plate 3.2). The lamp (which is the response: *e* in the diagram) can be turned on directly by switch a_u (unconditioned stimulus). It can be turned on also by switch a_c (conditioned stimulus) by way of a conditioning process that consists in closing a_c immediately after a_u. In this latter case, when the whole system has been conditioned, a_c will be connected to lamp *e* via three Baernstein circuits connected in a specific configuration or pattern. *What* that pattern is depends on the dial shift on the three manometers M_1, M_2, M_3. Each dial may assume one of three positions indicated by numbers 1, 2, and 3 (with their exponents) and thus close one of the three Baernstein circuits in parallel. So a particular closed circuit between a_c and *e* will be established. The shift of the manometer dials depends on the pressure wave traveling along pipe P, which is full of air, when the microphone membrane MF is set vibrating. The exact shape of the pressure wave will depend on the mode of vibration of the membrane. The different ways of setting the membrane into vibration represent the different 'stimulus patterns.'

The diagram shows a circuit that has been closed following one possible 'stimulation' of MF and the subsequent shift of the dials of the manometers. The circuit corresponds to the dotted line from switch a_c to light bulb *e* through 1', s'$_1$, 3", s"$_3$, 2"', s'''$_2$. A different pressure wave will close three other Baernstein circuits in a configuration that will not close the aforementioned circuit and will not evoke the conditioned response (lighting of *e*). The different 'stimulations' of membrane MF thus correspond to different stimulus patterns. This way, the machine 'discriminates' which pattern it is conditioned to and responds only to that one and not to others.

ganisms could be studied by one theory, and that mentalistic language had a role of its own in that theory. He treated the systems he studied as "general schemata," to be seen case by case as physico-chemical systems, as living organisms, and as electromechanical machines. If a system or an organism is able to modify its responses in interaction with the environment, we usually say that it 'knows' or has 'experienced' the effect of a given response; that it 'desires' to obtain a given result; that it 'infers' the way to get it through various 'trials'; and that it has a certain 'purpose.' But why use psychological or mentalistic language in describing the behavior of this kind of system? Rashevsky's answer is that description "in psychological terms [...] is justified by the circumstance that the above process of trials occurred *on a different level from the ordinary muscular reaction*" (p. 393, my italics).

We saw in Chapter 1 that Jennings maintained a comparable claim when thinking about non-human minds, those of animals. According to Jennings, an animal's reactions to the environment cannot be usefully described at the physico-chemical level; psychological or mentalistic language is needed to predict and control its reactions. Jennings did not explicitly dealt with the legitimacy of the psychological description of machine behavior, but on at least one occasion he emphasized that it was not enough to know the physical properties of a machine to predict and control its reactions; one needed to know its functional organization. Rashevsky was more explicit on this point because he had in mind a "inorganic" machine *designed or build to simulate mental functions*, a machine actually capable of changing its reactions in interaction with the environment Thus, he emphasized that, when one of these machines displays behavior of some complexity and unpredictability, it has to be described on another level than the physical one of producing a given sequence of responses. For example, in the case of a machine that learns by trial-and-error, like the system or organism described above, the level could be that of the mechanism Hull called the elimination of errors through reinforcement. Rashevsky pointed out explicitly that in cases like this the unprejudiced "external observer" interacting with the machine has no choice but to use psychological language, because he does not know *a priori* "with what 'purpose' a certain act is done by the machine" (p. 403).

It is worth noting that it is the relatively complex performance of these 'new' artifacts (i.e. their ability to change their internal organization) that suggested the appropriateness of mentalistic language in predicting and controlling their behavior. In the following chapters we will see this claim became increasingly popular.

4. Automatism and rudimentary forms of thought

The construction of inorganic devices that simulated simple selective learning might well be considered a success of the robot approach—"one more step," Ellson called it, when reviewing the recent history of the mechanistic approach in psychology from Stephens to Rashevsky (Ellson, 1935: 217). But on rereading the aforementioned conclusion of Hull's "Simple Trial-and-Error Learning," the impression one has is that Hull did not overrate the importance of those devices, which were limited to reproducing in fairly rough form some features of a very elementary form of variable behavior, i.e. simple trial-and-error learning. Hull pointed out that although this is a behavior which, if observed in an animal, would be called purposive by most psychologists, it certainly does not show "the type of purpose involving plan." His conclusion was that the construction of inorganic automatisms simulating this kind of purposeful behavior and other even more complex and "truly psychic" phenomena, such as insight, suggested a "radically new order of automaticity," though he did not go into detail about its nature (Hull, 1930a: 256).

Hull's theoretical and experimental work in the late 1920s and early 1930s tried to establish the frame within which this set of problems could be handled.[10] Here we shall consider only aspects of Hull's work that are connected with the "radically new order of automaticity" as a potential mechanistic explanation of "truly psychic" behavior. An important issue is the nature of an organism's internal representations of the outer world. Hull hypothesized that organisms are endowed with mechanisms for representing the world in varying degrees of complexity. In this section we shall describe some that Hull considered very important at the outset but then abandoned in favour of others that specifically concerned "truly psychic" phenomena, to which we will turn in next section.

Looking again at Figure 3.2a, let us consider the role of the proprioceptive stimuli in the redintegrative stimulus complexes, i.e. the s_i aroused in the organism by its responses to stimuli S_i from the outer world. The proprioceptive stimuli in the figure tend independently to evoke these responses through the new connections established with them. When these connections are established, the sequence of different responses R_i can be activated by the initial stimulus S_1 alone by way of the series of connections $S_1 \rightarrow R_1 \rightarrow s_1 \rightarrow R_2 \rightarrow s_2 \rightarrow R_3$. Hence a redintegrative organism has one fundamental feature: it can acquire the capacity to set off a sequence of responses even when the corresponding sequence of external stimuli is incomplete. In this case, it is stimuli inside the organism, the s_i, that complete the sequence of responses.

This is the core of Hull's representational theory: the organism acquires what he called a kind of "subjective parallel" of the outer world. It is as if "the world in a very important sense has stamped the pattern of its action upon a physical object," namely, the living organism (Hull, 1930b: 513). This pattern is a representation of the world inside the organism and has the causal power to control and guide its action. The biological value of this mechanism is easy to see. Take S_3 in the figure to be a seriously noxious stimulus that reaches the organism through a contact receptor, for example, an attack by a predator, and take R_3 to be an efficacious defense reaction, for example, flight. If, as is generally the case, the noxious stimulus also stimulates one of the organism's distance receptors, in our case the eye producing a visual stimulation S_1, and if the organism has past experience of noxious stimulus S_3, thereby acquiring the pattern $S_1 \rightarrow R_1 \rightarrow s_1 \rightarrow R_2 \rightarrow s_2 \rightarrow R_3$, then the organism can launch the sequence of responses R_i without waiting for the whole sequence of external stimuli S_i. The result is that the R-sequence will reel off faster than the S-sequence so that s_2 will evoke R_3 (flight) before S_3 (the noxious stimulus) has occurred. In other words, the organism is capable of responding with R_3 without directly undergoing S_3. These patterns or replicas constitute the physical causal mechanism whereby organisms acquire *foresight* and can deal with events in the outer world by *anticipating* them.

[10] See especially Hull (1929, 1930a, 1930b, 1931, 1932, 1934, 1935b, 1937).

The imprint has been made in such a way—Hull concluded—that a functional parallel of this action segment of the physical world has become a part of the organism. Henceforth the organism will carry about continuously a kind of replica of this world segment. In this very intimate and biologically significant sense the
organism may be said to know the world. No spiritual or supernatural forces need be assumed to understand
the acquisition of this knowledge. The process is an entirely naturalist one throughout (Hull, 1930b: 514).

So the organism's final response, once conditioned, may precede the stimulus that was
originally needed to evoke it. This response is unique in having an instrumental function
in the sequence of responses, i.e. to provoke a change in the environment, for example,
through the successful defense reaction. The other responses that precede it have a strictly *symbolic* function: they are "pure stimulus acts." In some cases, as in the anticipatory
reaction of flight in the foregoing, they may advantageously be reduced to a minimum.
"Short circuiting" is what Hull calls the mechanism for reducing pure stimulus acts (p.
519). This does not mean that pure stimulus acts have no significance. On the contrary,
they are responses that, through the medium of the proprioceptive stimuli they arouse,
serve to evoke other responses in the sequence and are indispensable to bring about the
final response. This way "the organism is no longer a passive reactor to stimuli from
without, but becomes relatively free and dynamic." Thus the pure stimulus act "emerges
as an organic, physiological—strictly internal and individual—symbolism," and instrumental acts are so transformed into a kind of *thought*. "Rudimentary" as it may be, this
thought is capable of some forms of anticipatory behavior in which the organism "can
react to the not-here as well as to the not-now." The completely automatic nature of this
"transformation of mere action into thought" ought to assure Hull a naturalistic explanation of the acquisition of knowledge, which is not any "kind of miracle." And again
this automatism throws down the gauntlet of "synthetic verification from inorganic materials" (p. 517).

It was a challenge worth taking up. In 1934 Norman B. Krim, an engineer impressed
by Hull's robot approach, submitted a thesis for the degree of Bachelor of Science in Electrical Engineering at the Massachusetts Institute of Technology in which he described
fourteen electric circuits of different complexity with which to simulate, more or less realistically, different features of the forms of learning Hull investigated.[11]

As an engineer, Krim's interest in the robot approach was twofold. There was theoretical interest on the psychological side, which involved the principal assumptions of
the robot approach (the mechanical model as a test of psychological theory and as a prophylaxis against vitalism) and highlighted the usefulness of demonstration models in
teaching psychology. And there was also a practical interest on the engineering side,
which consisted in seeing whether the study of the behavior of higher organisms might
be useful in designing electrical control circuits for some purposeful application. Krim
believed that the nervous system of higher organisms was "composed of very ingenious
nerve control circuits," and as such might be a source of inspiration for engineers and provide helpful hints for solving their problems. And this was not an isolated case. For example, in refining the new technology of television systems, an analogy with the retina
seemed to suggest ways of designing the system's "artificial eye" (Krim, 1934: 8). But

[11] Hull gave a copy of Krim's unpublished thesis to the Yale Library, where it can be consulted.

Krim's was fairly pessimistic about the prospect of a similar result in his own work at the time (p. 49).

Krim was familiar with the literature from Russell to Rashevsky, and some of the circuits he designed reproduced forms of learning that had been simulated by earlier electro-mechanical devices. Plate 3.5 shows the circuit for simulating automatisms at the root of what Krim, like Hull, called "rudimentary" forms of thought: acquisition of knowledge, foresight or anticipatory response, and evolution of pure stimulus acts.

5. "Ultra-automatism." Hull's "psychic" machine

Hull attributed great importance to symbolic or pure stimulus acts, because they were evidence of the "imprint" left by the organism's past history and made the organism freer from the pressures of the environment. The link between the automatism of pure stimulus acts and the plasticity of the organism's behavior was the premise that made it conceivable to build what he called a "psychic" machine.

> It is altogether probable—Hull wrote— that a "psychic" machine, with ample provision in its design for the evolution of pure stimulus acts, could attain a degree of freedom, spontaneity, and power to dominate its environment, inconceivable alike to individuals unfamiliar with the possibilities of automatic mechanisms and to the professional designers of ordinary rigid-type machines (Hull, 1930b: 517).

Despite Krim's simulation of some simple aspects of pure stimulus acts, Hull was not about to overestimate its significance for the construction of a "psychic" machine. His stance in behaviorism was becoming increasingly clear. His theoretical vocabulary increased with the addition of several hypothetical constructs and mechanisms intended to explain the high "degree of freedom" that the higher organisms, especially man, enjoyed *vis-à-vis* the environment. It is noteworthy that Hull took up the term from the Gestalt psychologists. Although he disagreed with them, he believed that they raised issues that were important for the study of behavior. At the same time, he considered Watson's approach to these problems unsatisfactory. Hull's investigations of the years under review here reflect this stance.

One example is Hull's approach to forms of selective learning that are more complex than selective learning in puzzle boxes, which he habitually referred to as "simple." He started going deeper into the features of one kind of selective learning that was receiving much attention in psychology laboratories at the time: that of an animal, usually a white rat, that through trial-and-error reaches the food at the end of a maze. The most common was the 'T' (or 'Y') maze, in which the animal encountered several choice points between a blind alley and the path to another choice point, until it finally reached the food. Each time the animal was put back at the starting point, it found its way to the goal by a quicker and surer exploration of the choice points and eventually avoided the blind alleys altogether. In maze learning the response that brought about drive reduction was not a single, specific act chosen from several possibilities, the usual procedure in the "simple" selective learning in the puzzle boxes, but a whole specific sequence or chain of acts, consisting of the animal's choices at the different choice points of the maze.

Hull subsequently called this form of maze learning "compound" selective learning.

Plate 3.5

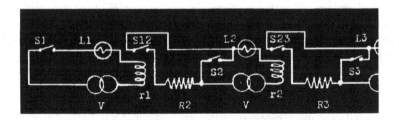

Acquisition of knowledge. As usual, the closed switch corresponds to a stimulus and the lighting of the lamp to a response. The circuits are arranged in sequences so that when switch S_1 is closed, because of generator V, lamp L_1 lights, and immediately afterwards switch s_{12} closes automatically because of relay r_1. If we now close switch S_2 while s_{12} is closed, lamp L_2 lights, and an auxiliary mechanism (not shown in the diagram) simultaneously lowers resistance R_2. In this way, we have 'conditioned' s_{12} to L_2. Likewise we can 'condition' s_{23} to L_3. By closing switches S_1, S_2, S_3 one after the other, the whole sequence of s_{ik} can be 'conditioned.' By repeating the operation several times, resistances R_2 and R_3 are gradually reduced so that it will suffice to close S_1 to light lamps L_1, L_2, L_3 one after another. The device is intended to simulate the way in which a living organism acquires the "imprint" or "pattern" aroused by the sequence of stimuli S_1, S_2, S_3 so that subsequently stimulus S_1 alone can automatically launch the sequence of responses L_1, L_2, L_3. One might say that the device behaves like an organism that 'knows' the world consisting of that sequence of stimuli.

Foresight. If switches S_1, S_2, S_3 are closed several times at minimum speed, lamp L_3 will ultimately light before S_3 is closed, because s_{23} is automatically closed before S_3. In this case, the device is intended to simulate the 'anticipation' of response L_3 to stimulus S_3, which originally was needed to evoke the response.

Symbolic or pure stimulus acts. If the final response in the two foregoing cases, the lighting of L_3, is seen as the sole response with which the device reacts to the environment, i.e., the only one with instrumental value, then L_1 and L_2 may be viewed as pure stimulus acts. Actually their sole function corresponds in the organism to supplying the stimuli that evoke successive responses in the sequence. The simulation, however, does not reproduce short-circuiting. L_1 (with its relay) and L_2 (with its relay) are needed in the circuit to bring about s_{12} and s_{23}, which are needed for L_3 to light when S_1 is closed. (From Krim, 1934, unpublished)

He believed, in contrast to behaviorists like Watson, that its explanation required other principles than the ones that sufficed to explain simple selective learning (Hull, 1942: 89).[12] As we saw, simple selective learning was based on elimination of error through reinforcement. In compound selective learning, as in maze learning, error consisted in going down a blind alley. In this case, however, the principle of reinforcement did not seem to explain how the animal learned to eliminate the blind alleys and fix its response on correct path choice. For whether the single choices at the choice points were correct or

[12] In particular Hull found Watson's law of frequency and the simple chain reaction hypothesis to be insufficient (Hull, 1930b: 524; 1932: 25).

not, the animal was rewarded when it finally reached the goal, so there was always rein-forcement.

Hull's answer was based on the so-called "goal gradient principle" and was consis-tent with the hypotheses of connectionism. The animal's learning of the correct path al-ways depended on the strength of the connections between S_D, the persistent stimulus aroused by the need for food, and the animal's different reactions. But the more times the animal went through the maze, the stronger were the connections of the choices that led the animal straight to the goal and avoided the blind alleys, and the weaker the connec-tions of the choices that led it astray down the blind alleys. This would explain the elim-ination of the blind alleys and why the animal learned the one correct path, the shortest one to the goal (Hull, 1932: 34-36).[13]

On closer examination, the animal might have an entire "family" of possible se-quences or chains of acts that could be arranged hierarchically according to how satis-factory they were in achieving the same goal. At the top would be the shortest path, the correct one. Thus, in addition to reinforcement and goal gradient, there would seem to be another principle governing compound selective learning, that of the "habit hierarchy family." It operated whenever there was more than one sequence of possible acts lead-ing to the same goal (Hull, 1934).

And that was not the whole story. In an animal that traversed a maze in which it had thoroughly learned the correct path, the shortest one, psychologists observed behavior that could not be explained solely by S_D, the persistent stimulus of the need for food, or by the proprioceptive stimuli produced by the animal's movements. There were reactions like mouth movements of a masticatory nature and acceleration of movement in prox-imity to the goal (where the food was), the simplification of some movements on enter-ing familiar paths in the maze, and vicarious trials and errors, that is to say, looking for clues to the right path at a choice point. So when a rat runs through a maze that is fairly familiar, its motor activity is partly a reaction to the future gustatory stimuli of the food waiting for it at the goal. Although these anticipatory or premature reactions depend on S_D, they cannot be explained by S_D. The representations or "imprints" left by the envi-ronment in this case are not the same kind that produced an anticipatory final response as exemplified by the reaction of flight in the foregoing. In that case, the representation led to a short-circuiting that eliminated the pure stimulus acts. Vice versa, the anticipa-tory reactions described above accompanied the animal's instrumental acts, namely, for-ward movement in a maze, and were not eliminated.

For Hull these reactions call forth a theoretical construct that is 'mediational' *par ex-cellence*, a construct between stimulus and response that is known as "anticipatory goal reaction," r_G as he designated it. As suggested by the maze learning example, r_G is an or-ganism's internal response to the stimulus of the need for food, which is S_D. It is a *prepara-tory* response on the part of the organism, the nature of which is linked to the response that would have been evoked by the corresponding stimulus (mouth movements in prox-imity to the goal is perhaps the simplest case). Like any act, r_G then arouses propriocep-

[13] Hull was later to add other explanatory principles (see, for example, Hull, 1942).

tive stimulation, which Hull called "goal stimulus" and designated s_G (Hull, 1931). It is a constant accompaniment to the course of action no less than S_D and is the authentic dynamic mechanism that makes the organism "hormic or purposive," as Hull was later to express it (Hull, 1942: 90).[14]

What he thought he found in the anticipatory goal reaction that aroused stimulus s_G was a physical mechanism that could account for the so-called "paradox of backward causation," which seemed typical of anticipatory action in purposive behavior. The paradox lay in the traditional difficulty of explaining how an idea, by definition mental and non-physical, could cause a physical action and how the idea, while representing the purpose or future end to which the action was directed, could cause an action *working backward* and thus guiding the subsequent course of the action. Consider the following: "I am reading and it grows dark. I think of turning on the electric light, and without hesitation that action is performed. The act here described is just as purposive as if I had deliberated and planned out every step in the procedure beforehand." [15] It is like witnessing a veritable inversion of the causal order: the future result of an act *precedes* the act itself in the chain of causation. Hence the appeal to the 'final cause' of traditional teleology, which supported a teleological explanation as opposed to a causal one.

In the next chapter we shall see that this paradox gave rise to several attempts to reconcile the teleological and causal explanations until the solution hypothesized at the advent of cybernetics. To stay with Hull, he attacked vitalist thinkers and what he called psychologists "dominated by metaphysical idealism," for whom the paradox could be resolved only by appeal to the non-physical principle of final causes. The principle of anticipatory goal reaction suggested a different solution to Hull. Anticipatory goal reaction did not have an instrumental function but a *symbolic* one, because its sole function was to produce a goal stimulus, which *precedes* the goal. So the anticipatory goal reaction plays the role traditionally ascribed to the ideas of guiding and controlling the sequence of acts of purposeful behavior. Yet it is a physical mechanism, since it consists of an action that was also a stimulus to action, so its effect, like its origin (produced by S_D), was physical and not mental in the sense of metaphysical psychology (Hull, 1931: 502-506).

But for Hull anticipatory goal reaction was not the sole physical mechanism to play a causal role in the cognitive activity of higher organisms (the role played by "what in the past have been called ideas"). Indeed, in the case of human beings he granted that it might be necessary to add several other principles. His theoretical and experimental work alike seemed to confirm the *automatic* nature of more complex forms of anticipatory be-

---

[14] Hull's choice of terms is significant, because the use of 'hormic' as a synonym for 'purposeful' was made popular by McDougall (1923a: 72), though in order to stress the irreducibility of purpose to any mechanistic explanation. But Hull made a point of identifying purpose with the goal stimulus s_G and not with the drive stimulus S_D, which we saw as the source of a different and more elementary kind of anticipatory behavior (see section 2 above). Mediational hypothetical constructs connected with anticipatory goal response were held in high esteem by Hull's followers, such as Hobart Mowrer and C. E. Osgood (see especially Mowrer, 1960a, 1960b). Grossberg (1982) discussed several difficulties concerning anticipatory goal reaction. See also Chapter 6, section 4.

[15] The example comes from Howard Warren, "A Study of Purpose" (Warren, 1916: 8), an essay that will be discussed in the next chapter.

havior, which are at the root of reasoning, planning and problem solving—i.e. the fact that they could be reduced to the principles of associationism. So in this case too there was "no magic." Not even insight eluded associationist mechanical explanation, as long as complex mediational constructs were allowed. In conflict with mentalist and Gestalt psychologists, Hull thought he had provided "a deduction of insight in terms such that it might conceivably be constructed by a clever engineer as a non-living—even an inorganic—mechanism" (Hull, 1935b: 231).[16] It looked as if the usual "synthetic verification from inorganic materials" might also be applied to higher behavioral processes. The robot approach was based on an empirical hypothesis: success in the inorganic simulation of the principles that explain the elementary behavior of organisms paves the way to future inorganic simulation of the principles that explains the "truly psychic" behavior of organisms.

Hull was always vague about his "psychic" machine. When he tried to be specific about the features of this automatic *but* "psychic" machine, as compared with existing machines, he defined it in negative terms: the machine's "ultra-automatism," as he called it, would *not* be like the automatism of such modern machines as the steam engine, the electrical motor, or printing machines, which were familiar through their extensive practical and industrial applications. Rather, as he wrote in 1929, in what now seem like prophetic terms, it was a matter of imagining an "utterly new and different order of automaticity" by which the "mechanical engineering of automatic machines will be revolutionized to a degree similar to the introduction of steam engines and electricity" (Hull, 1962: 828).

In concluding his 1931 description of the Krueger model, Hull had listed the problems that remained to be faced in the future construction of simulation machines in order to approach something like the "psychic" machine. According to the list, such a machine would have had to embody all the explanatory hypotheses of the behavior of higher organisms that he was formulating at the time. The construction of machines simulating organisms' "hormic or purposive" behavior seemed to him a far distant but not unattainable goal. So Hull wrote in a 1931 letter to Edwin Boring:

> I believe that we now know enough about the inner mechanics of complex trial-and-error learning, such as is found in a maze, to construct a mechanism which, given sufficient length of time, will learn any maze that a rat can learn. Moreover, I think we now have sufficient insight into the habit mechanisms underlying purpose and volition to be able to design machines which will have a degree of spontaneity and freedom in the sense of being able to over-ride adverse enviromental conditions, to manifest behavior which will satisfy not only all of McDougall's objective criteria of purposive behavior, but additional ones which McDougall hasn't thought of.[17]

[16] On this occasion Hull thought that psychologist Norman Maier had adopted Gestalt principles because the only alternatives he saw were naïve forms of associationism. At the same time, Hull once again staked out his distance from Watson's position and said that he had never argued that complex forms of behavior started out from reflexes. His idea was rather that "the *principles of action* discovered in conditioned reaction experiments are also operative in the higher behavioral processes" (p. 228 n.). For the development of Gestalt psychology, only mentioned here, see Ash (1995) and Poggi (1994).

[17] I am indebted to Laurence Smith for letting me having access to the 1931 exchange of letters between Hull and Boring (from Boring correspondence at Harvard Archives). On McDougall's criteria of purpose, see Chapter 4, pp. 135-136.

6. The advent of robotics and developments of Hull's simulation method

In the 1930s a brilliant electrochemical expert, Thomas Ross, designed automata harking back to Hull's robot approach. Ross's automata are mentioned by several designers of electromechanical animals in the cybernetic age, especially Grey Walter.[18] Ross designed machines that may well be considered the ancestors of a particular kind of robot, the mechanical maze-learner.

Ross got the original inspiration for his robots from a newspaper report on Baernstein's 1929 model. This was when Ross got in touch with Hull, to whom he then submitted what was immediately called a "thinking machine." Ross referred to Hull's approach when he described his work in an article for *Scientific American*, "Machines That Think," from which the photograph in Figure 3.4 is taken (Ross, 1933).[19] It was a kind of mechanical arm powered by an electrical motor that explored five parallel paths in a kind of vertical maze searching one after the other from entrance to exit. The goal was to reach the end of the fifth path. When put back at the starting position, the device did not repeat the full exploration of the five paths but aimed to traverse the fifth.

Very complicated circuits constituting the memory cells of this primitive robot were responsible for its performance. Ross noted that a machine capable of reproducing behavior "that may truly be described as intelligent" required much more complex mechanisms than his, and this ineluctably entailed the design of increasingly efficient and less cumbersome memory cells (p. 208).[20]

The memory system of another robot that Ross designed was not very sophisticated, but its basic mechanism inspired other designers of mechanical maze-learners (see Cahapter 5). The robot was completed in the summer of 1935 in collaboration with the psychologist Stevenson Smith and two technicians from the University of Washington in Seattle, Byron Sullivan and W.A. Dillman. When it was shown to the public it came to be known as the "robot rat."

Ross published a description of this robot a few years later in the *Psychological Review* (Ross, 1938). The robot was a three-wheeled vehicle a little more than a foot long and about seven inches wide. The vehicle had a battery-powered motor and ran through a maze consisting of a sequence of twelve 'Y'-shaped choice points, where the right branch led to a dead end. When the robot was put at the beginning of the maze for the first time, it explored the entire maze, having been set to try the dead-end right branch first, then go back and try the left branch, and continue its advance. When the robot was again put at the beginning of the maze, it went the whole way without 'error,' i.e. avoiding all the dead ends.

[18] See Chapter 5, section 2.

[19] The article was preceded by a note from the Editor of the journal, who introduced the "purely mechanical device" described by Ross as the fruit of the growing efforts of psychologists "to test their suspicion that […] thought is […] some purely mechanical process, nothing more." Referring to the dispute between mechanists and vitalists, he warned any reader uninterested in "philosophical problems such as the nature of thought" that he need not take sides in the dispute based on Ross's machine and consider it simply "good entertainment." After all, he argued, no experiment with so-called "thinking machines" had yet *shown* what thought was.

[20] Some memory cells are described in Ross (1935).

Fig. 3.4. Thomas Ross's mechanical arm 'learning' a vertical maze (from Ross, 1933).

The simple mechanism behind this automatic learning is shown in Figure 3.5. Omitting the details, the heart of the mechanism was a rotating disk D, the "memory disk." Before the robot entered the maze, all twelve tabs on the disk were raised, but the mechanism was designed so that when the robot took the dead-end path to the right, one of the tabs went down and a circuit was activated that prevented the car from turning right again at that particular split in the path. The robot's successful and unsuccessful 'trials,' its turn to the right and then to the left, were registered on the disk in the form of a pattern of twelve depressed and raised tabs. As the robot passed all twelve 'Y'-sections of the maze, the disk went through a complete rotation and arrived back at its starting position, but now the twelve tabs were in a pattern that prevented the robot from turning right. In other words, the correct path was 'imprinted' in the robot's memory disk, and afterwards the robot never made errors when going through the maze.

In Ross's description of this robot he mentioned what might be considered a vitalist thinker's main objection to the possibility of machines that could display learning: "that it is intelligent behavior—a machine could never do that" (Ross, 1938: 187). But Ross believed his machine did exactly that, which showed that it was unwise to set a limit to the possibility of reproducing intelligent behavior in a machine. In particular, he pointed out that his machine's behavior in the maze was indistinguishable from that of a living animal under the same conditions, thus alluding to a sort of test for learning ability in machines.

But there was one difference, and an obvious one, as Stevenson Smith also recognized: "no living organism can be depended on to make no errors of this type after only one trial" (quoted by Gray, 1935-36b: 423). It was the non-animal-like perfection with which the robot learned the maze that seemed to be a limitation of the model, at least if

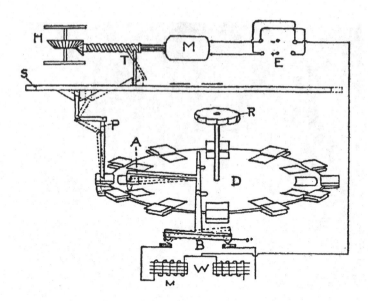

Fig. 3.5. The "memory disk" of the mechanical maze-learner built in 1935 (from Ross, 1938).

the simulation were to be psychologically plausible, a point that the Ross test clearly was not concerned with. Actually the Ross machine displayed no feature envisaged by the different learning theories we discussed: it did not forget, nor did it exhibit spontaneous recovery; and its performance could not be described by a hypothetical learning curve, the explicit aim of Ellson, for example.

It was Hugh Bradner at the Psychology laboratory of the University of Miami, Ohio, who pointed explicitly to the psychological implausibility of robot simulations at the time. He designed a machine conceived in a different fashion and proposed to simulate, among other things, the repetition of errors that occurs in animal maze-learning (Bradner, 1937). To achieve this particular performance, he equipped his machine with a device that was sensitive to an outside stimulus that interfered with learning. His moving robot could only 'learn' by trial-and-error to take the right path in a simple 'T'-maze consisting of a single choice point with two choices. But like all builders of machines to simulate some organism performance, Bradner looked to future improvements of his robot, which he mentioned in a rather intricate fashion, to make it capable of more sophisticated performance, such as moving through a more complex maze.

His robot was a cart twelve inches long and six inches wide with two wheels on a front axle, a driving wheel in the middle, and a steering wheel located near the rear, so that the cart could make very sharp turns. It was powered by a small electrical motor and moved through the maze at a constant speed of about six feet per minute. Bradner's description of how the robot operated is rather incomplete and imprecise. The decrease in resistance with the passage of current, followed by an increase with the lack of use, explained the robot's learning capacity. Bradner intended the robot to simulate the reinforcement effect and the repetition of error, but he also expected it to behave in accordance with Hull's goal gradient principle, by which an organism in a maze learns to choose the shortest path to its goal. For that to happen, it must be assumed that the right path of the 'T'-maze, which is the one Bradner's robot has to learn to choose, is shorter than the left path (Plate 3.6). Anyway, the working of the robot is based on *ad hoc* mechanisms that do not seem to have much to do with Hull's goal gradient principle.

Rather than continuing to describe how these robots work, it is worth noting the implications they had regarding Hull's "synthetic method." Ross, for example, was particularly clear about the idea of testing psychological hypotheses with simulative machines and about the exclusively *functional* nature of the organism-machine comparison.

> It is hoped—Ross said—that it may be possible *to test the various psychological hypotheses as to the nature of thought by constructing machines in accord with the principles that these hypotheses involve and comparing the behavior of the machines with that of intelligent creatures.* Clearly, this synthetic method is not intended to give any indication as to the nature of the mechanical structures of physical functions of the brain itself, but only to determine as closely as may be *the type of function that may take place between 'stimulus' and 'response'* as observed in the psychological laboratory or in ordinary uncontrolled learning and thinking. *Only analogies which will work when elaborately executed are sought,* not imitations of nerve, brain and muscle structure (Ross, 1935: 387, my italics).

The last italicized remark goes back to a point we have already noted, that a genuine model approach to the behavior of living organisms is not based on vague analogies between organisms and machines but on analogies that come out of the design and building of *functioning* artifacts. Ross distinguished this theoretical or simulative approach to machines, which might have implications for psychological research, from an engineering approach that explores the "fascinating possibility" of providing human beings with "intelligent" machines, which are different from traditional machines: a distinction which would be made clear many years later (see Chapter 5). Thus, he concluded

> Mechanical servants that will perform their duties without being directed or adjusted or preset as ordinary machines need to be may soon be possible as a result of recent research which aims to endow machines with intelligence of the sort possessed by living creatures (*ibid.*)

For his part, Hull had long since made it clear that the simulative approach underlying the synthetic method did not concern the reproduction of external features, as if one were building realistic-looking self-moving toys of the order of eighteenth-century clockwork automata. A mechanical model certainly did not have to salivate in order to say that it provided a satisfactory reproduction of Pavlov's conditioned reflex. Rather, what mattered was that the "functional relations between stimulus and response" (termed "essential functions" in the 1929 *Science* article) be organized along analogous lines in the machine and in the living organism alike. This would make it possible for the machine to be a test of the plausibility of a theory explaining the behavior of an organism.

Hull returned to the matter in the article "Mind, Mechanism, and Adaptive Behavior" and insisted on the anti-vitalist view underlying his "psychic" machine in keeping with a wholly explicit naturalistic reductionism (Hull, 1937). He was convinced that in present state of knowledge it was certainly unthinkable to "deduce" the postulates of his

Plate 3.6

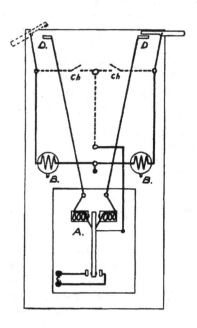

The 'brain' of Bradner's robot consists of two parallel circuits with two non-linear resistors with hysteresis B and a differential relay A between them. The resistors, two toluene-mercury memory cells like those Baernstein used, are set into the overall circuit in such a way as to increase their resistance when their control relays D in the front of the robot are opened. These relays act in opposition upon the relay A, which closes a circuit through one of two electromagnets and turns the steering wheel one way or the other.

The robot, in its course through the T-maze, enters one or the other of the two alternative paths. Given that the robot must learn to take the right-hand path, it must do so in such a way that it can subsequently 'remember' what it did. When the robot takes the left-hand path, it must 'forget' what it did, i.e. the memory cells B must go back to zero. In other words, more time is required between trials in the former case and less time in the latter. Bradner is not clear on this point. Anyway, one might suppose, considering Bradner's data on speed and performance times, that the right-hand path of the maze is *shorter* than the left-hand path.

In any case, to further 'reinforce' from outside the correct choice of the right-hand turn, left control relay D can be opened manually for a few seconds while the right one is kept closed. In addition, by activating from outside a device that closes the two chance switches *Ch* in the figure, the resistance of the two resistors B can be changed, thereby affecting their previous 'history' and causing incorrect responses to be made after a behavior cycle. (From Bradner, 1937)

behavioral theory as theorems in physics, in keeping with the "natural goal of science." So the idea of "complete scientific monism" could be considered "only as a working hypothesis." But meanwhile what he called "a kind of experimental shortcut" was possible. Mechanical models could be constructed that behaved as predicted by the axioms of his theory and would support the basic assumption of the purely physical nature of animal and human intelligence (p. 29 and n.). The models, of course, could not *prove* the truth of the theory, Hull pointed out elsewhere, but they would in any case be a test of its plausibility, "an argument in its favor," as Stephens put it.

> If we have a mechanical hypothesis of thinking—Hull concluded—and if we build a mechanical model following this hypothesis, and if our model executes behavior of a kind analogous to that which in the living animal we call mental behavior, then we can fairly claim that a machine can think—though we may be sure that the living organism is not the same *kind* of machine (quoted by Gray, 1935-36b: 424).

It was Ross who suggested how Hull's "experimental shortcut" might be understood. He said that while awaiting the "hoped-for ultimate success of physiologists" in explaining the cerebral structures of intelligence, psychologists should seriously consider the possibility of building artifacts functionally equivalent to the intelligent behavior of organisms:

> To find the *sufficient condition* for learning we should try to make a machine that will learn ... A very persistent mistaken attitude to work of this sort is the idea that the builder of a machine which will learn must think he has built a mechanism physically like that underlying human or animal learning. Nothing could be further from the truth. What is demonstrated by the physical *existence* of a performing machine is that a machine is capable of that kind of performance. It is not demonstrated, however, that only this sort of machine can produce the given effects; for *no truth is more commonplace in mechanics than that, in general, several alternative mechanisms, differing widely in superficial characteristics and forms of energy utilized, can produce the same end result* (Ross, 1938: 185, my italics).

The existence of a learning machine was thus a proof of *sufficiency* for the learning processes invoked in his explanation. Meyer before him found Russell's machine proof of this kind, proof that *nothing more* is required to explain learning than what suffices for building a learning machine. The approach of Ross and Hull was consistent with a form of functionalism suggested by their experience with the machines: a "commonplace in mechanics" that at the time apparently led Russell to see that his hydraulic devices might be replaced by other electrical ones to perform the same functions. The "independence from living protoplasm" of learning processes about which Stephens had spoken, explained, to repeat Hull's words, that "it is only a question how the material is organized that determines how it will behave."

7. What happened to the robot approach?

The first reference to the "psychic" machine appeared in the article Hull and Baernstein published in *Science* in 1929, and the last seems to have been in the 1937 paper "Mind, Mechanism, and Adaptive Behavior," in which Hull spoke of the "experimental shortcut" mentioned and, in a note, cited the work of Krueger, Ellson, Bennett and Ward (but no one else) as a "beginning" for the construction of a "psychic" machine (Hull, 1937: 29 n).

"What happened to 'psychic' machines?" was the question asked by one of the authors who edited sections of Hull's *Idea Books* (Ammons, 1962: 802). Actually, those sections of *Idea Books* do not clear away doubts about why Hull turned his back on the "psychic" machine project in the mid-1930s. Instead they give the impression that initially he was anxious to take over leadership of the project. For example, in 1930 he wrote in his *Idea Books*: "Fortunately my years of study and meditation on the subject will probably enable me to keep well ahead of the pack and be their leader and spokesman. My academic position as well as my age should aid in this" (Hull, 1962: 838). He also took account of the hostility the project might arouse. "I shall doubtless encounter sneers, criticism, and possibly even opposition from conservative and unimaginative individuals." Yet he seemed undeterred by these difficulties. "But if so, this can hardly be more than an incident," he concluded, "I must surround myself with a few sympathetic and intelligent individuals so as to protect myself from the negative suggestion associated with harsh criticism" (p. 829).

Which is actually what he tried to do. Hull collaborated with technicians and engineers, fostered the publication of the work of people doing research with various machines, established contacts with scientists like Rashevsky who seemed interested, put some of his machines on public display, and gave magazine interviews. Furthermore, he over-reacted when he felt that his "psychic" machine project was not taken seriously. In a response to minor casual criticisms that Boring had made of Krueger's model, Hull wrote in the above-mentioned 1931 letter to Boring (my italics):

> I must remember that the business of designing "psychic" machines is pretty young. I assure you that the model will really do all the things which have been stated in the article signed by Mr. Krueger and myself. I have a somewhat battered model in my office, which does these things whenever anyone wishes to see them. [...] We are working on the hypothesis that the complex forms of adaptive behavior ordinarily spoken of as mental are not necessarily associated with nerve tissue or even with protoplasm. This may be all wrong, and even profoundly absurd. On the other hand, it is just barely possible that it may be true. Who is there who will dare dogmatically to deny this possibility? At any rate, *the way to find out the possibilities in this direction is to proceed resolutely to realize them by actual trial. I have a fairly definite program involving successive steps in the evolution of these mechanisms.* I have indicated in an extremely sketchy manner something of the nature of this program in the latter part of the Krueger article.

However, there were not many scientists, aside from Rashevsky, who showed any real interest in Hull's project. Furthermore, Rashevsky never returned to the subject, especially during the cybernetics years. And psychologists behaved fairly coolly towards Hull's machines. Ernest Hilgard mentioned them in passing as a support of the mechanistic-materialistic stance of behaviorism (Hilgard, 1936: 551). Thorndike made passing reference to "the ingenious machines that modify their behavior by Stephens and Hull" (Thorndike, 1932: 314), while other behaviorists such as Watson or Skinner were not interested at all.

As to Boring, he claimed his real interest in "further developments" of Hull's models in his reply to Hull's letter, in which Boring seemed to appreciate the fact that Hull was "not under particular illusion as to models already constructed." Many years later, Boring, when listing the main models of the 1930s in his 1946 article "Mind and Mechanism," claimed that they were nothing but "paltry imitations" of the learning abilities of living organisms (Boring, 1946: 184). Actually, those models did not undergo the hoped-for developments. Boring had written his article because Wiener had challenged him "to describe a capacity of the human brain which he could not duplicate with electronic devices" (p. 178). Boring agreed that there was not such a capacity in principle, and pointed out that the design of "hypothetical" robots or the construction of "actual" ones would have compelled psychologists to avoid mystic, ambiguous mentalistic terms and to use rigorous operational definitions. Robots could usefully have this role in psychology until neurophysiology had so far advanced as to give a complete picture of the human brain; in any case, a robot whose performance was not distinguishable from that of a human would be "an extremely convincing demonstration of the mechanical nature of man and of the unity of sciences" (pp. 192-193): a conclusion which was in agreement with Hull's.[21]

Doubts about why Hull abandoned his "psychic" machine project were not completely dispelled by Laurence Smith's subsequent consideration of the unpublished sections of Hull's *Idea Books*. They confirmed Hull's initial enthusiasm, for in 1930 he even considered setting up a museum of "psychic" machines at Yale. The project also included an exhibit of designs for more complicated machines than the ones actually built, which, it was hoped, would attract the interest of physicists, chemists, physiologists, and engineers (Smith, 1986: 162). Smith's hypothesis is that in about 1935 Hull realized it was not worth pursuing a research programme that aroused no interest in official science, and then described his interest in "psychic" machines as "merely a hobby" not to be taken too seriously in public, at least in comparison with his work as an experimental psychologist (p. 358).[22] It must be supposed that, in the end, Hull gave in to the "negative suggestion" of criticisms that originally did not seem to bother him, and indeed provoked his strong reaction.

It was not until 1943, anyway, that Hull made explicit reference to his earlier ideas about the role of machines in psychology. In *Principles of Behavior*, certainly his most important work, he confirmed his hostility to any form of anthropomorphism and vitalism and recommended the robot approach as "prophylaxis against anthropomorphic subjectivism," while suggesting the following strategy:

> Regard [...] the behaving organism as a complex self-maintaining robot, constructed of materials as unlike ourselves as may be. [...] The temptation to introduce an entelechy, soul, spirit, or daemon into a robot is slight. [...] The robot approach thus aids us in avoiding the very natural but childish tendency to choose easy though false solutions to our problems by removing all excuses for not facing them squarely and without evasion (Hull, 1943: 27-28).

[21] In fact many psychologists considered Boring's article an apologia for mechanism, to the point that the term "mechanomorphism" was coined polemically to describe Boring's approach and Hull's alike, which culminated "in the rise of behavioristic psychology and in the construction of mechanical analogies of trial-and-error learning, conditioning, rats and sowbugs" (Waters, 1948: 138).

[22] There would seem to be support for this hypothesis in the testimony of George Gray, who after a meeting with Hull in 1936, wrote: "The construction of model psychic mechanisms is a fascinating diversion, perhaps some would call it a weakness to be indulged occasionally. [...] In his laboratory Dr. Hull has under way a huge program of research with living material. The theory of the conditioned reflex is being tested here through experiments on the habits of men as well as on those of white rats, dogs, and monkeys" (Gray, 1935-36b: 425).

Miller et al. (1960) quoted this passage in their successful *Plans and the Structure of Behavior* as an example of psychologists' growing faith in machines. But they missed the fact that the claim which seemed central to Hull's robot approach in the 1930s, that of the machine as a test of a psychological theory, is not even mentioned in *Principles of Behavior*, and that there is no reference in this book to the articles on the subject written in those years, in particular the ones Hull wrote in collaboration with Baernstein and with Krueger. Although there is an echo in the passage quoted, almost word for word, of some of Hull's earlier statements, the idea of the machine as a tool in theory building and testing seems to evaporate in the therapeutic function of the machine as a prophylaxis against anthropomorphism.

Hull had been dead for some years, since 1952, when Miller, Galanter and Pribram wrote about the robot approach. What is more striking than Hull's abandonment in the 1930s of the original "psychic" machine project is the fact that he did not think of going back to it in the following decade, when the intellectual climate was much friendlier because of the advent of cybernetics, and when the theory and technology of new machines had made decisive steps forward. In fact, Hull's *Principles of Behavior* was published the same year as three manifestos of the new-born cybernetics, namely the article by Rosenblueth et al. (1943), the one by McCulloch and Pitts (1943), and the book by Craik (1943). The point is that Hull was there at the birth of cybernetics and lived long enough to witness the development of its early projects, hopes, and disappointments, but he seems not to have been much involved. Omar Moore and Donald Lewis quoted the same above-mentioned passage from *Principles of Behavior* and pointed out the affinity between Hull's programme and that of the cyberneticians. Wiener, they concluded, "would characterize Hull's self-maintaining robot as active, purposive, teleological and capable of high-order predictions" (Moore and Lewis, 1953: 152). And Hull's original claims about "ultra-automatism" and non "rigid-type" machines seemed to take on new life in the negative-feedback machines that the cyberneticians proposed as new models of adaptation and learning. This was also Kenneth Craik's opinion, as we shall see in the next chapter. In 1943 Craik suggested that the robot approach was worth pursuing "even more unswervingly" than Hull had. What is more, the turn that cybernetics took when automatic control and computing machines came into use in the 1940s might have been seen as the realization of Hull's prophecy about the role that the practical applications of ultra-automatism might play in the behavioral sciences:

It is not inconceivable that in the demands for higher and higher degrees of automaticity in machines constantly being made by modern industry, the ultra-automaticity of the type of mechanism here considered [i.e. the "psychic" machine] may have an important place. In that event the exploration of the potentialities lying in this radically new order of automaticity would be comparatively rapid (Krueger and Hull, 1931: 268).

So what happened to the robot approach? Probably, Smith's hypothesis is the best we have. Hull was not satisfied with the qualitative method of early machine modeling because, under the influence of the neopositivism and operationism dominant in the United States in the 1930s and 1940s, he was increasingly attracted by a very different style of study. This was characterized both by logico-deductive rigor in the construction of psychological theory and by operational definitions of hypothetical constructs, measurement and quantification in experimental work (Smith, 1986: 223-224). This is actually the prevalent style of Hull's work in the period following the robot approach, and the influence of neopositivism and operationism is easy to see. Thus, when Hull abandoned the informal 'deductions' of his early experimental investigations, which dealt more with hypothetical connection-strengthening and response-tendencies in organisms than with actual predictive precision, he disregarded the rough predictive capability of the mechanical models. "If Hull had been satisfied to remain at this level of abstraction,—Smith concludes—he might have gone on to play a direct role in the establishment of modern cybernetics" (p. 222).

Yet it could not have been at all easy for Hull to repress his dream of a robot which was "active, purposive, teleological and capable of high-order predictions" and which Wiener would have found to his own liking. Sigmund Koch reports that a pre-publication draft of the *Principles of Behavior* "had the robot frolicking about through the course of an entire chapter. A series of questions were asked with regard to what conditions the design of a robot would have to satisfy, for various type of behavioral adaptation to occur." [23]

---

[23] Quoted by Smith (1986: 245 n.). See also Smith (1990).

CHAPTER 4

BEHAVIOR, PURPOSE AND TELEOLOGY

1. Introduction. Teleological explanations

We have mentioned the paradox of backward causation, which afflicted the explanation of purposeful behavior. This kind of behavior seemed to consist in an inversion of the causal sequence: the future or final result of an action (the end to which it is directed) *precedes* or *anticipates* the action. "A sequence entirely inadmissible in a world of pure mechanism," was how McDougall (1923a: 194) saw it. What was known as the metaphysical solution of the paradox always saw the end or the goal of an action as its 'final cause,' and teleological explanation was considered completely different from causal explanation.[1] Thus an unbridgeable gulf opened up between teleology and science, one that challenged the very plausibility of using teleological language in the scientific study of the behavior of living organisms.

The question of purpose and teleological or, generally speaking, mentalistic language has emerged in different contexts in our investigation into the discovery of the artificial. For those whom McDougall would have classified as supporters of Automaton Theories, the instinctive behavior of man and animals was nothing but chains of reflexes that were always *automatic,* no matter how complicated they might be.

For Loeb, for example, eliminating in this case subjective terms such as 'choice,' 'purpose' and so on meant doing a service on behalf of science. According to Meyer, the replacement of subjective by neurophysiological language was always the ideal at which a purely objective science of behavior should aim. Without supporting vitalism, Jennings had insisted instead on the need to use mentalistic language for the purpose of controlling and predicting the behavior of even the lower animals. He also used it in describing various phenomena in the *inorganic* world in order to show that it could be used objectively.

In Hull's robot approach, the notions of automatism and purpose did not seem incompatible, since machines could simulate at least "rudimentary" forms of anticipatory behavior. It was expected that a "psychic" machine would do better in the future and incorporate principles that explained more complex behavior, such as the principle of anticipatory goal reaction, which for Hull was the basis of purposeful behavior. Rashevsky explicitly legitimized the use of mentalistic and teleological language for the prediction of the behavior of the 'new' machines. Since these machines could change their internal

---

[1] The peculiarity of the teleological explanation has been debated at great length by philosophers, but it is not our purpose to discuss this point here. Moreover, among the many people who dealt with the issue during the years we are concerned with in the present chapter (the period before cybernetics), we shall refer only to some of those who were sensitive to the possibility of *extending* teleology to the processes of the inorganic world, and especially to machines. For aspects of the teleological explanation that are relevant to our purposes, there are the insightful analyses s by Boden (1972) and Zuriff (1985).

organization in response to stimuli from the environment, they could display a degree of unpredictability. Thus it was impossible to know *a priori* the 'purpose' of their responses and, in the case of more evolved future machines, whether they 'lied.'

It is usual to date the first modern attempt to reinstate teleology within scientific knowledge, so to speak, to the famous 1943 article by Arturo Rosenblueth, Norbert Wiener, and Julian H. Bigelow, "Behavior, Purpose, and Teleology." The three scientists seemed to be risking their very solid reputations, as Miller, Galanter, and Pribram remarked with some irony, when they claimed that machines with negative feedback display teleological behavior (see Plate 4.1). As the authors themselves remarked, at the time "teleological" was synonymous with "unscientific," and the 1943 article seemed to give the term new respectability in behavioral sciences (Miller et al., 1960: 42).

In their article, Rosenblueth, Wiener and Bigelow proposed a *general method* for studying a system or "behaving object" in its environment and a *classification* of the different kinds of behavior in the environment of such a system or object. Their aim was to give proper weight to the importance of the concept of purpose, which would allow an objective, albeit "restricted," definition of teleology; restricted because freed from the "vague concept of a 'final cause'" (Rosenblueth et al., 1943: 23).

The authors called their method "behavioristic." It centered on an observer who studies the relationships that a system maintains with the environment in which it is located, and its responses or "outputs" as a function of certain stimuli or "inputs." This study is independent of the specific nature and internal structure of the system, which may be studied by another, so-called "functional" method. From the point of view of behavioristic study, the system and its environment are inseparable. Indeed, they constitute a veritable single system. The classification of behavior that followed the statement of the behavioristic method proceeded in dichotomous fashion. Thus, it was possible to distinguish a class of behavior that could be classified as "teleological." This behavior was "purposeful" in the specific sense of being modified and guided by continuous (negative) feedback from the goal state. In other words, teleological behavior is controlled by the error of the reaction, i.e. "by the difference between the state of the behaving object at any time and the final state interpreted as the purpose" (p. 24).

The claim of the three authors was that teleological behavior so defined was observable not only in living organisms but also in *certain* machines. Tropisms were examples of telelogical behavior in the case of simple organisms, while in more complex organisms, activities such as the pursuit of prey were classified as teleological. Servomechanisms are machines that are endowed with negative feedbacks and as such can display teleological behavior, so that they may be considered "intrinsically purposeful" (p. 19). A simple thermostat that keeps room temperature fairly constant is an example, but so is a radar-controlled gun, in which information provided by radar about a moving target, an airplane, say, is constantly fed back to alter the gun's aim. However the behavior of a thermostat and the tropistic behavior of a simple organism are both different than the behavior of the gun-radar-airplane system and the predator-prey system. The latter behavior displays the ability of machine and organism alike to 'extrapolate' or 'predict' a *future* point in a trajectory described by the moving object (the target aircraft and the prey

Plate 4.1

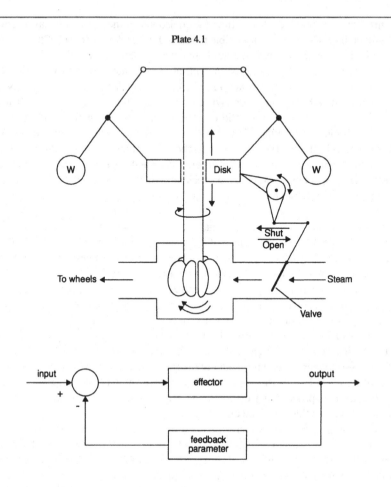

An example of a *negative-feedback* device is the centrifugal governor developed by James Watt (1736-1819), which is placed in a steam engine. Clerk Maxwell gave the mathematical treatment of governors in his famous 1868 essay "On Governors," which Wiener mentioned as the source that suggested the term 'cybernetics' to him (the word 'governor' is meant as the Latin corruption of the Greek word *kubernétes*, i.e. 'steersman')

Watt's governor (above in the figure) is placed in the steam-supply pipe, and monitors the amount of steam flowing to the wheels of the machine. The shaft of the device, guided through gears by the drive shaft, rotates, lifting the two weights (W). These pull up a disk, which, acting through a set of levers, vary the opening of a valve, which shuts as the weights rise and opens as they fall. In this way, the speed of drive shaft is kept fairly constant.

The block diagram (below in the figure) shows the functioning of the device, based on this principle of error correction (the circle indicates that the actual response is compared with the desired response, so giving the correction signal). When the counter-signal acts to augment the final effect instead of reducing it, one speaks of *positive feedback*.

respectively). So according to the authors, teleological (negative-feedback) behavior is subdivided into two classes: "non-extrapolative" or "non-predictive" and "extrapolative" or "predictive." [2]

An earlier article by Ashby, "Adaptiveness and Equilibrium" (Ashby, 1940) revealed an interest in feedback in describing purposeful behavior.[3] Here too the aim was to avoid "all metaphysical complications of 'purpose'" (p. 483). The guiding spirit behind the two articles might seem different. Ashby was not so much interested in reinstating teleological language, albeit in restricted form, as in "substituting," as he put it, the "vague" teleological notion of adaptation with a "quantitative" notion, that of *stable equilibrium*. Although in this case the distinction was probably more verbal than substantial, the formulation of the problem by Rosenblueth, Wiener and Bigelow was more provocative and was destined to give rise to a flood of discussion among philosophers and researchers in various fields, such as biologists, neurologists, psychologists and computer scientists, later on.

Even before the publication of these two articles, there were philosophers and scientists who had pointed out that certain artifacts endowed with what was later to be called negative feedback behaved in a way that an outside observer might interpret in teleological terms, and that this might corroborate the possibility of giving an objective, albeit variously "restricted," definition of teleology. While this claim raised problems of its own, it suggested that there was no need to appeal to the idea of a final cause to avoid the paradox of backward causation, and that in principle there was no contradiction between *mechanical* and *purposeful* processes, between machine and teleology.

In the present chapter, we shall examine these less familiar aspects of the discussion between science and philosophy about teleology in the years before the cybernetic era. In the last two sections of the chapter, we will argue that this discussion was clarified by the ideas of the control system and information transmission that emerged on the threshold of cybernetics. In this regard, we will pay particular attention to the role of Kenneth Craik. Partly because of his explicit references to the robot approach, Craik seems to mark the transition from the mechanistic stance of behavioral sciences in the early twentieth century to the stance that merged in the 1940s with the development of the theory and technology of automatic control.

2. Adaptation as equilibration.
Lillie and the "reconciliation" of teleology with science

A useful starting point for our investigation is Ralph S. Lillie's 1915 study of purposeful behavior.[4] His interest in processes of equilibration were in a line of research running from

---

[2] In describing Rosenblueth, Wiener and Bigelow's classification of behavior we have intentionally mixed description and examples given in their article with those in later writings by Wiener and other cyberneticians. Examples from warfare should come no surprise: as mentioned earlier (see pp. 6-7) cybernetics was given much impetus during World War II.

[3] Ashby did not use the term 'feedback' in this article (though he did soon after) to describe such behavior. Instead he used the term "circuit" in reference to the close relationship between organism and environment, and in this regard he mentioned von Uexküll's "functional circles" (see above, p. 18).

[4] Lillie was a physiologist who studied cell processes, organic growth, and metabolism. For his idea of "inor-

Spencer and Jennings all the way to the aforementioned remarks of Ashby. Lillie wondered how to "reconcile" the teleological description of living organisms, according to which they demonstrate purposeful behavior in adapting to the external environment, with their scientific study, namely study that is limited to describing them as material systems in an environment with which they interact. From the latter viewpoint, the systems have "peculiarities that may not ultimately be accounted for on the basis of [their] physico-chemical constituents alone" (Lillie, 1915: 590).

According to Lillie, the only way to reconcile teleology with the scientific study of organisms is to consider their behavior purposeful solely on the basis of what he called "external marks of purpose": these may give rise to an "objective" use of teleological language. Considered objectively, purposeful behavior is merely one of several regulation processes by which a complex physicochemical system adapts to the environment. It is a behavior that "is not in its general nature something distinctive of living organisms alone" (*ibid.*)

In Chapter 1, we looked in detail at an argument of this kind, the one that led Jennings to conclude that so-called "teleological" (regulatory) principles existed in the *inorganic* world too. Lillie described the living organism as a system that shares with a class of natural inorganic systems the feature of maintaining a certain structural stability despite variation in external conditions. And it is thanks to this feature that these systems tend to re-establish their initial conditions whenever they are disturbed. A flame is an example of this kind of "stationary system," as Lillie called it, which continually exchanges matter and energy with the environment. These systems thus maintain themselves in a state of dynamic equilibrium characterized by a twofold, constructive and dissipative process. Metabolism is simply a particularly complex way of maintaining that equilibrium and a specific feature of living organisms. Like Jennings first and Ashby later, Lillie considered the organism as inseparable from the environment, and the notion of dynamic equilibrium arises from consideration of their reciprocal influences.

In order to provide a "more precise" definition (p. 592) of the teleological notion of adaptation for organisms, all that is needed, in Lillie's opinion, is to translate such a notion into terms of "maintenance of equilibrium," or metabolic equilibrium in the specific case. Actually, Lillie suggested a classification of the organism's equilibration behavior that included a kind of purposive behavior, and somewhat anticipated the classification that Rosenblueth, Wiener and Bigelow proposed in their 1943 article.

In Lillie's account, the metabolic equilibrium that characterizes living organisms is maintained by a broad class of regulatory processes, some "internal," such as those that maintain body temperature (called "homeostatic" after Cannon), and some "external," concerning the organism's interaction with the environment. The latter are subdivided into "static" and "active" processes. The static ones cover such permanent features of organisms as body shape, pigmentation, and so on, in relation to *permanent* features of the environment. It is a stable correspondence between organism and environment that fos-

ganic models of growth," to which we shall refer later on, see Lillie (1922). In an interesting essay on problems in the philosophy of biology at the time, Joseph Needham included Lillie among the "neomechanists" (in part because of his 1915 article), who rejected the non-quantitative notion of teleology (Needham, 1928: 85 and 88).

ters the organism's very survival, its adaptation. Active processes also establish a stable correspondence of the same kind, but in relation to *variable* features of the environment, so that when the environment changes, those processes are activated to restore the organism's conditions of equilibrium.

There are two subclasses of active processes, the organism's "instinctive" and "intelligent" processes. In both kinds of process there is *the reference to some future situation* that characterizes purposeful action, and which therefore cannot be understood only in terms of present conditions. Strictly speaking, even reflexes imply a kind of reference to the future: for example, eating is a reflex action that might well be called "purposive" in assuring the organism the necessary energy reserve for future activities. But in this sense any action that fostered the organism's survival ought to be considered purposeful. For Lillie, a more interesting sense of purposive behavior regards a *specific* future situation that requires a *specific* sequence of actions to be performed (in terms of instinct, consider the bird that builds its nest). This "foresight," as he called it, distinctly characterizes instinctive and intelligent action alike.

As already mentioned, it is the reference to the future typical of purposive action that traditionally evoked the idea of a final cause. Rosenblueth, Wiener and Bigelow wanted to separate the notion of purpose from this very idea, because it required that teleology be defined in terms of the paradoxical and discredited "cause subsequent in time to a given event" (Rosenblueth et al., 1943: 23). Lillie too mentioned the metaphysical solution of the paradox, which consisted in postulating a special conscious agency, like Driesch's entelechy (Lillie, 1915: 607). Lillie's argument seems to have been not to restrict purposive action to conscious intelligence. He kept reference to the future as a feature of instinctive action and tried to free such a feature of every trace of the paradoxical by a move that went in the direction later indicated by Rosenblueth, Wiener and Bigelow, that of establishing an analogy between the action of organisms and the working of certain artifacts.

Resuming his thesis of adaptation as equilibration, Lillie gave a definition of instinctive actions that referred directly to their compensatory or regulatory nature as "automatic counter-processes," as he put it (p. 593). These are processes that "either continually or at intervals compensate or correct deviations from the balanced condition" (p. 603). It is a definition that, by the very terms in which it is formulated, leads almost naturally to likening instincts to what Lillie called "artificial mechanisms" of control, including thermostats, governors, and safety valves. In the case of organic and artificial automatic counter-processes alike,

[...] there is a permanent mechanism which gives a definite response to a certain change of situation. This response provides against a future contingency. What is remarkable is that the condition of action and its ultimate effect are exactly what we should expect them to be if the whole situation were under the control of some intelligent purposive agency (Lillie, 1915: 604).

According to Lillie, then, it is merely an illusion on the part of the "human observer" to see conscious prevision guided by a final cause or entelechy in the reference to the future that is typical of the instinctive action of living organisms. It is no more legitimate than ascribing such a feature to an artificial mechanism equipped with a regulatory device. And it was the very existence of artefacts with "automatic counter-processes" that convinced Lillie that it was possible to offer a teleological description from the viewpoint of the outside observer of an important class of behavior, that entailed in instinctive activity, without having to refer to the notion of conscious purpose.

But what of the other subclass of "active" processes, that of intelligent behavior? Lillie was rather vague in defining the relations between instinct and intelligence or between intelligence and consciousness in the animal world. As we saw, these subjects were hotly debated at the time, when it usually came down to contrasting the stereotypical or automatic character of instinct with the varied and modifiable character of intelligent action.

Lillie merely maintained a vaguely evolutionist and continuist thesis, similar to Jennings,' by which "intelligence" was synonymous with adaptive and self-regulating behavior. Thus, *every* response of the organism is always a function of change in the external environment. More evolved organisms have more complex and differentiated regulative-response apparatuses, which reach their "acme of development in the kind of behavior known as intelligent," without any need to assume an agency that operates on principles other than those of reflex and instinctive behavior (p. 607).

It is no accident that Lillie was skeptical about the possibility of finding in associative memory an objective criterion for singling out intelligence in the animal world, a thesis Loeb espoused with great conviction in those years. Loeb may have shared with Lillie the analogy between the instinctive behavior of organisms and artificial self-controlling devices (after all, a device of this kind was Hammond and Miessner's automaton), but it was that very analogy which made Loeb eliminate teleological and mentalistic vocabulary from the description of instinctive behavior and restrict it to behavior in which associative memory could be observed. On the contrary, once the teleological idea of adaptation had been defined with the language of equilibration, Lillie regained the possibility of speaking of purpose in a way that was objective, albeit restricted ("more precise" is how he put it), even about intelligent behavior.

Note that it is the claim about the nature of teleology that makes Lillie's thesis interesting for us, because it distinguishes his thesis from vague attention to equilibration as a property of life, which goes back at least to Spencer. Furthermore, against this very background an analogy had already been made between organic and artificial processes of self-equilibration.

In 1901 the sociologist Leonard T. Hobhouse took up the general principle that "life is a process of unceasing oscillation about an imaginary equilibrium point, departure from which tends of itself to set up processes which take the organism back again," and compared the self-equilibration of organisms with that of machines with automatic controls, for example, a steam engine with a governor.[5] Lillie proceeded along a less well-frequented path. Jennings, among others, had already indicated self-regulation as an objective feature of adaptive behavior. Now Lillie explicitly highlighted what had seemed the toughest aspect for the mechanist, that of reference to the future, and tried to study it objectively.

[5] Hobhouse (1901: 15). On Hobhouse, see Boakes (1984: 179-184).

3. Warren and teleology as a scientific problem

What is most interesting for us in Lillie's thesis was explicitly dealt with by Howard C. Warren in those very years, in particular in a set of three articles collectively entitled "A Study of Purpose" (Warren, 1916).[6] Warren's aim, as he had explained elsewhere, was to treat "teleology as a scientific problem," and to that end he suggested reforming the traditional teleological vocabulary. What had to be done for teleology was what psychologists had already done for intelligence. By referring intelligence to an organism's observable ability to improve its performance with experience, the term found an objective reference that made it undergo a "hopeful change in meaning" (Warren, 1914: 91). This way, the term 'intelligence,' formerly restricted to humans alone, could be *extended* to non-human animals without having to imagine, as Warren aptly put it, that there was "a man inside the dog" to explain the dog's intelligent behavior.

So Warren's project was to replace the "old anthropomorphic teleology" by a "natural teleology" (p. 94) in which the traditional concepts of choice, purpose and so on could be described in objective terms. This way, it would be possible legitimately *to extend* these concepts outside human conscious activity. "If we rid teleology of its anthropomorphic accretions, [...] there is no reason why the most thoroughgoing mechanist should not accept purposive events as a specific class of natural processes" (Warren, 1916: 6). In "A Study of Purpose," Warren suggested classifying the different kinds of purposive behavior according to three levels, corresponding to the "psychic," the "organic," and the "inorganic."

The *psychic* world is that of personal experience and human consciousness. In this case, an action is called purposive if there is conscious "forethought" about the result. Consider Warren's aforementioned example: if it gets dark when I am reading, the idea of turning on the light seems to cause an action that is performed as if I had deliberately planned each single step in advance.[7] Hence a "mental representation" of the result of an action occurs before the action is performed, since the image that "symbolizes" the action, as Warren put it, guides its planning and execution (p. 8). He does not dwell on this point, except to argue that the presence of the *subjective* mental image or "idea" can be ascertained directly through personal experience or inferred in other individuals from observed behavior or verbal reports. What he wanted to stress was that *reference to the future* was always a distinguishing *objective* feature of teleological behavior. Without appealing to conscious forethought, reference to the future nevertheless entails "anticipa-

---

[6] Unlike Lillie, who dealt with the problem of teleology within the framework of his biological and physiological studies, Warren considered the matter as part of his thinking about the role of psychology as science of behavior and the mind-body problem. Regarding the latter, he maintained the "double-aspect theory," a theory that McDougall in *Body and Mind* had classified among the Automaton Theories, alongside epiphenomenism and parallelism. The double-aspect theory shared with parallelism the negation of a strictly causal relationship between mental and brain processes and yet considered them not as two independent realities, but as two manifestations of a single reality, one regarded under the aspect of conscious or subjective experience, and another under the objective aspect to be drawn from the study of the nervous system (Warren, 1914). Warren described his intellectual life as a journey "from mysticism to mechanism." Many of his ideas about purpose, consciousness, and the very nature of psychology evolved in an increasingly marked mechanist direction.

[7] See above, p. 104.

tion" of the end result of an action. And it is this very presence outside the mental world of human experience, which is what psychology studies, that justifies the extension of the idea of purpose to the *organic* world, which is what biology studies. Let us now look at the phenomena of the organic world in which anticipation is present.

There were many, including Jennings, for example, who used the term "regulatory" to describe the changes we now call homeostatic and metabolic. But Warren, like Lillie, considered them in the particular sense of anticipation: "all the vital functions [...] are anticipatory; they prepare the organism for future conditions" (p. 34). Shifting attention to this aspect of regulatory activity allowed Warren to find "objective" examples of anticipation in those phenomena as well.

As for the behavior of living organisms, continuity in the evolutionary scale "from amoeba to man" (Warren and Jennings used the same description) is marked by increasing complexity of anticipatory behavior. The various degrees of complexity of the nervous system on the evolutionary scale account for the different degrees of complexity of this behavior, from reflex and instinctive action to intelligent and conscious action. Without presuming to have the last word in the ongoing dispute between vitalists and mechanists, Warren accepted the neurological hypotheses of the time as "working hypotheses" that helped to explain anticipation in the organic world without recourse to entelechy. He considered it a plausible hypothesis that the nervous impulse always followed the path of least resistance and that the *plasticity* of the nervous system made the formation and consolidation of new low resistance paths possible[8]. As we know from Chapter 2, in this way it is possible for the impulse to *deviate* from some paths to others which preserve a trace or 'memory' of its passage.

Warren considered this mechanism a sufficient physical apparatus to explain, for example, the capacity displayed by an animal endowed with distance receptors to anticipate a response (say, the flight reaction) *before* the appearance of the corresponding stimulus (contact with danger) (pp. 35-36). Initially, Hull was to refer to Warren in introducing his explanation of these anticipatory abilities of the organism in terms of "patterns" or "imprints" from the world.[9] But Warren was quite vague on the nature of the mechanisms underlying conscious forethought, and ultimately the solution he advanced could not be other than adaptionist: a more complex anticipatory mechanism such as conscious forethought has a greater adaptive advantage for organisms that have it, so that teleology may be considered "a scientific corollary of natural selection" (Warren, 1914: 94).

[8] "Intelligence is a function of the plasticity of nervous structure which enables a great variety of association to be formed. [...] The more intelligent or plastic a man is, the more his purposive thoughts are likely to be fulfilled. The fulfilment is not due to a directive agent within." Take the example of a chess problem: "A novice at the game will fail utterly to see the [successful] result. [...] The master rejects certain alternatives at once, and reaches the result of other alternatives instantly. But it is his experience that shortens the thought process, not a peculiar 'insight'. [...] The central nervous structure of the chess master, his repeated practice in forming the chessboard associations, seem sufficient to account for his greater speed and accuracy in reaching the conclusion. Is it not redundant to assume a psychomorphic factor of intelligence, and attribute to it some mysterious efficiency in bringing about the result?" (Warren, 1916: 48).

[9] See above, pp. 99-100.

4. Purpose in the natural world and in artefacts

Warren's analysis of the third level of his classification of purposive behavior, the *inorganic* level, is particularly interesting for us. His aim was to show that the notion of purpose as anticipation was not exclusive to the sphere of the living organism in its aforementioned two dimensions, mental and biological, but may also be *extended* to the inorganic. The mechanistic approach of natural teleology would at least be corroborated if cases of anticipation could be found in the inorganic world, where it would be odd indeed to invoke an entelechy to explain them. More generally, "in so far as this attempt is successful, the gap between inorganic and organic processes is bridged" (Warren, 1916: 68).

In Warren's classification, anticipation in the inorganic world refers to *natural* and *artificial* phenomena alike. Regarding natural phenomena, he admits he cannot identify "an *unquestionable* example of anticipation" (p. 61) in nature, even if there are natural phenomena that can be considered not too "fanciful" examples of anticipatory behavior. Among these he mentions the "complex interworking" of cloud formation and of the water level in a large river: in this case, the flow of the water is maintained "at a fairly constant level," Warren says (*ibid.*). It is, rather, among the second kind of phenomena in the inorganic world, the artificial ones, that Warren holds that he can more surely identify systems that exhibit anticipatory behavior. In this case he takes as examples, following Lillie, those artifacts that are capable of self-regulation, such as governors and thermostats. Let us examine some aspects of this teleology of the inorganic more closely.

The study of systems in which one can observe the loss or restoration of equilibrium became usual in the cybernetic age, when the generalization of the language of feedback to nature and the biological world, or within the human sciences, exercised considerable fascination. At the Conference on Teleological Mechanisms held in 1946, Evelyne Hutchinson, making reference to Wiener, reviewed various "circular causal systems" occurring in nature, from ecological ones to those identified by Lotka and Volterra in population dynamics (Frank et al., 1948).[10] The so-called "kybernetics of natural systems" (D. Stanley-Jones and K. Stanley-Jones, 1960) and the cybernetic models in ecology (Margalef, 1968) are examples of this kind of approach.

In Warren's day, descriptions of natural phenomena in terms of restoration of equilibrium were very popular and often "fanciful," and they reechoed various Spencerian themes. An example is the case of Stevenson Smith, who stated his notion, following the chemist W. D. Bancroft, of a qualitative "universal law," according to which "a system tends to change so as to minimize an external disturbance" (Bancroft, 1911: 92). According to Bancroft, this law was exemplified under various forms: in chemistry as Le Châtelier's law; in physics as the principle of least action, or Maupertius' theorem; in biology as the law of the survival of the fittest; in economics as the law of supply and demand. Bancroft considered even the heliotropism that Loeb studied a particular case of this law, since in this case the organism tends to "minimize the state of stress" (p. 102). Stevenson Smith, in turn, piled on examples of this "principle of auto-adjustment" a bit haphazardly, extending it to various natural phenomena, and even to simple feedback de-

[10] See above, p. 94.

vices. He spoke of "negative regulation" to indicate the process by which a system tends to remove the conditions that favor its stability, so that "correction is the result of the excess of process, or deviation from stability" (Smith, 1914: 323).[11]

But just where some generic extrapolations of the notion of equilibration might eventually lead was revealed in a book by the neurologist C. Judson Herrik, *The Thinking Machine* (Herrick, 1929). Warren had chided Driesch and the vitalists for basing their critique of the mechanism on a "narrow" notion of the machine: "there are machines and other machines; and our knowledge of mechanical possibilities is not yet complete" (Warren, 1916: 38 and 37). Herrick now levels the same charge against the anti-mechanists, and to refute them he finds nothing better than extending the notion of machine to include all things. The mental world, the organic and inorganic ones, both natural and artificial, thus appear to be populated entirely by machines endowed to various degrees with the ability of adaptation, understood as self-regulation and self-control. Machines are thus present in inorganic nature: the "natural" or "dead machines," such as the commonly mentioned large rivers that "adapt" their courses to the features of the environment, or the solar system; animals are machines, and the human body is a machine; so-called "artificial" things are machines: tools, airplanes, calculators, telephone networks, and many more. Even Bent Russell's device figures in this disorderly inventory as a machine endowed with memory.

One "artificial machine" was correctly classified by Herrick among those where "control is wholly automatic" (Herrick, 1929: 308). Actually, it is a simple mechanical animal described by Lotka in his *Elements of Physical Biology*. The main subject of Lotka's pioneering book was a generalized thermodynamics of living systems. The mathematical approach to the evolution of complex systems in terms of reciprocal equilibria led Lotka to try to extend his approach to fields other than population dynamics. These attempts seem to anticipate certain cybernetic trends, which we have just mentioned, and still others inspired by von Bertalanffy's general system theory. But it should be remarked that Lotka proceeds with extreme caution, not failing to detail the difficulties to which certain overly simplistic generalizations give rise. For example, in citing Bancroft's statement of the "universal law," which had so struck Stevenson Smith, Lotka deems it an interpretation of Le Châtelier's principle that is vague and lacking in explanatory value. Furthermore, he observes that, no less than similar statements that suggested applications to biological systems, it could be traced back to the Spencerian formulations, well known to be generic and unusable for authentically explanatory purposes (Lotka, 1925/1956: 283).

In the final chapters of his book, Lotka faces the problems of the mind-body relationship, of consciousness, and of teleology, taking up various claims from Warren, particularly the claim that anticipatory behavior could be, so to speak, the *minimal* objective feature of purpose, and as such could also be *extended* to certain artifacts. Lotka gave a description of a system endowed with a "correlating apparatus" in cyclical interaction with the external environment, which is shown here in the diagram in Figure 4.1.

---

[11] This idea of negative regulation, along with the complementary one of "positive regulation" (a sort of reinforcement caused in the system by favorable conditions that increase its stability), was then developed in Smith and Guthrie (1921), an important contribution to behaviorist psychology.

It consists of receptor and effector organs, and a set of "adjustors," which adapted the response of the system to its environment based, as Lotka put it explicitly, on "the information brought in from the receptors" (p. 339). Lotka believed that an apparatus of this kind would permit organisms to interact with their environment by displaying various forms of adaptive behavior.[12]

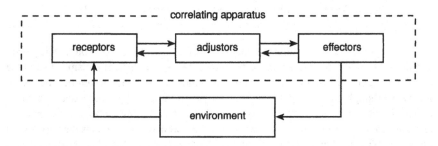

Fig. 4.1. A block-diagram showing the "correlating apparatus" described by Lotka.

The correlating apparatus, however, is not possessed solely by organisms: it can be embodied in the "mechanical beetle" of Figure 4.2. This very simple toy machine is equipped with two antennae of different lengths and has a small front wheel, set transversely to the direction of a larger rear wheel, operated by a spring-driven mechanism. When the machine runs around on top of a table, the longer antenna, the only one that has a function, prevents the front wheel from touching the surface until the antenna reaches the edge of the table. At this point the front wheel makes the machine change direction, and it continues moving without ever falling off the table, because the antenna "perceives" its edge, as Lotka put it.

Lotka sees in this toy machine an exemplification of the anticipatory mechanism that Warren had described: it permits the system to *depict* a possible future event. Taking up the same claim and terminology as Warren, Lotka says that if the purposive action is determined in humans by a psychic picture or a mental representation of a *certain future situation*, something of the sort occurs in the mechanical animal, though in a minimal form. The front wheel, "about as simple an example of an adjustor as can well be imagined, [...] 'construes' the information furnished by the receptor antenna," changing the behavior of the artifact (p. 342). As Lotka points out, the antenna, by "apprising" the artifact of a feature of the environment (the edge of the table), is the receptor that, roughly if one so wishes, "depicts" *in* the artifact a possible future event (p. 341).

[12] The correlating device shown in Figure 4.1 is actually a simplified schema: it does not include the "elaborators," whose function, says Lotka, is "to combine and further elaborate the crude information furnished by the senses" before it is translated into action by the adaptors. The elaborators can be seen as a kind of memory system, which attains particular complexity in human beings (Lotka, 1925/1956: 339-340). Thus one passes from "rigid or automaton type" behavior to "elastic type" behavior, which "we experience in ourselves subjectively as *free choice* between alternative courses of action" (pp. 350-351).

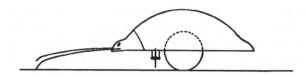

Fig. 4.2. A very simple self-controlled mechanical animal (from Lotka, 1925/1956).

This is perhaps the first time that the notion of representation, or a picture, has been transferred from the description of the teleological behavior of an organism to that of the teleological behavior of an artifact, a point to which we will have to return. The lesson that Lotka thought could be gathered from the functioning of the mechanical beetle was that its very simple *anticipatory* teleological device could be described *without making reference to the notion of a final cause* (p. 383). As we have seen, this is the very lesson that Rosenblueth, Wiener and Bigelow would gather from the 'new' negative-feedback machines.

5. True and derivative teleology

In "A Study of Purpose," Warren raised some doubts that give us occasion to probe more deeply in our analysis of the teleology of the inorganic. We have already seen how very cautious Warren was in tracking down phenomena in inorganic nature showing effective (not "fanciful," he said) anticipation. Now he starts to wonder about the actual *explanatory* role of teleological language in the description of such phenomena: why should one talk of *anticipation* in their presence? The use of teleological language in describing these phenomena might *add nothing* on the explanatory level to their description in physical terms. More exactly, they would be explained adequately and completely without introducing terms like 'purpose' or 'anticipation,' which, if used, would be completely metaphorical in this case. Here is Warren's doubt:

> But does [an anticipatory phenomenon in inorganic nature] involve *real anticipation*? Does not the causal relation describe it fully? In such cases does the future outcome *add any new meaning* to the successive stages of the process? (Warren, 1916: 61, my italics).

This problem of the legitimacy of teleological descriptions could also be raised with regard to the anticipation present in the inorganic world of *artificial* phenomena, i.e. those artifacts built by man and endowed with self-regulation. But regarding these Warren raises a different problem, though linked to the first, namely, that of the *origin* of their purposive behavior. According to Warren, the existence of self-regulated artifacts suggests how "mechanistic processes *may* fall into the purposive type." Actually, the contradiction stated by Driesch between machine and teleology does not exist in this case: who, Warren asks, would attribute a special entity, an entelechy, to a governor because this displays anticipation, the essential feature of purposeful behavior? Here, however, there is a new doubt. The importance of these artifacts as *true* instances of the teleology of the inorganic should not be exaggerated, since purpose is "built up" into them, as Warren puts it, *by the human designer*: it is the latter who "originates" the purposeful behavior of the artifacts, which "do not *of themselves* assume the purposive type of activity" (pp. 61-62).

The idea that the functioning of machines always has a purpose having its origin in the intentions of their builder is a philosophical commonplace.[13] With reference to the new self-regulated machines, the idea had been formulated by Hobhouse. He distinguished "two forms in which purpose may operate." The first form is the purpose of the machine, which, however, is revealed to us *from the outside* by the intention or by the "purposive mind" of the designer of the very machine, who brings its various parts together so as to gain a certain end. The second form of purpose is that manifested by the organism, which seems directed *from the inside* towards a purpose, in the sense that its parts are intrinsically brought together so as to constitute an "organic unity" characterized by self-maintenance and growth (Hobhouse, 1913: 301). Certainly, Hobhouse admitted, if we consider "an arrangement as a self-acting machine," say a governor, "we shall be forced to recognize in [it] something of the organic character," i.e. the fact that its different parts function in a mutual relation, collaborating in the accomplishment of a purpose, its self-maintenance. Even in this case, however, "the organic character disappears entirely when we consider its genesis," given that the machine is always the product of a designer and, furthermore, that its *organic* nature is more apparent than real (p. 309).[14] In general, therefore, it should always be possible to decide if one is in the presence of a "mechanical adjustment which simulates teleology" or in that of a case of "genuine teleology" (pp. 313-314).

Without going back to any particular 'new' machine, it would then be McDougall who, in *Modern Materialism*, would neatly distinguish "true teleology," which involves the presence of a mind, from the "derivative teleology" of artifacts, or "pseudo-teleology." The latter, no matter what kind the artifacts are, displays "a purposiveness which derives from, supplements and extends, the purposive actions of its designer and operator" (McDougall, 1929: 41).

In the next section we will look at McDougall's position on purpose. However, the presence of a conscious mind had been considered a distinguishing feature of purpose by other authors to whom we have already referred, for example James. In a little-known 1878 essay, while examining Spencer's notion of adaptation, James had distinguished the point of view of consciousness, or subjective experience (the personal interest of the agent in adapting in order to survive in a given situation) from that of the knowledge of the object on the part of an observer (the objective description given of the agent which adapts in order to survive). The latter is based on the purpose *attributed* to the agent and on *inferences* concerning his behavior in relation to a future situation (the result of the adaptation). That is, in the latter case it is the "outside spectator," as James calls him, who "measures what [he] sees going on by [his] private teleological standard, and judges it

---

[13] Only certain points concerning the issue we deal with in this chapter are touched on here. In general, the problem would bring us back once again to the debated question of the peculiarity of teleological explanation.

[14] The reference to self-regulated machines like the governor is, in any event, rather incidental in Hobhouse's text, which is concerned with identifying the distinctive marks of the teleological explanation as compared to the causal one.

intelligent." But this is a "hypothetical" teleology. In other words, the observer *may* use teleological or mental terms to describe and check the behavior of an agent to which he attributes a purpose, that of survival, but he does so only by considering the *external* results, those which can be objectively considered, of his behavior ("the reactions or outward consequences of the interests"). Conversely, in the first case, that of the point of view of consciousness or, we could say, of true teleology, James states that the use of "non-mental terms" is not merely inappropriate but impossible, because in this case an "absolutely new factor" is present, that represented by the agent's *subjective* interest (James, 1878: 62-65).

These distinctions more or less explicitly challenged the role of an "objective" teleology, one based on the *third-person ascription* of ends to the system, whether it be an organism (a human or a non-human animal) or a machine, on the part of an outside observer, who makes inferences about the behavior of the agent. Questions about the subjective purposes of the system did non enter into the scope of inquiry in this teleology. Such questions, instead, referred to a direct experience of the purpose, a *first-person knowledge* of it, and as such had to be placed at the level of the conscious, subjective experience of that purpose. In this regard, James emphasized a point that is of interest to us: it was only this kind of first-person purposiveness that made mentalistic language, the use of "mental terms," unavoidable, given the presence of that "new factor," conscious subjectivity, which made all the difference. We can consider this a possible answer *in nuce* to Warren's doubts: reference to the future as such in alleged purposive systems in the *inorganic* world did not add any "new meaning" to causal explanation. Especially with regard to artifacts, Warren himself admitted that their importance as actual examples of teleology should not be exaggerated: they did not have, and could not have, any *autonomous* purposes of their own. The purposes of artifacts found their origin in their designer: a pseudo-teleology, as McDougall finally decreed.

It is no surprise that in 1950, when cybernetics had already officially been born, the philosopher Richard Taylor, taking exception to the theses maintained by Rosenblueth, Wiener and Bigelow in their 1943 article, insisted on precisely those problems of objective teleology which revolved around Warren's doubts: for example, whether teleological language could not be renounced in the description of feedback machines, and up to what point the observer's judgment could justify the attribution of purpose to a system, whether organic or inorganic (Taylor, 1950a; 1950b).

Regarding the first problem, Taylor objected that the teleological description of self-regulated machines invoked by the three authors *adds nothing,* from the explanatory point of view, to the description of them in causal terms used in physical processes. When it is said that a missile "seeks" the target, teleological language is being used in a metaphorical sense, precisely as in the case where attributions of purpose are made regarding many other systems with which one often interacts. For example, do we not say that a plant "seeks" the light or "follows" the sun? (Taylor, 1950a: 315-16)

Rosenblueth and Wiener answered Taylor, insisting on the usefulness and necessity of teleological language in the description of the behavior of *certain* machines (those with feedback). To say that a missile "follows" its target, they concluded, "simplifies and clarifies" an equivalent description in mechanical terms.[15] The choice of this "humanistic" terminology, while it does not carry with it any reference to final causes, does underscore the pertinence of a *unified* study of the behavior of organisms and machines (Rosenblueth and Wiener, 1950: 321), which is, in fact, the true goal of Wiener's cybernetics.

Taylor raised then a second objection, which touched directly on the other problem we have mentioned, that of the observer's role in attributing a purpose to a system, and hence the role of his interests with respect to those of the system itself. Taylor objected that defining purpose, as his opponents had already done in their 1943 paper, in terms of behavior observable by an outside observer did not clarify what the *true* purposes of the system might be, or even if it had a purpose. The system or agent could manifest from time to time the *same* behavioral sequence (drive a car at a passer-by, for example) and nevertheless be motivated by intentions that *differ* (to run him over, to frighten him, and so on) or even by *no* intention or purpose (because of distraction). More than this, defining teleological behavior as a "search controlled by negative feedback" implied that the goal oriented the behavior of the system by using feedback signals (as in the example of the predator following its prey and that of the target-seeking missile). The definition could not, therefore, satisfy the case of *non-existent* goals (the Holy Grail, say) which, as contents of the agent's beliefs or desires, 'orient' his behavior towards an end (Taylor, 1950b: 329). This was Taylor's conclusion as to the necessary and sufficient condition in order appropriately to regard a behavior pattern as purposive:

> There must be, on the part of the behaving entity, i.e. the agent: (a) a desire, whether actually felt or not, for some object, event, or state of affairs as yet future; (b) the belief, whether tacit or explicit, that a given behavioral sequence will be efficacious as a means to the realization of that object, event, or state of affairs; and (c) the behavior pattern in question. Less precisely, this means that to say of a given behavior pattern that it is purposeful, is to say that the entity exhibiting that behavior desires some goal, and is behaving in a manner it believes appropriate to the attainment of it (Taylor, 1950b: 331).

But in their previous reply Rosenblueth and Wiener had already remarked the "behavioristic" stance of their approach to purpose: as such it starts "from the nature of the act, not from the study of or from any speculation on the structure and nature of the acting object" (Rosenblueth and Wiener, 1950: 323). The observer is the one who *attributes* a purpose to the system, whether it is an organism (a predator following its prey) or an artifact with feedback (a target-seeking missile). The notion of purpose, therefore, is not absolute but *relative to the observer*, to his interests and goals. Different observers can evaluate differently the degree of purposefulness in a system's behavior, and the same observer can judge a certain behavior as purposeful or as purposeless depending on the different interests at the moment. Rosenblueth and Wiener thus avoid "speculating" on what the purposes of the system might be and, especially, in the case of an artificial system, on the fact that they might be derived from those of its designer. Insisting

---

[15] As Mowrer will testify, the practice of describing how servomechanisms work by attributing 'mental' qualities and 'intelligence' to them was common among operators. He himself showed how the description of a servomechanism in mental terms recalled that of the behavior of a mouse at a choice point in a maze (Mowrer, 1960b: 221).

on the purposes of the designer as the *true* purposes was irrelevant from their point of view, since these purposes might not coincide with those of the artificial system.[16]

We will return to a discussion of this problem later, in the concluding chapter. Now it is of interest to point out how the analyses that the philosophers and scientists mentioned here made of the reinstatement of teleology took place in a context not too distant from that in which the cybernetic pioneers and their first critics were moving. To summarize, let us restate the main claims debated before and after the publication of the 1943 paper.

The "objective" analysis of teleology, which permits us to credit its use in science, means (a) that the system, whether organic or inorganic, is to be considered an inseparable part of the environment; (b) that the purposeful behavior of such a system is to be studied in terms of behavior that can be detected from outside; (c) that teleological vocabulary should undergo a revision which would refer to a notion of teleology in some way "restricted"; this notion would allow one to find examples of purposeful behavior in organisms as well as in inorganic nature and in certain artifacts, which would make the vitalist interpretation of purpose all the less dubious. These claims were contested on the grounds (a) that to consider the system solely in its reciprocal relations with the environment does not reveal the intentions of the system, and, therefore, (b) that the outside ("behavioristic") analysis of purposeful behavior ignores the true purposes of the system and, as a result, (c) that teleological vocabulary is used in this case, if not improperly, at least metaphorically and not in an explanatory way. In the case of artifacts, whatever sort they might be, one should not ignore the fact that their ability to manifest purposeful behavior derives from the human designer.

6. Learning and teleology: Perry, McDougall and Tolman

Up to this point, we have examined some attempts, prior to the dawn of cybernetics, to explain what had been assumed to be the fundamental or essential feature of teleological behavior, backward causation, without invoking so-called 'metaphysical' notions like final causes or entelechies. In those cases, recourse was made to 'objective' notions, which should replace metaphysical ones with respect to their explanatory power. The objective character of these notions, which should have made it possible for teleology to refer not solely to aspects of the subjective experience of purpose, was thought to be supported by the fact that those notions allowed for an interpretation in teleological terms of certain inorganic phenomena, in particular the functioning of certain machines.

Even the philosopher, Ralph B. Perry, in the years on which we are focusing, tried to give an objective definition of purpose which would make it possible to restore teleological vocabulary. He, too, referring to Lillie, used examples of self-regulating arti-

---

[16] "The emphasis on human purposes is irrelevant. The purpose of the designer of a radar-controlled gun may have been to have the gun seek an enemy plane, but if the gun seeks the car of the commanding officer of the post, as the officer drives by, and destroys it, surely the purpose of the gun differs from that of the designer. Indeed, this would be an excellent example of cross-purposes" (Rosenblueth and Wiener, 1950: 318). Taylor later returned to the issue of teleological explanation in reference to cybernetic artifacts as well (Taylor, 1966). At the time, however, the discussion had already moved on to more complex artifacts, such as computer programs of early AI (see Chapter 5), which Taylor showed no signs of considering. As we will see, it is precisely computer programs which will suggest new ways to take up again the problems argued by Taylor.

facts.[17] Unlike Lillie and other authors we have mentioned, however, Perry set himself the task of establishing at what point the use of teleological vocabulary really cannot be renounced and is not simply an option for an outside observer. According to Perry, teleological vocabulary should demonstrate its peculiarity with respect to causal vocabulary, without being incompatible with it.

To say that teleological vocabulary cannot be renounced in explaining *certain* behaviors of a system means that any explanation of such behavior in causal terms is not sufficient: it needs, as Perry put it, "some additional factor" which, without being a mysterious agency, identifies in that behavior those objective features that make it purposive (Perry, 1917a: 359-360). To take up Warren's terminology once again, it would be necessary to clarify why the causal explanation of that behavior is not complete, and what "new meaning" is added by teleological explanation. As we will see, this led Perry to exclude the possibility that the essence of purpose could be identified with an activity determined by the future, or with the anticipatory tendency of adaptive behavior, as Lillie and Warren, for example, maintained. A little in keeping with these authors, Perry defined the notion of adaptation in terms of the restoration of a disturbed equilibrium, but he distinguished the *adaptation* processes from those of *learning*, finding in the latter the peculiar and objective mark of purposeful behavior.

In analyzing the adaptation processes, Perry pointed out an important distinction, that between the *tendency towards equilibrium*, in which case the system returns to a certain state when the disturbance from outside ceases, and the *tendency to maintain equilibrium*, in which case the system possesses a specific "mechanism of recovery which is released whenever the system rises above or falls below a certain zero point, and the effects of which are equal in quantity but opposite in sign to those of the disturbing agency" (Perry, 1917b: 488). With regard to the first case, the classic example of a stationary system is that of a candle flame, already mentioned by Lillie, which became famous because it also was used by von Bertalanffy (1968) and by the popular philosophy of general system theory. In the second case, that of equilibrium maintenance, *the only one in which it is possible to speak of adaptation*, Perry brings together all those processes that Lillie defined as those of "internal" equilibration, afterwards called homeostatic, and part of the "external" equilibration processes, i.e. reflexes or tropisms and animal instincts. According to Perry, even artificial mechanisms such as the governor or the thermostat, by satisfying the definition above, are part of this same class of processes, which he calls "compensatory adjustments." These examples seem to suggest to Perry that a distinction should be made between the principles of physical equilibrium in dynamics and the principle of control by means of negative feedback, which is embodied in an ordinary servomechanism. We will return to this point later (see section 7), to point out how, through this distinction, one might avoid the vagueness characterizing certain aforementioned discussions about teleology and inorganic or "dead" machines, as Herrik had called certain self-equilibrating natural systems (rivers seeking their way, and the like).

These compensatory adjustments are nothing but a first class of adaptive processes,

[17] Famous as the founder of American philosophical neo-realism, Perry made important theoretical contributions in the field of psychological behaviorism.

actually the simplest ones. Perry describes two others. There is the class of "progressive adjustments," in which the organism does not act to restore an equilibrium disturbed from outside, but establishes a relationship with the environment that makes it possible to achieve a state of equilibrium previously not possessed. This is the case in the processes of organic growth, or certain animal instincts, like searching for food. Finally, there is the class of "preparatory adjustments," in which the disturbance is forestalled by a reaction of adjustment which anticipates its effect, as happens in certain protective instincts, for example, flight in the face of danger.

Perry includes these three cases of adjustment in a single class which he calls "complementary adjustment." In these three cases, for self-regulating artifacts as well as for organisms, it is always possible, in his opinion, to use teleological and mentalistic terminology. But *precisely* because a building equipped with a heating boiler and a thermostat "may be said in respect of temperature to be 'adapted' to [the] environment," we still cannot conclude that we are in the presence of a genuine case of purpose. Rather, we are still dealing with purpose only in a "broad sense" (p. 488), and we are thus using teleological language in a way that we could call metaphoric or non-explanatory.[18] But are there, Perry asks, cases where teleological and mentalistic language *cannot be renounced*?

To begin with, all the adjustments included in Perry's classification discussed up to this point, i.e. the complementary ones, he defines as "automatic." We have discussed the acceptance of this very common term among neurologists and psychologists. It was used to define those behaviors that manifest the same property of both reflexive and instinctive action: the organism, or the artifact, *adapts* to its environment through behavior which produces a constant result. In Perry's definition, a behavior is "automatic" when, given a certain stimulus, the response can be deduced as a dependent variable with respect to the environment by applying a constant rule. But there also exists a "non-automatic" behavior, in which the response is an independent variable. In this case, some responses lead to the result while others do not, and the former are selected by the organism *with a view to the result*, as happens in the trial-and-error learning process described by Thorndike (Perry, 1918: 2-3). Now it is the notion of "task" that is the genuine mark of purpose in Perry's conception: bringing a task to completion implies that the means needed to achieve a given purpose must be established. Each step takes into account both future expectations and past experience, i.e. the result obtained. This kind of behavior was defined by Perry as "plastic," because different choices are possible in it, choices that explain the "docility" or the "margin of modifiability" that objectively justify teleology and the use, not merely metaphorical, of teleological language (p. 12).

We can, therefore, identify the automatism described by Perry with a system equipped with a feedback control mechanism, which, as such, does not involve *learned* changes in its behavior. Actually, what Perry called "compensatory" adjustment corresponds to the "non-predictive" or "non-extrapolative" teleological behavior of the authors of "Be-

---

[18] Taylor stressed how Perry's claim anticipated the criticism that he would make, as we have seen, of the feedback analysis of purpose (Taylor, 1950b: 329 n.). But the issue seems to have been more popular than one might suppose. For example, in the early 1930s the psychologist Stanley Gray used the thermostat as an example of a machine showing purposeful behavior (Gray, 1932: 273).

havior, Purpose, and Teleology." And one notes how both the examples given by Perry and those usually given by the cyberneticians are the same, in the case of organisms as well as that of machines: tropisms, as well as instincts, in the first case; thermostats, governors and the like in the second.

Beyond such affinities, there remains a basic difference: for cyberneticians teleology was restored by automatic control machines, but for Perry one cannot speak properly of teleology in the case of automatic adjustment behaviors, *whether* in organisms *or* in machines. Conversely, mentalistic or teleological language is used properly only in cases of "plastic" or "modifiable" behavior. Despite the important specifications Perry made about the concept of equilibrium in the context of teleological disputes and his careful examination of adaptive behavior, his conclusive statement seems to be quite usual. In fact it is not too distant from the traditional Spencerian canon, which had already been summarized by Lloyd Morgan through the distinction between *automatic* regulatory processes, which can be observed in instinctive behavior, and *plastic* regulatory processes, which can be observed in intelligent behavior.[19]

One who never agreed with the thesis of the automatic nature of instincts was McDougall, who considered them true examples of purposeful behavior, no less than those actions in which learning takes place. After *Body and Mind*, McDougall had come back on different occasions to radicalize the conflict between mechanism and vitalism: the conflict between causal and teleological explanation was, after all, just an aspect of it. The very titles of some of his well known essays reflect this radicalization: "Purposive or Mechanical Psychology?" (McDougall, 1923b), "Men or Robot?" (McDougall, 1926). In these works, as in the later *Modern Materialism* already mentioned, McDougall extended his criticism to some of the authors we have mentioned in this chapter, reasserting, especially against Warren, the causal efficacy of mind in the foresight of future actions (McDougall, 1929: 189). This was a thesis he had developed more organically in his *Outline of Psychology*, where he considered backward causation, which constitutes a paradox for the mechanistic thinker, to be a *distinctive* property of the mind instead, and a peculiarity of the teleological explanation by comparison with a mechanistic or causal one: "The essential nature of Mind," he had concluded, "is to govern present action by anticipation of the future in the light of past experience; to make, in short, effects precede and determine their cause" (McDougall, 1923a: 195).

This conclusion followed his formulation of the six famous "marks of behavior" (pp. 43-46). McDougall considered behavior peculiar to living organisms. The six marks he defined consisted of: (i) spontaneity of action; (ii) persistency of activity independently of the continuance of the stimulus which initiated it; (iii) variation of direction of persistent movements; (iv) cessation of activity when an action is completed and one finds oneself in a new situation; (v) anticipation or preparation of the results of an action; and finally (vi) improving the action when it is repeated in similar circumstances. This last mark regarding the *improvement* of performance refers to learning, while the first five define purposeful behavior. McDougall denied that one could deal with them without making reference to the subject's experience, or *extend* them to the inorganic world by means of the different above-mentioned 'objective' criteria. On the contrary, he held that

---

[19] See above, p. 13.

the five marks of purposeful behavior, while they could not be satisfied by reflex actions, were actually satisfied by instinctive ones.[20]

Edward Tolman attributed to Perry the intuition of a definition of purpose that was "purely objective and behavioristic," since it is objectively inherent in every behavior that involves purpose. Nevertheless, Tolman felt that it was possible to give an objective definition of purpose that was less restrictive than Perry's, i.e. one which would refer more generally to behavior in which, in each trial, an organism *persists until* a given end is reached, without having to consider improvement in its performance in a later behavior cycle, which is usually identified as learning. For example, the avoidance reaction of simple organisms, like those studied by Jennings, would be a case of purpose, even if in a later behavior cycle there were no sooner appearance of that reaction (Tolman, 1925: 36). In these cases, the purpose to be achieved is *part* of the persisting action, and the use of teleological language is, therefore, unavoidable: it is not metaphorical nor can it be eliminated, but neither does it refer or allude to a mysterious mental entity.

Tolman agreed, then, with McDougall in believing that the sixth mark of behavior, that related to learning, was not necessary to define purpose: the first five were enough, those which he considered, however, as objective marks of a specific behavior, a purposeful one, i.e. one requiring that its description "include a reference to the position or nature of the goal-object" (p. 37). This last specification is very important, and in it can be summarized the difference between McDougall's *intentional* teleology and the *objective* teleology of the other authors we have considered in this chapter, including Tolman: McDougall *inferred* purpose from those five characteristics; the others could *identify it* with them (or, in the case of Perry, with learning).

Tolman's "intentional behaviorism" constitutes a particularly original chapter in the history of the sciences of mind in the early twentieth century, one that today seems like a sort of cross-contamination between the behaviorism of his day and the cognitivism that followed. Tolman rejected Thorndike's connectionism and distanced himself from various forms of behaviorism of the time, from that of Watson to that of Skinner and Hull. It was Tolman who, in a well-known article, would clarify the difference between the concept of learning as the modification of sensory-motor or S-R connections, the thesis which he attributed to Hull, and his own concept of learning as the reorganization of sensory or perceptual processes. In the latter case, the organism, for example the rat in the maze, does not learn a series of movements corresponding to reinforced connections, but learns a "cognitive map," that is to say, a representation of the problem in relation to the goal and the means available to achieve it. This cognitive map, therefore, refers to the language of purpose in an essential way, and it calls up a different metaphor of the brain: this "is far more like a map control room than it is like an old-fashioned telephone exchange" (Tolman, 1948: 244).[21]

---

[20] On the basis of this concept taken from psychology, which McDougall called "hormic" or "intentional," he elaborated a theory of instincts as "sources of energy," which he illustrated by making use of some mechanical analogies. On McDougall and the ethological approach of the models of Konrad Lorenz and N. Tinbergen, see Smith (1960). On McDougall's concept of purpose, also in relation to that of the other authors mentioned in this chapter, see Boden (1972).

[21] Tolman's distinction can be traced back to that, later made canonical by Spence (1951), between S-R, or *associationist*, psychological theories and S-S, or *cognitive*, psychological theories.

Tolman does share with Hull, however, a concern with the theoretical concepts of psychology, which could be understood as "intervening variables" between stimulus and response. This concern was the result of their common interest in neo-positivist epistemology in its liberalized form, which recognized the role of the theoretical hypotheses of science.[22] Hull, for his part, had taken up the distinction supported by Tolman between a *molecular* explanation of behavior, the study of observed or hypothesized neurophysiological mechanisms, and a *molar* explanation of behavior, the study of the laws that could be derived from an analysis of the behavior itself by introducing intervening variables between stimulus and response. Hull dealt with molar study with a mathematical style, which had come to mark his approach, and which was foreign to Tolman.[23]

In 1939 Tolman described a mechanical animal, the "schematic sowbug"—a "hypothetical robot," as Boring put it, because the exact design of its working was not specified (Boring, 1946: 191). Compared to the robot approach that had occupied Hull for years, this was an incidental experiment in Tolman's investigations. He too, however, proposed the sowbug as the scheme of a machine that exemplified a theory, that of vicarious trial-and-error learning (Tolman, 1939). Tolman described the behavior of the sowbug as tropistic in Loeb's sense, because it automatically oriented itself towards the source of stimulation. In the case where two stimuli were in competition, a white square and a black or gray one, the sowbug oriented itself in the direction of the first stimulus rather than the other, according to "hypotheses," as Tolman put it, that could be reinforced or weakened. Miller et al. (1960: 59) defined the sowbug as "a perfectly respectable feedback mechanism": there were, in fact, different feedbacks that guided the sowbug's orientation, both tropistic and discriminative, in which vicarious movements were present.

7. Craik's symbolic theory of thought and synthetic method

In recent times, the cognitive psychologist Philip Johnson-Laird has proposed a distinction between "Cartesian automata" and "Craikian automata," named after the psychologist Kenneth Craik (Johnson-Laird, 1983: 400 ff.).[24] Craikian automata, in contrast to Cartesian ones, have a sensory system capable of encoding stimuli from the environment and machinery capable of using this information to construct what Johnson-Laird calls "representations of the external world." These representations guide the behavior of the automaton by means of feedback loops with the environment (see Figure 4.3). Johnson-Laird gives as an example of a Craikian automaton, albeit primitive and incomplete, a very simple robot devised by another cognitive psychologist, Christopher Longuet-Higgins. The robot is provided with two wheels, which are both its sensory and motor organs, and the world in which it moves is the surface of a table. It possesses a representation of the table in the form of a sort of rudimentary map in miniature, actually a

---

[22] On the influence of neopositivism on Hull and Tolman, and in general on their different concepts of psychology, see Smith (1986).

[23] We will not enter here into a discussion of the so-called "conceptual nervous system" to which Skinner made reference as a different level of research for psychology (see Mecacci, 1979).

[24] On Craik, see Zangwill (1980) and Gregory (1983).

piece of stiff paper placed inside it, which has the same shape as the table. Thanks to a simple mechanical device, the robot's position at any moment on the table is made to correspond on the piece of paper. When the robot reaches the edge of the table and is about to fall off, thanks to the presence of this internal map, or small-scale model, a circuit is closed, sounding an alarm bell, which warns the human observer of the danger. The schema of Lotka's correlating apparatus, which we showed in Figure 4.1, brings to mind, in a simplified form, Johnson-Laird's block-diagram of a Craikian automaton, and the robot described by Lotka can be considered an example of Craikian automata *ante litteram*, even if such a robot is endowed with a rather different representational device. As we have seen, its representational device is as special-purpose as it is effective: a depression in the external world (the table's surface) is "translated," Lotka said, "into a downward tilt in the angle of repose of the mechanical toy beetle" (p. 342).

Johnson-Laird pointed out that his notion of representation has a forerunner in the notion of model formulated by Craik in a book that soon became well known, *The Nature of Explanation* (Craik, 1943). Here, Craik formulated a hypothesis on the nature of thought which, as we shall see, deals with a number of questions at the core of the discovery of the artificial. According to Craik, thought is, first of all, "prediction," and prediction consists of three steps: "translating" processes in the external world, perceived by means of a sensory system, into an internal, simplified or small-scale model; drawing from this model the possible inferences by means of appropriate machinery; and "retranslating" this model into external processes, i.e. acting by means of a motor system (pp. 50-51).

The model, as Craik put it, is a symbolic "parallel" of the external world, whose "essential features" it retains. By means of symbols and symbolic processes, to the degree that these establish a relationship of *parallelism* with the world, the agent is able to build an internal representation of external events and processes, in order to make predictions and to *anticipate* the result of an action. This definition is intentionally general and, as we shall see, has to be worked out.

According to Craik, building symbolic models of this sort is a capability of the nervous systems of living organisms, but also of certain machines. In the case of the nervous system's representational capabilities, Craik is unavoidably very vague, limiting himself

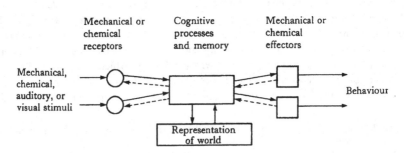

Fig. 4.3. The block-diagram of a Craikian automaton, showing feedback loops, according to Johnson-Laird (1983).

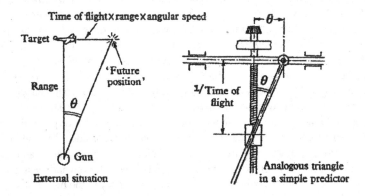

Fig. 4.4. The external situation (on the left) is represented in a simple predictor
of an automatic anti-aircraft system (on the right) (from Tustin, 1953).

to hypothesizing the existence of neural patterns in which impulses coming from outside
are organized, along the usual "lines of least resistance" at the synaptic level (p. 60): it is in
such patterns that concepts or perceptions of objects are represented. In the case of machines,
he explicitly mentions the new machines of the time: among others, radar-controlled anti-
aircraft systems and calculating machines such as Vannevar Bush's differential analyzer.
These are analog computing machines, in which external processes are represented as the
positions of gears and the like. These physical dispositions were considered by Craik as *symbols* capable of playing a causal role in determining the behavior of machines.

To clarify Craik's claims, we should firstly mention the mechanism in Figure 4.4, tak-
en from an article published during the cybernetic age. Its author, A. Tustin, describes the
simplest mechanism for *foreseeing* the future position of a moving target, a mechanism
used by an automatic anti-aircraft system such as those mentioned by Craik. This "predictive" or "extrapolative" feedback mechanism (precisely in the sense of Rosenblueth,
Wiener and Bigelow) constantly duplicates, as Tustin puts it, the triangle whose vertices
are the gun, the target and its future position in a "small-scale representation" (the Θ angle is the same in both cases). Based on data perceived by a sensory system, this representation, or "image," as Tustin called it, is kept at all times in correspondence with the
relevant features of the changing external situation and, by continuously modifying itself,
determines through the motor system the direction of the gun's aim (Tustin, 1953: 27).[25]

In describing this kind of teleological, predictive behavior, Tustin thus uses a representational terminology that had at the time entered into common parlance among cyberneticians, and that Craik would probably have accepted. However, Craik had in mind
more then this when speaking about the representational capability of both organisms and
machines. In his taxonomy, prediction and purposeful activity through servomechanisms

[25] The article by Tustin, an engineer, was requested by the British Psychological Society, so that he might
explain to what point brain mechanisms could be described in terms of the new calculating and control devices.

and negative-feedback mechanisms, such as that in Figure 4.4, are the lowest of the possible forms. In the world of organisms, Craik exemplified these forms with the usual cases of danger avoidance or feeding actions. He sketched this taxonomy in a work published posthumously, *The Mechanism of Human Action*, where he again dealt with the representational theory previously developed in *The Nature of Explanation*.[26]

In *The Mechanism of Human Action*, even more explicitly than in that earlier book, Craik investigated both the capabilities and the limits of devices endowed with different (negative and positive, quantitative and qualitative) feedbacks. We shall deal with some of these in the next section. Now we would mention one form of predictive and purposeful behavior higher than that in Figure 4.4, one Craik considered as underlying cognitive activities such as problem solving, invention, concept formation and discovery, which involve ideas or abstract images of the ends to be achieved and the agent's previous knowledge, beliefs, desires and expectations. Contrary to the behavior sequence in Figure 4.4, in this kind of activity representations are not directly and continuously linked to events occurring in a changing environment, but can be manipulated by the agent fairly independently of incoming stimuli. In the one case the agent's responses are evoked only by outer objects though actual sensory stimulation, but in the other those responses are evoked mainly by patterns of previously experienced stimuli. In Craik's own words:

> While on the one hand we find that as a rule mere objects evoke, in themselves, little response, anything which in the light of our previous knowledge puzzle us or defeats our insight or suggests new possibilities may evoke a very definite response. We want, then, to find some scheme in which our various experiences combine to reproduce *patterns in us which sometimes begin to flow into one another, or run up against one another, and evoke them* [...] These inner patterns are, as it were, *active replicas of outer object*—capable of acting in a dynamic way which the real objects often do not. When these patterns fuse or compete *it suggests possibilities of discovery and solution, or of perplexity and unsolved problems, in the outer world* (Craik, 1966: 72, my italics).

The "scheme" mentioned is suggested by Craik's own representational theory. One instance in which such a scheme is at work is the planning of a sequence of actions leading to a goal, where the agent must choose among different, possibly opposite, moves by selecting incoming stimuli, and does so on the base of his previous knowledge or experience, expectations or desires. All these items suggest to the agent what Craik calls the "possibilities" of actions, in this case the possible alternative courses of action that the agent can evaluate without actually trying them and thus without suffering the consequences (think of the usual example of chess playing). Another instance is invention, where man produces an artifact (say, a steam engine) combining in a novel way the "possibilities" of objects existing in nature (heat, water, and so on). In such cases, Craik concluded, agents use *"mental models of a possible event in the external world."*[27]

[26] Craik started working on *The Mechanism of Human Action* in October 1943, after completing *The Nature of Explanation*. *The Mechanism of Human Action* is a lengthy sketch for a second book, which was never finished (Craik died in 1945 at the age of thirty-one in a car accident in Cambridge). The manuscript was published with other texts, most of them previously unpublished, selected by Warren McCullock, Leo Verbeek and Stephen Sherwood, and collected in a volume edited by the latter, which includes a bibliography of Craik's works (Craik, 1996). See Craik (1966: 89-90) for the explicit statement of different kinds of purposive activity.

[27] As for other authors we discussed earlier in our investigation, for Craik the function of consciousness is to permit greater flexibility in the activity of organisms.

These higher forms of purposeful activity could be included among those mentioned by Taylor when he objected that Rosenblueth, Wiener and Bigelow's definition of teleological behavior as behavior controlled by the error of the reaction could apply only to the seeking of objects physically existing in the outer environment (negative feedback machines would not be able to seek absent or non-existent objects). Thus, according to Taylor, one must consider the agent's desires and beliefs in order appropriately to regard his behavior as purposeful. In fact, Craik's inner models or patterns refer to goals (objects), such as those in planning or in invention mentioned above, that are clearly are not present in the here-and-now, and might be non-existent. An inner representation as a *mental model* does not necessarily need to carry information directly from outer existing goals, and could be viewed as an hypothetical entity explaining the role of experience, beliefs and so on in agents capable of fairly high-level activities.[28] According to Craik, however, in these cases too one's activity is directed by the *discrepancy* between the actual situation and that represented as a goal through the inner model or pattern, and thus this kind of higher purposeful activity, as well as others, does not seem to entail "any power intrinsically outside the scope of mechanisms" (p. 90).

Craik tried to justify this last statement by again comparing the functioning of nervous systems and the calculating machines of his time.[29] Clearly, he was aware that none of these machines could even distantly compete with the flexibility and spontaneity of the behavior of living organisms. Nonetheless, according to Craik, machines share with organisms, at least in certain cases, the important feature of manipulating models in trying out alternative courses of action *before* making a decision. His favorite example is that of a computing machine simulating the development of strains in a bridge. Such a machine "parallels" and so "is able to 'give account of' or 'predict'," as he put it, phenomena regarding, for example, the strength of the bridge, before we actually try it (by sending a train over the bridge) (Craik, 1943: 95, and see 52). More generally, "only this internal model of reality—this working model—enables us to predict events which had not yet occurred in the physical world, a process which saves time, expense, and even life" (p. 82).

In sum, in this case also the causal role of symbols in machines, in some of its essential features, can be compared to the causal role played by the nervous system in the behavior of organisms when making inferences or drawing implications regarding events in the world.

"Implication" would be the power of [the] neural mechanisms to operate each other as the real events act causally on each other [...] Implication would thus be *a kind of artificial causation in which symbols connected by rules represent events connected by causal interaction.* [...] Assuming then the existence of the external world I have outlined a symbolic theory of thought, in which *the nervous system is viewed as a calculating machine capable of modelling or paralleling external events,* and have suggested that this process of paralleling is the basic feature of thought and of explanation (Craik, 1943: 63 and 121, my italics).

[28] Gregory pointed out that, in *The Nature of Explanation,* Craik answered the criticism that internal models might not be needed, stressing that they were necessary for explaining *cognitive* processes (Gregory, 1983: 236).

[29] Lashley's interference pattern theory suggested to Craik the hypothetical neurological substrate of his dynamic patterns or models, although he believed that the "old theory of different resistance pathways at synapses" could make up for certain insufficiencies in Lashley's theory (Craik, 1966: 73).

This "symbolic theory of thought" was later involved in a representational theory of the mind viewed as an information processing system. In this form, as we will see in later chapters, the theory is even today the subject of dispute. Craik's symbols, however, are analog representations, not the symbol structures of the digital computer programs of AI.[30] Although Craik's notion of symbolism and dynamic models seems to have been fully developed in that context, it could appropriately be regarded as a crucial advance with respect to previous speculations regarding the role of 'symbolism' in thinking, as this role had been pointed out by various authors, for example Warren. That notion can also be seen as an original development of the representational mechanism that Hull described in order to explain the capacity for foresight in both an organism and a machine endowed with different "degrees of freedom" with respect to the environment. Hull had already spoken of a *parallelism* between the external world and the internal "patterns" or "replicas" of the organism. In minimal or "rudimentary" forms, this parallelism enables the system interacting with the environment to manipulate inner states (patterns, replicas) before operating upon it, by evaluating possible choices without suffering the consequences of those actions.[31]

The novelty in Craik's symbolic theory of thought is the full-blown notion of a system processing and controlling the flux of information coming from the environment—a system that could be exemplified using Johnson-Laird's block-diagram. Such a system was suggested to Craik by his profound competence in the field of automatic control. The "theory of the human operator in control systems," which he was developing in a more systematic form at the end of his brief life, is the keystone for understanding his approach to animal and human behavior. In some pages written in 1945 and published posthumously (Craik, 1947; 1948), man, as an element of a control system, is described as a "chain" that includes a sensory device, a computing and amplifying system and a response device. He observes as follows:

> Such considerations serve to bridge the gap between the physiological statement of man as an animal giving reflex and learned responses to sensory stimuli, and the engineering statement in terms of the type of mechanism which would be designed to fulfil the same function in a wholly automatic system (Craik, 1948: 142).

This claim is fully in agreement with Wiener's newly-emerged cybernetics, according to which "the operation of the living individual and the operation of some of the newer communication machines are precisely parallel" (Wiener, 1950: 13). And the parallelism was given by their common possession of the "chain" of items pointed out by Craik, consisting of sensory-computing-actuator devices—in a word, by their being "Craikian automata."

Craik's concept of man as a computing and control system was a radical simplification. It cut out various ethical and general philosophical aspects that Craik, however, touched on in *The Nature of Explanation*. As he made clear elsewhere, the role of "[bridg-

---

[30] On this point, see Gregory (1983). Before Johnson-Laird, just about all the founders of AI, such as Minsky, Newell, Simon, insisted, from different points of view, on the centrality of Craik's claims when developing their cognitive computer models.

[31] See above, p. 100.

ing] the gaps between [...] physiology, medicine and engineering" had to be assumed by psychology (Craik, 1945: 24), obviously appealing to this functional notion of a computing and control system, of which organisms and machines are different realizations.

What Craik called the engineering statement of man was then the focus of research that was driven by military applications. The usual example of the anti-aircraft gun, mentioned by Craik, no less than by Wiener, is not fortuitous. Craik's scientific activity, like that of Wiener and so many other pioneers of automatic computing and control, was always buttressed by participation in the projects of the armed forces during the Second World War. As Grey Walter recalled:

> The first notion of constructing a free goal-seeking mechanism goes back to a wartime talk with the psychologist, Kenneth Craik, whose untimely death was one of the greatest losses Cambridge has suffered in years. When he was engaged on a war job for the Government, he came to get the help of our automatic analyser with some very complicated curves he had obtained, curves relating to the aiming errors of air gunners. Goal-seeking missiles were literally much in the air in those days; so, in our minds, were scanning mechanisms (Walter, 1953: 82).

Perhaps better than any other, Grey Walter's testimony allows us to place the figure of Craik within the climate where cybernetics was born. Wiener himself would recall anti-aircraft guns and scanning mechanisms as the issues at the center of much research in the war years (Wiener, 1948/1961: 26-29). In fact, they constituted Craik's main occupation in that period.[32]

While the symbolic theory of thought Craik developed in *The Nature of Explanation* has always occupied front stage, in the background there remained his investigations into the automatic control systems as tools for studying organism behavior, taking into account the results of the psychology and neurology of his day. This has reinforced the image of Craik as the forerunner of information processing theories, but it has prevented certain of his brilliant intuitions from being placed in their right context.

With the aim of highlighting this point, we come back to an issue in *The Mechanism of Human Action* that we have already touched on. In this posthumous work, Craik stated that he wanted to carry forward the robot approach "even more unswervingly" than Hull had (Craik, 1966: 80). In his earlier *The Nature of Explanation*, he had mentioned Hull's conditioning models (Craik, 1943: 52), but in this second text Craik is more explicit. These references to the robot approach allow a better evaluation of Craik's ideas and, at the same time, an understanding of who it is that might have picked up those vague formulations

---

[32] See for example Craik (1945). It is singular that, in reconstructing the history of the origins of cybernetics, Wiener does not cite the name of Craik. This is even more singular if one recalls that Wiener, referring to his trip to England in 1947, just two years after Craik's death, remembered that he visited the Psychological Laboratory at Cambridge, where he had "a very good chance to discuss the work that Professor F.C. Bartlett and his staff were doing on the human element in control processes involving such an element" (Wiener, 1948/1961: 23). This was precisely work which, in psychological investigations and in wartime applications as well, had found in Craik its most active protagonist alongside Bartlett. As Bartlett said, Craik was the "key man" in the scientific research organization of the British army (see the obituary notice Bartlett wrote for Craik, republished in Craik, 1966). Craik's pioneering role in the psychological research between engineering and neurology during the war was stressed by those who developed so-called *engineering psychology* or *human engineering*, in which the role of the human operator in control systems was studied (see, for example, Sinaiko, 1961).

of the "psychic" machine that Hull himself had let drop at the time. Craik, in fact, seems to be placed at the confluence of the results of behavioristic psychology (or better, of the "mechanistic tendency of modern psychology," to use Baernstein and Hull's phrase) with the then recent development of automatic control theory and technology.

Actually, the simulative methodology of the robot approach might have inspired the proposal with which Craik opens *The Mechanism of Human Action*. Here he distinguishes between two methods for studying behavior and learning in living organisms: the "analytic" method, which is concerned with the anatomical and neurophysiological structure of organisms, and the "synthetic" method, which is at the root of the construction of models simulating different functions of organisms. The latter method is based on the possibility of identifying what Craik called "the general principles" which are common to living organisms and machines, both being considered as complex adaptive systems which use energy supplied from outside in order to maintain a state of dynamic equilibrium.[33] By identifying these general principles, the synthetic method seems thus to be the one that best characterizes the enterprise of psychology, which has to "bridge the gap" between the biological and engineering statements of man.

Craik subscribed to Hull's claim that the robot approach put one on guard against the error of vitalism (Craik, 1966: 10). Now, however, the argument against those who, as Hull wrote in 1931,[34] are "unfamiliar with the possibilities of automatic mechanisms," or limit themselves to considering "ordinary *rigid-type* machines," takes more precise form as an argument against those who reject the modeling method on the basis of a narrow notion of the machine, or of "a limited range of machines": those machines, watches and the like, that have deliberately been built to be "*rigid* in their behaviour and *lacking in feedback*" (pp. 11 and 19, my italics). McDougall is unfailingly cited as one of these people. Even though McDougall died in 1938, he was still playing the role he had always personified, that of the anti-mechanist *par excellence*. Craik objected that the *new* feedback machines, such as servomechanisms, were the best answer to the question of backward causation raised by McDougall. These machines work on the basis of the result attained, and thus they show what the origin of purposeful behavior could be (p. 12). Feedback, in this way, becomes the keystone of biological and psychological mechanism, the new context in which certain disputes that we have touched on seem to become more definite. Think of Hull's vague reference to "ultra-automatic" machines, or Warren's even more vague rebuke to those who adhere to vitalism on the base of a "narrow" notion of the machine. But Craik's interest in the robot approach, or actually in an approach based on the *new* machines, should not be reduced to its generic anti-vitalist function.

In *The Nature of Explanation*, Craik had already raised a question which has resurfaced

[33] See Craik (1966), especially the Introduction and Chapter 3. The phrase "synthetic method" recalls that used in the context of the robot approach to indicate the method for building 'inorganic' or 'artificial' models. Craik's distinction between "analytic method" and "synthetic method" has nothing to do directly with other methodological distinctions of the same tenor, such as that of Jennings (see Chapter 1, section 4). Rather, at least in certain aspects, Craik's 1943 distinction recalls that between "behavioristic" and "functional" method, stated by Rosenblueth, Wiener and Bigelow in the same year, even if Craik was not aware of their article (see Zangwill, 1980: 10).

[34] See above, p. 101.

several times in our investigation, especially in the present chapter: do any examples of adaptation and anticipation exist *outside* the world of living organisms? Or, if one prefers to use Craik's terminology: is the essential feature of *symbolism* (that is, the ability of certain processes to parallel each other) also present in the inorganic world? We already know that Craik's answer is 'yes' as far as artifacts like automatic control devices and calculating machines are concerned. As for the world of nature, Craik seemed to think that there were no substantial differences between that and the world of artifacts. In both cases, for example, the usual forms of hysteresis can be detected. "Everything bears some mark of its past," was his radical conclusion, "and the difference between the 'memory' of a stone and [that] of one of Hull's conditioned reflex models is only one of degree" (Craik, 1943: 83).

It may be surprising that Craik too offers, though cautiously, the usual example of water that, in seeking its way, gradually digs a channel: "the *material* of symbolism—the parallel mechanisms—seems to be there" (p. 41). The specification that follows is, however, important and is a sign of the times: these systems in the world of nature, Craik says, lack actual receptors (and effectors), as well as information control and processing devices. They thus lack something like a nervous system, or a functional analog of the latter—in a word, they are not true Craikian automata.

This important distinction would be clearly stated later on during the cybernetic age. For example, Donald MacKay would distinguish between the "passive" and the "active" sense of being *directed* towards an end state. Water seeking its way is an instance of the passive sense of the term (already stressed, as we have seen in our investigation into the discovery of the artificial, from the days of Spencer and James onwards). In this case there is not "a distinguishable process of *control*," as in the case of a system endowed with a feedback device, where the system reacts because it has received information as to a certain situation—a reaction that need not have occurred if information had *not* been received, as MacKay (1952: 65) emphasized. MacKay's above distinction, which we saw adumbrated by Perry, seems to be clear to Craik in the form of the distinction between a system that tends to return to its previous state of equilibrium and a system acting on the basis of the discrepancy between its disturbed state and some *assigned* state of equilibrium, such as a servomechanism.[35]

In sum, Craik's own knowledge of the features of computing and information processing systems (the sensory-control-effector items in the "chain" mentioned above) seems to make him rather cautious about considering examples from the world of inorganic nature as, as it were, *complete* instances of symbolism. The already meager examples from the world of nature illustrated in *The Nature of Explanation* were virtually

[35] See Craik's discussion in Craik, 1966, pp. 12-16. According to MacKay (1952), 'purpose,' like 'directed,' has both a passive and an active sense—and this too has consequences for some of the questions touched on earlier in this chapter. The passive sense of purpose is that of "function," and in this "it can be predicated of almost everything, and its use sometimes leads to confusion, as when pontifical statements are made that *the only purposes a machine can have are the purposes of its designer*" (p. 66 n.). The active sense is that of "intention." This objection was made by the philosopher R.J. Spilsbury, who actually seemed to repeat against MacKay the same objections that Taylor had made against Rosenblueth and Wiener, particularly that about the impossibility of describing as feedback-directed the search for *non-existent* goals See Chapter 7 for further discussion of both these points.

abandoned in *The Mechanism of Human Action*. Craik's attention now concentrated on the "general principles" that justify the use of the 'new' feedback-based machines as simulation models of the performance of organisms. This point seems of particular importance in order to understand Craik's position, and it is also of great interest, because it captures the real novelty of using machines to study behavior, which afterwards became widespread. In fact, the principles that lie at the basis of the organism-machine analogy, rather than the analogy as such, play a central role in the synthetic method. This point had already been stressed in *The Nature of Explanation*:

> It is perhaps better to start with a definite idea as to the kind of tasks mechanism can accomplish in calculation, and the tasks it would have to accomplish in order to play a part in thought, rather than to draw analogies between the nervous system and some specific mechanism such as a telephone exchange and leave the matter there. A telephone exchange may resemble the nervous system in just the sense I think important; *but the essential point is the principle underlying the similarity* (Craik, 1943: 52-53, my italics).

In building a behavioral model, therefore, we cannot limit ourselves to establishing superficial analogies between organism and machine and then "leave the matter there," without worrying about the general principles common to the functioning of the organism and the machine. Craik's criticism of the "various 'robots' which have been specifically designed to imitate living creatures" in *The Mechanism of Human Action* can be explained thus: many of these robots are systems lacking any kind of feedback; others, and among them Craik mentions the robot described by Bradner in 1937, seem to be built according to *ad hoc* principles and are based on "a very arbitrary, and rather unbiological, type of feedback," which has nothing to do with the actual features of animal learning (Craik, 1966: 20-21).

These criticisms suggest that the synthetic method, according to Craik, has no hope of succeeding in explaining the behavior of organisms if it does not take into account the knowledge gained using the analytic method. A reading of *The Mechanism of Human Action*, though not easy given that it is an incomplete text, shows that, in Craik's judgment, once the organism has been described as a control and computing system, in constructing models one must introduce relevant *constraints* so as not to make the simulation *ad hoc*, a mere imitation of exterior behavior traits. The source of constraints for these models is a biological one, and it consists first of all in the study of the nervous structure and functions of organisms. The laws that psychologists derive from the behavior of organisms cannot fail to take this study into account. The synthetic method, therefore, is not an exclusively *molar* approach to behavior, one indifferent to the neurophysiological mechanisms underlying behavior. Rather, the synthetic method *marches side by side* with the study of the organism at the analytic level to identify those mechanical models that are biologically plausible and that take into account, in particular, empirical evidence and hypotheses at the neurophysiological level.

This interpretation of Craik's claim, while doing justice to the functionalism that inspires the synthetic method, for which organisms and machines are realizations of the same "general principles," shows how the introduction of the "engineering statement" in explaining the behavior of organisms did not mean that psychology did not have to take the "physiological statement" into account. This explains the caution with which Craik, even as he was declaring his adherence to the robot approach, referred to some typical hypothetical entities in molar approaches to behavior, i.e. to "psychological entities such as habits, drives, and instincts" (p. 80). This also explains certain of his criticisms of explanations of maze learning based on "generalized descriptions of the macroscopic phenomena of learning" which do not even attempt "to suggest an actual mechanism which would account for the phenomena in terms of physics or physiology" (p. 87).

At various points in *The Mechanism of Human Action* Craik again runs through the attempts on the part of psychologists and neurophysiologists to identify laws and hypotheses that would take into account, in varying degrees, different actual mechanisms of that kind: from the law of use, in which learning is due to a weakening of resistance in nervous connections after repeated stimulation, to Thorndike's law of effect; from the theory of the synapse as an element with variable resistance to various hypotheses on physical-chemical mechanisms for transmitting nervous impulses. The problems and authors that Craik confronts are actually familiar to us from our investigation. In Craik's work, we find the appeal to Spencer and to the equilibration processes; the claim about learning mechanisms as the products of natural selection; McDougall's drainage theory regarding the association mechanisms; the problem of the formation of nervous connections and the inadequacy of mere repetition to explain it (with the usual image of the "river [that] wears itself a channel"); the role of reinforcement, pleasure and pain, of satisfaction and discomfort. We find, in particular, the "dilemma," as Craik puts it, of whether the two classic forms of learning, those of Pavlov and Thorndike, one by conditioned reflex and the other selective, or by trial-and-error, must refer to different explanatory mechanisms, or if they cannot instead be traced back to a single principle.

This is the context in which Craik's interest in learning must be placed. Having rejected the unification of forms of learning supported by Hull, Craik tried to suggest the *different* neurophysiological mechanisms that could be hypothesized as underlying those forms of learning and the *different* functional principles that these mechanisms could share with learning machines. Craik credited Hull with constructing models of conditioned reflex that succeeded in simulating at least some features of the specific neural mechanism that one might suppose was involved in conditioning: the facilitation, for example, by an active S-R connection (provoked by the unconditioned stimulus), of a second active S-R connection (provoked by the conditioned stimulus), in such a way that the stimulation of the latter converges with the response of the former. As an example of Hull's model which worked according to this hypothesis, Craik mentioned an electric circuit that closely resembles that constructed by Krueger and Hull in 1931 (p. 53), which we have described in Chapter 3 (see Plate 3.1).

Unlike these investigations into learning by conditioning, those concerning selective or trial-and-error learning in puzzle boxes and in mazes had been carried out, according to Craik, on a "high or psychological level" (we could say on a molar level): these investigations thus shed little light on the actual neurophysiological mechanisms involved (p. 47). This also came about because of the greater complexity of selective learning, in which the circular process that distinguishes Thorndike's law of effect is present, a process in which the effect of the response feeds back to the stimulus that had provoked it. For Craik, the fairly definite notions used in the conditioning experiments are lost in this case: in a more complex form of learning, such as selective learning, it is necessary to take into account the *consequences* of an action, which become an essential component of the very stimulation conditions.

It is at this point that the synthetic method comes into play: the newly-emerged field of control and computing systems comes to the rescue of psychology. Craik maintained that one possible approach to the study of more complex forms of learning, such as selective learning, was suggested by the examination of some war problems which he had studied, such as 'tracking,' or the activity of a human operator in following a moving object using various controls. In this activity, complex processes are involved, such as, to use Craik's words, "anticipation, prediction, grasping of a problem, calculation of the future," and the new error-actuated machines or servomechanisms were designed precisely to "replace man" in those activities (pp. 47-48).

The engineering statements and the physiological statements of these circular processes seem, then, to refer to a common language. "Thorndike's Law of Effect, and the analogy of 'error-actuated' devices, suggest that we must look for the facilitating or inhibiting agent in the *results* of the first transmission by the sensory-motor arc, that is by the pleasure or pain, other sensations or lack of them, and conduction or non-conduction in other neural pathways, which follow the first action." So it is necessary to go back to "a mechanism for the cyclical action, feedback restoring force, or call it what you will, *which will bridge what is otherwise a gap in our theory of learning and the design of our learning robot*" (p. 83, my italics). Let us see to what extent that would have been possible at the time.

8. Learning and feedback

Craik's attention to a field of research, *avant-garde* in his day, such as that of the new feedback machines came together with his knowledge of traditional issues related to equilibration processes in the organic world, a subject to which we have returned at various points. On the one hand, there are the results of the study of the body's homeostatic mechanisms, of known and hypothesized neurophysiological processes, of pleasure and pain mechanisms; on the other, there are the results of electrical engineering in the field of automatic control machines. All these seem to have suggested to Craik that living organisms and machines could share a tendency to favor the functioning of those "error-actuated" devices in their possession that restore equilibrium.

In the case of the nervous system, Craik shares the connectionist neurological hypothesis, which he translates into the traditional terminology of equilibration processes: the goal to be attained during trial-and-error learning can be considered a *state of equilibrium* of the organism; therefore, the resistance of those nerve connections whose effect is to favor the attainment of that state decreases, while the resistance of the others increases. According to Craik, various factors participate in this process, from hormonal ones to those of pleasure and pain.

In the case of machines, a device for cyclical action or for the restoration of equilibrium comparable to that found in the organism is a feedback device. While Craik remains vague concerning the physiological equilibration mechanisms underlying the law of effect (which is understandable, given the scanty empirical evidence on the subject at the time), he is more exhaustive in discussing the *different* kinds of feedback that could provide a possible foundation for an analogy with the machine.

Simple negative feedback systems, for example, are unable to try another response if the first one does not succeed. In this case, the feedback is simply "quantitative," as Craik called it, given its ability to act only on the *quantity* of the disturbance. Such feedback cannot simulate any form of complex learning, much less one where a change in the *type* of response can be observed following the effect, with the consequent elimination of unsuccessful responses and the fixation of the correct response.[36] It is the correct response that can be viewed as the element that returns the system to a state of equilibrium, which is precisely what happens in Thorndike's selective or trial-and-error learning, as Craik viewed it. To have a machine, therefore, that is capable of learning as a nervous system would, a cyclical action device is needed that acts so as to *modify its own functioning*, thus changing the *type* of response. The machine, that is, has to be provided with what Craik called "qualitative feedback" (p. 17).

Craik was aware that the machines of his day, nothing more than analog computors and automatic control devices, had very rudimentary abilities in simulating flexible forms of learning behavior. In *The Nature of Explanation* Craik reviewed various perceptual and cognitive abilities of organisms so that he could demonstrate that the differences between their performance and that of various electro-mechanical devices and computing machines were differences in degree, not in principle.[37] Moreover, as he observed, even the flexibility of animals and humans in their interaction with the environment has its limits (for example, those imposed by their anatomy or by their more or less limited cognitive ability). "It takes generations of selective evolution," he had concluded, "to modify non-nervous structure, and generations of men to evolve new machines and techniques" (Craik, 1966: 59). Since, therefore, only the future evolution of machines would be able to satisfy the requirement for a machine that could actually learn, Craik held that it might be useful to start exploring the abilities of some existing machines. For example, the construction of an electro-mechanical system that could discriminate between different types of responses, a precondition for selective learning, could take its inspiration, in his view, from automatic telephone exchanges (p. 17).

---

[36] Once more Craik is fully aware of issues that would be dealt with during early cybernetics. "Learning," Wiener would stress, "is a most complicated form of feedback, and influences not merely the *individual action*, but the *pattern of action*" (Wiener, 1950: 69, my italics). See also Walter (1956) for a discussion on learning versus simple feedback devices in organisms and machines.

[37] Craik had not limited himself to analyzing the performance of the new feedback machines; rather, he had considered the most varied analogies between the sensory-motor and computing apparatuses of organisms and machines. For example, with regard to the ability to respond differently to the same stimulation depending on the state in which both organism and machines are found, he had observed: "an animal responds differently to food if it is hungry or satisfied, my typewriter responds differently to pressure on a letter-key according to whether the shift-key is depressed or not" (Craik, 1943: 70). Note that his is the same example Jennings used to illustrate the "parallel conditions" that can be observed in machines and living organisms (see above, pp. 23-24). In the case of the analogy Craik proposed, the *spontaneity* of the change in internal state on which Jennings had insisted did not come into play.

In *The Nature of Explanation*, Craik referred to the telephone exchange as something that could share an important functional principle with the nervous system. The telephone exchange of our day is a familiar and highly evolved device. The one to which Craik referred is rather primitive. It was provided with electromechanical uniselectors that *search* for a free line, *trying* among those that are available, with the *goal* of establishing contact with the specific telephone number requested by the user: the uniselectors pass from one line to the other, and they stop automatically when they find one that is not busy. In *The Mechanism of Human Action* and in other posthumous writings, Craik analyzed the power of qualitative feedback. He described various refinements and various forms of 'memory' which would put the network of connections in a position to improve its own performance over time, thus showing at least some basic features of selective learning and predictive purposeful behavior.

An automatic telephone exchange had already been mentioned by Lotka to exemplify an artifact equipped with a more complex correlating apparatus than that of the mechanical toy beetle (Figure 4.1), precisely because that artifact could make *choices*. Referring to a 1923 telephone exchange, Lotka deemed it one of the most evolved correlating apparatuses of the time, and he pointed out that, being automatic, it "eliminates the 'operator' at the central offices" (Lotka, 1925/1956: 342). This observation explains the growing interest of researchers in automatic control in mechanisms which, as Craik had already said and as Wiener would later say, "usurp" mental functions like calculation and prediction from man: these are not, therefore, simply menial functions as in the mechanisms of earlier times.[38]

It was in early cybernetics that the telephone exchange would become a common subject in discussions about machine learning. In general, the reference model was that of a complex feedback network provided by various memory devices, in which the messages had to be sorted in the most 'expert' way possible by means of various channels or "associative trails." Since the switching mechanism could *control its own activity* so as to make the best choice in relation to external conditions, it would be described as a system equipped with a further or second-order feedback. In teleological terms, it is a feedback system that does not simply *seeks* its goal, but *sets* itself new goals.[39]

---

[38] Wiener (1948/1961: 6), and see above p. 6. These analogies had the purpose of showing how a certain technology could permit the simulation of elementary forms of learning, based on the common principles of which Craik had spoken. They are more exacting analogies than the connectionist ones between nervous connections and telephone lines advanced by Thorndike, Hull and many others, and used by James himself in his *Principles* to introduce the mechanistic hypothesis on associative paths (see above, p. 53). Note that McDougall, in his argument against "mechanistic psychology," had gathered from the most recent mechanical analogies for the functioning of the nervous system the aspect of the elimination of the "intelligent purposive operator," as he put it, by the automatic telephone exchange. He considered it as the elimination of the mental entity which Descartes had left to supervise neurological mechanism in the case of human beings (McDougall, 1923b: 275-276).

[39] Boring stressed the analogy of the telephone exchange with phenomena related to learning when listing the properties of the hypothetical human-like robot (Boring, 1946: 180-181). But see the analyses of this point by the sociologist Deutsch (1951-52) and by the pioneers in operation research Churchman et al. (1957, Chapter 4). Deutsch took the above-mentioned phrase "associative trails" from Bush's article on associative memory, which afterwards enjoyed great popularity (Bush, 1945). Churchman and Ackoff (1950) dealt with Rosenblueth, Wiener and Bigelow's claims in the 1943 article.

This distinction between feedback of different orders brings to mind the point we introduced in Chapter 1, when we distinguished a machine endowed with a single, invariable decision rule from a more complex machine endowed with a set of decision rules.[40] The first machine includes a single feedback loop between sensory apparatus and motor apparatus, a loop that causes a change of state in the machine in the course of *one and the same behavior*. A machine of this kind is capable of responding in a constant manner to a change in its environment; it self-corrects its behavior without changing its internal organization. The second machine includes a further feedback loop, which this time changes the machine's internal organization. The choice of the decision rule has as its effect a *change in behavior*: the machine can *try* various responses to react to a disturbance coming from the environment, and it can *select* the successful response.

Figure 1.4 shows a diagram for a machine of this kind, one which Ashby defined as a "little ultrastable system" (Ashby, 1952/1960). The first feedback loop in such a system, that between the sensory apparatus and the motor apparatus, functions continuously and quickly: the sensory-input parameters vary almost continuously. The second loop, however, functions intermittently and rather slowly: it goes from the environment to the essential variables which influence some parameters which change only from trial to trial. We can identify this latter as a kind of second-order feedback loop.

Ashby maintained that it was this feedback that made the system *ultrastable*, i.e. at the same time automatic, or mechanical, and selective, or capable of spontaneous changes (p. 134). He described a machine, the well-known "homeostat," which functioned according to the principle of ultrastability. The homeostat persists in its action *until* it succeeds in eliminating a disturbance from the environment, thus exhibiting the objective mark of behavior that Tolman defined as teleological.[41] Even before introducing the homeostat, and using a different terminology, Ashby had concluded that a machine of this new kind, i.e. able to change its organization, shows how adaptation by trial-and-error, at least in its simplest forms, "is in no way special to living things, [...] it is an elementary and fundamental property of matter" (Ashby, 1945: 13). In other words, the new machine reduces the oft-theorized distance between *organic* and *inorganic* systems.

In the cybernetic era, the ultrastability of the homeostat was considered significant with respect to the stability of simple feedback mechanisms precisely because it simulated some features of the variability and spontaneity of responses that are typical of animal behavior (see for example Sluckin, 1954). The ability to vary these responses lies, in fact, at the core of a machine that learns or that acquires new habits, that is, one which not only changes its own behavior, but improves it over time by reducing, for example, the number of errors.

In our investigation into the discovery of the artificial, we have seen that, in many

---

[40] See also Apter (1970, Chapter 4) for an insightful discussion.

[41] The homeostat had already been described by Ashby earlier (Ashby, 1948). The homeostat, and more generally the notion of homeostasis, gave rise to various discussions among psychologists in the 1950s: for further details see Cordeschi (1988). Mowrer (1960a; 1960b) investigated the relationships that ultrastability and other cybernetic notions had with earlier learning theories, both Thorndike's and Hull's connectionist ones and Tolman's 'cognitive' one. A similar aim was that of George (1961). Regarding the influence exerted by cybernetic concepts in the field of biological regulation, see, for example, Hassenstein (1970).

analyses of animal behavior, the opposition between *automatism*, or rigidity, and *plasticity*, or the ability to make choices, had been described in terms of control mechanisms that are not only different from each other but also incompatible. The conclusion had been that *automatic* and *selective* are mutually exclusive, and that an *intelligent automatism* was "a contradiction in terms." Conversely, some artifacts, from the days of the robot approach to the dawn of cybernetics, seemed to manifest some simple behaviors that were *both* automatic and selective. Craik's qualitative feedback and Ashby's ultrastability, introduced to simulate through machines behaviors of this sort, are notions that have to be placed within the tortuous process of clarifying the concepts of adaptation, automatism and control in living organisms and in machines.

CHAPTER 5

CYBERNETICS AND THE ORIGINS OF ARTIFICIAL INTELLIGENCE

1. Introduction. The turning point

In the previous chapters we identified various stages in the discovery of a novel strategy in the study of mind and behavior, suggested by 'new' notions of the machine. More than once we alluded to cybernetics, especially in Chapter 4. We mentioned there claims made by Rosenblueth, Wiener and Bigelow in their 1943 paper, emphasizing the role that began to be attributed to feedback in the study of various aspects of organism behavior. That paper is usually considered the manifesto of what Wiener called cybernetics, i.e. the study of "control and communication in the animal and the machine" (Wiener, 1948/1961).

But "Behavior, Purpose, and Teleology" was not an isolated herald of cybernetics. In 1943, Craik published *The Nature of Explanation*, and in the same year Warren McCulloch and Walter Pitts published a memorable article that would deeply influence both cybernetics and computer science (McCulloch and Pitts, 1943). "Certain ideas were in the air," was Seymour Papert's comment (Papert, 1968: 136). This is even clearer if one considers Ashby's 1940 article mentioned earlier and, in a different context, Jean Piaget's analysis of equilibration processes (Piaget, 1941), which broadly anticipated the concepts and methods of cybernetics, whose terminology Piaget was later to adopt.

As McCulloch would later recall, at that time he and Pitts were unaware of the results that Claude Shannon had already published (Shannon, 1938). And yet, McCulloch and Pitts applied the same tool used by Shannon, Boolean algebra, to investigate a quite different domain. They introduced networks consisting of "formal" neurons, simplified analogs of the neurons in the brain, functioning according to the all-or-nothing law (a neuron does or does not fire according to whether the intensity of the impulses it receives does or does not reach a certain threshold), whereas Shannon modeled the components of electric circuits, functioning according to a similar law (a relay closes or opens according to whether the current does or does not reach a certain intensity). Shannon's work would prove decisive in designing the circuits of digital computers. Though they knew nothing of Shannon's work, McCulloch and Pitts were perfectly aware of Alan Turing's. In 1936, Turing introduced the abstract computing machines that bear his name, and explicitly construed a universal machine which could simulate, with appropriate encoding, any computation carried out by any Turing machine (including, of course, the universal one) (Turing, 1936-37). These Turing machines came to be considered as the more general abstract model of every physically realized general-purpose digital computer. McCulloch and Pitts concluded that every net of formal neurons, if furnished with a tape and suitable input, output and scanning systems, is equivalent to a Turing machine (McCulloch and Pitts, 1943: 132).

From the early 1940s through to the mid-1950s, many other events signaled a turning point in the very understanding of the concept of machine, in the construction of actual machines and in man-machine interaction. Let us briefly consider some of those events.[1]

In 1941 Konrad Zuse built the Z3 electro-mechanical digital computer in Germany, and in 1944 Howard Aiken built another, the Mark I, in the United States. Research on wartime applications of computers was funded by generous as well as self-serving grants, and was repaid by rapid advances. While the defeat of Germany interrupted Zuse's work, in England and the United States the realization of large digital computers was relentlessly pursued, through the mobilization of extraordinary talents and resources. Already in 1943 the COLOSSUS computers, used to break German military codes, were functioning in England. Though these machines were dedicated to performing this kind of task, they were more evolved than the aforementioned computers—they were, among other things, completely electronic, i.e. with vacuum tubes replacing the electro-mechanical relays. This technological progress would make data processing really fast for the first time, leading to so-called first-generation computers. As they were blanketed by the strictest military secrecy, it was only from the mid-1970s that one began to learn about the characteristics of these machines, designed and built by a group headed by the mathematician Max Newman, and including I.J. Good and Donald Michie. Turing himself contributed to breaking the code of the legendary German machine ENIGMA. In the second half of the1940s, he would participate in two different projects for large computers: ACE (Automatic Computing Engine) at Teddington and MADM (Manchester Automatic Digital Machine) at Manchester.

In the United States, the construction of an electronic computer was completed in 1946. Its designers, J. Presper Eckert and John Mauchly, from the University of Pennsylvania, called it the Electronic Numerical Integrator and Calculator, or ENIAC. It was the largest computer ever built, and it is usually considered the first general-purpose computer. It was precisely within the ENIAC group that one of the most decisive events of these turning-point years came about. One of the consultants to the ENIAC project was John von Neumann. Few texts are as famous in the history of computer science as the *First Draft*, written by von Neumann in 1945. There, adopting McCulloch and Pitts' symbolism, he described the architecture of a newly-conceived general-purpose computer, which would remain basically unchanged over the years to come. Not only were data stored in its main memory; instructions to handle data, or programs, were stored there, too, and thus became as readily modifiable as the data themselves. The first large stored-program general-purpose computer, however, was built in Cambridge, England, by a group headed by Maurice Wilkes at the Mathematical Laboratory: in 1949 they completed the EDSAC (Electronic Delay Storage Automatic Calculator). In the United States, a stored-program general-purpose computer, the EDVAC (Electronic Discrete Variable Automatic Computer), was completed, on the design of von Neumann and others, in 1951.

Between 1954 and 1955, the first programming languages were introduced. After the Turing machine and von Neumann's architecture, they are, according to Allen Newell and

---

[1] For events, characters and texts in the history of computer science that are mentioned below, see Goldstine (1981), Hodges (1983), Metropolis et al. (1980), Randell (1973). See also the web site http://vlmp.museophile.com/computing.html.

Herbert Simon, the third crucial milestone in the history of computer science as it progressed towards AI (Newell e Simon, 1976). This new discipline, officially launched at the now celebrated Dartmouth seminar in 1956, aimed at reproducing by means of computer programs behaviors that, if observed in human beings, would be considered 'intelligent.'

The themes that will be dealt with in the main body of this chapter can be traced back to these turning-point years. First of all, we examine some artifacts of cybernetic robotics, attempting to identify their engineering significance, since they embody automatic control and electronic principles, and their theoretical significance, since they seem to embody some of the principles of the behavior of living organisms as well. This twofold source of interest, as we will see, remains a constant in the history of artificial modeling up to our day. Then, after isolating some stages in the ongoing influence of information-processing concepts over the psychology of the early 1950s, we will follow the coming of age of the 'intelligent' computer up to the first appearances of AI and of what Newell and Simon called Information Processing Psychology. Our chief goal, in this and the next chapter, is to emphasize, together with the radical novelties, the elements that these investigations share with certain experiments, methodological perspectives and philosophical assumptions whose discussion occupied us in the previous chapters.

2. Cybernetic robotics

The technology underlying Hammond and Miessner's automaton, the phototropic dog Seleno whose performance had so struck Loeb, was exploited for wartime applications during the First World Word.[2] The circumstances surrounding some of the best-known cybernetic synthetic animals was no different. Notwithstanding the toy-like character of Grey Walter's *Machina speculatrix*, or "tortoise," one should not forget that two of its main characteristics, negative feedback and scanning, were at the center of experimentation that matured in the context of the Second World War. The first exemplars of the *Machina speculatrix* were implemented towards the end of the 1940s at Bristol, where Grey Walter worked in the Physiology Department of the Burden Neurological Institute. The tortoises were undoubtedly the most popular cybernetic robots, and were exhibited on several occasions (Walter, 1950; 1951).[3]

The *Machina speculatrix* shared with other robots of the period the appearance of a three-wheeled cart. The front wheel was both for propulsion and for steering. Furnished with a photoelectric cell (its first sensor) mounted on the cart, the machine manifested a form of positive tropism. In the dark it explored its surroundings by circular movements, but quickly headed towards any light source striking its photoelectric cell. The variable behavior of this machine depended on the combined operation of two motors (the circuit in Plate 5.1 accounts for such operation). Unlike Hammond and Miessner's phototropic

---

[2] See Chapter 1, pp. 5-6. There are reports of similar automata presented at Paris in 1929 and at New York in 1939 (de Latil, 1953: 266). Devices exemplified by these artifacts, mounted on torpedoes, were used by Germans against Allied ships during the Second World War (Nemes, 1969: 164).

[3] An exemplar has been restored by Owen Holland (see the web page of the Intelligent Autonomous Systems Engineering Laboratory of Bristol at http://www.uwe.ac.uk./facults/eng/ias).

Plate 5.1

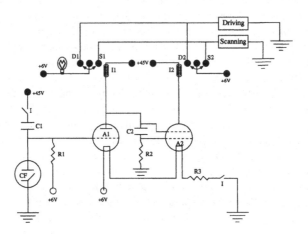

In this simplified circuit diagram of Grey Walter's *Machina speculatrix* there are two distinct electrical circuits. The upper circuit feeds the two motors D (DRIVING) and S (SCANNING), which are activated by the double-throw circuit breakers of electromagnetic relays R1 and R2. The lower circuit controls the opening and closing of the two relays. This second circuit consists of two amplifiers, A1 and A2, activating relays R1 and R2. When A1 is conducting, relay R1 is closed; when A2 is conducting, R2 is closed.

The conductivity of amplifier A1 depends on the voltage present on its control grid. If it is greater than zero, A1 conducts; if, instead, it is close to or less than zero, A1 is cut off. To the grid are connected the resistance R1 and the photoelectric cell CF. In the dark, the photoelectric cell CF does not conduct, and the grid is polarized through R1, resting at a positive voltage. In the presence of light, CF conducts, the grid voltage goes down towards zero and A1 is cut off.

The conductivity of A2, on the other hand, depends both on the conductivity of A1 and on the R2-C2 circuit. Let us suppose that A1 is conducting: in this case C2 and the screen grid of A2 have a low positive voltage (~10 V), while on the control grid the voltage is zero, since R2 is connected to ground. Therefore, A2 conducts. If, in this phase, A1 stops conducting because light impinges on CF, then the voltage on C2 rises to ~45 V, and A2 keeps conducting. If, afterwards, A1 resumes conducting, then the voltage on C2 returns to ~10 V, but since the capacitator was charged earlier at 45 V, it now applies a negative pulse to the control grid of A2 while discharging through R2. During this discharge, A2 will be cut off (the control voltage will slowly rise from −35 V to 0 V). When the discharge is finished, A2 will start conducting again.

Finally, depending on the position of the relays, the machine exhibits different behaviors. For example, when the machine finds itself in the dark, the amplifiers A1 and A2 conduct, with the effect of closing the contacts S1 and D2, and the machine *goes forward* and *steers*. If the machine encounters a light, A1 stops conducting and R1 closes on D1, causing the machine to go *forward* without steering because contact D2 is active. If, during this movement, the machine once again finds itself in the dark, A1 starts conducting again and S1 closes once more, while A2, for a period of time t=~R2C2, is cut off, thus closing S2, and hence the machine *steers* without progressing. After the discharge, A2 starts conducting again and, therefore, again switching from S2 to D2, so that the machine *goes forward* and *steers*.

machine, Grey Walter's moved away from light, if the latter was too intense or bright, and stopped at a certain distance from it, thereby avoiding the fate of the moth in the candle, as Grey Walter remarked in his popular book, *The Living Brain* (Walter, 1953: 84). Furthermore, if placed before two lights of the same intensity, the machine did not show any sign of 'neurosis,' to use the term which, in the days of the robot approach, Ellson had used to describe certain behaviors of his learning model (Plate 3.4). Thanks to its scanning device, the machine went first towards one and then towards the other light source. If it bumped against an obstacle, a mechanical switch (its second sensor) detected the jolt and inserted a condenser between the output and the input of its central amplifier. It thus became an oscillator, suppressing its phototropic and scanning behaviors and giving way to a backward-forward and left-right movement that in the end enabled the machine to dodge the obstacle with a reasonable rate of success.

Much like Ellson's model, the machine reserved some surprises for its designer, as it produced a piece of behavior that had not been explicitly foreseen. For example, the tortoises manifested "self-recognition" (in front of a mirror) and "mutual recognition" (when two exemplars met each other), and these abilities were discovered accidentally, because a pilot-light mounted on each machine turned on to indicate when the steering-servo was in operation. Recalling the wartime applications of phototropic feedback devices, Grey Walter noted that the machine could be transformed into a self-directing missile, with some simple modifications and by inserting a second photoelectric cell (p. 202). In other words, the tortoise would lose its interesting exploratory abilities, and behave like Hammond and Miessner's phototropic dog.

Grey Walter was profuse in his use of psychological terms when he described his machine as "spontaneous," "purposeful," "independent" and able to "recognize" itself and other individuals of the same species, as well as to exhibit a food-searching instinct (it automatically went towards its 'nest' to recharge its batteries when they were about to run out). He admitted that all this could be seen as nothing but a series of tricks; nonetheless, an outside observer, let us say a biologist, would have used just this mentalistic terminology had he witnessed this behavior in real animals. In fact, Grey Walter pressed on to emphasize the fact that behaviors so close to those of a living organism had been obtained with a *minimal* number of units corresponding to nerve cells. In his robots there were two miniature valves, two relays, two sensors, one light-sensitive and the other touch-sensitive, and two effectors. The latter were the two small electric motors which enabled the machine to go forward and to steer, respectively.

The machine's circuitry did not include a true form of memory, except for a delay of about one second in returning the central circuit from its oscillator configuration, which allowed it to escape obstacles, to that of the amplifier, with which its tropistic and exploratory behavior resumed. What really mattered was the presence of a feedback loop in which the environment was one of the two components, the other being the machine. As for its memory characteristics, Grey Walter observed, his "two-element synthetic animals" were not, therefore, comparable with Ross' 1935 robot rat, which was equipped with a "memory disk" (see Figure 3.4). He then designed a more refined electrical circuit, with which his synthetic animals would have been able to 'remember' and 'forget.'

This so-called *Machina docilis*, besides having the 'sight' and 'touch' of the *Machina speculatrix*, was equipped with a small microphone, which corresponded to 'hearing,' and it could manifest a simple form of learning by conditioning to an auditory stimulus.

In *The Living Brain*, Grey Walter emphasized the differences between his tortoises and other existing electro-mechanical robots. He recalled Ross' robot rat of the 1930s, as well as the more recent robots of Shannon and R.A. Wallace, and Ashby's homeostat. While his robots were able to move about freely in their surroundings, Ross' and Wallace's moved along rails; Shannon's could only move in a maze, and Ashby's homeostat simply tended to restore equilibrium, without manifesting any motor activity in a real environment (pp. 80-81).

The homeostat, the machine that gave rise to ultrastability, a notion we have mentioned several times, simulated a process of adaptation by random selection.[4] Shannon had designed two robots which seemed to exemplify an evolutionary development of the primitive robots Ross had built fifteen years earlier. The first was a sort of moving mechanical finger that 'learned' to reach its goal by touching the walls of a maze. Shannon described its characteristics at the Macy Conference on Cybernetics in 1951. This was the eighth of ten extraordinary interdisciplinary meetings held between 1946 and 1953 around Wiener's cybernetic project. Some of the best talents in the most diverse fields of research, from mathematics to computer science, from biology to psychology and other human sciences, attended these meetings. Plate 5.2 reproduces the design of Shannon's machine (Shannon, 1951). With respect to Ross' 1935 mechanical finger (Figure 3.5), Shannon's description shows the development achieved by the design of commutation and control circuits, which allow for more complex behaviors in the machine, including the ability to 'learn' a large number of mazes.

This is equally evident in Shannon's second machine, where he replaced the finger with a mobile object that explored a maze similar to the first one. This is the electro-mechanical mouse that Grey Walter mentioned, just a two-inch bar magnet on which three wheels were mounted. It was moved by an electromagnet placed under the metal floor of the maze. Operated by small motors, the electromagnet dragged the mouse around; the latter, by getting ahead in the maze or running into its walls, caused the electromagnet to move in the various possible directions in a way akin to the action of the mechanical finger in the maze in Plate 5.2. Indeed, the operation of these two machines is controlled in the same way. A circuit composed of two sets of forty and fifty electric relays respectively was housed underneath the floor of the maze: the first set controlled the sequence of the mouse's movements, the second recorded them. In brief, the two sets of relays were organized as the control unit and the memory unit of a digital computer, respectively.[5]

Wallace (1952) used similar control and memory principles to build another mechanical maze-learner mentioned by Grey Walter. Wallace referred to Ross as the first who had tried experiments of this kind. This machine was a cart approximately thirteen inches long and four inches wide, moving along a rail equipped with switches, which

[4] A more elementary machine devised by Ashby consisted of a circuit equipped with selectors bringing about a simple conditioned reflex (Ashby, 1950).

[5] A short description of this device can be found in the June 1952 issue of *Electrical Engineering*, pp.671-672.

Plate 5.2

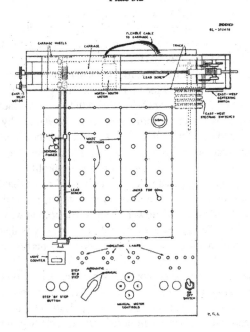

Shannon's maze-solver machine (from Shannon, 1951) took the form of a panel, on which was placed a maze of 5x5 squares, the sides of which can be left open or closed in different ways by means of movable barriers. In this way, different mazes can be obtained (the machine is seen from above in the figure, and various switches and indicator lights are shown in the lower section of the panel).

The "sensing finger," anchored to a cart which can be seen in the upper section of the panel, can be moved by two motors in four directions: to the right and to the left by the first motor, forward and backward by the second. When placed at the starting point for the first time, the finger begins to explore all the squares systematically in the following way. Going to the center of each square, it moves consecutively in each of the four allowed directions until it bumps against a wall, and then resumes its movement in a different direction or moves on to another square. Proceeding in this way, it reaches the goal, consisting of a pre-established square in the maze and recognized as such by the circuit. Each square of the maze is associated with a pair of relays, which can memorize one of the four possible directions. The direction that is remembered is the one used by the finger to leave the square the last time it visited that square. This is the "exploration strategy," as Shannon put it. When the finger reaches its goal, the motor turns off, a lamp mounted on it lights up and a bell rings. At the same time, a relay operates and locks in, and from then on the machine operates by following the "goal strategy": if brought to the starting point manually, the finger moves, avoiding the blind alleys of the maze, until it reaches the goal. Thus it follows the path it had memorized on the basis of cues concerning the exit from each individual square previously visited.

The machine is capable of other performances. For example, if the finger is placed in a part of the maze it has not yet explored, it fumbles around until it reaches a known region, and from that point on follows the path that will take it to the goal.

formed a branching maze with two paths at each choice point and six levels of branching. Its receptors signaled the starting position, the choice points, the dead-ends and the goal, while the effectors included a motor, the commands to operate the switches (to turn right and left), and a reverse function to pull back from a dead-end. Its 'brain' consisted of a small digital computer, which included a control unit and a memory. In the control unit, ten relays, by operating the switches and the reverse function, directed the cart in the different possible directions (forward, backward, right and left). The memory was composed of six relays, which allowed the machine to 'remember' the paths taken to reach the goal, which consisted of one of the final branches at the sixth level. The machine systematically explored the maze (it is not clear from the description whether by a depth-first or a breadth-first search), halting at the goal. In a subsequent trial, the machine headed directly for the goal. Unlike Shannon's machine, it was able to remember one maze only.

The mechanical maze-learners belong to a relatively prolific species. We will just mention two of them. The first was an electro-mechanical robot that learned relatively complex mazes. It was equipped with a memory disk which, according to its designer, was similar to that of Ross' robot rat (Howard, 1953). The second was built in Vienna by Eier and Zemanek (1960). Perhaps even more prolific were Grey Walter's tortoises. Their descendants had refinements involving both sensory-motor performance and a control unit and memory.

An early such descendant is the phototropic robot Squee, built by Edmund Berkeley and some of his collaborators between 1950 and 1951, and exhibited on various occasions. It was able to distinguish between steady and pulsating light sources, and to perform the following activities: *search* the floor for 'nuts' (in reality golf balls), which were illuminated by the steady light source; *head*, after collecting them with a spoon-like tool, towards the pulsating light source, located in its 'nest'; *deposit* the nuts in the nest, and then resume its search, attracted by the steady light source (Berkeley, 1951; 1952). The functioning of the robot was based on electric circuits of various degrees of complexity. Indeed, according to Berkeley himself, this was its most significant feature: the 'perceptual' and 'reasoning' abilities of the robot had been obtained using electric circuits fulfilling the rules of Boolean algebra, in the spirit of Shannon's 1938 work (Berkeley, 1959: 23).[6] Plate 5.3 describes a particularly simple Boolean circuit, involved in the association between light perception and movements (the robot's ability to discriminate between different light sources is not included) (Berkeley, 1952: 57).

The accurate amateur presentation of Timothy, another phototropic robot, suggests how the activity of building such synthetic animals was turning into a smart hobby (Kubanoff, 1953).[7] Timothy followed a light source until its batteries ran low and put it into a 'hungry' state: it then changed behavior, becoming sensitive to a second light

---

[6] For a first introduction to the Boolean logic machines of the period, see Gardner (1982). Some of them are described in the book by Nemes (1969). Completely different in nature was the small electric computer built by Berkeley to exemplify the functioning of the so-called "giant artificial brains," the first vacuum tube computers. It is described in a series of articles: see, for example, Berkeley and Jensen (1950). *Giant Brains or Machines That Think* was the title of one of the books Berkeley dedicated to this subject (Berkeley, 1949).

[7] The author explained: "Tim was originally constructed as a toy for my daughter but finally emerged as a full-fledged problem in cybernetics" (p. 35).

Plate 5.3

The 'sensations' of Berkeley's robot Squee, which influence its movements, are provided by its two photoelectric cells, which correspond to its right and left eyes. So, let R equal the truth value of 'Squee's right eye sees light,' and let L equal the truth value of 'Squee's left eye sees light.' Squee's behaviors can be described as follows: 'Squee is steering clockwise,' 'Squee is steering counterclockwise' and 'Squee is not steering,' with C, U, N equaling their respective truth values.

The problem is this: how does Squee behave in one of these three ways based on its sensations? There are four possible cases: neither of Squee's eyes sees light; only Squee's left eye sees light; only Squee's right eye sees light; or both of Squee's eyes see light. This is summarized in the following table:

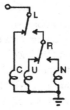

Case	R	L	C	U	N
1	0	0	1	0	0
2	0	1	0	1	0
3	1	0	1	0	0
4	1	1	0	0	1

(for example, in Case 4, both of Squee's eyes see light; therefore, Squee does not steer in any direction but heads straight for the light). We have, then, by applying the rules of Boolean algebra (where '$-$'stands for 'not,' '$\cdot$' stands for 'and,' and '$\vee$' stands for 'or'):

$$C = -R \cdot -L \vee R \cdot -L = -L$$
$$U = -R \cdot L$$
$$N = R \cdot L.$$

In other words: (a) Squee steers clockwise when the left eye does not see light; (b) Squee steers counterclockwise when the left eye sees light but the right eye does not see light; (c) Squee does not steer at all when both eyes see light. If we suppose that C, U and N correspond to an equal number of relays, then the circuit diagram of Squee's behavior is that reproduced next to the table. (From Berkeley, 1951)

source, flashing at a certain rate, which came from a 'nest' whose position had been memorized beforehand. It went to this nest, where it recharged its battery. The robot exhibited various behaviors evoking those of an animal. For example, if the flash rate and its duration were changed, the robot, after some 'hesitation,' was able to 'adapt' to the new situation.

Another machine inspired by Grey Walter's robotics is *Machina versatilis*, of which two different examples were built in the United States in 1956 (Sutherland, Mugglin and Sutherland, 1958). Its designers stressed that the machine's simplest behaviors strictly reproduced the tropistic behaviors described by Loeb. However, a more interesting performance resulted from a circuit designed to simulate the behavioral unpredictability that characterizes learning in the presence of a choice between mutually exclusive alternatives, when this choice presents an element of randomness. The "learning probability circuit" of *Machina versatilis* exploits a feature of neon tubes: their ignition voltage, in addition to a marked hysteresis, presents a degree of randomness, because the starting of the discharge depends on the fluctuations in the state of ionization of the gas in the lamps.[8] Three of these lamps are inserted in the circuit, only one of which can remain lit at any given time. The voltage change at the lamp terminals, due to the discharge of the condensers, can cause one of the two lamps that are off to be turned on and the one that is on to be turned off. The lamps, which reproduce in the circuit the various opposite responses of an organism, turn on alternatively at random, and the probability that each might stay on longer, thus representing the chosen response, is regulated by the discharge current through the condenser and their resistors. These resistors are, in fact, thermistors around which heating wires are wound. The ensuing change in the resistance value of the thermistors brings about learning in a probabilistic way.

The three authors observed that Shannon's mouse did not manifest any behavior of this sort, because it 'learned' its task after just one cycle of attempts, without committing any errors thereafter (Wallace's robot did the same). As we saw in Chapter 3, it was this kind of criticism of robots like Ross' that prompted Bradner to design a maze-learner that 'learned' by trial-and-error (Plate 3.7). It is worth noting that the authors were especially interested in developing communication processes that could be established within a "society of [...] mechanical animals." Their aim was to reproduce some "cooperation or analogous group behavior" more complex than the mutual recognition of which Grey Walter's tortoises were capable—some game-playing behavior, for example (Sutherland et al., 1958: 7). This is perhaps the first time in the discovery of the artificial that anyone expressed an intention to create social or cooperating behavior among real robots.

Synthetic animals spread all around the world: various examples were built in Austria, France, Hungary and the Soviet Union, some of which are described by Nemes (1969).[9] Other ingenious models were the fruit of the collaboration between the Hungarian A.J. Angyan and a Viennese research group. Of these Viennese models, Nemes describes only the least innovative, a tortoise differing from Grey Walter's mostly in that transistors replaced vacuum tubes.[10] In a 1961 work, however, the Viennese researchers described five tortoises, endowed with circuits of increasing complexity: two were just like Grey Walter's, and three novel ones exhibited more complex behaviors. This group of three included the *Machina reproducatrix*, built in Hungary in 1955. It was displayed by Angyan at the famous Teddington Symposium in 1958 (see Angyan, 1959). Responding to one light stimulus and two acoustic stimuli, this machine manifested various aspects of conditioning, from stimulus generalization and discrimination to extinction, in addition to habituation phenomena. The second new tortoise was the *Machina combinatrix*, resulting from

[8] In a simpler form the properties of neon tubes were used many years earlier to reproduce, among other things, the phenomenon of inhibition in a circuit where two lamps were inserted and switching one on caused the other to be turned off (Richardson, 1930).

[9] These included a phototropic robot built in Hungary in 1950. An artificial "protozoon" described by Nemes goes back instead to 1920.

[10] This model was presented by Heinz Zemanek at the first Cybernetics Congress at Namur in 1956. He also described a homeostat built in Vienna (Zemanek, 1958). At the same Congress, Silvio Ceccato introduced Adamo II (Ceccato, 1958), a mechanical model simulating some mental operations. It was completed at Milan in 1956, in collaboration with Enrico Maretti (Maretti, 1957). See also footnote 16.

a series of learning experiments in Vienna, both on living animals and on the earlier tortoise of Angyan. This second tortoise was able to learn by combining two conditioned reflexes. One of its modified versions was the third new robot (Zemanek et al., 1961).

3. Mechanical models and theories of behavior

As the very appearance of the robots we have mentioned suggests (some of them are reproduced in Figure 5.1), none of them was designed to mimic the outward appearances of living animals. The designers of the *Machina versatilis* emphasized this explicitly, referring to the mechanical toy-beetle described by Lotka, which managed not to fall off the table on which it moved (Figure 4.2). "The important thing," they concluded, "is not whether it looks like a beetle [...], but rather that we have here a mechanism with a built-in 'instinct' for self-preservation in a hostile environment" (Sutherland et al., 1958: 7). On his part, Wallace thought that, with his maze-learner, he had made a contribution to an explanation of learning characteristics in the spirit of Wiener's cybernetics (Wallace, 1952: 121). Many of these robots, however, mimicked animal behaviors without illuminating the underlying functional principles that could justify the analogy between an organism and a machine. For this reason, those who were more concerned with the theoretical aspects of simulation considered such robots as mere byproducts of the cybernetic enterprise.

Dennis Gabor, for example, rejected the idea that good models of learning might be found either in the "too trivial" behaviorist models of the conditioned reflex (Gabor, 1956: 5) or in Shannon's electro-mechanical mouse, which "appears to learn from experience, but in reality it is the maze which remembers, not the mouse" (p. 3)[11]. Gordon Pask's negative judgment was more careful: almost all cybernetic robots, and especially maze-learners, merely imitate *responses* of organisms, without embodying *functional principles* common to organisms and machines. Only one machine, the homeostat, was clearly significant according to Pask. Notwithstanding its evident limitations, it pointed to the right level of abstraction for cybernetic modeling, since ultrastability, in its essential features, is an organizing principle that Ashby recognized in both brain and machine (Pask, 1961: 17). These criticisms rehearse in some respects those that Craik had leveled against Bradner's mechanical maze-learner and other robots of his day: these machines had been built without taking into account "general principles," as Craik put it, that must inspire the construction of models.

In fact, the interest that some pioneers of cybernetics and control theory had in certain simple artifacts lay in the practical applications that they exemplified in miniature, so to speak. In short, these projects were more engineering than psychology lab experiments. This is especially evident in the case of Shannon: working at that time as a mathematician for the Bell Telephone Laboratories, he had used for his maze relays tried out on telephone switchboards.

[11] Gabor does not mention a particular example of behaviorist models, but he gives an electrical circuit diagram that resembles those we have examined, especially in Chapter 3. In opposition to the behaviorist models, he offers as "a new stage in the understanding of conditioned reflexes and of association in general" the models of Wilfried Taylor, which we will touch on below (see Chapter 6, section 1).

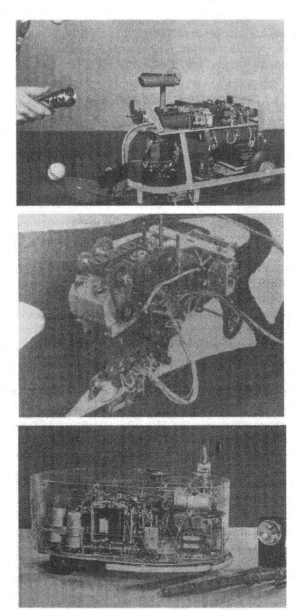

Fig. 5.1. Robots from the 1950s. Above: the phototropic robot Squee of Edmund Berkeley, which gathered
golf balls (from Berkeley, 1951); the *Mechano trolley* of Alfred Uttley, connected to a computer based
on conditional probability (see Chapter 6) (from Andrew, 1958); the *Machina reproducatrix* of A.J. Angyan,
which can be 'conditioned' to different luminous and acoustic stimuli (from Angyan, 1959).

In other cases, an interest in these simple devices grew out of the opportunity to explore the principles of automatic control in general, and negative feedback in particular. In tortoises and other robots we mentioned above, there was experimentation with automatic control principles within the framework provided by the early developments in electronics (see Plate 5.4). And sometimes there was no lack of surprises, as the potential developments in this field were only beginning to be glimpsed. It is instructive in this regard to read Shannon's presentation of his maze-learner at the 1951 Macy Conference on Cybernetics. He was frequently interrupted by questions and observations from surprised and curious listeners of the caliber of Bigelow, MacKay, McCulloch, Margaret Mead, Pitts, and Rosenblueth, to mention only a few. What aroused their interest, just as in the case of Grey Walter's tortoises, was precisely the extreme simplicity of the device

---

Plate 5.4

Electrical engineering and electronics

The cybernetic machines designed by Grey Walter and other robot builders of the time should be placed within the context of the development of electronics, characterized by the advent of the so-called active components: first vacuum tubes, then semiconductors, such as transistors and, at present, integrated circuits.

At its beginning in the 1930s, electronics was sometimes designated the low-current part of electrical engineering, to set it apart from the technology of large electric machines, which were considered high-current. This distinction, based on current intensity or on the power involved, now appears to be of secondary importance compared to the really innovative phenomenon that characterizes electronics, i.e. the *control* of electric quantities by other electric quantities. Before the advent of active components it was possible to control one current with another only by means of electro-mechanical relays. The electrical machines that we have examined in previous chapters for the most part use relays as their central components. Such relays had extremely important applications in the sectors we have mentioned, such as telephone exchanges and the control and memory units of the first digital computers, as well as in some cybernetic artifacts, such as those designed by Shannon. Nevertheless, their performance remained quite limited.

Vacuum tubes made it possible, for the first time, to distinguish between the *signal*, consisting of low current, or information, and the *action*, represented by high current, or energy or motion. At first glance, it seemed that the simplicity and flexibility of the way the tubes worked were due to the gradual, or analog, behavior of these devices as compared to electro-mechanical digital relays. It is not, however, so much the distinction between the analog and the digital that helps us to understand the importance of tubes as control devices compared to relays, as a kind of *universality* that characterizes active components in general. Despite efforts to achieve a high level of standardization, by far the great majority of the pieces used in mechanical or electro-mechanical assembly must be designed *ad hoc*, starting from materials that are not very structured. Furthermore, the control of one mechanical quantity by another is, as a rule, complicated and specific to a given mechanism (one thinks, for example, of a pendulum). In the context of electronics, however, tubes or transistors, resistors, capacitors, inductors and power sources are the *sole* elementary components, with which it is possible to build almost all electronic control and communication systems.

reproducing complex and theoretically elusive phenomena involving memory, learning, and the ability to integrate various sensations. This explains Grey Walter's approach, which might seem naive today, of presenting his robots as suggestive of the complexity of life. In fact, compared with other mobile robot designers, Grey Walter was more attracted by the idea that these machines embodied a theoretical hypothesis: what explains behavior of a certain complexity is not so much the number of the base units as the wealth of their connections.

The fact that machines were more stringently used for testing theoretical hypotheses was particularly evident in some of the models and robots designed by engineers and psychologists in the 1950s.

As a development stemming from his previous studies with Rosenblueth and Bigelow, Wiener raised the problem of explaining the tremor of subjects affected by Parkinson's disease. This tremor differs from intention tremor, a pathology resulting from an injury to the cerebellum, present in voluntary or purposeful behavior, which the three authors had interpreted as a malfunction of the negative feedback discussed in Chapter 4. For example, intention tremor prevents a patient from bringing a glass to his mouth and drinking from it. On the contrary, the tremor caused by Parkinson's disease can manifest itself at rest, in a condition known as the shaking palsy of old men: indeed, if the patient tries to perform a well-defined task, so that there is a purpose, the tremor from Parkinson's disease tends to disappear. This tremor had been construed as the result of a second, so-called "postural," feedback. Therefore, what is manifested in both cases is feedback which is excessive, giving rise to oscillations in behavior. But, and this was the hypothesis endorsed by Wiener, the tendency to amplify excessively, caused by the postural feedback of Parkinson's disease, was countered by voluntary feedback, which was able to bring the postural feedback back out of the zone where oscillations were triggered.

Wiener suggested the possibility of embodying this principle in a machine, so that a "demonstration apparatus which would act according to our theories" would be available, as he said in his popular book *The Human Use of Human Beings* (Wiener, 1950: 191), where a machine of the sort is described. This is a simple robot, built by Henry Singleton, a small car moved by a motor, with two driving wheels in the rear and a steering wheel in the front. The robot, equipped with two photocells and appropriate negative feedbacks, could display the two behaviors of positive and negative phototropism, depending on whether its purpose was to seek the light or avoid it. Under the proper conditions, it could even manifest these two antagonistic purposeful behaviors in an oscillatory manner, and the oscillations always increased. This was the analog of the intention tremor. Furthermore, due to the presence of a device that created the second, postural feedback, the robot could manifest a marked oscillatory movement, but this time in the absence of light, i.e. in the absence of the machine's goal. This behavior, which could be made to correspond to the tremor caused by Parkinson's disease, was due to the fact that the second feedback was antagonistic to the first and tended to decrease in amount.

A quantitative model of the brain which would be, at the same time, a theory of behavior, a tool for neuropsychological research and a template for building "mechanisms possessing intelligence" was proposed by an engineer, Edgard Coburn, in a series of articles published in the *Psychological Review* (Coburn, 1951; 1952; 1953). This model, which he called the "Brain Analogy," was based more on behavioral data than on anatomico-physiological data. In this sense, it was put forward "to simulate function, not structure, of organic nervous systems" (Coburn, 1951: 155). Coburn also commented on the physical construction of the model, and his interest was primarily aimed at the "*principles* of intelligent mechanisms" (p. 156).

In these statements, we recognize a functionalist approach to the study of organism behavior that has come to light since the start of our investigation, to emerge more and more explicitly in various authors. This functionalist stance did not prevent Coburn from adopting a cautious attitude towards molar approaches to intelligence and learning. His line of reasoning reminds one of Craik's argument. Coburn pointed out that, though starting from a molar level approach (i.e. one based on the study of a 'hypothetical' nervous system rather than the actual features of neurons), he was led to consider the underlying neural mechanisms in order to provide an adequate formulation of the *general principles* of conditioned reflex learning. And in order to identify a "physically realizable structure" that would satisfy those principles, he was forced "to dig deeper into the [neural] mechanisms, even though the complexities appear to be multiplied, and consider the elementary properties of neurons" (Coburn, 1952: 459).

An explicit functionalist choice, within the context of a radically molar option with respect to Coburn's, lays at the base of the mechanical model developed by the psychologist J.A. Deutsch. It was a maze-learner, and unsurprisingly the only robot of the kind to be spared by Pask's above-mentioned criticisms. Deutsch's functionalist choice, in fact, directly concerned the relation between psychological *theory* and mechanical *model*. He presented his theory as an "abstract" or "formal system," capable of various "interpretations" or "realizations," which could be either an organism or a suitably organized machine, provided that either would behave as predicted by the theory. The machine could be made of various components, such as mechanical gears, vacuum tubes or transistors, as long as they were organized according to a common principle (Deutsch, 1954: 7). Deutsch's functionalism characteristically refused to introduce "physiological speculations" into psychology, on the basis of the conviction that any success in the latter should not defend on progress in neurology (even if, in perspective, neurology will have to provide the foundational basis of psychology).

The theory that Deutsch describes as a "formal system" actually posits a fundamental "unit" that underlies all behaviors, from the simpler to the more complex ones. The latter turn out to be "chains" of these units. The unit Deutsch postulates is composed of five elements, having three types of relations towards each other, as shown by the block diagram reproduced in Figure 5.2. (Deutsch, 1953: 305).

According to the "psychological interpretation" of this theory, or actually of the block diagram in Figure 5.2, the central structures, or links, of an organism, when activated by an *internal* drive, provoked, for example, by the need for food, or by an instinct, in turn activate some effectors, which cause a change in the external environment. The latter can activate a specific receptor or analyzer, which transmits a feedback signal to the central structure of the organism, modifying its activation threshold, just as an automatic con-

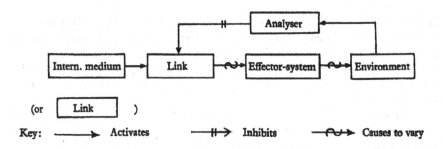

Fig. 5.2. J.A. Deutsch's 'unit,' with the feedback loop of information coming from the analyzer
(from Deutsch, 1953).

trol system would.[12] In tasks of a certain complexity, like searching for the way out of a
maze, the behavior of an organism is brought about by a "chain" of these units, connected through the central structures. By means of "semineurologic" terminology, as he
called it, Deutsch described rules that modify the resistance of the connections between
the links of the various units involved in the solution of a task, like maze-learning by a
rat. After running through the maze repeatedly, the rat has recorded a specific chain of
units, which establishes a genuine internal representation or map of the situation. This
chain of units is a purposeful mechanism, whose goal is to satisfy the organism's drive
(in this example, taking food at the end of the maze) by solving the task.

But this theory can also be "interpreted" in terms of vacuum tubes, relays or mechanical contrivances, by constructing a model that "embodies" the theory, as Deutsch
put it, and is capable of learning as predicted by the theory itself (Deutsch, 1954). Deutsch
schematically describes a robot whose 'brain' consisted of twenty-three relays and six
uniselectors. Appropriately connected, they physically instantiated the chain of units that
were needed to provide internal representations of different mazes (in fact, the machine
was able to learn two).

Donald Broadbent included Deutsch's approach within the area of psychological theorizing that introduced information theory concepts into psychology.[13] These concepts,

[12] The theory summarized in this block diagram tries to explain a conative behavior, i.e. one motivated by
an instinct or by a drive corresponding to *internal* physical states of the organism: the *external* stimulus concludes, not causes, a behavior (Deutsch, 1953). The Figure is also reproduced in a book (Deutsch, 1960), where
the author expounds his theory more systematically, comparing it with others, especially that of Hull on the
one hand and that of Tinbergen, Lorenz and the proponents of homeostatic models for conative activity on the
other (see Hinde, 1960, for a discussion of the models in the theories of Lorenz and Tinbergen, in addition to
those of Freud and MacDougall, which latter we have already mentioned). A discussion of Deutsch's positions
within the context of behaviorism is provided by Broadbent (1961).

[13] For the applications of information theory in psychology, a reference text of the period is Attneave (1959).
The so-called "British approach to information processing," that of Colin Cherry and Broadbent himself, is mentioned by Gardner (1985). Broadbent, after studying engineering, was in Cambridge for a long time, having
arrived there in 1947 at the Psychological Laboratory directed by Bartlett, two years after Craik's death. Broadbent has more recently again taken up information-processing models in the light of developments in simulative models (see, for example, Broadbent, 1984).

according to Broadbent, who pioneered their systematic use, were suitable to describe a general system that could select incoming information by means of "sensory channels," as well as store and process that information. These concepts could apply to a human being and an appropriately organized mechanical model alike. The flow diagram of Broadbent's information processing system is shown in Figure 5.3 (Broadbent, 1958).

Broadbent described the mechanical model as "a theory expressed in material parts rather than in abstract symbols such as words or mathematical expressions" (Broadbent, 1957: 205). Therefore, his modeling methodology departed from mathematical and quantitative psychological theorizing, which he felt to be prevalent at the time in behaviorist psychology. As an example of such theorizing, he mentioned Hull, then evidently known solely for his quantitative investigations, which followed the modeling approach of the 1930s (Broadbent, 1956: 354). For Broadbent, however, the function of the mechanical model was, above all, to render more precise and, at the same time, more understandable to psychologists theories formulated in terms of relatively "unfamiliar" information-processing concepts. This is precisely what he did with his attention model, a 'Y'-shaped tube which exemplified various features of the information flow through sensory channels. After all, Broadbent's view of models was quite narrow (the model was, first of all, an "expository device"), and he made it very clear that he had never built a model in any physical sense (Broadbent, 1957: 214).

A more central role for models in psychological theory construction was suggested by the psychologist Benjamin Wyckoff (Wyckoff, 1954). His starting point was a law qualitatively formulated by Skinner: discriminative stimuli function as secondary reinforcement in conditioning (for example, a light can function as a discriminative stimulus if the stimulus that provokes the conditioned response is always accompanied by that light). Wyckoff formulated Skinner's law as a *quantitative* postulate, but he encountered various difficulties in drawing, from that single postulate, the implications needed to predict the various phenomena observed in conditioning with a discriminative stimulus present. To solve this problem, he thought he would build a mechanical model that functioned according to that postulate and observe its behavior.

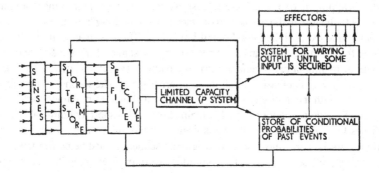

Fig. 5.3. The information-flow diagram in Broadbent (1958).

The resulting machine drew Wyckoff's attention to errors in the theory formulated as a single postulate, and suggested how to correct them: the introduction of a second postulate, formulated in quantitative terms as well, allowed one to derive the interesting phenomena observed experimentally. At this point, a *second* model, modified so as to incorporate both postulates, behaved in accordance with the requirements of the new theory. In its modified version, Wyckoff's model is an analogue electronic device that uses thyratron timer circuits. The model enabled one to reproduce various experimental situations of conditioning in the presence of a discriminative stimulus. In this way, a cycle was established involving the testing of the theory and its improvement, by constructing a model, which was in turn improved in the later version.

In Wyckoff's view, the model's chief role was to reveal the "shortcomings" of a theory (p. 95), those missing mechanisms that had to be postulated in better approximations of an explanation of behavioral data. In his opinion, a purely verbal formulation of the theory could not satisfy this need. As Coburn had already concluded, one had to "drop verbalization, which conceals inconsistencies [of the theory], and substitute physical structures which expose them" (Coburn, 1952: 458).

4. The intelligent computer

One trend in the research of the turning-point years, as we pointed out at the beginning of this chapter, endeavored to reproduce intelligent behaviors of human beings by means of digital computer programs. This was the origin of AI. In cybernetic circles, there was widespread skepticism about the possibility of reproducing with digital computers the ability to learn as well as the spontaneity and complexity of behavior in living organisms. Ashby, Grey Walter and MacKay, to name a few leading figures, regarded the computer as a machine which, unlike living organisms, manifested an entirely preprogrammed and, therefore, rigid and inflexible behavior.[14] Precisely during those years, however, computer design made some decisive steps, which began to make one think of the computer as an 'intelligent' machine, even though it is so different from the human brain.

In addition to the developments in computer science and technology we already mentioned, it is appropriate to recall here at least two features of programming that immediately came to the fore in the discussion of "mechanical thinking": the processing of nonnumerical data and so-called conditional branching. The first feature transformed the computer from a calculator (capable of performing the standard arithmetic functions) into a symbol manipulator or general-purpose machine (i.e. it became capable of performing a large variety of tasks, not simply numerical ones). The second feature endowed the computer with the ability to make a decision or a choice from among various alternatives, taking into account previously obtained results (in short, conditional branching establishes that, if a given condition has been satisfied, then a certain sequence of instructions must be performed; otherwise, another sequence must be performed).

These features today seem such a commonplace of programming that it may appear

[14] See for example, Ashby (1948); MacKay (1951; 1962); Walter (1953).

dull to insist on them. But even though they had already been described by Charles Babbage in the nineteenth century,[15] when they were first actually tried on computers, there was a feeling that the notion of a program was more powerful and general than one could have thought. The EDSAC computer, fully realizing those features, had just been built by a group led by Wilkes at Cambridge, England, when Anthony Oettinger, also then at Cambridge, wrote two of the first 'intelligent' programs for it. These programs were able to modify their performance on the basis of experience, or to 'learn' (Oettinger, 1952).

With one of those programs Oettinger tried to simulate the formation of a habit by reinforcement. The machine was given an integer whose value corresponded to the intensity of an incoming stimulus. The machine responded in turn by printing another integer, corresponding to one of a finite number of possible responses. At the beginning, it responded to the stimuli by randomly printing a number, or by printing an X instead if the stimulus was too 'weak' to elicit a definite response. For every response, the experimenter in turn expressed his approval or disapproval by communicating an integer to the machine. The machine was programmed in such a way that, if the response received approval, the probability increased that this response would be presented again immediately afterward; otherwise the probability decreased. Using cyclical applications of this rule, it was possible to train the machine to respond with a given number, and in the course of its training its errors became less frequent.

Oettinger's program shows how, at that time, the designer of so-called "thinking machines" was still under the influence of the behaviorist and associationist approaches to learning that we dwelt on in previous chapters. And, in fact, Oettinger's references also include, alongside the main pioneers in computer science and cybernetics, authors from the pre-cybernetic period, including Hull, with his 1930 article on trial-and-error learning, and Craik's *The Nature of Explanation*.[16] But Oettinger's research was more directly influenced by three papers that had appeared in the immediately preceding years. The first was an article by Shannon, "Programming a Computer to Play Chess," in which the author insisted on the importance of non-numerical applications of digital computers, with the game of chess as an example (Shannon, 1950). The other two were authored by Turing and Wilkes, respectively, and concerned "mechanical thought," or the intelligence of computers.

Turing's article, "Computing Machinery and Intelligence," was destined to become one of the best-known and most frequently cited texts in the literature, both for profound insights that anticipated future developments in computing machines and for what Turing called the "imitation game" (Turing, 1950). There were three participants in the game: a man, a woman and an interrogator. The latter, by asking the most varied questions and receiving the answers in a standard form on two different terminals, had to guess which was the man and which the woman. Turing imagined that, in giving his answers, the man

---

[15] Pratt (1987) gives a lively introduction to Babbage's projects, as well as to previous projects (like those of Pascal and Leibniz) and later ones (like the undertakings of Turing and the pioneers of computer science).

[16] Hull's article, "Simple Tiral-and-error Learning," was mentioned several times in Chapter 3. We discussed in Chapter 4 how Craik's 1943 book was destined to become a privileged reference text in the literature on intelligent machines that came after it.

would try to fool the interrogator, while the woman would try to help him. He proposed, therefore, to substitute a machine for the man, in fact a general-purpose digital computer, and to see how it would manage in the game, i.e. to what extent it would manage to fool the interrogator. Would the latter, Turing wondered, be mistaken in identifying his fellow players "as often" as when a man, and not a machine, played the game? He intended this question, posed as it is "in relatively unambiguous words," to replace the more popular but misleading one, "can machines think?" (p. 433). Wilkes, taking up the imitation game in his article, "Can Machines Think?," maintained that, to believe seriously that one could "simulate human behavior" using a computer, it would be necessary to design a "generalized 'learning' program," i.e. a program able to learn *any* subject chosen by the programmer—a very distant goal, given the performance of the programs that had been devised so far (Wilkes, 1951).

Oettinger held that his programs provided partial responses to the requirements set by Turing and Wilkes. Far away as they were from demonstrating the "generalized" ability to learn indicated by Wilkes, these programs still managed to improve their performance in certain specified tasks. They would have been able, therefore, to pass at least "restricted versions," as he put it, of the imitation game. Oettinger thus seems to be the first to interpret the imitation game as a sufficiency test (a "criterion," he called it) in evaluating the performance of *particular* computer programs in limited domains. It is in this interpretation that the imitation game, known as the *Turing test*, would become more popular afterwards.

Note that Oettinger stressed that he used the computer to simulate certain *functions* of the brain, not its physical *structure*, and that "Turing's criterion" could serve only to verify the existence of a *functional correspondence* between the computer and the brain (Oettinger, 1952: 1261). We have already noticed a functionalist stance in Coburn and Deutsch. We could call it *machine functionalism*, i.e. the claim that organisms and machines can be studied from the viewpoint of their common functional organization. This is an idea that, in fact, was suggested by the very study of machines: it is possible to build "the same machines, showing the same reactions, from a different kind of material, with different properties," to put it in Jennings' quite broad formulation. In a more evolved context, a statement of this sort was, for Ross, the "commonplace in mechanics," as it was for Ashby, who spoke in this regard of "isomorphic machines" (Ashby, 1956: 94).[17] It is with the advent of the computer that machine functionalism takes a different form, based on the idea of a general-purpose machine. As Oettinger pointed out, there are many ways of realizing a given set of functions. A device able to learn by conditioning could be "synthetized," as he put it, in a physical structure or a "special machine" different from EDSAC (Oettinger, 1952: 1261-62). But a "universal digital computer" like EDSAC has the interesting property of being able, "when provided with a suitable *programme*, to mimic arbitrary machines in a very general class" (p. 1243).

Oettinger's insights touch upon other central issues in the incoming computer simu-

[17] The attribution of this form of functionalism to Jennings, as we made clear in Chapter 1, is related to the interpretation of his action system. See above Chapter 3, section 6, as regards Hull and Ross. We will later return to a discussion of the various forms of functionalism, particularly in Chapter 7.

lation of mental functions. For example, Oettinger observed how the non-numerical (i.e. symbolic) nature of computers should appeal those who, "like psychologists and neuro-physiologists, are interested in [their] potentialities [...] as models of the structure and functions of animal nervous systems" (p. 1244). Further, his interpretation of the conditional branching instruction in programs was particularly engaging for many of them. Even Shannon, in the article mentioned by Oettinger, had spoken of conditional branching as a procedure that put the machine in a position of *deciding* or *choosing* between different alternatives based on previously obtained results (Shannon, 1950: 264). But Oettinger emphasized that this aspect was crucial for his programs, because it allowed them "to organize new information meaningfully and to select alternative modes of behaviour on the basis of this organization" (Oettinger, 1952: 1247).

As one can easily see, this is simply a matter of a computer like EDSAC being able to simulate the behavior of an analogue feedback device. But it was precisely cybernetics that had exalted the *discriminative* capabilities of these devices, and, as we have seen, Rosenblueth, Wiener and Bigelow were the ones to introduce the psychological language of 'choice,' of 'purpose,' and so forth, into the description of these artifacts. One invitation to make a cautious, to say the very least, use of psychological terms suggested by conditional branching, such as 'decision' or 'discrimination,' let alone 'thought,' came from a later article by Wilkes (1953). On the one hand, Wilkies recognized the importance of conditional branching in designing learning programs, like those Oettinger had just designed. On the other hand, he pointed out that the use of these psychological terms was simply metaphorical, and that it was "a fantastic suggestion" that a machine should be able to pass what he called the Turing "test" in its generalized form (p. 1231).

This latter article by Wilkes was republished in one of the most widely-read scientific periodicals of the day, the *Proceedings of the Institute of Radio Engineers*, in a special issue of October, 1953, *The Computer Issue*. This provides an excellent testimony to the level of computer design and technology achieved at the time. Wilkes' article was followed by one by Shannon, "Computers and Automata," a review of computer performances comparable to those of humans (Shannon, 1953), and by a long series of papers that presented the digital computer in all its aspects, from programming to hardware. In several of these papers there were glimpses of the advantages stemming from the imminent spread of transistors, which, by replacing the cumbersome and unreliable vacuum tube, would characterize much more advanced second-generation computers.

The building and dissemination of computers, which were mostly designed in the academic world, in the United States and Europe was substantially sponsored by industry. In the United States, IBM had already supported Aiken's project. At the start of the 1950s, almost at the same time as Ferranti in England, IBM began selling the 701 computer, which was carefully described in the *Computer Issue*. This was the first in a series of electronic general-purpose, stored-program computers which could be used for theoretical research purposes, had industrial applications, and quickly turned IBM into the leading company in the field. This was the computer on which Arthur Samuel, then holding a research position at IBM and the author of the opening article for the *Computer Issue*, ran his first programs for the game of checkers in 1952.

In April of that same year, 1953, the tenth and last Macy Conference on Cybernetics was held in New York. McCulloch delivered the closing address, a "Summary of the Points of Agreement Reached in the Previous Nine Conferences on Cybernetics" (McCulloch, 1953). These points included his and Pitt's formal networks and Turing's results, but no mention was made of the emerging use of the computer as a general-purpose machine and its possible role in the cybernetic programme. If one compares the papers at this Conference with the articles contained in the *Computer Issue* of that same year, one can sense two worlds that were very far apart.[18]

Another conference, in which McCulloch himself participated, eventually came to grips with the prospective role of computers in the mind and brain sciences. Together with Oettinger, the neurologist Otto Schmitt, and Nathaniel Rochester, director of research at IBM, McCulloch was one of the four main speakers at the Symposium on *The design of machines to simulate the behavior of the human brain* (McCulloch et al., 1956). This was organized in 1955 by the IRE National Convention. Those invited included John Mauchly, Walter Pitts and Marvin Minsky. The report of this Symposium, which precedes the official birth of AI at Dartmouth by one year, is illuminating. It is a unique inventory of the main issues involved in building intelligent machines, of methodological approaches, ambitions and difficulties that would move to the forefront in the following decade, and in some cases even in more recent times.

In the background or at the center of the issues debated at the Symposium were the first computer programs, either in operation or merely in their experimental stages, which imitated human performance or competed with it. Some programs had already been illustrated by Shannon in his article in the *Computer Issue*, and Oettinger, in his talk at the Symposium, mentioned others. There were, first of all, programs that were able to play different games fairly well: the program for checkers, suggested by Turing to Christopher Strachey, who published a report in 1952; that of D.W. Davies for tic-tac-toe, which ran on a DEUCE computer; and that for nim. The NIMROD electronic computer, built by Ferranti, had played nim with visitors to the scientific exhibition at the 1951 Festival

---

[18] Heims (1991) has reconstructed some points in the evolution of cybernetics during the years of the Macy Conferences, which were held between 1946 and 1953 (see also the essays in Dupuy et al., 1985). The original multidisciplinary programme of Wiener underwent various developments. The Congrès International de Cybernétique organized at Namur in Belgium beginning in 1956 was the stage for the different contributions coming from different experiences and countries. In England, the ARTORGA (ARTificial ORGAnisms) association, founded at the initiative of Oliver D. Wells, distributed among its members, starting at the end of 1958, a bulletin that carried various debates. Members of this association included Ashby, George, Pask, Stafford Beer (Messadié, 1961). In Italy, in addition to those research centers more directly influenced by Wiener's ideas, like that of Eduardo Caianiello (see Chapter 6 below), mention should be made of the proposal for a so-called "third cybernetics" advanced, in the context of the Italian Operative School, by Silvio Ceccato. In this very context occurred the publication, between 1947 and 1964, of the journals *Sigma* and *Methodos*, both containing contributions from leading figures in cybernetics from around the world (Somenzi, 1987; see also Somenzi, 1956). In France mention should be made of a pioneering figure like Louis Couffignal, while other developments concern the so-called "second-order cybernetics" of Heinz von Foerster (these and other developments are documented in van de Vijver, 1992). These experiences deserve separate treatment, just like the relationship between cybernetics and research programmes like the general system theory of von Bertalanffy (1968). Finally, one should not forget the influence that cybernetics has always continued to exercise on biological and neurological research, by means of various specialized journals over the entire second half of the twentieth century.

of Britain, where it was displayed together with Grey Walter's tortoises.[19] Then there were the aforementioned programs by Oettinger, and a more recent one by Rochester. The latter, with John Holland and others, had proposed to simulate on an IBM 701 the theory developed in the 1949 book, *The Organization of Behavior*, by the psychologist Donald Hebb. He viewed learning, following in the wake of the associationist tradition, as the strengthening of connections among neurons, or groups of neurons, which are repeatedly and simultaneously activated (Hebb, 1949).

In the Symposium sharply diverging views were discussed. Pressed by Pitts, Oettinger clarified his own claim about the distinct interests aroused by the digital computer: on the one hand, it could be used to test neurological theories about the functioning of the central nervous system, thus simulating both brain structure and functions; on the other hand, it could be used to simulate "higher mental functions," without imitating what is known or hypothesized about brain structure. Oettinger pointed out that the most successful simulation of living functions had usually been achieved by means not used by organisms, thus attaining superior performances of those functions: "for example, while the flight of birds undoubtedly stimulated man's urge to fly, human flight was achieved by significantly different means." As for digital computers, they perform arithmetic operations using computational processes different from those of humans, and it can be expected that "many machines of the future will continue to have only a functional resemblance to living organisms" (see McCulloch et al., 1956: 242).

As an example of the first, more neurologically oriented research Oettinger mentioned Rochester's program, in which "the digital computer may be programmed to simulate the neuron network with its environment" (p. 241). Rochester had presented his program at the Symposium, insisting on a methodology that proposed "to use modern automatic calculators to test some aspects of some of the theories of how the brain works" (p. 244). Figure 5.4 shows the methodological cycle illustrated by Rochester, which includes a true process of model testing and revision. It goes from formulating the model as a computer simulation of a theory of the brain, to determining the implications of the model, to testing them, and finally to using data to prove, disprove, or modify the theory. This is the cycle he had tried out on Hebb's theory, which, as Rochester emphasizes, had to undergo some changes as suggested by the computer simulation.

Much debated at the Symposium was the issue raised by Schmitt: if it was to be demonstrated that machines could give a realistic simulation of brain behavior, they had to imitate the flexibility of reasoning shown by humans. Thus, computers would have to use a "gray" logic, as Schmitt called it, not the rigid, bivalent, or "black-and-white" logic that characterize them. This would allow them to grasp ill-defined or abstract concepts, as well as to exploit the incomplete, conflicting or partially inappropriate knowledge usually available in real life, particularly when humans make real-time decisions.

I believe—Schmitt concluded—[...] that we are taking an unbalanced view of the problem, based on the phenomenal success of the large digital machines, and are thereby depriving ourselves of a tremendous complementary development of more brain-like machines (see McCulloch et al., 1956: 245).

[19] Turing was among the visitors to this exposition of the marvels of the new machines; he played against the computer, and won (Hodges, 1983: 428).

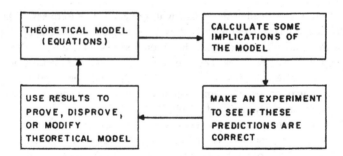

Fig. 5.4. The methodological cycle proposed by Rochester in 1955, where the computer is used
to test Hebb's learning theory (from McCulloch et al., 1956).

In this sense, Schmitt was not satisfied by computer simulations in the manner of
Rochester either, nor by the way McCulloch and his associates "have gone a long way
to associate digital-computer significance with known brain functions." These were
generic statements which, nevertheless, in the discussion that followed Schmitt's talk,
took more specific form in the issue of how plausible or not it was to credit computers
with common-sense knowledge. Schmitt's skeptical conclusions were counterbalanced
by Oettinger's optimistic claim:

> With computers—Oettinger concluded—it seems to me that we are able in principle, by the use of ap-
> propriate programming or designing of structure, to build in one swoop the whole background of explicit ex-
> isting knowledge" (see McCulloch et al., 1956: 249).

It is an issue, as one can see, that is at the core of much current investigation of the
matter. In a brief discussion with McCulloch, finally, Minsky declared that he was skeptical about the state of models with "distributed memory," and he refused to think, as it
had been suggested, that a good example of such models would be a machine equipped
with the simple self-organizing capabilities of Ashby's homeostat (p. 251). This, too,
was a issue bound to return to the fore again and again in the future.

5. The origins of Artificial Intelligence

The 1955 Symposium was being held while Samuel was completing the implementation
of a new checkers program on an IBM 704, shown on television in February the following year and later acknowledged as a milestone in machine learning research. He developed some of Shannon's earlier insights on chess programming, but he chose checkers because its rules were simpler, effectively making the game tractable for a computer. The study of decision-making behavior in games was assigned a leading role in the
research lying at the origin of AI, and had a major impact on early methodological approaches. It is, therefore, rewarding for us to examine its premises and main developments
in some detail.

Shannon had started to think about a computer program for chess around the middle of the 1940s. Turing had something to say on this subject too: along with Good, he had sketched a chess program akin to Shannon's in its fundamental features (Hodges, 1983: 213-214).[20] Shannon's program, which he described in the aforementioned article "Programming a Computer to Play Chess," was based on the idea of evaluating the best move using a look-ahead analysis of alternative moves, based on a procedure called *minimax* (Shannon, 1950). This procedure had its origins in the initial formulations of mathematical game-theory, a subject on which von Neumann had been working since the 1920s. The chess player had become a common metaphor in the analysis of decision-making, with its classic formulation in the book von Neumann published in 1944 together with the economist Oskar Morgenster, *Theory of Games and Economic Behavior*.

In their terminology, chess, like other games we have mentioned, such as checkers, nim or tic-tac-toe, is "univocally determined." One way to represent it is the *game tree*, which is generated, starting from an initial position or node, by first considering all the legal moves of the first player (the Level 1 nodes, reachable from the starting node by applying the rules of the game), then all the countermoves of the adversary (the Level 2 nodes), and so forth. A perfectly rational player, in fact an omniscient one, would be able 'to see' the complete game tree and therefore to choose the best sequence of moves by evaluating the end consequences of each alternative move. It would be enough for him to assign distinct values to the terminal positions, corresponding to win, loss and draw, then to go backward up the tree applying the minimax procedure, i.e. establishing at each node which branch leads him to a position of maximum advantage for him and minimum advantage for his adversary, until he arrives at the alternatives of his first move and makes his decision. In practice, this exhaustive, or "brute force," strategy encounters an insurmountable difficulty with the combinatorial explosion of possible moves, which Shannon calculated to be of the order of 10^{120} in the case of chess.

For this reason, Shannon proposed his first change to this strategy, which consisted of generating nodes at different levels of the game tree only up to a pre-established depth, then assigning set values to the nodes thus attained and evaluating the paths backwards using a minimax-based *evaluation function*. As such a procedure was radically inefficient, Shannon raised the problem of how to improve it so as "to develop a tolerably good strategy for selecting the move to be made" (p. 260). He suggested the inclusion in the program (more precisely, in its evaluation function) of some selectivity criteria directly stemming from investigations by Dutch psychologist Adrian de Groot into chess masters, who made their analyses by 'thinking aloud' during the game.

The most in-depth study on implementing the evaluation function is owed to Samuel. His program for checkers, before evaluating a position, checked its memory to see whether it had already evaluated it, so as to save time. This elementary form of rote learning, already tried out in simple tasks by Oettinger in his programs, was made more powerful by Samuel, so that storing an evaluated position would increase the program's lookahead ability. Consider the case in which the program looks ahead for three moves, i.e.

---

[20] The chess playing machine build by Leonardo Torres y Quevedo was able to play an end game with a rock and king against a human opponent's king. See Bowden (1953: 286), and the article in in *Scientific American* (November, 1915) mentioned in C. Eames and R. Eames (1990: 67).

the look-ahead search is always terminated at Level 3 before evaluating the resulting board positions. Now, if the program was to encounter a board position evaluated in a previous look-ahead search and stored in memory, it could take advantage of this, and, in fact, the program looks six moves in advance rather than three, i.e. the search reaches Level 6. In this way, the program could be given "the ability to utilize stored information in a different context from that in which it was obtained" (Samuel, 1959: 44).

Shannon's reference to de Groot also suggested an approach fairly different from Samuel's: combinatorial explosion could be confronted by studying *human* decision-making processes more closely. Now these processes were a central object of interest for Herbert Simon. He had already relinquished the normative approach of game theory, i.e. the analysis of the choices or the strategies that the rational agent *should* adopt in order to reach the optimal solution to a given problem. Instead, he introduced the *psychological* dimension into the study of choice, through an analysis of the decision-making behavior that characterizes a real agent. This is conditioned both by his own internal limits (concerning, for example, memory or the ability to process information) and by the complexity of the task environment. Developing this non-normative point of view, in 1947 Simon published *Administrative Behavior*, a book rounding out investigations that would be rewarded many years later with the Nobel Prize for Economics (Simon, 1947). The chess player was still the metaphor for the rational agent's behavior, but, in Simon's view, such a metaphor referred to the "bounded rationality" of a real problem-solver, or "administrative man," rather than to the omniscient abstract rationality of an idealized *Homo oeconomicus*. Internal limits and the complexity of the external environment, vividly illustrated by the game of chess, allow a real agent to use not the best strategy in the choice of moves, but only incomplete strategies, which are more or less "satisfactory," to use Simon's term.

These ideas set the stage for Simon's 1952 hypothesis of a chess program based on the implementation of these satisfactory strategies, which he placed the heart of human problem-solving processes, rather than on the refinements of Shannon's evaluation function. At that time, Simon was already in contact with Allen Newell, who was analyzing decision-making processes at the RAND Corporation. Newell had attended the lectures of the mathematician George Polya. The latter, in his 1945 book, *How to Solve It*, regarded the problem-solving processes as "heuristic," i.e. based on cues and various expedients, an idea that closely resembled Simon's satisfactory strategies. Newell recalled that a program made clear to him the great potential of the computer as a non-numerical machine: in 1954, Oliver Selfridge, who had been Wiener's assistant at MIT, had completed a program that could recognize patterns, such as letters of the alphabet. Newell then decided to try out the computer's symbolic processing ability using the game of chess.[21] In January 1956, however, Simon wrote a letter to de Groot saying that he and Newell, having set aside the chess program project, were instead about to conclude a project for a theorem-proving program in sentential logic (see Simon, 1991). In the meantime, Clifford Shaw, a gifted expert in programming, had joined him and Newell.

Newell, Shaw and Simon initiated a major development in AI research, the comput-

---

[21] This testimony from Newell was collected by McCorduck (1979).

er simulation of human problem-solving processes, also known as "Information Processing Psychology." We now examine this approach in some detail, as it affords us an excellent opportunity to exemplify a strategy in the study of mind that was made possible by computers. Furthermore, by reconsidering the various proposals characterizing the simulation methodology discussed in previous chapters, it will become clear how the new strategy proposed by these three authors preserves certain aspects of the former approaches that are anything but marginal, while radically altering its overall framework.

According to Newell, Shaw and Simon, the human organism and the computer program that simulates it are different realizations of a single system, the "Information Processing System" (IPS). From 1955 on, the IPS was made the center of their research. Figure 5.5 shows the block diagram of the IPS, with its input organs, or receptors, and output organs, or effectors, its processor, or control and computing unit, and its memory. Other diagrams, like those of Deutsch and Broadbent, had been described in terms of information processing, but a crucial feature sets the IPS apart: it involves computer programs as a tool for building and testing psychological theories.

The Information Processing Psychology, like other research programs in early AI that we will touch on in the next chapter, primarily focused on control issues. Like chess or other games, the logic theorem proving that Newell, Shaw and Simon analyzed could be represented as a tree. But this tree (or "maze," as they called it at first) was different from game trees representing the moves of two opposing players. Newell, Shaw and Simon's formulation marks the origin of what would later be known in AI as *state-space representation*. The search for a solution is seen, in this case, as the search for a path in the tree. This path, obtained by applying suitable operators, leads from a node, representing the initial state, to a terminal state, the goal or solution to the problem. In principle, if it were possible to explore exhaustively all the paths stemming from the initial state, sooner or later one would arrive at the solution required (supposing one exists). It would suffice to establish an *order* in which to visit the nodes, thus establishing a procedure for finding all successor nodes of a given node. Newell, Shaw and Simon call this the "British Museum algorithm." But this procedure does not take into account the combinatorial ex-

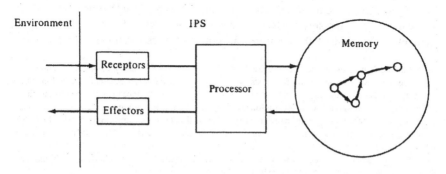

Fig. 5.5. Allen Newell and Herbert Simon's Information Processing System
(from Newell and Simon, 1972).

plosion of the state space. The human problem-solver never applies a procedure of the sort, following instead procedures that make use of partial information, or cues, to *select* the rules that appear to be most suitable for solving the problem. According to the three authors, a computer program, to control the combinatorial explosion, would have to embody such selective or "heuristic" procedures.

The Logic Theorist (LT), devised by Newell, Shaw and Simon between 1955 and 1956, was the program based on this insight, which Simon mentioned in his letter to de Groot. LT managed to prove about forty theorems of the sentential calculus of Bertrand Russell and Alfred Whitehead's *Principia Mathematica*. The routine lying at the core of the program and accounting for its success was a variant of a procedure that was later known as "means-ends analysis." Its chief, eminently *teleological* feature, was that of being goal-guided. Instead of systematically applying the rules of sentential logic (a 'blind' procedure, giving rise to a combinatorial explosion), the routine, by matching the sentential formula representing the initial state, i.e. the theorem to be proved, to the sentential formula representing the final state, i.e. the solution, selected only the rules most likely to eliminate the differences between the two formulas. The solution strategy involved generating a sequence of formulas progressively *more similar* to the final-state formula. The routine, called "similarity test," worked heuristically: a mechanized selective procedure had been made available, but applying the procedure was no guarantee that a solution to the problem would eventually be arrived at. In logical terms, it was not a complete proof procedure.[22] The control routine implemented in LT was soon tried out in various task environments and refined in various programs, giving rise to *heuristic programming*, one of the main achievements of early AI.

The first proof given by LT was printed by the JOHNNIAC computer in August 1956. LT, however, had already played a leading role in the summer seminar organized in June 1956 by John McCarthy, Minsky, Rochester, and Shannon at the Dartmouth College, in Hanover, New Hampshire. The meeting's aim was to examine "the conjecture that every aspect of learning or any other feature of intelligence can in principle be so precisely described that a machine can be made to simulate it," as one reads in the document, in which the Rockefeller Foundation was asked for financial support.[23] The main researchers actively designing intelligent computer programs were present at Dartmouth: in addition to the meeting's promoters, we have already mentioned Newell, Simon, Selfridge, and Samuel.[24] After Dartmouth, the historical centers of AI research would be formed: at

[22] At the time, the authors of the LT contrasted algorithms (by which they meant complete procedures that, as such, guarantee a solution, if a solution exists) with heuristics (incomplete procedures that, therefore, do not guarantee a solution). They suggested that the loss of completeness was the price to pay in order to gain the *efficiency* that algorithms (such as the British Museum algorithm) could not ensure in controlling the combinatorial explosion. Later developments in research would lead to different evaluations (see Cordeschi, 1996). The book by Nilsson (1971) was the first systematic approach to heuristic search, which we are here considering in its germinal state.

[23] The original document of the Dartmouth Summer Seminar can be found in http://www-formal.stanford.edu/jmc/history/dartmouth/dartmouth.html.

[24] This classic volume by Feigenbaum and Feldman (1963) gathers together the research of the various leading figures at Dartmouth and those who were the first to continue it after them.

Carnegie-Mellon University with Newell and Simon, at MIT with Minsky, and at Stanford University with McCarthy. In England, Turing's legacy was taken up by Michie at Edinburgh before AI research spilled over into other European countries.

At Dartmouth McCarthy discussed with the authors of LT a significant aspect of their program. LT had not been written in machine language (i.e. through finite sequences of binary digits corresponding to the absence or presence of an impulse), but in a *higher-level* language. Newell, Shaw and Simon had realized the difficulty of writing programs for complex tasks directly in machine language. The need for a program that would translate into machine language instructions in a language that was closer to natural language had been recognized for some time. In the early 1950s, significant progress in this direction had been made by Heinz Rutishauser and Corrado Böhm in Zurich. In 1954, an IBM research group, headed by John Backus, finally completed FORTRAN (FORmula TRANslator), the first higher-level programming language. The IPL (Information Processing Language) of Newell, Shaw and Simon, however, had its own characteristics, tailored to handle the complexities of heuristic programs. Its underlying inspiration was list programming, taken up again by McCarthy in 1958 with his LISP (LISt Processor), which was meant to remain the main AI programming language for a long while.[25]

The authors of LT had their own distinctive idea about how to apply the newly-conceived heuristic programming. This became, in their hands, the core of a simulative methodology marking a turning-point in the history of the sciences of the mind. Briefly, this simulative methodology was as follows. Human subjects were asked to solve a problem, such as to prove a theorem, 'thinking aloud.' The selective, or heuristic, problem-solving procedures they used were recorded in a verbal protocol, identified and then implemented in a program under the form of routines (or better, hierarchies of routines), like the above-mentioned means-ends analysis routine. A comparison of the verbal or thinking-aloud protocol and the program's trace should show whether, and to what extent, the simulation was having success, i.e. whether, and to what extent, problem-solving processes performed by humans and programs were the same.

An important aspect of this simulative methodology was that the program had to take into account the effective *limits* of the human problem-solver, those limits in memory, data-processing speed and so on, that characterize Simon's notion of bounded rationality. The program, therefore, had to satisfy some *constraints* in order to be a realistic simulation of the problem-solver's behavior from a psychological point of view. It was not enough that human and machine performance were found to match, or that the machine could provide the same answers as the human. Something more was required: the protocol-trace comparison had to ensure that the problem-solving *processes* were as close as possible in both cases.

This was the condition that immediately set Information Processing Psychology apart from other AI approaches. The very use of the term *heuristics* by Newell, Shaw and Simon revealed noticeably different aims. Other AI approaches aimed at reproducing intelligent performance in a heuristic program without additional constraints, freely ex-

[25] See the essays on the development of the first programming languages in Metropolis et al. (1980).

ploiting the computer's characteristics, such as computation speed and memory capacity. Thus, Newell, Shaw and Simon felt that the Turing test was a comparatively "weak" test, because it did not take the identity of *processes* into consideration. Protocol-trace comparison was indeed a "test of simulation that is much stronger than Turing's test" (Newell and Simon, 1959: 33).[26]

Newell, Shaw and Simon did not consider a computer program as a metaphor of human behavior, but as a model providing a test of the hypothesis that the mind is an information-processing system. More precisely, the model took the form of a program of a peculiar kind: *to explain* a given problem-solving behavior meant *to build a program step by step simulating that behavior*. The program was considered to be a highly *specific* behavioral theory, concerning the behavior of an individual human problem-solver: a *microtheory*, Newell and Simon would later say. It was distinguished from the *general* theory of human information-processing, a body of qualitative generalizations culled from a study of individual simulative programs, or microtheories. These generalizations dealt with the information-processing system (an adaptive system with the wide abovementioned limits), the task environment (whose structure determines the possible structures of the problem space) and the problem space (whose structure determines the possible heuristic strategies or programs) (Newell and Simon, 1972).

To be a good explanation, the computer trace had to approximate the verbal protocol as closely as possible. When the program ran on the computer, it became possible to identify its lacunae, then suggest modifications to improve it and find in its performance confirmation or disproof of the general theory as well. LT, for example, when compared with the verbal protocols of individuals grappling with problems in sentential logic, demonstrated the need for a "modified version," as the authors themselves later stated. The name that would be given to this new version is now well-known: this is the General Problem Solver (GPS). The program, equipped as it was with suitable heuristics, such as means-ends analysis, was judged by its designers to be, in many respects, a good simulation of the verbal protocol of a human individual grappling with a problem in sentential logic.[27]

Simulation of behavior achieved by means of the human protocol-computer trace comparison set the methodology of Newell, Shaw and Simon apart from previous sim-

---

[26] And for this reason, the defeat of a human being by a computer that plays chess, as in the case of the Deep Blue program that beat Kasparov in 1997, while interesting, is not a particularly significant result from the point of view of those (first of all, Simon) who remained interested in the psychological realism of simulation (on Simon and coworkers' investigations of chess playing, see p. 178 above). "Dissimilar processes yield similar conclusions": this is, moreover, the comment of the designers of Deep Blue, who emphasized the "contrast in styles" between man and machine during the match (as one can read on the IBM site at http://www.research.ibm.com/deepblue/meet/html/d.2.html).

[27] See Newell, Shaw and Simon (1962). This article, actually written in 1958, contains the first written report of GPS under a different name, and of a comparison of a thinking-aloud protocol with a computer trace (as mentioned by Newell and Simon, 1972: 885-886). Means-ends heuristics became typical of a program like the GPS in the form of a procedure analyzing a problem into simpler sub-problems, whose solution leads to that of the main problem. The original matching procedure of the LT could be seen as a form of this heuristics, and appeared to be such for the three authors. Later analyses have reconsidered the relationships between the procedures and the possible forms of representation (see again Nilsson, 1971). The qualification *general* applied to GPS refers to the original hope that it could be made into a versatile problem-solver, i.e. be as subject-independent as possible.

ulative proposals, which had already claimed the central role of models in the construction of behavioral and brain theories. A methodology based on model testing and revision had been maintained and applied by Wyckoff in the context of analogue simulation. He paid attention to *quantitative* theory formulation, however, which was completely foreign to the authors of GPS. In the context of digital simulation, this methodology was applied to the computer program written by Rochester and his collaborators (John Holland was one of them) to simulate Hebb's learning theory. Computer simulation, the authors concluded, shows that "some models are unworkable and provides clues as to how to revise the models to make them work" (Rochester et al., 1956: 88).

Significantly, the method of model testing and revision proposed by Rochester was positively evaluated by Newell and Simon, with regard both to the "verbal description" of the theory originally given by Hebb and to its later "mathematical analysis" (Newell and Simon, 1963: 396-397). They believed that a theory expressed in the form of a computational model was, in general, the best alternative both to verbal (qualitative) descriptions and mathematical (quantitative) analyses of behavior. But unlike Broadbent and others, who agreed on similar distinctions, Newell and Simon held that the modeling method did not simply arise from the need to clarify a theory. In fact, it was an almost obligatory choice: given the complexity of the phenomena under study, as far as cognitive processes are concerned, "we have a greater chance of building a theory by way of the computer program than by a direct attempt at mathematical formulation" (Simon and Newell, 1957: 81). On the other hand, purely verbal formulations of the theory could hide its inconsistencies or lacunae. Newell and Simon were no less sensitive to this problem than other behavioral scientists mentioned above. However, substituting verbal formulations with physical structures or models that could bring to light the inconsistencies of the theory, to use Coburn's slogan, meant for Newell and Simon *formulating the theory in terms of a program*. This could submit the theory to a sufficiently rigorous test.

A new level of analysis was now available to psychology, the building of simulative programs, an intermediate level between the (molar) level of overt behavior and the (molecular) level of neurophysiology. New kinds of theoretical constructs to study the mind, those of information processing, were thereby introduced. As Newell, Shaw and Simon pointed out in an article in the *Psychological Review* directly aimed at the psychological community, this type of construct was the basis for behavioral models that made no appeal to traditional associationist notions of "trace," "fixation," "excitation," "inhibition," and the like. These notions referred back to an overall view of the nervous system as "a relatively passive electrochemical system (or, alternatively, a passive switchboard)"—in fact, the view we discussed in previous chapters. They certainly recognized that these mechanical models had been motivated by the "struggle against vitalism," but they continued:

> The invention of the digital computer has acquainted the world with a device—obviously a mechanism—whose response to stimuli is clearly more complex and 'active' than the response of more traditional switching networks. It has provided us with operational and unobjectionable interpretations of terms like "purpose," "set" and "insight" (Newell, Shaw and Simon, 1958: 162).

Newell, Shaw and Simon thus entered headlong into the debate, which at that time divided psychologists, about the problems of the experimental and operational method, the building of psychological theory, and the relationship between the study of mind and neurological research. Concluding their article, they sketched an effective portrait of psychology in that period, describing it as in the grip of a "polarization" between behaviorism and Gestaltism, a badly paralyzing polarization according to the diagnosis of many psychologists.[28] The three authors pointed to a novel and enticing escape route: one had to recognize, as the Gestaltists required, the complexity of the investigated object, the mind, at the same time asserting the need for serious scientific standards, as the behaviorists claimed. This could be done by using the *new* method for operational control of psychological theories, one based on building simulative programs.

This proposal met the needs of many psychologists, who gave the impression that they had found, to use Tolman's phrase, their "place in the sun" with respect to the work of neurologists. They felt psychology was finally independent from neurology, and for a good reason. Since information processes could be thought of as realized in different physical stuffs, such as brain and computer hardware, the mind is *independent* of the specific realization or instantiation of that structure as a biological brain.[29] As Figure 5.6 shows, the comparison between a human being and a computer is not possible at the level of their different structures. The comparison can be carried out only between computer traces (for example, of GPS) and human protocols, which both suggests the existence of a *common functional organization* and is the actual source of the aforementioned *constraints*. The success of the comparison justifies the very enterprise of psychology as a science: the computer simulation of human mind.

Here is a wise paradox! After the dark years of behaviorism, the mind had been re-consigned to psychologists by machine-builders. Man, seen as a symbolic information-processor, became the leading player in the new Information Processing Psychology, a genuine "science of the artificial," according to the famous wording later used by Simon (1969).[30]

The kind of functionalism that had already emerged in early discussions of the intel-

---

[28] Hebb, for example, had spoken ironically of the opposition between a behaviorist "Right," which "favors parsimony of explanatory ideas, a simple or mechanical account of behavior, and definiteness even at the cost of being narrow," and a Gestaltist "Left," which is "prepared to postulate more freely and can better tolerate vagueness" (Hebb, 1951-52: 48). See also below, pp. 216-217.

[29] Establishing a "bridge," as Simon occasionally put it, between Information Processing Psychology and neurology was something postponed for the future. Indeed, Information Processing Psychology could, in the meantime, allow for progress in psychological research, without having to wait for progress in neurology: after all, genetics did not have to wait for progress at the 'microlevel' of the processes underlying genes and chromosomes in order to develop into a science. The issue, therefore, of the relationship between psychology and neurology was addressed by the authors in the framework of reductionism "in perspective," typical of the hierarchy of levels of science theorized by liberal logical positivism (Simon, let us recall, was a student of Rudolf Carnap in Chicago). This view had long been popular among psychologists, as we have had occasion to emphasize in our investigation. Newell and Simon stated explicitly their view of behaviorists like Hull and Tolman and the legacy of logical neo-positivism (see, for example, Newell and Simon, 1972, Chapter xxx). Ericsson and Simon (1981) placed the use of verbal reports in information-processing modeling within the framework of the different positions taken by behaviorists and Gestaltists concerning introspection.

[30] The influence of Newell, Shaw and Simon's claims on psychologists could easily be documented: it is sufficient to mention the book by Miller et al. (1960), which has been cited several times. *Artificial* systems are, for Simon (1969), those systems (organic and inorganic) that, even in their limits, exhibit capacities for plasticity and adaptation to changing environments: they are *designed* to fit themselves to those environments.

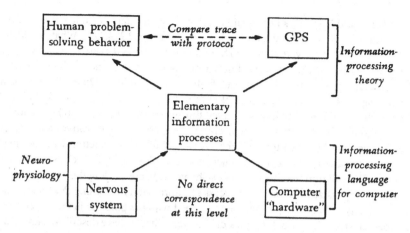

Fig. 5.6. The functionalism of early AI: information processes can be realized using different material structures, the nervous system and computer hardware. The elementary information processes are assumed to be common to humans and computer programs (from Simon, 1961).

ligent computer now took specific form as some demanding consequences. The point is now explicitly the program's ability to manipulate symbol structures. These are *representations* and, together, have a *causal power*, i.e. they can *stand for* very different objects and, moreover, when manipulated through the rules, they *generate* other symbol structures. Since they are manipulated through those rules solely as *physical* structures, their causal power does not imply an appeal to something non-physical. This kind of functionalism seems to suggest a materialistic solution to some of the enigmas of the mind-body problem. On the one hand, it removes plausibility from vitalism; on the other hand it makes room for a physicalist theory of mental representations which is very different from those discussed in previous chapters.

In Chapter 7, we will return to a discussion of this kind of functionalism, which became popular within AI, and of the issue of the *constraints* of the behavioral models. In the meantime, it should be said that Information Processing Psychology shared an anti-behavioristic bias with all early AI, or at least the part that offered itself as a new science of mind. Minsky, for example, insisted that AI had reintroduced mentalistic and teleological language in psychology as proof of its anti-behaviorist thrust (Minsky, 1968: 2). The suggestion from cybernetics of using a purposive language to describe feedback machines' behavior was, therefore, transferred to describing programs' performance. After all, the possibility of automating choice had been struck upon by Oettinger, and this led him to talk of "learning" and "discriminative" abilities in programs. The new and more evolved heuristic programs of early AI seemed to develop these potentials. These programs presented themselves as complex hierarchies of procedures that were both *automatic* and *selective*, and thus confirmed the feeling that there was no longer any reason for the contrast between these two terms. But unlike the simple artifacts of cybernetics, they aimed at reproducing the cognitive processes of human beings.

"What would McDougall have said to Ashby's homeostat?" wondered the philosopher Wladyslaw Sluckin on the threshold of AI (Sluckin, 1954: 35). What would McDougall have said to Newell, Shaw and Simon's GPS? This is the question that Margaret Boden seemed to pose in more recent times in discussing whether and to what extent GPS, with its means-ends heuristics, could satisfy the criteria that in McDougall's view, as we saw in Chapter 4, were characteristic of purposeful behavior (Boden, 1972: 118-119). McDougall would probably have answered this question by referring to his distinction between "true" teleology (that of the machine's designer) and "derivative" teleology, or "pseudo-teleology" (that of the machine). A closely related distinction was later made with regard to AI programs that were much more complex that those we have mentioned up to now. We will turn to this point too in Chapter 7. In concluding the present chapter, we wish to emphasize how the early success of Information Processing Psychology, and more generally of heuristic programming, carried with it a polemic judgment concerning cybernetic modeling. Looking back on the events that we have described, Newell and Simon concluded:

> Although the tortoises aroused considerable interest and have been further developed by other investigators, they appear no longer to be in the main line of evolution of psychological simulations. The interesting properties they exhibited could be rather easily simulated by digital computers, and the digital simulation lent itself to greater elaboration than did the analogue devices (Newell and Simon, 1963: 385-386).

Nevertheless, these models seemed to Newell and Simon to be "existence proofs," demonstrating that there are mechanisms capable of certain kinds of behavior, such as goal-seeking and learning, usually considered to be characteristic of organisms (p. 401). LT itself, before it was replaced by its GPS modified version, was considered by its authors a sufficiency proof at the very least: the proof that one was not forced to invoke something else, something non-physical, to explain certain higher processes that characterize the human mind (see for example Newell and Simon 1959: 5). In these remarks we see the renewal of a recurring wager, one urged on by the idea that the 'new' and more versatile machines that become available can be used to overcome the opposition between the mental and the physical, between the organic and the inorganic.

CHAPTER 6

NEW STEPS TOWARDS THE ARTIFICIAL

1. Introduction: symbols or neurons?

While denying the relevance of cybernetic robotics, Newell and Simon pointed out that, besides symbolic information-processing modeling, another, different line of research was being pursued at the time, which would use formal models that simulated the properties of neurons and of their organization into nets (Newell and Simon, 1963: 392). In fact, at the time of writing, this line of research was well established, and some of the events in its development were touched on in previous chapters. Rashevsky had tried, at the end of the 1920s and later in his 1938 *Mathematical Biophysics*, to analyze various physiological and neural phenomena mathematically. In 1943, McCulloch and Pitts introduced Boolean algebra to describe nets consisting of formal neurons. In 1949, in *The Organization of Behavior*, Hebb formulated his law on the modification of nerve connections during learning. Nets of formal neurons, with connections that could be modified through rules of this kind, have been simulated on computers since the early 1950s.

These nets were trained to solve simple tasks of pattern recognition and classification, tasks which have always been at the center of attention in studies of human and animal behavior. Some of the pioneering contributors in this field were Alfred Uttley and Wilfrid Taylor in England. Uttley designed, and then perfected in later versions, a model that can be described as a formal net which learns to classify sensory patterns. The model used conditional probability to reconstruct a pattern on the basis of previous 'experience' (Uttley, 1954). Taylor was more interested in neurological evidence. He supplied the nets with an associative memory, training them to associate different patterns through their repeated presentation (Taylor, 1956). Both Uttley's and Taylor's models were able to exhibit simple forms of the conditioned reflex. Uttley, in particular, built hydraulic and electronic models of learning (Uttley, 1959), the latter consisting of computers that were also connected to mobile robots (see Figure 5.1).

Two machines realized by two United States researchers, Oliver Selfridge and Frank Rosenblatt, were destined to become particularly popular among psychologists. Both were presented, together with Taylor's and Uttley's machines, at the Symposium on the Mechanisation of Thought Processes, one of the most important meetings in the history of cybernetics and early AI. Held at Teddington in 1958, its participants included neurologists and psychologists such as R.L. Gregory, experts in computer programming such as Backus, cyberneticians such as Angyan, Ashby, McCulloch, MacKay, and Pask, and leading figures at Dartmouth such as McCarthy and Minsky.

Selfridge's Pandemonium was the machine that had already drawn Newell's attention: it discriminated between and classified sensory patterns consisting of letter-shapes and was composed of a hierarchy of units, called "demons." These cooperated at different levels, in order to recognize the features of a sensory pattern, which they then clas-

Plate 6.1

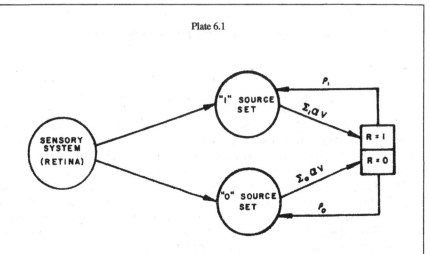

A very simple Perceptron discriminates between the presence (1) or absence (0) of a feature. It consists of three layers (the figure shows the Perceptron described by Rosenblatt at the Teddington Symposium in 1958: see Rosenblatt, 1959). Each element in the first layer, which represents the sensory system (an analog for a retina), is randomly connected to one or more elements in the second layer, the association system. The latter consists of association cells, or A-units, whose output is a function of the input signal α (which is either 1 or 0 in our case) and of a "value" v, a variable quantity that makes the output signal changeable over time (a form of memory, as Rosenblatt called it). The A-units are grouped into two source sets, whose outputs are therefore $\Sigma_1\alpha v$ and $\Sigma_0\alpha v$. These are able to activate the response unit, which constitutes the third layer. The two sets of A-units are called, respectively, 1-source set and 0-source set. The A-units in the first set elicit the response (R=1), the others do not (R=0).

Now if R=1, a connection ρ_1 is activated which gives feedback as a reinforcement signal for all the A-units in the 1-source set. If R=0, a connection ρ_0 is activated, which gives feedback as a reinforcement signal for all the A-units in the 0-source set. When a stimulus is given to the visual system, the output signals from each of the source sets are summed, and the sign of the difference, $\Sigma_1\alpha v - \Sigma_0\alpha v$, determines whether the response is 1 or 0: if the 1-source set sends the stronger output signal, the response will be 1; if the 0-source set sends the stronger output signal, the response will be 0.

sified (Selfridge, 1959). Rosenblatt's Perceptron also learned to discriminate between and classify sensory patterns, but it was a differently-conceived machine, one where the psychological tradition of connectionism met neural networks *à la* McCulloch and Pitts. The units in Perceptron that allowed it to learn were neurons inspired by McCulloch and Pitts. However, they were endowed with "values," as Rosemblatt called them, which, varying over time, constituted a form of 'memory' for neurons.[1] In the early descriptions of Perceptron, like the simple one (Plate 6.1) presented by Rosenblatt at the Teddington

[1] We know that the need for a model of neural plasticity consisting of units provided with some form of 'memory' had already been addressed by earlier and more primitive modeling approaches (see Chapter 2, section 5).

Symposium, learning was essentially based on reinforcement rules, which made the correct response more likely when the stimulus was repeated (Rosenblatt, 1959). Other experiments led to the formulation of the Perceptron supervised-learning rule, which was used to adjust the 'weights' of the net connections when the response was incorrect, and to leave them unchanged when it was correct.

At Teddington, Rosenblatt rejected the possibility of using digital computers as models of the brain. With critical remarks that recall those of Schmitt, who feared that the brain-computer comparison would be an obstacle to the designing of "more brain-like machines" (see above, p. 175), Rosenblatt emphasized that digital computers, being based on binary logic, are not able to handle incomplete information effectively. Since they are "designed to follow rules" (p. 423), they might be able to play games like chess fairly well, but not to reproduce the intelligence and learning characteristics of living organisms, lacking as they do spontaneity and self-organizational abilities. Ashby, in Rosenblatt's judgment, was the only one who had proposed a machine that possessed these characteristics, but Perceptron, though inspired by the homeostat, had greater ambitions: it was not conceived just to maintain a system in equilibrium, but to process "meaningful information" (p. 424).

Rosenblatt's contribution was diametrically opposed to that of Minsky, who at Teddington carried to its extreme consequences the disagreement that we saw surfacing among the builders of intelligent machines even before the official birth of AI. After presenting the emerging heuristic programming as the study of "syntactic processes involving the manipulation of symbolic expressions," Minsky, who had himself been involved with neural nets earlier, now expressed his skepticism about neural-net and self-organizing models. In his opinion, they were somewhat successful at simulating some elementary forms of adaptation and learning, but inadequate when applied to higher cognitive processes. These were starting to be successfully simulated using symbolic systems equipped with a complex hierarchic organization like heuristic programs. It would be more worthwhile, Minsky concluded, to dedicate oneself to what "some of us call 'artificial intelligence'" (Minsky, 1959: 24- 26).[2]

The later development of the "sciences of the artificial" will turn out to be heavily influenced by this clear contrast in methods and goals. As it is, the advance of AI during the quarter-century after Teddington, marked the decline not only of the robotics of synthetic animals, but also of neural nets like Perceptrons and of self-organizing systems, exemplified *in nuce* by Ashby's homeostat. All these research areas are usually placed under the heading of cybernetics. However, the very development of AI during that quarter-century, in fact up to our own times, cannot be seen as the history of a homogeneous

---

[2] It should be recalled that Minsky's original interests were aimed precisely at neural nets and self-organizing systems. In 1951 he, along with a former classmate, Dean Edmons, and thanks to financing obtained by George Miller, had built a machine consisting of a net of forty-plus artificial neurons (actually, vacuum tubes) linked randomly. The machine learned a path through a maze by means of a reinforcement rule like Skinner's. This machine is mentioned by Minsky under the name of Snarc (Minsky, 1987: 76). Minsky himself recalls how this experience helped convince him of the difficulty in capturing the nature of intelligence using machines of the sort, essentially self-organizing random nets (see also the testimony collected by Bernstein, 1978).

line of research. On the contrary, it seems to be marked by strong internal tensions, by a multiplicity of research programmes and proposals, even mutually conflicting ones, some of which succeeded, some of which failed or were abandoned, and some of which were taken up again in different times and contexts. The so-called renascence of neural nets, beginning in the early 1980s, is to be viewed, therefore, in an ever-changing context, and the same can be said for those research trends that came to maturity at the same time or shortly afterwards, such as ALife. Conceptually related to the cybernetic tradition, those trends have once again taken up, but in a very different context, certain issues in connectionism and robotics of the 1950s.

In this chapter, we discuss these contrasting developments in the sciences of the artificial, developments which marked the final decades of the twentieth century. We will return in the next chapter to the thread of events that marked the stages of what we have called, synthetically, the discovery of the artificial.

2. Meaning and knowledge: some difficulties for AI

We have mentioned how, from the very origin of AI, the term *heuristics*, when applied to selective procedures in a program, was used in two very different ways. In its first sense, the term referred to the *most detailed simulation possible* of human cognitive processes, and it characterized Newell, Shaw and Simon's Information Processing Psychology. In its other sense, the term referred to the possibility of obtaining the *most efficient performance possible* from programs, by allowing also for typically non-human procedures, such as those where the computer can excel.

Before Newell, Shaw and Simon made the term 'heuristics' popular in AI, procedures which might have been defined as heuristic in the *second* of these senses had already been tried out experimentally. The first among them were the procedures that allowed Samuel's program to play checkers despite the combinatory explosion of moves. Although not specifically conceived for this purpose, given the simplicity of the task environment, certain selection procedures present in Oettinger's programs could also be considered heuristic.[3]

The fact that two tendencies, reflected in this double meaning of the term heuristic, coexisted in AI was immediately clear. In 1961, while discussing a presentation of GPS given by Simon during a seminar at MIT, Minsky drew a distinction in AI research between those who were willing to use "non-human techniques" in constructing intelligent programs and those, like the Carnegie-Mellon group, who were interested in simulating human cognitive processes.[4] The different aspirations that characterized these two ten-

---

[3] Though Oettinger did not use the term heuristics, he mentioned Polya's *How to Solve It* among the references of his 1952 paper.

[4] Minsky emphasized that these two tendencies were distinguished "in methods and goals" from a third tendency, that which "has a physiological orientation and alleges to be based on an imitation of the brain," i.e. neural net and self-organizing system approaches. He confirmed the negative judgment on the latter tendency that he had already expressed some years earlier at the Teddington Symposium, on the basis of the inability of such models to tackle complex cognitive tasks. At the MIT seminar, Simon essentially agreed with Minsky. Simon's talk and the discussion that followed it are in Greenberger (1962: 114-129).

dencies in AI had an influence on its later evolution, although the two meanings of the term heuristic often tended to be mixed together. On the one hand, LT itself was originally motivated as a study of the *efficiency* of heuristic procedures; on the other, the best source of inspiration for refining heuristic programs remained, as Minsky recognized, the human mind. It should also be said that experimentation with heuristics in AI soon took directions other than that of the selective search in the state space that we mentioned in the previous chapter, giving rise to an extremely varied range of proposals, projects and experiments.

Something new could be perceived even in one of the AI programs conceived in the Dartmouth days, since its programmers had undertaken to handle the combinatory-explosion problem in a style noticeably different from that of simple state-space representation. This was the Geometry Theorem Machine, a program that ran in 1959 on an IBM 704. It was written in a modified version of FORTRAN by Herbert Gelernter and other programmers from the Rochester group. The machine demonstrated a number of Euclidean plane geometry theorems, using a stratagem already pointed out by Minsky at Dartmouth, where Gelernter was present.[5]

In the early AI programs mentioned so far, which played games or proved theorems, the *meaning* of the symbols was usually not considered. Earlier versions of GPS, for example, made a mere pattern matching: different physical patterns of symbols (in fact, well formed formulas of sentential logic) consisting of letters (sentential variables) and of signs like '∨', '⊃' and so forth (logical connectives) were compared; then the appropriate operators (rules of logic) were applied to eliminate certain differences among those patterns, "as though [such patterns] were so many pieces of wood or metal," as Simon would later say (see Simon and Siklóssy, 1972: 2).

The novel feature of the Geometry Machine was that, while applying, in order to prove a theorem, means-ends heuristics in the form of a decomposition of the problem into simpler sub-problems, it did not, as LT or GPS did, use only the so-called 'syntactic' methods of pattern matching between sentences to guide the search. The machine also had access to a geometric figure (coded as a list of coordinates) that corresponded to the statement of the theorem. When the machine generated a sub-problem, it compared the result to the figure and discarded it immediately if it was incompatible with that figure: "if you like, [this] is the seat of our artificial intelligence," Gelernter concluded (Gelernter 1959: 143). Later experiments convinced the authors of the Geometry Machine that it could even compete with a human being in a "restricted" form, as they said (almost echoing Oettinger's words about Turing test), i.e. a form limited to geometry theorem-proving (Gelernter et al., 1960: 158). The reason for their enthusiasm is easy to state. It was felt that the Geometry Machine used a 'semantic' interpretation of geometry theorems to control the search—and wasn't this the way a human theorem-prover did it?

In fact, the early AI syntactic approach was consistent with the developments in Noam Chomsky's transformational linguistics. AI and transformational linguistics enjoyed a privileged relationship from the outset. Over time that relationship become more and

---

[5] See, however, Gelenter's later explanation of this in Siekmann and Wrightson (1983).

more strained, even though Simon still remembers with pleasure how, in the same IRE convention at MIT in 1956, while he and Newell presented the implementation of LT, Chomsky was expounding the outlines of the linguistic theory that he would publish the following year in *Syntactic Structures* (Chomsky, 1957). With this book, Chomsky declared the primacy of syntax in the study of language, a primacy that later research always comes to term with. The early approaches to automatic natural-language processing in terms of syntactic parsers of sentences owe much to Chomsky's ideas. Moreover, transformational grammar attracted the attention of those who were working on the development of programming languages and their compilers.

Work in machine translation, even anticipating the official birth of AI, assigned a leading role to the computational aspects of syntax, while semantic problems were deliberately set aside. Machine translation emerged almost at the dawn of digital computers and enjoyed a surge of interest in the immediate Post-War period, due, above all, to the work of Warren Weaver. In these earlier experiments on machine translation, the computer, already well-proven in deciphering military codes, did not go much beyond substituting one word for an equivalent one in another language, using a bilingual dictionary, following grammatical rules, and reducing semantics to a study of some statistical regularities.

Oettinger had been among the first to put this kind of approach into practice. After moving to Harvard from Cambridge, England, from the mid-1950s onwards he launched a project to design a computer program that could translate from Russian into English. In the next ten years, research centers were started more or less everywhere—in Western Europe, in the Soviet Union and in Japan. Despite the mobilization of human and financial resources, after some initial success machine translation seemed to have arrived at a deadlock. In 1966, following the so-called ALPAC report, grants were cut off in the United States. Oettinger himself, deeply disappointed, quit machine translation. In the end, he wrote a preface for one of the texts which would later become a point of reference for every critic of AI, *What Computers Can't Do*, by the philosopher Hubert Dreyfus.[6] An ironic twist of fate: Oettinger had been one of the favorite targets of the invectives against AI contained in a volume published earlier, this time by an engineer, Mortimer Taube, *Computers and Common Sense: The Myth of Thinking Machines* (Taube, 1961).

Another pioneer in the field, Yehoshua Bar-Hillel, has discussed the difficulty that best summarized the reason why what was initially referred to as "fully automatic high quality translation" failed. We can express it by running through one of his examples (Bar-Hillel, 1960: 158-163). Given the sentence 'The baby looked for his box and the box was in the pen', a native English speaker, understands it "automatically," as Bar-Hillel put it: he *knows* that here 'pen' refers, not to the writing instrument, which we will call PEN, but to a play-pen, say PEN1. How could a machine translate the sentence correctly into another language, without *knowing* what is being discussed? Similar cases can be mul-

---

[6] This book, which aroused much discussion, has been reprinted with updates and variations on the theme of what computers *cannot do*, up to the most recent edition, with the revised title of *What Computers Still Can't Do* (Dreyfus, 1992).

tiplied at will. The moral: a good translation from one language to another, but more generally a good *understanding* of languages, cannot disregard the meanings suggested by the context nor the common-sense knowledge about the relationships that could exist in the real world between the objects mentioned (such as pens and boxes in the example). Now, is it possible, or is it completely impossible, as Bar-Hillel concluded, that this kind of knowledge might be represented in a computer program?

The idea of resorting to a computational device that took into account the associative connections between words in a dictionary, in order to make the use of the lexicon more flexible, was developed precisely in the context of machine translation. In the 1950s and 1960s, it was tried by, among others, Silvio Ceccato in Italy and Margaret Masterman in England.[7] Starting with his doctoral thesis in 1966 under Simon at Carnegie-Mellon University, M. Ross Quillian introduced "semantic networks," whose developments have proved to be most fertile up to the present. Quillian's aim was, more generally, to construct a psychologically plausible model of semantic memory, which, when implemented in a computer, would reproduce some aspects of the human ability to understand a text and to draw inferences based on a body of knowledge. This is a crucial point where AI started to move away from Chomsky. According to Quillian, his model demonstrated that the entire set of problems linked to the *understanding* of a text in natural language (whether it was a matter of parsing it, translating it, or interpreting it in order to answer questions) could not, generally, be handled exhaustively by appealing to syntactic properties only. The crucial problem, Quillian said, was "extracting a cognitive representation of a text's message," an undertaking concerned with the *meaning* of the words. Hence the central role he attributed to semantic memory.

Quillian conceived of semantic memory as a network divided into "planes," the portions of network nodes that represent the word meaning in the lexicon. To represent the two meanings of the word *pen*, for example, Quillian would have used two different nodes, called "patriarch nodes": PEN (*writing instrument*) and PEN1 (*play-pen*). These two patriarch nodes are connected to each other by "associative links." To each patriarch node corresponds a distinct plane, structured as a hierarchy of nodes subordinate to that patriarch node. Each plane is in turn connected by associative links to other patriarch nodes belonging to other planes: in the above example, to BABY and BOX. When the above sentence is read, the activation of the BABY node *spreads* towards all nodes connected with it. Thus PEN1 and PEN2 are activated in turn. Quillian gave some computational procedures to establish whether the associative links between some nodes are more direct than links between other nodes. The result is, in our case, that PEN1 is more directly connected than PEN with BABY in the context of the sentence.

Quillian's work was published in *Semantic Information Processing*, a collection of essays edited by Minsky (1968), together with a series of research reports carried out at MIT during the first half of the 1960s, exploring various aspects of knowledge representation in programs. Minsky admitted that Quillian's insights were not far off from those of the "earlier associationists," and, considering our investigation of the discovery of the

---

[7] The history of machine translation is given by Hutchins (1986).

artificial, this may seem particularly evident.[8] Nevertheless, Minsky insisted on the fact that, in Quillian's case, these insights were translated into "much more concrete proposals," i.e. in computational procedures. By taking up Bar-Hillell's very example, Minsky concluded that Quillian's program provided an early answer to the objection that "machines can't do semantics" (p. 22).

Other programs described in *Semantic Information Processing* have become well known. ANALOGY by Thomas Evans recognized analogies between simple geometric figures; STUDENT by Daniel Bobrow answered some elementary questions posed in algebra world problems; SIR (Semantic Information Retrieval) by Bertram Raphael answered some questions that entailed knowledge of logical relationships, such as set-theory membership and inclusion, and of some of their properties, such as transitivity of inclusion. This allowed the program to draw a number of inferences, relative to a very limited domain, that were not explicitly coded in its data base. Knowledge was represented in the program through a number of pre-established "templates" such as ** *is a part of* **, where nouns can be substituted for the variables **. Using these templates, the program matched the sentences given in input and, by applying the substitution and quantification rules of logic, showed that it 'understood' sentences like 'a finger *is a part* of a hand.' Understanding the meaning of a sentence, according to Raphael, consisted in an automatic process that was summarized as recognizing the objects in the sentence and placing them within a specified relationship. The possibility of resolving some very simple semantic ambiguities by means of this procedure—in the sentence from the earlier example it cannot be that *a box is in a pen* in the meaning of PEN—led Minsky to conclude that semantic approaches of this kind could begin to tackle the problem of common-sense knowledge. They had capabilities that seemed go beyond the syntactic approaches suggested by linguistics, as well as those based on simple heuristic search in the state space. According to Minsky, the very "excellent results" (p. 19) obtained using the semantic model of the Geometry Machine suggested this line of research.

Simon had independently arrived at similar conclusions. With his student Jeffrey Page, he published in 1966 an analysis of thinking-aloud protocols of subjects dealing with algebra world problems of the sort handled by Bobrow's STUDENT. The experimental data revealed that different subjects used different strategies, and these were associated with different problem representations. In particular, some subjects used semantic information coming from figures or diagrams as auxiliary information not explicit

---

[8] Compare the above example to the way that James, referring back to his neurological hypotheses (see Chaper 2, section 2), explained the associations of words in memorized verses. The same word, *ages*, appears in two verses of Locksley Hall: 'I, the heir of all the *ages*, in the foremost files of time,' and 'For I doubt not through the *ages* one eternal purpose runs.' But when these two verses must be recited from memory, normally one does not commit the error, while reciting the first, of following the word *ages* with the words 'one...' instead of 'in.' Even if 'ages', James observed, in the abstract can establish an associative connection both with the words 'one...' and with the words 'in...,' in fact the former and the latter are not evoked solely by 'ages', but also by the set of words that precede it: "then the strongest line of discharge will be that which they *all alike* tend to take" (James, 1890, vol. 1: 567-568). Put otherwise, the words that precede 'ages' constitute a *context* (as Pillsbury, 1911: 144, put it when he illustrated this example) that activates one association instead of another.

in the problem statement but useful in solving the problem. These points had not been considered in Bobrow's program.

Clearly, Page and Simon's aim was quite different from Bobrow's. Following the methodology of Information Processing Psychology, Page and Simon were attempting to achieve a detailed computer simulation of various processes used by humans in solving algebra world problems, thus testing their theory, while Bobrow's intention was an investigation in AI, i.e. to build a program that could communicate with people in a natural language within that problem domain. As such, Bobrow's program was considered by Page and Simon a "gross test of sufficiency" for their theory, because the program's performance roughly resembled that of some human problem solvers. As the authors observed, "the flight of airplanes does not much resemble the flight of birds, except in the fact that both can sometimes stay aloft" (see Simon, 1979: 203). Therefore, once the *sufficiency* of the theory is checked, the next step is the stronger test of comparing human and computer problem-solving *processes*. It is the standard procedure of theory building and testing we have already discussed, that Page and Simon described as a "forward motion" towards progressively more adequate explanations of behavior.[9]

The "simple tree-search paradigm," as Simon was then calling heuristic search in the state space, had thus given its very best in the building of intelligent machines, and future programs had to be able to make ever more extensive use of information that could help to solve a problem (Simon, 1972: 270). According to Simon, Chomsky's distinction between *competence* (abstract linguistic knowledge) and *performance* (the realization of that knowledge in specific linguistic abilities) tends to disappear in natural-language understanding programs. Several research projects conducted at Carnegie-Mellon between 1965 and 1969 documented this approach (Simon and Siklóssy, 1972). A program by Stephen Coles, for example, used semantic information contained in a picture corresponding to an ambiguous sentence to decide which of the various possible syntactic analyses of the sentence was correct with respect to a given context. Laurent Siklóssy's program used a fairly analogous procedure. The program was given a picture of a certain situation, represented in a LISP-like functional notation. When a sentence in a natural language that described what was in the picture was also given to the program, it used the pictures as clues to the meaning of the sentences, thus simulating a child who is learning a language. Like a child, the program was able to make inferences about the vocabulary and other sentences of that language.

"Hybrid" systems of this kind, as Simon put it, cashed in on the lesson learned from the Geometry Machine (Simon, 1972: 273). The latter did not contain one and only one representation of the problem space, that of the state space; it also contained another one

---

[9] See Chapter 5, section 5. The example of flight (an analogy already stressed by Hull: see above, p. 85) has become popular in AI. It was used by Oettinger, but, unlike Paige and Simon, with the aim of stressing the mere "functional resemblance" between organisms and machines, which as such does not concern the resemblance of *processes* (see above, p. 175). See Chapter 7 for a discussion of this point. Drawing the analogy with fly (aircraft do it well without imitating birds), Ford and Hayes (1998) argue that the goal of AI is not that of imitating *human* intelligence, but that of seeking a *general* theory of intelligence, including machines, animals and humans.

in the form of a "semantic space," that of the geometric figures. The efficiency of the program derived from its use of both representations. The problem of search control, concluded Simon, was now connected to that of knowledge representation.

The performance of Joseph Weizenbaum's ELIZA, a program implemented during those same years at MIT, was based on a procedure similar to SIR's template matching: in ELIZA, the words in the input were associated with key-words codified in the data base. The program managed to converse with a human being, simulating, at least up to a certain point, the behavior of a psychotherapist. ELIZA was the most popular language-understanding program of those years because, in some cases, it seemed to satisfy the usual "restricted version" of the Turing test: some of the patients who interacted with the program mistook it for a real human therapist. From this result Weizenbaum drew some pessimistic—and even worried—conclusions about the AI undertaking in a book which became very popular (Weizenbaum, 1976). Actually, this result threw light on the ambiguities inherent in the Turing test in its restricted version, which certainly was not the one that Turing had originally imagined. It also demonstrated how risky it was to aim at defining 'artificial intelligence' by relying on mere functional resemblance.

Apart from Weizenbaum's evaluation, 'semantic' programs such as ELIZA really were not very semantic. Their performance was restricted to very limited domains, and their knowledge resided in the templates or in the key words provided by the programmer. The syntactic analysis itself consisted of simple *ad hoc* procedures. Other programs, such as Quillian's or Siklóssy's, raised instead a crucial problem for later AI research: that of constructing systems capable of handling knowledge through suitable representations, or models, of the world, whether that be general common-sense knowledge or domain-dependent knowledge, and capable of doing so with human-like flexibility. As we shall see, this would mean significantly different things depending on the medium chosen to represent knowledge and how flexible that medium was.

It was a student of Simon's, Edward Feigenbaum, who highlighted the importance of MIT and Carnegie semantic information-processing programs of the 1960s for the purpose of knowledge representation. In a talk at the 1968 Information Processing Conference, after sketching a survey of AI research in the 1960s, he envisioned the AI prospects for the following decade (Feigenbaum, 1969).[10] At that time, however, Feigenbaum was conducting his own research project. From Carnegie-Mellon, where in 1959 he had completed, under Simon's supervision, EPAM (Elementary Perceiver And Memorizer), a program that simulates the human processes involved in memorizing nonsense syllables, Feigenbaum had moved to Stanford and his interests had changed.[11] At Stanford he met Joshua Lederberg, a Nobel laureate in genetics. Starting in the mid-1960s, these two launched a project that would open up a new field in AI, with commercial consequences that could not be foreseen at that time. As Feigenbaum pointed out in his 1968

[10] Feigenbaum's survey shows the hegemony of the United States in AI research in problem solving, heuristic programming, and semantic information processing. However, he mentioned other research areas that also had "a rightful place under the umbrella of 'artificial intelligence'," such as pattern recognition, bionics and neurophysiological information-processing models (p. 1008).
[11] Feigenbaum's 1961 presentation of EPAM is in Feigenbaum and Feldman (1963).

talk, where he presented the first results of research he had conducted with Lederberg, their project lay in what he considered "the mainstream of AI research: problem solving using the heuristic search paradigm" (p. 1016). There was at least one fundamental difference, however: the chosen task environment was not a toy problem or a (fairly) well-defined problem of the kind which had been the subject of heuristic programming up until then, i.e. logic, chess, and various games or puzzles. On the contrary, their program tackled a task where specialized knowledge is needed, a task similar to induction and hypothesis formation in a scientific problem, namely, identifying the molecular structure of unknown organic compounds.[12]

The flow diagram of the program was a cycle that reproduced observation, inductive hypothesis formation, prediction and testing according to the canonical procedure of the "Baconian" scientific method, as Michie described it in the discussion that followed Feigenbaum's presentation at the Information Processing Conference. In this version, the program, written in LISP and called DENDRAL (DENDRitic ALgorithm), was composed of a "Hypothesis Generator" and a "Predictor." As its authors would later point out, these two parts of DENDRAL reflected the 'generalist' approach of GPS, as they embodied the generate-and-test method, i.e. the 'weakest' general-purpose search method, as it was conceived by Newell and Simon (Feigenbaum et al., 1971: 169).[13] The Generator (the generating part) defined the problem space of DENDRAL as a hypothesis space in a way, Feigenbaum observed, that was totally analogous to that of a legal move generator in a chess program. The generation of hypotheses about molecular structure could be exhaustive, being based on an algorithm already identified by Lederberg. In its turn, the Predictor (the testing part), which tested the hypotheses and selected those that were plausible, was called an "expert," but a very general expert, since its competence was in the theory of mass spectrometry. One of the main novelties in the program was that the Predictor did not examine all the hypotheses produced by the Generator using Lederberg's algorithm, but only one of its subsets, chosen by a "Preliminary Inference Maker." This was the real "specialist." The authors called it the "Planner," which operated on the basis of knowledge and special-purpose heuristic rules related to the mass spectrum and the atomic elements of the molecule one sought to identify.

DENDRAL is considered the root of the family of 'expert systems', a name readily given to those AI systems that made extensive use of specialized knowledge to attempt to solve complex and real-life problems. It was considered fairly distant from GPS, to the extent that this used general problem-solving methods and general problem representation. DENDRAL, however, according to its authors' own intentions, was a study in the tradeoff between *generality* and *power* of heuristics, and this was also the aim of the analysis of GPS by Ernst and Newell (1969). Feigenbaum's conclusion was that general heuristics, the GPS-like 'weak methods', proved effective when they were associated with some special-purpose heuristics, i.e. related to a certain body of knowledge (Feigenbaum et al., 1971: 188). In this form, weak methods have continue to constitute the back-

---

[12] The (actually fuzzy) distinction between well-defined and ill-defined problems has been much debated in AI: see for example Simon (1973). And among games, chess can be seen as a knowledge-rich domain .

[13] A classic discussion of weak methods in heuristic search is in Newell (1973).

bone of various heuristic-search AI systems. Some later experiments on DENDRAL, for example, concentrated on search constraints to be imposed on the Planner.

Michie, on the occasion we have already mentioned, called DENDRAL an example of "epistemological engineering." Feigenbaum later opted for "knowledge engineering," which has now entered the jargon as identifying one of the critical points in expert systems research: how to transfer into an AI program the wealth of heuristic knowledge that characterizes a human expert. Feigenbaum also mentioned the distrust that DENDRAL initially encountered among 'generalists.' The latter, even without adopting the original formulation of GPS, believed that AI had to search for those general principles of intelligence which could be transferred into machines. It must, however, be said that before the development of large computer memories, which began in the 1970s, the management of extensive knowledge bases like those required by expert systems was not a pursuable goal. Only after that period would expert systems be successful in spreading into the most diverse fields, from medicine to geology, from engineering to computer-aided instruction, and often be transformed into as many commercial products.

3. Common-sense problems for computers

The programs realized from the *generalist* standpoint, which the authors of DENDRAL criticized, included, in addition to GPS, a program whose prototype McCarthy had outlined many years earlier, at the time of the Teddington Symposium (McCarthy, 1959). The Advice Taker, as it was called, was conceived as a general or multi-purpose problem-solving system, formulating plans and drawing inferences based on a sufficiently extensive body of knowledge, while also making use of 'advice' provided by its programmer. The Advice Taker shared GPS's aspiration to generality, with one fundamental difference: logic was not merely one of the subjects handled by the program, but the very medium or language for representing heuristics and the body of knowledge related to every subject. In fact, this was all to be represented in the form of first-order logic sentences, assumed as axioms or premises, and their consequences were to be inferred by the rules of logic.

Other programs of the period, like GPS or the Geometry Machine, managed to perform in domains requiring a high level of human intelligence, for example in theorem proving. On the contrary, the Advice Taker should have exhibited capabilities that were closer to those of the average human: planning actions, drawing inferences, taking decisions based on common-sense reasoning in real-life situations (like reaching an airport from home in order to board an airplane, as in the example discussed by McCarthy). "A program has common sense," McCarthy claimed, "if it automatically deduces for itself a sufficiently wide class of immediate consequences of anything it is told and that it already knows" (p. 78).

One early attempt to implement at least some of the characteristics of the Advice Taker dates back to 1964 and is owed to Fisher Black. Minsky included it in *Semantic Information Processing*, warning that it was the "least 'semantic' paper in this collection"

(Minsky, 1968: 5).[14] The aspiration to generality that characterized the Advice Taker was taken up again after the formulation of a particularly promising new procedure for automatic theorem proving. This was J. Alan Robinson's resolution principle, which one of McCarthy's students, Cordell Green, incorporated into a question-answering program, QA3. Making inferences based on Robinson's principle, or rule, the program was able to generate answers to questions asked by the user and related to various subject areas. It was, therefore, a program based on logic and designed to be general, or subject-independent (Green, 1969).

Behind Robinson's result there is an entire path beaten by researchers interested in a kind of automatic theorem proving which did not have as its goal the simulation of human information processing pursued by Newell, Shaw and Simon. Instead, it made use of earlier findings by logicians like Thoralf Skolem, Jaques Herbrand, and Gerhard Gentzen. Hao Wang had already questioned Newell, Shaw and Simon's claims about the efficiency of the heuristics (understood as incomplete procedures) of LT. Between 1958 and 1959, Wang implemented on an IBM 704 three algorithmic procedures, both correct and complete, which in a few minutes proved theorems of the sentential and predicate calculi in the *Principia Mathematica*, thus showing itself to be much more *efficient* than LT. The subsequent research by Martin Davis and by Hilary Putnam and Dag Prawitz culminated in Robinson's classic 1965 article, where he described a logical calculus without axioms but with a single rule of inference, called "resolution," which was proved to be correct and complete.[15]

For some years most of the research on automatic deduction concentrated on resolution, which came to be associated with a kind of general-purpose theorem proving that made very little use of domain-dependent information and even less of heuristic procedures that were not of a syntactic nature. In this way, so-called 'refinements' of resolution were introduced, above all in their twofold form concerning constraints and the order to impose on the generation of particular clauses. A change of course took place in the first half of the 1970s, when dissatisfaction with the results achieved in research on resolution refinements rekindled interest in a kind of theorem proving less sensitive to the requirement for completeness and more attentive to heuristic procedures inspired by human problem-solving methods. Such theorem proving was going to be less syntactic

---

[14] In the same collection we also find an extended and modified version of McCarthy's talk at Teddington, where the Advice Taker had been presented by him as "a joint project with Marvin Minsky" (McCarthy, 1959: 78). Minsky himself, in his talk at Teddington, mentioned the Advice Taker as a joint project with McCarthy, concerned with the problem of common-sense knowledge (Minsky, 1959: 34). This commonality of McCarthy's and Minsky's methods in confronting this problem was growing weaker at the time (see also below). As Minsky later recalled, "[McCarthy and I] agreed that the most critical problem was how minds do common-sense reasoning. McCarthy was more concerned with establishing logical and mathematical foundations for reasoning, while I was more involved with theories of how we actually reason using pattern recognition and analogy" (Minsky, 1987: 323).

[15] In its simplest form (concerning sentential variables), the rule states that from two well-formed formulae consisting of disjunctions of atomic formulae or their negations, $A \vee \neg B$ and $B \vee C$ (the "parent clauses"), it is possible to infer the "resolvent" $A \vee C$ (the clause consisting of the disjunction of the non-complementary constituents of the parent clauses).

and more bound to domain-dependent knowledge. W.W. Bledsoe, after initially working on refinements, "made the switch," as he put it, with greater conviction, returning in
part to the statements on heuristics by Newell and Simon and by Gelernter.[16]

Resolution paved the way, however, to a new style of programming, introduced by Robert
Kowalski and known as 'logic programming.' This uses a refinement of resolution that is
correct and complete and altogether very efficient for a particular and important class of formulae, the Horn clauses.[17] This refinement was incorporated in PROLOG (PROgrammation
en LOGique), the programming language developed during the first half of the 1970s in
some European Universities, at Edinburgh and, with Alain Colmerauer, at Marseilles.

The difficulty of extending QA3's performance, when common-sense problems of a
certain complexity and large data bases were present, discouraged Green from continuing to pursue the goal of a question-answering system that was "general, formal and de-
ductive," as he stated initially, with reference to Advice Taker (Green, 1969: 184). As Mc-
Carthy later observed, it was these unsuccessful experiences in controlling the reasoning that led to programs like STRIPS (STanford Research Institute Problem Solver) and
its successors (McCarthy, 1988: 301). In STRIPS, designed in 1969 at the SRI (Stanford
Research Institute) by Richard Fikes and Nils Nillson, knowledge was once again represented using first-order logic, and deduction was again entrusted to resolution, but
planning was executed using an evolved version of the GPS's means-ends heuristics.

In 1971, again at the SRI, the authors of STRIPS, in collaboration with Raphael, used
their program for representing knowledge and for controlling a robot that moved around
in a real environment. Shakey was the robot's name.[18] In the previous decade, at Stanford, at MIT and at Edinburgh, experiments had been conducted regarding the automatic manipulation of simple blocks arranged on a table. The so-called 'hand-eye' systems
were equipped with a mobile arm and a television camera that provided images to a computer. Shakey was the most successful attempt of the time to build a mobile robot. The
robot was a radio-controlled cart equipped with a television camera and some bumper
switches. The sensory information provided by the camera was converted into symbolic representations in first-order logic, on the basis of which the robot constructed a detailed general model of its environment. The planning of STRIPS was used to construct
plans and make decisions based on this symbolic representation of the world. Shakey was
able to move around only in very limited and well pre-arranged surroundings, where it
managed to avoid obstacles and to move large solid items.[19]

---

[16] Bledsoe (1977: 2). On the origins and developments of resolution and its refinements, see Cordeschi
(1996) But above all see Bledsoe and Loveland (1984), which also contains Hao Wang's testimony. The contributions by the mentioned authors (including Robinson's), which marked the origin of automatic theorem proving, have been collected by Siekmann and Wrightson (1983).

[17] A Horn clause is a formula with at most one positive constituent, of the form $A \lor -B_1 \lor ... \lor -B_n$.

[18] A description of Shakey is given by Raphael (1976), where one also finds the description of what was called
'Hopkins' Beast,' a robot built at the Johns Hopkins University in the early 1960s, whose performance was similar to that of Grey Walter's tortoises.

[19] Shakey's performance was such that one of the traditional supporters of AI research in the United States,
the DARPA, interested at the time in military applications for robotics, decided not to continue to finance the
project. Newquist (1994) reconstructs matters related to the various sources of financing in AI research.

One of the difficulties that had discouraged Green, but that the SRI group had overcome with STRIPS, at least in Shakey's very limited performance, is the *frame problem*, formulated by McCarthy and Patrick Hayes (McCarthy and Hayes, 1969).[20] The frame problem occurs during the execution phase of a plan. Since the aim is to provide a formal representation of the agent's knowledge of the world, and since the world changes during the execution of a plan, it always seems necessary to describe, using suitable axioms (the so-called "frame axioms"), even those aspects of a situation that do *not* get modified by the action. Going into the execution of the plan, this inevitably translates into a proliferation of axioms that, if controllable in the case of simple toy problems, becomes more and more uncontrollable in the case of problems dealing with the complexity of the real world. A robot that moves around in the physical world faces a problem of this sort, and Shakey was able to resolve it only because it moved about in a circumscribed and pre-arranged environment.

In their article on the frame problem, however, McCarthy and Hayes made a clear distinction between the problems raised by the *control* of the inferences, which they called the "heuristic problems," and the problems related to the *representation* of knowledge in a formal language, which they called "epistemological problems." While an attempt was made with STRIPS to confront the heuristic problems, McCarthy's interest was always directed towards the epistemological ones. Indeed, the solution of the latter, or at least their correct formulation, seems to him preliminary to the solution of the former. In this sense, for McCarthy the Advice Taker was never realized, and probably never would be unless the aspects of logic needed to capture the *non-monotonic* character of common-sense reasoning were clarified first.[21]

In a common-sense situation, the initial information is usually incomplete, or the environment changes, so that acquiring new information can cause previously inferred conclusions to become incorrect and in need of elimination. This cannot happen in traditional, or *monotonic*, logic. The canonical example of a simple non-monotonic reasoning starts from the acceptance of the following inference: if x is a bird (premise), then x can fly (conclusion). But if one comes to know that x is an ostrich (a further premise), one has to reconsider the conclusion previously accepted. It is in the non-monotonic *epistemological* approach to reasoning that McCarthy's proposal for "circumscription" should be placed. This presents itself, in real life, as a "rule of conjecture," as McCarthy called it, which, in the presence of incomplete information, as in the example above, justifies the fact that one "jumps" to certain conclusions. The idea is *to circumscribe* as "anomalous" potential exceptions to a typical situation, like the one stated by the sentence 'if x is a bird, then x can fly.' In this case, the property of 'non-flying' is anomalous with respect to 'being a bird,' and thus such an anomalous property is circumscribed. In other words, we assume

---

[20] As the two authors pointed out (p. 468), the article was in part a reply to the criticism of McCarthy's contribution at the Teddington Symposium by Bar-Hillel, who had emphasized that the Advice Taker project contained several unclear philosophical (and "pseudo-philosophical") assumptions. (But Bar-Hillel's criticism on that occasion was leveled more generally at the very plausibility of the project. The *Proceedings* of the Symposium provide documentation of a lively discussion.)

[21] Giunchiglia (1995) deals with the entire span of McCarthy's research, beginning with the Advice Taker.

that it has the smallest possible extension with respect to the information at one's disposition. The sentence in the example, therefore, gets reformulated as the following rule: 'if x is a bird, and x is not an anomalous bird, then x can fly.'

These epistemological problems provided the background for a whole series of research projects, which were then called 'logicist', on the use of logic as a medium to represent the common-sense knowledge which is the core of the agent's model of the world.[22] However, these investigations rarely provided suggestions for actual implementation or, in general, for the solution of heuristic problems. Thus one often witnessed a proliferation of investigations into various forms of circumscription and non-monotonic rules, which also led to some defections. Such was the case of Drew McDermott, who abandoned research on non-monotonic logic through, as he put it, a "critique of pure [logicist] reason" (McDermott, 1988). Interesting but controversial results were also produced by the study of other forms of logic: modal, temporal, fuzzy. In particular, through the latter, introduced by Lofti Zadeh, an attempt was made to grasp those features of common-sense reasoning, regarding for example concept formation, difficult to deal with through binary logic—a problem raised at the very beginning of computer simulation of cognitive processes in terms of "gray" logic.[23]

Antithetic to the logicist position on the representation of common-sense knowledge was the proposal advanced by Minsky in a 1975 article, which would become widely-known as the 'frame paper' (Minsky, 1975). In this paper, Minsky endeavored to establish a "new paradigm" for representing knowledge as opposed to the "dominant paradigm of the past" (p. 259), that of the simple heuristic search in the state space. He then proposed a data structure which he called a "frame." The core of this idea was certainly not new. Notions of the sort, as Minsky himself noted, were already popular among psychologists (Barlett's "schema," for example). Furthermore, frames could be considered a development of Newell, Shaw and Simon's IPL "schemas" and Quillian's semantic networks.[24]

In the early 1970s, the most influential among analogous proposals was Roger Schank's theory of "conceptual dependency" (Schank, 1972), which was equally anti-Chomskyan and anti-logicist. Schank's theory confirmed the limits of some of the natural-language understanding programs of the previous decade. For Schank, the negative model *par excellence* was ELIZA, a collection of tricks, he said, that make a program ape the understanding of word meanings. His aim was to explain natural-language understanding as a cognitive phenomenon through computational processes that were psychologically plausible. He proposed to identify a small set of elementary notions, or semantic primitives, using which it would be possible to construct the representation of mean-

[22] See the texts collected by Bobrow (1980), which also contains McCarthy's article on circumscription. Pylyshyn (1987) is a collection of significant essays on the frame problem.

[23] See above, p. 175. In section 5 below we shall see, however, how both non-monotonic and fuzzy logic have found some successful applications in knowledge representation and in control of recent mobile robots, which are far more complex than Shakey. Other investigations dealing with implementing systems based on McCarthy's approach have been made by Fausto Giunchiglia and coworkers (see for example Bouquet and Cimatti, 1995).

[24] According to McCarthy (1977: 1040), the use of the term 'frame' by Minsky, a term which McCarthy had previously used concerning the frame problem, seemed to "confound matters."

ing for any English verb. The sentence, therefore, was analyzed, making explicit its representation in terms of semantic primitives. In fact, this was the central axiom of the theory: two sentences that are identical in meaning, even if they contain different words or have different structures, share a single representation in terms of semantic primitives.

Schank's theory had important consequences for machine translation, as Schank's early programs, like MARGIE and SAM, demonstrated. The semantic primitives, held to be common to all natural languages, constituted a sort of *interlingua*. Therefore, the ability to translate sentences was not considered any different from the ability to understand them or to parse them. The central point was the existence of a representation which, for sentences of equal meaning, is the same in all languages. The original dream of a "fully automatic high quality translation" having vanished, concepts such as Schank's semantic primitives mark the start of a renewed interest in automatic translation.

It was when Schank passed from constructing a program that could understand (or translate) single sentences to constructing one that could understand (or translate) entire stories that he found he had to take common sense into account. One problem concerned the knowledge needed to draw meaningful inferences from the union of different sentences in a story, so as to make explicit the beliefs and expectations implicitly raised by the context.[25] To tackle this and other problems, Schank and Yale psychologist Robert Abelson endowed SAM (Script Applier Mechanism) with "scripts" (Schank and Abelson, 1977). To give some idea of what a script is, we prefer to refer back to Minsky's frame paper. The frame has become the prototype of various related notions, including scripts, whose aim was to tackle the problem of common sense through knowledge representation structures that were psychologically plausible.[26]

Let us reformulate one of Minsky's examples. When opening a door inside a house with which we are not familiar, we usually expect to find a room with features that are more or less recognizable or predictable. Now these features are referred to a body of knowledge organized in the form of prototypes (the *typical* room). The data structures which reflect this flexible and altogether very integrated way of using knowledge, which is typical of human beings, can be described as "frame systems." Therefore, the 'room frame' is a cluster of information that includes, listed in appropriate "slots" or "terminals," the *generic* features of a room, such as having a certain number of walls and windows, a ceiling, and so forth. There could be various *kinds* of rooms: dining rooms, bedrooms, etc., each of them constituting in its turn a frame with more *specific* features, again listed in appropriate slots. And John's dining room might well be quite different from Mary's in various details, but it will always be part of one and the same *kind* of room frame, whose properties it *inherits* in keeping with a mechanism already present in Quillian's semantic networks.

Minsky's description in the frame paper (referring mainly to visual experience) was at times obscure. However, he described methods that activate or deactivate frames at various levels of specificity, opening up the possibility of modifying frustrated beliefs and expectation, should the need arise. For example, according to Minsky the correct way to

---

[25] Recall Bar-Hillel's example mentioned above in section 2.

[26] Early interest in frames began with their appearance in the comments of Fikes, Hewitt and Schank in Schank and Nash-Webber (1975). A development of the idea of a frame system was later given by Minsky (1987).

tackle the typical exceptions in common-sense or non-monotonic reasoning is the use of "defaults." They establish generalizations that constitute beliefs presumed true until proven otherwise (or in the absence of needed information). A default for the number of walls of a room could be the number '4', but a room with a collapsed wall still belongs to the 'room frame.' In an appendix to the frame paper, Minsky launched an attack on the logicist approach, which, in his opinion, had been led astray by logical problems of consistency and completeness and was unable to tackle the flexibility of common-sense reasoning which is so evident in human beings.

There has never been overall agreement on how reasonable Minsky's opposition between psychologically plausible and logicist representations is. One response from the logicist side came from Hayes (1979), who tried to translate the formalism of semantic networks and frames into first-order logic, to demonstrate its basic equivalence with the formalism of logic. The point is that, whereas for some researchers frames are nothing but sets of declarative sentences, for others they have been a way out of the opposition, theorized by McCarthy, between epistemological and heuristic problems. Frames, like scripts and other analogous notions, have also suggested how to settle the dispute between 'declarativists' and 'proceduralists', which divided the AI community in the 1970s. In brief, according to the declarativist thesis, supported mainly by logicists, knowledge is, first of all, 'know that': it consists in having available a body of sentences, and rules to infer other sentences. For the proceduralist thesis, however, knowledge is, first of all, 'know how': it consists in having available procedures for the *use* of the knowledge itself. It is possible to endow frames with procedures of the latter kind, called 'attached procedures': for example, in the room frame, one could *attach* to the slot 'number of walls: 4' a procedure for recognizing, when circumstances so require, the wall of a circular room.

A program that might be considered a telling example of the proceduralist theses is SHRDLU, built within a project on natural-language understanding by Terry Winograd at MIT in 1971. SHRDLU is a simulated robot capable of coherently performing actions within a simulated environment, where blocks of various forms and colors are placed on a table—a 'microworld', as these groups of geometric solids, on which much AI was performed in those years, came to be called. SHRDLU correctly executed various orders, which were input in English, pertaining to the movements of blocks on the table. Upon request, it also explained in English why it had behaved in one way rather than in another. It was also able to resolve ambiguities in orders, by referring back to the way the blocks were arranged and asking, if necessary, for confirmation of its interpretation of the context. To do so, SHRDLU integrated the syntactic and semantic analyses of sentences with a small body of knowledge about the objects and the properties of the microworld. Thus it became possible to deal with those aspects of meaning that were inaccessible to the programs of the 1960s (which, as we have seen, were based mostly on the comparison of templates and key words). SHRDLU had, in fact, an internal model of the microworld, and its knowledge of such an environment was represented, not in a declarative form, but in a procedural one. In other words, each word in its vocabulary corresponded, not to an explicit definition, but to a short program, whose execution checked whether the use of that word in the given context was correct or not (Winograd, 1972).

Knowledge representation in procedural form, as typically used by SHURDLU, was made possible by MICRO-PLANNER, the high-level language in which it was implemented. This was a section of PLANNER, conceived by Carl Hewitt at MIT in 1971, where the part involving control (or heuristic, in McCarthy's sense) was, so to speak, integrated with that involving representation (or epistemological).

A differently-motivated approach to natural-language understanding is UNDERSTAND, a program developed by Simon and John Hayes during the 1970s. This program started as an investigation into computer simulation of human behavior. The subject's task was to understand problem instructions in a natural language; the program, starting from these very instructions, constructed a representation for the problem. Actually, the natural-language statement of the problem was translated by the program into a particular list-processing representation. The authors explored several issues connected to this activity—for example, how changes in problem instructions induce changes in problem representations, when the subjects are given problems that are "isomorphic" (i.e. their legal moves can be mapped between them in a one-to-one fashion).[27]

A wide-ranging criticism of the microworld practice, the hegemony of knowledge representation, and human behavior simulation, in short, of the whole approach of AI research in the 1970s, was formulated by David Marr. He raised his criticism while working in computer vision, a field that had long been considered secondary in early AI. Even today, Marr's ideas, despite some recognized limitations, seem to mark a watershed in the brief history of computer vision, and they have left important traces in more recent tendencies in cognitive research.[28]

Invited by Minsky and Papert, Marr arrived at MIT from England in 1973, as a neurophysiologist convinced that vision was too complex a subject to be left to the resources of his discipline alone. At MIT there had been a long tradition in vision research, connected to the interest in robotics that we have mentioned, and stimulated by Minsky in particular. After a false start, in which computer vision was considered a secondary problem, which could easily be solved once the general principles of intelligence were discovered, a more promising path seemed to be found. At the beginning of the 1960s, Larry Roberts had passed from studying recognition and classification of two-dimensional patterns, usually in the form of letters, which was typical of traditional pattern recognition, to studying the description of three-dimensional scenes, which a robot would decipher while moving around in a real environment. Such a real-world task met with difficult problems, such as edge detection, correcting distortions due to perspective, adjusting to variations of light intensity, and making sense of texture. Roberts used different geometric solids, and his pioneering work was continued at MIT with the investigation of the 'block worlds' by Adolfo Guzman, David Waltz, and Patrick Winston.

Marr rejected the microworld strategy, because it could not be extended to real-life scenes. Furthermore, he held that the major part of research in this field was in agree-

---

[27] See the papers on UNDERSTAND collected in Simon (1979, Chapter 7).

[28] See Kosslyn (1994: 35-39) for an insightful discussion of Marr's original approach, and the book in general for the developments of research in visual mental imagery.

ment with the AI philosophy of those years, which he equally rejected. In order to make an artificial system able to understand a scene, the AI researchers usually tried to endow it with explicit representations and heuristics, in other words, with 'top-down' special-purpose knowledge, which the system would have to use to recognize the components of the scene itself. In keeping with some of the results in neurophysiological research, Marr's idea was instead that the *physical* features of the objects, not the system's knowledge of those objects, were what guided 'bottom-up' their identification within the first two stages of visual perception, which constitute "early vision." In the first stage, the system extracts information from an object about the properties of the two-dimensional image, using, for example, edge detection, and thus obtaining a "primal sketch" of the object. In the second stage, the system, based on this sketch, processes information related to the object's depth and orientation, thus obtaining a "$2^{1/2}$-dimensional sketch." Only the processing of the latter into a "3-dimensional model" of the object, which is the third stage, or that of "high vision," requires the intervention of the system's knowledge. Such knowledge guides it in identifying, for example, *what kind* of object is present in the scene. Tomaso Poggio has defined as "reversed optics" the study of this process for reconstructing three-dimensional images starting from two-dimensional ones.

In a book published posthumously, *Vision*, Marr maintained that the *computational theory* of vision is, first of all, interested in identifying physical constraints and functions (*what* is being computed and *why*), while the choice of the kind of *representation* and of the particular *algorithms* to manipulate them involves another level of analysis (*how* computation actually runs). This distinction corresponded, according to Marr, to Chomsky's distinction between the competence level and performance level. Marr's third level is that of the *implementing* of the algorithm in a particular hardware (Marr, 1982: 22-27). Results from psychophysiology and neurology could influence the choice of particular representations and algorithms. Thus, Marr recognized an interaction between the neurosciences and AI research that goes beyond early AI's original indifference towards neurology.

Based on this theoretical assumption, which went beyond the problems raised by computer vision in a strict sense, Marr criticized the AI leading researchers of the 1970s: Winograd and the proceduralists because they confused two levels, the computational and the algorithmic (even though some did so deliberately, as we have seen); Schank and Minsky because they worked exclusively on the *mechanisms* of representation, and therefore at the algorithmic level, neglecting the computational one; Newell and Simon because, when they deluded themselves that they were simulating human behavior, in fact they were "mimicking" it by means of *ad hoc* procedures—hence they, too, chose the wrong level of analysis (pp. 342-247). Many of the criticisms that Marr raised hit tender spots in the AI research of those times, first among them the difficulty of representing knowledge using data structures like frames or scripts as soon as one abandons the usual microworlds. This was a difficulty that, going beyond the dispute between logicists and anti-logicists, raised again the problem of common-sense knowledge, the true *bête noire* of AI. It was this problem that, in the end, discouraged Winograd himself from pursuing his own research (Winograd and Flores, 1986).

The subject of Marr's criticism of the simulation of cognitive processes was *Human Problem Solving*, the monumental *summa* in which Newell and Simon had collected the results of their investigations in the field of Information Processing Psychology (Newell and Simon, 1972). Notwithstanding Marr's criticism, a lot of empirical evidence regarding human cognition was given in Newell and Simon's work. They had also experimented with a version of the production rules (which, in the general form of 'IF condition, THEN action,' specify the condition whose presence determines that one or more actions take place). Incorporated in so-called 'production systems,' rules of this sort were widely tried for representing knowledge in expert systems, beginning with MYCIN, a system used to diagnose blood diseases.

We find Newell and Simon together once more in 1975. In their Turing Award Lecture, they stated the Physical Symbol System Hypothesis (PSSH), which can be viewed as a refinement of the IPS hypothesis of early Information Processing Psychology. According to the PSSH, the necessary and sufficient condition for the intelligence of a system, whether organic or artificial, is its ability to transform symbolic expressions into others by means of explicit rules (Newell and Simon, 1976). Nevertheless, their main research interests were changing.

Newell continued to work on production systems. In his opinion, they could suggest a general or "unified" architecture for intelligence, which would gradually cover the whole domain of cognition and replace ordinary psychological microtheories. Newell believed he could find a confirmation of this in the early 1980s, when, with his students John Laird and Paul Rosenbloom, he began implementing SOAR. This was conceived as a single architecture for several cognitive tasks, which were formulated as a search in the state space. SOAR proceeds by selecting and applying suitable operators to transform the initial state into a succession of states that lead to the desired state, the goal or solution of the problem. When an "impasse" is reached in the course of this process, one due, for example, to the difficulty of deciding which operator to apply, SOAR generates a sub-goal whose solution frees it from that impasse. This is then added to the list of rules as a new rule, and constitutes a new "chunk" of knowledge, which can be used in the future if the same kind of impasse occurs. Chunking is, therefore, a learning mechanism that generates new rules, indeed SOAR's sole learning mechanism (Newell, 1990). Work on SOAR absorbed Newell up until his death in 1992. It is even now being continued by his group, giving rise to many reservations in the AI community, above all with regard to the very possibility of assuming a unified architecture for the whole domain of cognition.[29]

Simon, together with numerous collaborators, pursued the investigations into computer simulation models of cognitive processes, following the standard methodology of testing the predictions of the models by running the computer and comparing its performance with human behavior. Many of these investigations are better known among psychologists than among AI researchers, and gave valuable insights into classical issues in psychology such as perception, memory structures, forms of learning, induction, concept formation and discovery.

[29] See for example the reviews of Newell (1990) in the 1993 issue of *Artificial Intelligence*, p. 343 ff.

Early Information Processing Psychology had not progressed very far in accounting for perceptual phenomena. As Simon recalls in the above mentioned letter to de Groot, it was the difficulty in handling visual perception when programming a chess-playing machine that first convinced him and Newell to prefer the implementation of a theorem-proving machine as LT.[30] De Groot's own experiments had shown the relevance of perceptual processes when the expert human player is occupied in gathering information about the chess position before choosing the move. The eye movements of the human player thus became the subject of Simon's investigations in the mid-1960s and the 1970s. The PERCEIVER program was designed by Simon with his student Michael Barenfeld to simulate eye movements in the light of experimental data on expert chess players; the MAPP (Memory-Aided Pattern Perceiver) program was designed by Simon and Kevin Gilmartin to simulate expert recognition of chess patterns as it had been investigated by the psychologist William Chase and by Simon himself.[31]

On the whole, these investigations marked a significant stage in the development of psychologically plausible simulation models. They showed how certain perceptual abilities, pointed out as 'holistic' by Gestalt psychologists, could be simulated by programs embodying assumptions about human-perception processes. Furthermore, a convergence was stated between the theory of problem solving and psychological theories of perception processes.

MAPP combined the mechanisms of PERCEIVER with those already experimented with in EPAM, Feigenbaum's 1959 program, which we mentioned above. Simon implemented, with Feigenbaum and several coworkers, various versions of EPAM, which have been at the center of lively discussions among psychologists and AI researchers. In fact, EPAM become a long-running research project on memory structures and learning. EPAM had been conceived as a theory (actually, a detailed computer simulation) of the behavior of single individuals in the task of memorizing nonsense syllables, usually composed of three letters, in serial lists or associate pairs. Nonetheless, the ambition has been to extend EPAM gradually to encompass different tasks, even in more knowledge-rich problem domains such as chess, so that most of the mechanisms used in EPAM to explain many perceptual, memory and learning phenomena could be extended to many individuals, with different previous experience and task interpretation. Simon has always pursued this kind of "middle-size" theories of cognition, as he put it, but he sees recent versions of EPAM as being in the mainstream of cognitive theories which are more and more general or broad, if not "unified" in Newell's sense (Richman et al., 1995: 309).[32]

[30] Simon (1991), and see above, p. 178.

[31] See the papers collected in Simon (1979, Chapter 6) and, for a discussion including MATER, an earlier chess program by Simon and his student George Baylor, see Newell and Simon (1972: 765-783).

[32] Newell himself discussed the relationships between EPAM and SOAR (see Newell, 1990: 341-345). Actually, the search for a tradeoff between *individualized theories* (the computer simulations of a single performance) and *generalized theories* (the search for invariant psychological laws) goes back to the early days of Information Processing Psychology (see Chapter 5). Other papers on EPAM are in Simon (1979; 1989). The last volume also includes other investigations by Simon and coworkers from the China Academy of Sciences on memory structures and verbal learning in native Chinese speakers. These investigations significantly confirm the findings coming out from research in native Western languages speakers.

The experimental investigations of law finding or induction through heuristic search in sequences of letters that Simon had conducted with Kenneth Kotovsky, starting in the 1960s, can be viewed as the first steps towards computer simulation of scientific discovery processes.[33] Along with other researchers, Simon implemented various programs that rediscovered concepts and laws in different scientific disciplines (Langley et al., 1987), a project currently in progress. Some of these programs used weak methods, or general heuristics such as means-end analysis, and small knowledge bases. The BACON program represents an extreme case, very close to GPS. BACON rediscovers, among others, Kepler's third law using general or weak methods that identify regularities in the available data, without making any reference either to the meaning of such data or to assumptions about their structure. Furthermore, the ability of fourteen subjects to find regularities in the same data that had been given to BACON was investigated. The analysis of the thinking-aloud protocols of the successful subjects showed that the heuristic they used in identifying regularities in data were similar to BACON's (Qin and Simon, 1990).

A further step in the research on discovery processes was made in a less commonly investigated field, that of collaborative discovery. Usually, information-processing research had focused on how an individual processes information. Okada and Simon (1997) sought to investigate whether information processing is different when people work together. They compared the ability of single individuals with that of pairs of individuals in discovering scientific regularities with the aid of experiments. Pair of individuals were more successful in such a task, and explanatory activity was facilitated. Generally speaking, Simon's conclusion is that his early claim has been confirmed: *creative* discovery is nothing mysterious, but a form, though a complex one, of problem solving.

If one considers DENDRAL a scientific discovery program, then BACON might be placed at the opposite extreme. A program that might occupy an intermediate position between BACON and DENDRAL is AM (Automated Mathematician), designed by Douglas Lenat at Stanford around the middle of the 1970s. In a sense, Lenat's original inspiration seemed to be at the opposite extreme to expert systems. He wanted "to save the umbilicus" (Lenat, 1983a: 244) that tied the program to the human expert (the issue of knowledge engineering). Lenat's aim was to approximate "the ideal tradeoff between generality and power" (Lenat, 1979: 263): almost a quote from DENDRAL's authors. He tried to check whether, or to what extent, the program was able to learn on its own by gradually increasing its knowledge, starting from a general knowledge base. This included several elementary concepts (such as 'set,' 'truth value' an so on) and several heuristic rules. The latter enabled the program to rediscover numerous mathematical notions, including Goldbach's conjecture, which was introduced after rediscovering prime numbers. This knowledge base, without being comparable to that of a typical expert system, was still far from BACON's austerity.

Lenat became aware that one of the main causes preventing AM from making further progress was its inability to introduce, or 'learn,' new heuristics. After moving to

---

[33] See the papers in Simon (1979, Chapter 5). As a simple example of law finding, suppose you are presented with the sequence of letters A B M C D M ..., and asked to find the law that generated it.

Carnegie-Mellon, he dedicated himself to a new program, EURISKO. This was endowed with heuristic rules that enabled it to introduce, not only new concepts, in the style of AM, but also new heuristic rules, or "meta-heuristics" (Lenat, 1983b). The idea of a *meta-level* for representing the rules that a program could use to decide which rules of the object level to apply, or in which order, can be considered an evolution of the idea of implementing control through the use of heuristic procedures, an idea that comes from early AI. Meta-rules had been tried out in systems like SOAR and Randall Davis' TEIRESIAS, an expert system assisting entry of data into large databases. In other cases, such as Richard Weyhrauch's FOL, meta-theoretical knowledge is transferred to the object level by means of 'reflection principles,' to make the proof generation more efficient.[34] When speaking of reflection or of meta-level and self-reference, one inevitably thinks of *consciousness*, a subject about which, except for some speculations about possible reflexive architectures, AI has not produced appreciable results.[35]

Not even EURISKO had the success that Lenat hoped (some limitations of both AM and EURISKO have been discussed by Lenat and Brown, 1984). In the end, he agreed with Feigenbaum's criticism of expert systems. Briefly put, expert systems lack the general knowledge that characterizes common sense, so that their performance, based as it usually is on strictly domain-dependent knowledge, rapidly degrades. Lenat thus launched the CYC (enCYClopedia) program in 1984, a long-term project so ambitious that it has left many skeptical about its very plausibility. CYC should be provided with a large knowledge base derived from a number of encyclopedia entries, together with that general common-sense knowledge which must be presupposed in order to understand those entries. The final aim is to give the program all the common-sense knowledge, represented in explicit form, that it will need to understand any other encyclopedia entry (Lenat and Feigenbaum, 1991).[36]

Machine discovery programs, however, are currently at the forefront of several research groups. For example, Simon Colton, from the Edinburgh Mathematical Reasoning Group, has implemented the HR (Hardy-Ramanujan) program, which rediscovers mathematical concepts with an impressive performance. An example is 'refactorable numbers' (i.e. numbers where the number of divisors is itself a divisor, such as the number 9, which has 3 divisors, and of which 3 is a divisor). These numbers have many interesting properties, and when introduced by the HR program, these numbers were unknown to the program's author, although they had been introduced, and their properties judged interesting, by human mathematicians (Colton, 1999).[37]

[34] Maes and Nardi (1988) provides an introduction to these subjects.

[35] The issue is discussed in Trautteur (1995).

[36] CYC attracted the interest of MCTC (Microelectronics and Computer Technology Corporation), a national consortium that was supposed to prepare the US response to the Japanese project for 'superintelligent' fifth-generation computers programmed using PROLOG (launched in 1982 with 855 million dollars spread over ten years, the project was soon drastically reduced). Afterwards, CYC aroused the interest of various business enterprises, which allocated financing of 25 million dollars: CYC basically represents the hope for a generation of expert systems with a completely new conception (see Newquist, 1994).

[37] Implications of machine discovery for traditional epistemological and philosophical problems have been dealt with by Thagard (1988). Dartnall (1994) includes different points of view on the matter.

4. The origins of cognitive science. Old and new connectionism

The PSSH certainly did not uniformly characterize the AI undertaking. Newell and Simon considered it an empirical hypothesis, but it was often seen, both inside and outside the AI community, as a radical claim or an act of faith. The PSSH, however, summarized the original aspirations of AI as a science of the mind, and influenced, in variously weakened forms, the evolution of a new discipline, cognitive science. The latter was consecrated at a conference in San Diego, organized in 1979 by the Cognitive Science Society. This had already been publishing a journal and had received generous grants from the Sloan Foundation. Participating in the conference were psychologists, linguists and philosophers, besides Minsky, Newell, Schank, Simon, and Winograd. In fact, cognitive science brought together many of the ambitions of Information Processing Psychology and of AI as a science of mind, to such an extent that, at the conference, Simon backdated the birth of cognitive science to 1956.[38]

The new discipline had to stake out its own space in its relationship with AI. Two books, published almost simultaneously by Zenon Pylyshyn and Philip Johnson-Laird, aimed to do so. There are some things that the two authors share, together with a majority of the researchers in the field. Both maintain a computational theory of mind, i.e., briefly, the general claim that cognition is essentially computation of symbol structures, and both reject the Turing test, because this considers the program's performance without taking into account the cognitive processes involved. Moreover, both dealt with the problem of which *constraints* to impose on cognitive models, for example, limits of memory, errors, or reaction times. Although early behavior simulation was deemed for the most part pure "mimicry," in Marr's sense, one feels in these claims a flavor of the Information Processing Psychology heritage. Otherwise, Pylyshyn's approach is altogether different from Johnson-Laird's.

In *Computation and Cognition*, Pylyshyn outlined his distinction between "cognitively penetrable" and "cognitively non-penetrable" processes (Pylyshyn, 1984). The latter characterize the agent's cognitive architecture. Pylyshyn seemed to move in the direction of Chomsky and Marr, though with some uncertainty (he declared he was also inspired by Newell). Chomsky and Marr's modularity hypothesis on mind had already been carried to its extreme consequences by Jerry Fodor. He conceived the mind as a cluster of modules, corresponding to perception systems and language, which are not influenced by "central" processes or high-level knowledge. In his view, cognitive science, as a computational science of mind, can only concern itself with modules, while central processes, being cognitively penetrable, i.e. influenced by beliefs and expectations, or common-sense knowledge, remain impracticable for it. The whole of such knowledge constitutes, in fact, a boundless holistic network, which cannot be computationally analyzed (the frame problem is one of the major difficulties in this regard). According to Fodor, this explains the failures of AI, which fooled itself into representing common-sense knowledge by using data structures like frames or scripts (Fodor, 1983).

[38] Simon (1980: 34). Pictures of the origins and some developments of cognitive science are given by Gardner (1985) and Bechtel et al. (1998).

In contrast, in *Mental Models*, Johnson-Laird formulated the notion of 'mental model,' a new data structure with which to represent the knowledge and expectations, even subjective ones, of human beings. Johnson-Laird had begun to experiment with mental models in syllogistic reasoning. He distinguished the general theory of mental models from computer programs, which embody the fundamental hypotheses of the theory. Such programs are not to be considered experiments in either computer simulation or AI; rather, these programs are important for developing the general theory. In fact, between the theory of mental models and the programs that develop parts of such a theory a "dialectical process" is established that could give rise to experimentally testable predictions and to revisions of the theory itself (Johnson-Laird, 1983).[39]

But Pylyshyn already had to argue in his book against the validity of proposals for new architectures of cognition, alternatives to those inspired by the PSSH and advanced by so-called "new connectionism" (Pylyshyn, 1984: 71). He was referring to a collection of essays edited in 1981 by James Anderson and Geoffrey Hinton, *Parallel Models of Associative Memory*, which foreshadowed the revival of neural nets.

Opposing methods and goals had already appeared within the community of researchers in intelligent machinery at the 1958 Teddington Symposium, as we remarked above. However, both the proponents of neural-net models and those of symbolic models (the imitators of the brain and the manipulators of symbolic expressions, to repeat Minsky's words) continued to attend the same meetings for a while.[40] While AI was achieving its early successes in heuristic programming, various Perceptrons were being realized by different researchers, even outside Rosenblatt's group, for example, the PAPA machine by the group directed in Italy by Gamba et al. (1961). Starting at the end of the 1950s, Bernard Widrow and Marcian Hoff designed and refined other machines similar to Perceptrons, such as Adaline, using the so-called delta rule as a learning algorithm.[41] While networks using Hebb's rule had already been simulated on computer by the Rochester group in the mid-1950s, Widrow and Hoff's Adaline was a neural net built out of actual circuits.

During the 1960s, research on neural nets seemed to step back in the face of the various AI research programs that we have discussed. The now-famous book by Minsky and Papert (1969), which demonstrated the limitations of then-existing Perceptrons in discriminating very simple visual stimuli, was blamed for the demise of neural nets. In fact, the causes of this phenomenon are much more complex, and we say something about them in the next chapter. One should remember that various researchers, nevertheless, continued to work on neural nets in several countries. Anderson himself and Teuvo Kohonen developed insightful analyses of linear associative memories; Stephen Grossberg for-

[39] The notion of mental model is explicitly related, in Johnson-Laird's intentions, to Craik's internal model (see Chapter 4, section 7). In the next chapter we will return to a deeper examination of some of the most debated issues in cognitive science.

[40] For example, in the three interdisciplinary conferences on self-organizing systems held between 1959 and 1962, which witnessed the participation of various protagonists of the Teddington and Dartmouth meetings. See Yovits and Cameron (1960), von Foerster and Zopf (1961), Yovits et al. (1962).

[41] In short, the delta rule uses the discrepancy that exists between the desired pattern and the actual pattern to change the weights of the connections during learning.

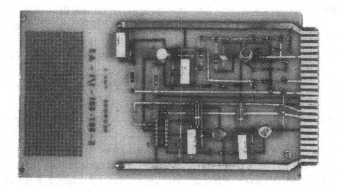

Fig. 6.1. An electronic simulator of a neuron in the DIANA neural-net machine, built during the late 1960s at the Institute of Cybernetics founded by E. Caianiello in Naples (courtesy of E. Burattini).

mulated neural models of conditioning, harking back especially to Hull's learning theory; Eduardo Caianiello, with his mathematical theory of nerve processes, inspired various neural-net learning models, like the conditioned reflex models by Tadashige Ishihara and the neural-net electronic simulator DIANA (Burattini and Marciano, 1969) (see Figure 6.1). Caianiello also influenced the work of neurologists like Valentino Braitenberg.[42]

The so-called renascence of neural nets in the 1980s thus took place in ground that had remained fertile. Nevertheless, this renascence was marked by at least two crucial events, accompanied by the development in those years of computers with great computing power, allowing them to simulate neural nets of increasing complexity. In 1982, John Hopfield proved that symmetrical neural nets necessarily evolve towards steady states, then interpreted as attractors in the dynamic system theory, and that they can function as associative memories (Hopfield, 1982). In 1985, David Rumelhart and his collaborators published a series of investigations inspired by an approach using parallel distributed processing (PDP) of information. They showed how a learning algorithm based on error correction, known as backpropagation, made it possible to overcome the chief limitations of neural nets described by Minsky and Papert (Rumelhart et al., 1986). These limitations were shown to be effective only for nets with a single associative-unit layer, like the simple Perceptron in Plate 6.1, not for multi-layer nets, i.e. for nets with more than one layer of association units, 'hidden' between the input layer and the output layer.[43]

[42] The texts of Anderson, Caianiello, Grossberg and Kohonen have been reprinted in Anderson and Rosenfeld (1988) and Anderson et al. (1990). See also Caianiello (1968) and Grossberg (1982).

[43] One net of this kind is a multi-layer feed-forward net, i.e. a net in which the associative ('hidden') units belonging to several separate layers have unidirectional connections between them, going from the layer of the input units to that of the output units. The backpropagation rule intervenes to change the weights of the connections between the hidden units, going backward from the error, which is calculated at the output units. It should be recalled that Rosenblatt, before his sudden death in 1972, had anticipated the formulation of various aspects of this rule.

With the revival of neural nets, learning was again an issue at the forefront of the study of intelligence, as it had been for all associationist psychology and the behavior modeling that were the focus of our investigation up until the advent of AI. AI had long since preferred to concentrate its efforts on studying mechanisms responsible for intelligent performance, such as heuristic search or knowledge representation. One had to wait until the end of the 1970s, when SOAR, AM and EURISKO were designed, for learning to arouse true interest again within the AI community.[44]

Investigations in AI and in new neural nets have coexisted during recent decades, but they are often in conflict, because of the dispute between philosophers and psychologists as regards the different computational architecture proposed by these two approaches, now called, respectively, "classic" or "symbolic," and "connectionist" or "subsymbolic" (Smolensky, 1988). A survey of this debate lies beyond our scope, but at least one point should be stressed here.[45] A great euphoria characterized the connectionism of the 1980s: after the revival of neural nets, connectionism immediately offered itself as an alternative 'paradigm,' capable of resolving the difficulties of symbolic AI that we have discussed earlier in this chapter. Such a euphoria was destined to diminish very quickly in the face of empirical evidence. It had to be admitted that essentially the objection Minsky raised at Teddington in 1958 still stood. Connectionist models, just as in the days of early Perceptrons, continued to do best in handling elementary activities, like pattern recognition and classification or associative learning. They failed, however, in handling higher cognitive functions, like complex inference-based reasoning. As Anderson and Rosenfeld wrote in *Neurocomputing*, a collection of key texts in the history of neural nets, "at present, our networks, even after thirty years of progress, still act 'brain damaged.' It is an open question as to whether severe modifications of network theory will have to be made to handle these highest cognitive functions" (Anderson and Rosenfeld, 1988: 91).

One serious attempt to come to grips with the current limitations of connectionism dates back to 1989, when the *Workshop on High-Level Connectionistic Models* was held at New Mexico State University. An analysis of the foundations of connectionism was made through a comparison with the so-called 'symbolic paradigm' of AI during a lively debate, and a tentative *vademecum* of the strengths and limitations of the two approaches was drawn up by Michael Dyer (Figure 6.2). Different experimental proposals aiming at integrating the two approaches in connectionist-symbolic or "hybrid" systems were put forward. These proposals had the value of showing how the symbolic-vs-subsymbolic dispute could lead to possible synthesis instead of head-on collision (Barnden and Pollack, 1991).[46]

[44] Evidence of this new interest is given in the *Machine Learning* collection (Michalski et al., 1983), which afterwards became a publication that periodically documented the extensive variety of AI investigations of learning.

[45] We will touch on some other issues in the dispute in the next chapter. Bechtel and Abrahamsen (1991) is an excellent introduction to all the principal arguments in the symbolic-vs-subsymbolic dispute, and also to the learning algorithms for neural nets which we mention in the text.

[46] See Hilario (1995) for a taxonomy of hybrid systems. This more 'cognitive' trend in research on hybrid systems should, however, be distinguished from other proposals for hybrid systems, whose aim is to build more efficient AI systems. In these cases, a neural net is associated with an expert system to reduce the more or less rapid degradation of the latter's performance in the presence of incomplete data (see Gutknecht and Pfeifer, 1990; Burattini et al., 2002). Hofstadter (1995) and Sun and Bookman (1995) collect several investigations in symbolic-connectionist systems that are relevant to different extent from the cognitive viewpoint.

Purely Symbolic	Purely Distributed Subsymbolic	Capability
-	+	knowledge integration
-	+	smooth variation
-	+	intermediate representations
-	+	reconstructive memory
-	+	self-organization
-	+	associative retrieval
-	+	robustness to noise & damage
-	+	associative inference
-	+	adaptive learning
+	-	variables & bindings
+	-	schemas & roles
+	-	constituent, recursive structure
+	-	infinite generative capacity
+	-	defaults & inheritance
+	-	instantiations (types/tokens)
+	-	reference/pointers
+	-	memory management
+	-	intratask communication
+	-	metareasoning
+	-	explanation-based learning
+	-	complex sequential control

Fig. 6.2. Successes (+) and failures (-) of symbolic and subsymbolic models in reproducing various kinds of intelligent performance according to Michael Dyer (from Barnden and Pollack, 1991).

Clearly, only empirical research can solve the open question concerning the "severe modifications" to be imposed on neural nets to make them capable of handling higher cognitive tasks. But where possible, a good strategy for assessing the adequacy of symbolic and connectionist theories is to compare their capabilities in explaining human behavior in the same tasks. Following this strategy, Richman and Simon (1989) compared McClelland and Rumelhart's connectionist model of human recognition of visual patterns, such as four-letter words, with a version of EPAM handling the same task. The comparison showed that EPAM fits the experimental data on human subjects at least as well as McClelland and Rumelhart's model. Thus, tasks such as pattern recognition, which are usually considered "connectionism's forte," as Bechtel and Abrahamsen (1991) put it, and Dyer's own *vademecum* suggests, can equally well be performed by symbolic models simulating human responses under a variety of conditions. The claim that parallel-processing models could simulate human pattern recognition better than a serial processor such as EPAM has been refuted in this case.[47]

We shall touch on the issue of simulation methodologies in the next chapter. At the

[47] This was the claim by Barsalou and Bower already refuted by Feigenbaum and Simon (see Simon, 1989: 145-166).

moment we are interested in returning to the issue of connectionism to briefly clarify various stages in its evolution.

In *Neurocomputing,* the two editors emphasized that both Rosenblatt and, before him, Hebb used the term 'connectionist' in presenting their own research (Anderson and Rosenfeld, 1988: 41 and 91). This fact struck them because they were looking at the connectionism of the 1980s, in which they were authoritative protagonists. To them, Rosenblatt and Hebb seemed rather like their precursors. But, of course, Rosenblatt and Hebb, in using that term, were looking to the past. For Rosenblatt, connectionism was linked to the tradition of English empiricism, to which he attributed the conception of memory as a network of connections, where phenomena like Hebb's cell assemblies or Hull's anticipatory goal response could take place.[48] These phenomena give rise to the problem of how new connections in the nervous system could be used during learning, a problem on which we have dwelt at length in earlier chapters. The solution Rosenblatt offered when presenting Perceptron in the *Psychological Review* is still that "new stimuli will make use of [the] new pathways which have been created, automatically activating the appropriate response" (Rosenblatt, 1958: 387). In his turn, Hebb, in presenting his own theory as "a form of connectionism" (Hebb, 1949: xix), was referring to a tradition that went back to Hull and Thorndike, who, as we know, had defined his approach as "connectionist."

It would have been only correct to grant some space in *Neurocomputing* to Thorndike and to acknowledge him as the inventor of the term 'connectionism.' Hebb referred back to Thorndike, frequently emphasizing both their mutual affinities and differences, to the point of considering his own approach "an attempt to fill in the gap left by Thorndike's treatment" of the physiological processes implicit in the law of effect (p. 177). And when he defined his own theory as "a form of connectionism," he called it "one of the switch-board variety," using a metaphor that, as we know, was shared by Thorndike, Hull and other associationist psychologists and neurologists. In fact, Hebb's connectionism was an instance of that variety with its own peculiar features, but in a sense that Anderson and Rosenfeld do not seem to consider. The point is that Hebb stressed central *autonomous* processes, and S-S connections between various brain sensory-areas, rather than simple S-R connections, as early connectionism did. This is what Hebb himself deems the chief novelty in his associationist theory with respect to the "old idea," as he put it, of the strengthening of connections between neurons or between systems of neurons repeatedly active at short time intervals (p. 70). This is precisely the connectionist law that now bears Hebb's name, and he seemed to be surprised by the general attention paid to it, since he felt, and not wrongly, that it was the part of his theory that was not completely original).[49] In fact, it is Hebb's theoretical constructs (cell assemblies, phase sequences, and so forth) that distinguish his connectionism from the early one. After all, he placed himself in an intermediate position, between the earlier "connectionists" and those that he

[48] A cell assembly consists of a group of neurons arranged in a circular connection, or a 'ring,' which Hebb hypothesized was the basis for the intervening processes between S and R (see below). On Hull's anticipatory goal response, see Chapter 3, pp. 103-104.

[49] See Milner (1993). An insightful evaluation of the role of Hebb's theory in cognitive research, which goes beyond the association law that bears his name, is given by Amit (1995).

called the "configurationists," among whom he included Lashley, Tolman and the Gestalt proponents of central processes (p. 59).

But if we are interested in the search for the roots of modern connectionism, we can push back even further, because Thorndike's connectionism was nothing but a particular version of psychological and neurological associationism. Anderson and Rosenfeld opened *Neurocomputing* with some passages from James' *Principles of Psychology*, emphasizing the 'Hebbian' spirit of his habit law. In Plate 6.2 we list James' habit law along with other statements of this law which we mentioned in our investigation into the dis-

---

Plate 6.2

Laws of association from Spencer to Hebb

The law in virtue of which all physical states that occur together tend to cohere, and cohere the more the more they are repeated together, until they become indissoluble [...] is the law in virtue of which nervous connections are formed. When a change in one part of an organism is habitually followed by change in another; and when the electrical disturbance thus produced is habitually followed by a change in another; the frequent restoration of electrical equilibrium between these two parts, being always effected through the same route, may tend to establish a permanent line of conduction—a nerve (Spencer, 1855, p. 544 n.).

In consequence of two [nervous circuits] being independently made active at the same moment, [...] a strengthened connection or diminished obstruction would arise between these two, by a change wrought in the intervening cell-substance (Bain, 1971/1873, p. 119).

When two elementary brain-processes have been active together or in immediate succession, one of them, on reoccurring, tends to propagate its excitement into the other (James, 1890, vol. 1, p. 566).

An association of two groups of neurons means a change at the synapses which constitute the physiological boundary and points of contact between the neurons of one group and those of the other (i.e., physiological contact, not necessarily physical contact); a change of such a nature that thereafter any excitation can spread more readily across the synapses from one group to the other. Such a change, such a diminution of the resistance at the synapses, seems to be the normal result of the passage of the excitation process across them (McDougall, 1901, p. 607).

Whenever any two neurones chance to act together a connection is formed between them, the original gap is bridged, and they come to form part of a new pathway. [...] Learning [...] is a process of making easier the passage of an impulse from neurone to neurone (Pillsbury, 1911, p. 52).

When any neuron or neuron group is stimulated and transmits to or discharges into or connects with a second neuron group, it will, when later stimulated again in the same way, have an increased tendency to transmit to the second neuron group as before, provided the act that resulted in the first instance brought a pleasant or at least indifferent mental state. If, on the contrary, the result in the first case was discomfort, the tendency to such transmission will be lessened (Thorndike, 1919, pp. 165-166).

When an axon of a cell A is near enough to excite a cell B and repeatedly or persistently takes part in firing it, some growth process or metabolic change takes place in one or both cells such that A's efficiency, as one of the cells firing B, is increased (Hebb, 1949, p. 62).

covery of the artificial, ending with Hebb's famous statement.[50] As can be seen, a 'Hebbian' law, if one passes over neurological differences, could be found almost everywhere among psychologists. But of course we could go back even further in our search for the roots of modern connectionism, reaching back, for example, to the English empiricists, mentioned both by James and by Rosenblatt himself.[51] And we could go back still further, because, whether rightly or wrongly, psychological associationism is made to date back to Aristotle. And indeed the second volume of *Neurocomputing* opens with a passage from Aristotle on memory (Anderson et al., 1990).

To avoid the slightly anachronistic flavor of these searches for precursors, in which the differences between positions that are often distant in time tend to disappear, the reader could reconsider some points in the analysis we attempted in earlier chapters. To mention but one example, in the case of James' 'Hebbian' law, the simultaneous activation of two nervous centers, which gives rise to the *formation* of a new path, is explained in terms of drainage: for there to be drainage, as we have seen, *two* centers must be active, and the drainage channel goes from the one that has just discharged, where an exuberance of force is present, to the one that is discharging, which is capable of 'attracting' it. On the other hand, the physical mechanism for *reinforcing* those connections, which, after Hebb, was interpreted as a variation in weights, is different for James, as it generally is for other drainage theorists, from the physical mechanism of connection formation: the connections, once they are established *via* drainage, get reinforced through use. Together with the growth of behaviorism, it is probable that it was precisely the discredited drainage metaphor that contributed to the almost total eclipse of James in discussions about the neurological bases of learning, which were then monopolized by Thorndike's and Watson's heirs. Thus, among the earlier connectionists who paid attention to the central neural processes Hebb acknowledges Hull and also Pavlov (Hebb, 1949: 5), while James is not even mentioned, perhaps because he is too distant from neuron theory and too close to discredited hydraulic analogies.

It is a fact, however, that Hebb is well-known to researchers in neural nets and to connectionists above all for his statement of the association law. In the 1950s, this law was used in a quantitative formulation as a synaptic plasticity rule, or learning algorithm, in many neural-net models, such as Uttley's and Taylor's models, which we have already mentioned. An illuminating review of these models was offered by Hawkins (1961). In the 1970s and the 1980s, Hebb's law or modified versions of it were embodied in many models to reproduce various phenomena of classic conditioning. Although conditioning may seem a rather old-fashioned topic, in fact it remained at the center of research even in the following decade. As Mignault and Marley (1997) observed in a complete survey

[50] These pre-Hebbian statements listed in Plate 6.2 (with the exception of that by Pillsbury, an author frequently mentioned by Hebb) were discussed in Chapter 2. Crovitz (1990) points out affinities and differences between James' associationism and that stressed by new connectionists. He also quotes a 'Hebbian' rule formulated by Tolman (p. 172), but Tolman's statement is actually not a neurological postulate, but a psychological one, thus regarding just the association of ideas.

[51] Actually, there is a long sequence of anachronistic analyses of the history of connectionism. Insightful analyses of different points in this history are provided instead by Aizawa (1992), Savage and Cowie (1992), Walker (1990).

of these investigations, the issues raised by conditioning have come to be at the inter-section of different research areas: animal learning, behavioral neuroscience and new connectionism.[52]

As for animal learning and neuroscience, investigations conducted using ingenious methodologies have shown how it is possible to identify nerve circuits and physiologi-cal mechanisms of conditioned reflex learning in simple organisms such as *Limax* and *Aplysia*. They are two invertebrates with nervous systems of about 10000 and 20000 neu-rons, respectively. As for new connectionism, while the backpropagation rule has been used as a learning algorithm in multi-layer feed-forward nets, the descendants of Per-ceptrons, Hebb's law has been employed in Hopfield's nets with associative memory.[53] Hopfield himself, with other researchers, using nets with associative memory and Hebb's law as the learning algorithm, simulated various characteristics of the conditioned reflex studied in *Limax* by neurologists (Gelperin et al., 1985; Tesauro, 1986; 1990). Experiments have also been performed using computational models of *Aplysia*, which embody a learn-ing law different from Hebb's (Hawkins, 1989; Blanzieri, et al., 1996).

Contemporary neural-net models of learning constitute an actual advance when com-pared with early-connectionism models, both in the 1930s and in the 1950s and 1960s. With the aim of stressing this point, we shall discuss the use of these new models in the simulation of certain learning abilities of the above- mentioned simple organisms.

Until now we referred to Hebb's law without explicitly mentioning its quantitative statement as a learning algorithm, which was popular with new connectionists. In fact, the associative learning explained by this law requires a very simple cellular mechanism. To obtain a good number of simple conditioning features, for example, a neural circuit composed of three neurons is sufficient, two for the stimuli, conditioned and uncondi-tioned, and one for the response to be conditioned. In a slightly more complex form (with two conditioned stimuli), this circuit, using Hebb's law as its learning algorithm, is de-scribed by Tesauro (1990) in the diagram shown in Figure 6.3.

The circuit contains one sensory neuron for each stimulus (the conditioned ones, CS_1 and CS_2, and the unconditioned one, US) and one neuron for the motor response. X_i and Y represent the activities of the individual neurons (actually, they are variables that rep-resent the short-term average firing rate of the neurons, and at any point in time they take on the values 0 or 1, depending on whether the corresponding stimulus is present or ab-sent). The strengths of the synapses are indicated by weights w_i. In this case, it is as-

---

[52] One should note that the received view of conditioning we are dealing with here, i.e the strengthening of a connection through repeated pairing of stimuli, has been criticized by Gallistel (2000). Starting from exper-iments on the dead-reckoning mechanism in simple animals (see in this chapter, section 4), he interprets con-ditioning as an entirely symbolic information-processing procedure. In his view, the associative connections could be replaced by decision variables whose value depends on certain rate estimates, which are "symbolic quantities in the head, repositories of remembered information, not conducting links" (p. 1190). This is a less popular hypothesis on conditioning, a field in which the associationist trend in neural-net modeling is domi-nant. Nonetheless, it is accepted by neurologists such as Gazzaniga (1998), who in his provocative book main-tains an anti-associationist stance with regard to the physical mechanisms of learning.

[53] Unlike multi-layer feed-forward nets, the units of Hopfield's nets can also be connected by means of loop connections. The relationships between the research on classic conditioning and new neural nets are described to good effect in Savage and Cowie (1992).

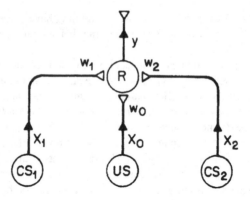

Fig. 6.3. A simple neural circuit for Hebbian conditioning composed of three neurons, each corresponding to a stimulus, unconditioned (US) and to be conditioned (CS_1 and CS_2) (from Tesauro, 1990).

sumed that the weights w1 and w2 are small at the outset and can vary during the learning phase according to Hebb's law, while w0 is assumed to be a large, fixed constant. A well-known quantitative statement of Hebb's law is given by the equation:

$$\dot{w}_i(t) = eX_i(t)Y(t),$$

where the dot indicates the time derivative and e is a numerical constant. Tesauro shows how, from this plasticity rule (or better, from one of its generalizations), it is possible to obtain many properties of conditioned reflex. For example, simple conditioning can be produced in the circuit of Figure 6.3 if the conditioned stimulus, CS_1, is presented and then immediately followed by the unconditioned one, US. Doing so produces the simultaneous activation of the *presynaptic* neuron CS_1 and the *postsynaptic* neuron R, the response to be conditioned that was originally solicited by the US. Therefore, the weight w_1 of the synaptic connection increases, and it continues to increase according to Hebb's law if the stimulation of CS_1 and US is repeated, until CS_1 alone (that is, without the stimulation of the US) produces the response. The description of the basic circuit for simple conditioning that Tesauro puts in Hebbian terms, i.e. of simultaneous pre-postsynaptic activation, is the same as that given in the connectionist models of the 1950s and 1960s. Hawkins, for example, making use of a circuit very similar to that of Figure 6.3, had shown how the strength of the variable connections could be calculated both by means of the Perceptron rule for changing weights or by means of Uttley's conditional probability (Hawkins, 1961: 38).

A cellular mechanism different from that hypothesized by Hebb, but which still allows for associative learning, was identified and studied, in the 1970s and the 1980s, in *Aplysia,* one of the simple animals we have already mentioned. *Aplysia* became well known due to the investigations into its nervous system by Eric Kandel and his collaborators. In this cellular mechanism, the activation of the neurons involved in the learning phase takes place, not at the *pre-postsynaptic* level, as Hebb's law states, but only at the *presynaptic* level. More exactly, according to this different law, the connection between two neurons can be strengthened even without the activation of the postsynaptic neuron, as long as a third neuron, the so-called "modulator" neuron, is active at the same time as the presynaptic one. Kandel and his collaborators classified this cellular mechanism among "non-Hebbian" ones (Hawkins et al., 1983).[54]

In earlier chapters we saw how the rough mechanical models in the early decades of the twentieth century reproduced, more or less realistically, some of the features of the conditioned reflex. In Plate 6.3 we show how, within certain limits, it would also be possible to use them to simulate the most general features of both Hebbian and non-Hebbian cellular mechanisms of conditioned reflex. In fact, these early-connectionist models can already be seen as machines that embody *different* theoretical postulates or hypotheses, those exemplified in the three neural circuits reproduced in Plate 6.3. However, the impossibility of making quantitative predictions and the difficulty of reproducing certain of the more complex, or higher, features of conditioning do not allow, altogether, any direct improvements of these rough models to simulate more complex behavior, or to better fit experimental data on real animals—for example, suggesting the exact shape of the learning curve in a particular animal. The highly generic prediction power of these models cannot be compared even to that of the simple basic model of Hebbian conditioning shown in Figure 6.3, given the precise quantitative statement of the learning law that this model embodies.

This basic model uses a generalized Hebb rule as a learning algorithm and local representations (such that a single neuron corresponds to a single sensory stimulus, as Figure 6.3 suggests). Actually, the model can be improved, as shown by Tesauro. He started from this model to show how it can simulate many principles of conditioned reflex learning. These are general principles, however, that are likely to apply to most organisms, and the model says nothing specific about how conditioning occurs in a particular animal. Nonetheless, such a model constitutes the basis for more complex models which may satisfy the latter requirement (Tesauro, 1990: 86). An example is the LIMAX model, essentially a Hopfield associative-memory net with Hebb's law as a learning algorithm (Gelperin et al., 1985). It is able to reproduce a class, both broad and specific, of particular features of behavior in an organism such as *Limax*, the other invertebrate we mentioned earlier. The performance of the LIMAX model is also due to the computational resources which have become available during the last twenty years. These have made it possible for the computer simulation of neural nets to perform in a way that cannot be compared with that possible in the 1950s and the 1960s. LIMAX uses, furthermore, distributed sensory representations to simulate certain aspects of *Limax*'s behavior, especially those dependent on sensory stimuli related to smell and taste (see Plate 6.4).

To make LIMAX fit experimental data regarding the animal's behavior even more closely, Tesauro later modified it. He introduced into the part of the model dealing with the evaluation of sensory stimuli as attractive or aversive, for the purposes of a suitable motor response, a multi-layer net with hidden units, which is trained using the backpropagation rule. Only then did the model exhibit certain abilities to react like a real animal, both to individual sensory stimuli, for example different food odors, and to their

[54] Churchland and Sejnovski (1992) offer a complete taxonomy of Hebbian and non-Hebbian learning rules.

Plate 6.3

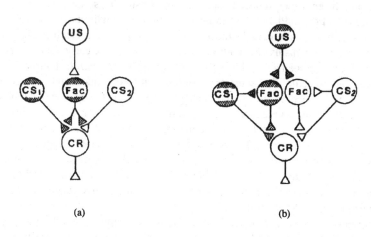

(a)   (b)

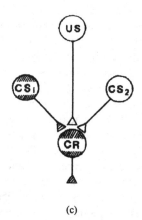

(c)

Hawkins et al. (1983) described three different forms of synaptic facilitation that produce classical conditioning (in these figures, the active neurons are shaded). These are: (a) presynaptic facilitation by means of a modulator inter-neuron (present in *Aplysia*); (b) "conventional" presynaptic facilitation (by means of stimulus summation); (c) pre-postsynaptic activity dependent (or "Hebbian") facilitation. At least in their general lines, these three forms of synaptic facilitation can be realized using some of the models we have already seen.

Krueger and Hull's model (1931), which we described in Chapter 3, reproduces some of the qualitative features of the Hebbian conditioning represented in circuit diagram (c), especially the pre-postsynaptic activity that produces a strengthening of the concerned connection. We can describe the generically Hebbian functioning of Krueger and Hull's model if we observe how, in the figure reproduced in Plate 1 in Chapter 3, during the simultaneous or double stimulation of S_1 (the conditioned stimulus) and S_u (the unconditioned stimulus), the battery E remains more or less at a constant potential, while E_1, the accumulator that initially was discharged, gradually gets charged. More precisely, following this double stimulation, lamp L is lit (the response to be conditioned) and nearly *at the same time* E_1 starts to charge. In this way the model simulates the effect that activating the pre-postsynaptic connection has on the conditioned stimulus and the conditioned response, an effect consisting of an increase in the charge of E_1 if the double stimulation is repeated several times.

Besides simple conditioning (the one we have just illustrated), we know that Krueger and Hull's model more or less realistically reproduces other properties, corresponding to those Tesauro drew from Hebb's law, in the circuit diagram reproduced in Figure 6.3 in the text, such as compound conditioning (regarding the two conditioned stimuli C_1 and C_2), second-order conditioning (where C_1, once it has been conditioned, can be used in the later conditioning of C_2), and the extinction of response (when the US is lacking).

The different cellular mechanism that permits associative learning in *Aplysia* is represented in circuit diagram (a).

In this case, the conditioning can be explained on the basis of the following postulate: the modulator or facilitator neuron, 'Fac' in the diagram (a), when activated by an unconditioned stimulus US, produces a greater *presynaptic* facilitation in a neuron CS_1 if it has already been activated by a conditioned stimulus. Therefore, the presynaptic facilitation induced by the unconditioned stimulus US is amplified by a previous stimulation of CS_1. In the end, the CS_1-CR connection has been strengthened to the point that CS_1, without the US, is always sufficient to produce the response, CR. This is a non-Hebbian law, because it involves activation only at the *presynaptic* level, and not activation at the *pre-postsynaptic* level, as is the case of Hebb. In fact, the diagram (c) that Kandel and associates use to exemplify a case of Hebb law is precisely the one in Figure 6.3, that of Tesauro.

A second simple model of conditioning from the 1930s, that of Baernstein and Hull (1931) described in Chapter 3, reproduces at least some conditions of the *non*-Hebbian postulate of Kandel and associates, exemplified by diagram (a). In fact, Baernstein and Hull's circuit, reproduced in Plate 2 of Chapter 3, is explicitly constructed in such a way that the activation of S'_c must occur before the activation of S_u because the latter could influence the conditioning process. Therefore, the 'facilitating' effect of S_u on the response R (i.e. the lighting of the lamp) does *not* occur if the connection between the latter and S'_c has not been involved beforehand. This feature of the circuit is due to the presence of the U-shaped tubes. Specifically, if S'_c does not activate tube C_1 beforehand, it does not have a 'facilitating' effect on the later stimulation of S_u.

Finally, a third simple model, which is familiar to us as well, reproduces some features of a different kind of presynaptic, and therefore *non*-Hebbian, facilitation which Kandel and associates called conventional, to distinguish it from the kind they had identified in *Aplysia*. This is shown in diagram (b), where greater presynaptic facilitation occurs by means of the summation of the stimuli, both conditioned and unconditioned. With those limitations that we already know, Bent Russell's net of transmitters, described in Figure 7 of Chapter 2, reproduces the conventional mechanism of stimulus summation at the *presynaptic* level that gives rise to conditioning: the stimuli S_0 and S_1, when presented one after the other, exert on the response, by means of the transmitter involved, a presynaptic 'facilitation' action that is greater than it is when they are presented separately.

Plate 6.4

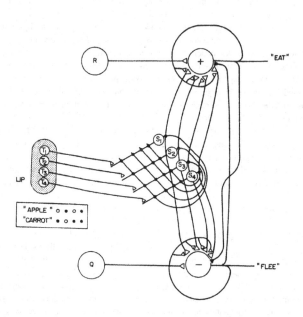

The LIMAX model consists of three major parts: (1) a group of receptors $T_1, ..., T_N$ (analogous to the taste receptors in the animal); (2) a Hopfield net consisting of the neurons $S_1, ..., S_N$; (3) a learning control/motor output system consisting of two neurons, R and Q, corresponding to the unconditioned stimuli, and of two neurons, + and -, corresponding to the same number of motor activities: in the animal, 'eating' and 'fleeing,' respectively. (In the figure $N = 4$, but in the actual simulation of the model $N = 100$.)

The net is where categorization and memory reside. It functions by converging toward a state belonging to a set of stable states (attractors) determined by the synaptic weights between S_i and S_j (in the figure these are indicated by the black dots between the axons and the dendrites of the neurons $S_1, ..., S_4$). These weights are computed using the Hopfield rule, and they constitute the memory of LIMAX. The net is activated by receptors in such a way that each 'flavor' is codified by a distribution of the activity of all the receptors. The figure exemplifies those corresponding to the flavors *apple* and *carrot*: this is a distributed representation, not a local representation.

The learning control/motor output system is, instead, local: the two +/- neurons are the single elements that trigger the entire eating/fleeing behavior. These neurons, mutually inhibited (as indicated by the black synaptic buttons in the figure), are subject to Hebbian learning together with the neurons in the net, $S_1, ..., S_4$. In the presence of a conditioned stimulus consisting of the net response to the input given to the receptors, the unconditioned stimulus, consisting of neurons R or Q, is activated. After several paired stimulations of the conditioned stimulus and the unconditioned one, the Hebbian synapses of the + and - neurons enable the activation of the respective neuron in response to the conditioned stimulus alone. (From Gelperin et al., 1985)

mixtures. Tesauro emphasized this process of model refinement and improvement through an interaction with experimental research on real animals, holding that this modeling strategy is particularly useful when anatomical or physiological data are not fully available (Tesauro, 1990: 100). We have already discussed some antecedents of this methodology.

This brief overview of a trend in contemporary neural-net modeling should clarify the sense in which models such as LIMAX and its modified versions could be considered case-studies in "computational neuroscience." This is what Sejnowski et al. (1990) call neural-net research aimed at building "simplified models of the brain," i.e. artificial net models that try to grasp how the nervous system works, without necessarily taking into account the biological plausibility of the simulation, as the so-called "realistic models of the brain" try to do. Tesauro, for example, is more interested in the elegance and power of the algorithms employed in his modified version of LIMAX than he is in the biological plausibility of the proposed implementation scheme. He believes that algorithms "should not be summarily dismissed from the domain of biological relevance merely because they do not have immediately obvious neurobiological correlates" (Tesauro, 1990: 97). He thus uses the backpropagation algorithm, even though he agrees that it is biologically implausible. In keeping with Hopfield's approach, Tesauro separates the part of the model dealing with representation and categorization of sensory stimuli from that dealing with evaluation of the stimuli and generation of the appropriate motor responses, even if he recognizes that this is a doubtful separation from a biological point of view.

Biological plausibility is the aim of the non-Hebbian computational model of *Aplysia* described by Hawkins (1989), which is closer, therefore, to the "realistic models of the brain." Hawkins' model proposes to simulate neurons actually identified in the animal's nervous system and not hypothetical neural circuits, composed of formal units and governed by *ad hoc* learning algorithms. Nothing could be farther from the PDP connectionist approach, as Hawkins himself emphasizes. Hawkins considers each individual neuron as a complex computational system, capable of various phenomena of synaptic plasticity, from habituation to the basic features of conditioning. Only the higher-order features of conditioning are explained by network interactions. The model is, therefore, always subject to the test of physiological data (it is an "analytical model," as Blanzieri et al., 1996, state, developing this kind of approach). After all, Hawkins concludes, "nervous systems are still the best computers we have for many tasks, and we can probably learn much more from them" (Hawkins, 1989: 242)

Gerald Edelman's "synthetic neural modeling" is another simulation research-project inspired by criteria of biological plausibility, and very critical towards both symbolic AI and connectionism. Along with various collaborators, Edelman has developed the computer simulation of automata capable of integrating some sensory modalities. Although certain aspects of the performance of these automata could be reproduced more simply using neural-net models, one should note that the *complicated* aspect of Edelman's automata is due precisely to his interest in the biological plausibility of the simulation. For example, the computer-simulated automaton Darwin III, which is endowed with a mobile eye and a four-jointed arm, has a nervous system consisting of no less than 50,000 neuron-like units of fifty different kinds, linked by about 620,000 synapse-like connections (Reeke et al., 1989).

Edelman's automata embody the principles of his theory of neural Darwinism, according to which epigenesis and learning are the result of an evolutionary process that selects different groups of neurons during the organism's development and interaction with the environment. He considers machines as tests of this theory, and even as the basis for a more ambitious project: that of arriving by steps, though the construction of artifacts of increasing complexity and realism, at the unveiling of the enigmas underlying some forms of consciousness.[55] Both the claim that the model could test theoretical hypotheses and the claim that the model should increasingly improve its performance in reproducing complex organic phenomena are among the methodological assumptions that Edelman shares with simulation strategies different from his own, of which our investigation has provided various examples.

These modeling approaches, with their criticism of connectionism, were not isolated cases. Starting at the end of the 1980s, new research areas set out to tackle issues where connectionism, no less than traditional symbolic AI, met with difficulties, such as evolution, development and the dynamic interaction between the system and its environment. We are alluding to ALife and situated robotics.

5. Artificial Life and the development of robotics

In order to consider ALife, it might be useful to take a step back to the days when the artificial or physical imitation of the essential features of living protoplasm was a popular line of research among biologists. Above all at the close of the nineteenth century, some successes in obtaining "synthetic protoplasm" were interpreted as defeats for vitalism. In fact, they promised "a bridge from the inorganic to the organic, from the physical to the vital," as Jennings summed it up in a survey of experiments to simulate the behavior of some species of amoeba in the laboratory (Jennings, 1904: 625).

Although interest in this kind of experiment has waned, the methodology inspiring them is the same as that which has always been at the core of the discovery of the artificial. Jennings summarized it effectively as follows. While studying certain organic phenomena, hypotheses are stated about the physical causes of them; one then goes on to build an artificial simulation of those phenomena that functions according to those hypotheses; if the simulation succeeds, the hypotheses gain, at the very least, more plausibility. The success of inorganic simulation might represent notable progress towards explaining organic life phenomena. Nonetheless, it still remains to be seen, Jennings observed, whether the hypothesized physical causes are actually *the same* in the model and

[55] On Edelman's claim about consciousness, see Reeke's essay in Trautteur (1995). For a criticism of Edelman's notion of categorization and a different claim about consciousness, see Rosenfield (1992). Neural Darwinism, however much it was suggested to Edelman by his original experience as an immunologist, finds its place in the history of selectionist attempts to explain learning. An explicit example of such attempts is Thorndike's theory of competition between neurons: see above, p. 55. As for Ashby, Simon defined Ashby's conception as "neural darwinism" (Simon and Newell, 1956: 78).

in the living organism, or whether the model is a mere imitation, one based on an external or misleading resemblance to the living organism (p. 626).

This general observation remains valid for any approach to simulating the performance of an organism. *Substituting* a function of an organism by using an artifact is an important result from the point of view of building machines that are increasingly good at 'usurping,' to repeat Wiener's term, the functions of the organism. Nonetheless, this is not the equivalent of *explaining* that function through a model that is capable of reproducing the essential features of the organism. For example, this was the *caveat* that distinguished Newell and Simon's simulation approach from other AI approaches. The latter were interested in reproducing human performance in a program, regardless of the *constraints* that it would have had to satisfy in order to be a psychologically plausible model of certain cognitive processes.

In the next chapter we will come back to a discussion of this problem, which is certainly among the hottest in current human and animal behavior modeling. For the time being, we would point out that it was perceived as a real difficulty very early on in the discovery of the artificial. Summarizing some of the experiments of his time, which have been mentioned in our investigation, Joseph Needham concluded with an observation that referred back to this problem. This observation is reminiscent of Jennings' criticism. Needham emphasized that an artifact that *substitutes* man in a mental task, or more generally an artificial imitation of life, does not necessarily function according to the same principles. He drew from that a skeptical conclusion with regard to the explanatory value of simulation as compared to that of the neurophysiological analysis to the living being. In his own words:

> Combinations of oil drops with acids may be made to exhibit most of the phenomena shown by the Protozoa, the mechanical beetle of Lotka never falls off the table, the Robot chess-player of Torress y Quevedo is rarely in error, and as for the automatic telephone operator it is difficult to see anything more perfect could be designed as a substitute for human intelligence. *But the fact that these imitations of life function so well does not prove that their mechanisms are the same as those of living brain, it only suggests that*; and therefore physico-chemical hypotheses derived from actual physiological data are the more interesting (Needham, 1929: 153, my italics).

In this passage, Needham mentioned the physical imitation of simple organisms like Jennings' amoeba. The organic amoeba has been described as a small, chemically active mass of viscid fluid which takes in oxygen and other substances from the water, and expels excreted substances into it. The so-called "artificial amoeba" could consist of a drop of chloroform; when put in water, it exhibits some behaviors imitating those of a living amoeba, for example, its selective ability to envelop certain solid particles as food and not certain others when it comes into contact with them. In the case of the artificial amoeba, the explanation of the phenomenon is given by the capacity for adhesion between certain solid objects on one side and the chloroform and water on the other. Those objects that adhere more to the chloroform than to the water are enveloped by it, while the others are expelled. Jennings showed how the explanation of the real amoeba's behavior in these terms would be misleading. Indeed, the taking in of food by the animal occurs by means of its active capture together with a small quantity of water. Therefore, the fact that it 'chooses' certain particles and not certain others cannot be explained by differential adhesion. The artificial amoeba is an imitation based on an external resemblance, and it does not grasp what Jennings called the "essential features" of the natural phenomenon (Jennings, 1904: 636).[56]

While these experiments were certainly useful in weakening vitalism, a much more important line of research was undermining its very basis. Among chemists and physiologists in the nineteenth century, vitalism was summarized in the conviction that the stuff constituting living beings has peculiar features: it consists of *organic* compounds. This seemed to give legitimacy to the idea that a vital force was present in these compounds, making it impossible to reproduce them in the laboratory. The synthesis of urea obtained by Friedrich Wöhler in 1828 made a dent in this conviction, opening the way to several experiments on organic compound synthesis. Among experiments of this kind should be mentioned the building of models that simulated increasingly detailed properties of the living cell in the laboratory. After the experiments on osmosis carried out by Wilhelm Pfeffer in 1877 by using artificial membranes, various characteristics of the permeability of the cell membrane were reproduced.

In these cases, as in others that we have considered, physiologists built an inorganic model that embodied their hypotheses about the physical causes of the selective permeability exhibited by the cell membrane. This model constituted a kind of test for those hypotheses, and it backed the claim of the futility of invoking vital forces to explain membrane selective permeability. Perhaps the best known model produced in a laboratory is Lillie's artificial nerve cell, an iron wire immersed in a solution of nitric acid, which exhibited various responses typical of nerve tissue (for example, irritability after passing a certain threshold of stimulation, if electric current passes through the wire). Now we move on to the 1920s and the 1930s. Other models of living cells, this time mathematical models, were formulated by Rashevsky. His goal was to use these models to simulate, besides phenomena of hysteresis, the "essential feature" of the cell, as he defined metabolism in *Mathematical Biophysics*.[57] Rashevsky clearly explained the "asymptotic" or "gradual approximation" to the real cell through his models:

> We start with a study of highly idealized systems, which, at first, may even not have any counterpart in real nature. This point must be particularly emphasized. The objection may be raised against such an approach, because such systems have no connection with reality and therefore any conclusions drawn about such idealized systems cannot be applied to real ones. Yet this is exactly what as been, and always is, done in physics.

[56] Jennings had conducted various experiments on "artificial amoebas" (Jennings, 1902). The skeptical conclusions he drew from them are evident in *Behavior of the Lower Organisms*: even the amoeba has an action system, though rudimentary, and its behavior can be influenced by its previous history (see Chapter 1, section 4).

[57] See Rashevsky, 1938/1960, vol. 2: 182. On Rashevshy's claims on hysteresis as a physical feature of learning, see above p. 95. A popular but effective review of attempts to construct "machines which imitate life," i.e. physical and mathematical models of cell properties, between the 1920s and the 1930s was given by Gray (1935-36a), before his review, mentioned earlier, of the "thinking machines" of the robot approach (see p. 85 n. 3). Lillie's model of the nerve cell was later criticized by Rosenblueth and Wiener, since, to explain a phenomenon like nervous conduction, the model invoked a physical phenomenon that is, in its turn, the subject of conjecture, as was the case at the time for conduction in metals (Rosenblueth and Wiener, 1945: 89). But see Lillie (1928) for more detailed analyses of artificial models of physiological phenomena.

The physicist goes on studying mathematically, in detail, such nonreal things as 'material points,' 'absolutely rigid bodies,' ideal fluid,' and so on. *There are no such things as those in nature.* Yet the physicist not only studies them but applies his conclusions to *real things.* And behold! Such an application leads to practical results—at least within certain limits. This is because within these limits the real things have common properties with the fictitious idealized ones! (Rashevsky, 1938/1960, vol. 1: 1).

Many years later, with experience in cybernetics behind him, Michael Apter defined "artificial life" as a research area that stretched from bionics to a possible future robotics of "entirely autonomous" mobile artifacts. Apter also harked back to a term used by Uttley, *autonomics,* to indicate the building of "autonomous self-supporting systems or [...] artificial living systems." These had to be able to extract energy from the natural environment and to transform it for their own survival, as living organisms do. Early, very partial realizations of machines that could function in this way were, according to Apter, some "chemical machines" that were the subject of pioneering studies in chemistry during those years. Among these are the so-called artificial muscles; by imitating the way some organic muscles work, they were able to convert chemical energy directly into mechanical energy. Apter also considered Grey Walter's robots to be rudimentary autonomous systems because of their ability to wander about in the environment and to extract directly from it the energy needed to recharge their own batteries (Apter, 1970: 155).

Apter's artificial life thus made reference to very disparate experiences. It is no accident that Apter appears in the early systematic bibliography on ALife, edited by Christopher Langton. Langton used this name (without, incidentally, mentioning that it had already been used by Apter) to baptize the new research area officially born at the Interdisciplinary Workshop on the Synthesis and Simulation of Living Systems, held at Los Alamos in 1987. ALife had assembled researchers from different fields, from computer science to biology to the study of complex systems (Langton, 1989).

The key concept of ALife is identified by Langton as "emergent behavior." This expression refers to the dynamics of a complex system, in which behavior emerges out of the organized interaction of a large number of simpler units (p. 2).[58] The metaphor invoked by Langton is the well-known one of the ant colony, whose complex organization is the result of the multiple cooperative interactions of individual components, without the intervention of centralized control. This metaphor seeks to suggest an antivitalistic formulation of the problem of emergence, and it can at the same time be used to clarify ALife's relationship with the biological sciences. In explaining life, according to Langton, biology starts "at the top," considering the organism as a complex biochemical machine;

[58] It should be mentioned that, within AI research, a similar philosophy inspired Distributed AI. Officially born at the American meeting dedicated to it in 1980, Distributed AI has its background in the 'blackboard' system, a database shared by different cooperating modules and endowed with specialized knowledge. HEARSAY II, designed in the 1970s at Carnegie-Mellon as a speech-recognition system, is considered even now one of the most successful examples of this kind of architecture, which has also been tried in some expert systems. Distributed AI has insisted on the cooperative aspect of knowledge management, but also on the social dimension of knowledge and of action. For example, Hewitt gave a formulation of Distributed AI referring to "open systems," so called because, in order to make headway against the partial information available to them, they cooperate collectively, also using various problem-solving strategies (Hewitt, 1991). In general, multi-agent systems are a current research area in AI.

it then goes *analytically* downwards from there, until it reaches the levels of the cell and of the molecule. ALife starts instead "at the bottom," considering the organism as a large population of simple machines, and it works *synthetically* from there, constructing aggregates of simple objects that interact mutually and non-linearly in support of global, life-like dynamics. In this sense ALife is interested in the *"formal* basis of life" (p. 2).

Thus the ALife notion of artificial life refers to the thesis, well known to reader, of the identity of functional organization in a different stuff, whether organic or inorganic. This had been pointed out, for example, by Simon in *The Sciences of the Artificial* (Simon, 1969), and Langton gives him great prominence. However, he points out that, in the case of ALife, it is the constituents that are *artificial*, not the features of the emerging phenomenon. The computer can be used to simulate, say, the behavior of a flock of birds in flight, and the constituents of the simulation are "artificial." Nonetheless, simulated birds, no less than the "natural" birds, are "two instances of the same phenomenon": *flocking*, right up there with flocks of geese and flocks of starlings. The "big claim" of ALife is that, given the identity of the functional role, the artificial realization of an emerging phenomenon (flocking behavior, in the example) is "genuine life," although "made of different stuff than the life that evolved here on Earth" (Langton, 1989: 33).

In his search for the roots of ALife, Langton also mentioned the clockwork automata of seventeenth century mechanism. These, however, have nothing in common with the concepts of self-organization and autonomy which he places at the center of ALife. Some pre-cybernetic machines discussed in our investigation at least made an effort to grasp such concepts. Along with these machines, the models we just mentioned, those proposing to synthesize the living cell, could also be mentioned among the forerunners of ALife. Indeed, it is to experiments on osmotic pressure and artificial cells in Pfeffer's time that the ALife research in the field of so-called "synthetic biology" refers (Zeleny et al., 1989).

Langton's reference to cybernetic robotics as an antecedent to ALife can be taken for granted. Grey Walter, after being judged negatively by Newell and Simon in the early 1960s, now gets his revenge. An "imitation of life"—that is what he called his own tortoises; and Langton was struck by those same aspects of Grey Walter's robotics that led Apter to talk of *artificial life*. Moreover, Braitenberg, in an elegant "essay of synthetic psychology" that has now become a classic of ALife, had already described numerous hypothetical robots (as Boring might have defined them), which seemed to be a recapitulation of Grey Walter's dream. Braitenberg suggested how, by gradually complicating a very simple basic model that reproduced tropistic behaviors like those studied by Loeb, one could obtain synthetic organisms with increasingly complex behaviors describable in terms of 'memory,' 'learning,' 'curiosity' and so on (Braitenberg, 1984). Some of the pre-cybernetic machines we mentioned in our investigation had already simulated behaviors comparable to those of Braitenberg's "vehicles": from Hammond and Miessner's phototropic automaton, which had impressed Loeb, to Tolman's schematic sowbug and Bradner's learning robot. The performance of the latter, based on conductance variation with temperature (see Plate 3.7), recalls Braitenberg's vehicle equipped with 'Mnemotrix,' a device that could embody the same principle.

Langton's reference to cybernetic robotics emphasized how ALife, though primari-

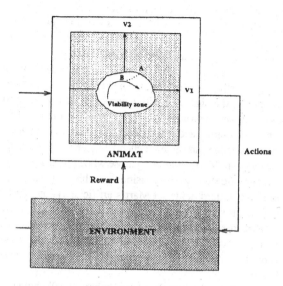

Fig. 6.4. The dynamic interaction between an animat and its environment. The adaptation consists of a corrective action (preprogrammed or learned, for example by means of a reward from the environment) such that the animat begins at point B to avoid crossing at point A its viability zone, associated with the two essential variables V1 and V2 (from Meyer and Guillot, 1994).

ly concerned with computer-simulated agents, was also concerned with *real* artificial agents or systems. As early as the mid-1980s, Stuart Wilson had used the expression "artificial animals," or "animats," to refer both to simulated animals and to real robots whose behavioral rules are inspired by those of living animals. Both in the former case and in the latter, what matters is that these systems are "complete systems," i.e. systems that engage in a dynamic relation with the environment (whether simulated or real) in which they are located and which they must confront in order to survive, or to adapt, or to learn. These systems are thus considered "holistically," and since it is not possible to simulate human intelligence holistically, the animat approach is firstly concerned with animal-like systems at a low level (Wilson, 1990: 16). Figure 6.4 shows what is meant in this approach by a dynamic relation. Everything, beginning with the terms employed, evokes Ashby's ultrastable system (see Figure 1.4) as well as earlier claims we mentioned about the organism and environment as an inseparable unit.[59]

Our brief inroad into ALife is certainly not enough to document its various interests, but at least it provides an idea of its chief methodological creed, consisting in the *bottom-up* simulation of organisms' behavior, i.e. simulation starting from low-level organic phenomena, such as adaptation and simple forms of learning. Neural-net models also

[59] See also Beer (1995) for a treatment of this point.

were concerned with these phenomena, thus establishing a bridge with the neurosciences. But ALife focuses on other phenomena, such as the emergence of life, biological evolution and development, thus establishing a bridge with several other disciplines, such as genetics, evolutionary biology and development biology.

While ALife researchers often consider neural nets as a sub-domain of their discipline, they explicitly oppose the so-called *top-down* approach of AI. In their view, this approach consists in simulating the higher cognitive processes involved in problem-solving tasks (such as chess or theorem proving), or in tasks where the agent must have a body of knowledge regarding a simulated world (as in the case of microworlds), or must have both common-sense knowledge and subject-dependent knowledge (as in the case of expert systems). As we have seen, Marr was among those who argued against this approach, bringing into prominence the study of early vision. Now his proposal seems limited in its turn. For example, Dana Ballard held that Marr's artificial vision had confined itself to the study of static and passive systems, without considering the dynamic aspects of visual perception. Ballard instead proposed to consider more closely the relations that the agent undertakes with the world. To that purpose, he emphasized "personalized" representations, which could be situated in a context and be relative to the observer's interest (Ballard, 1991, 1993).

In the case of mobile robots, early AI researchers usually hold that the problem of robot interaction with the real environment might be solved if one could adequately represent in a program the knowledge that enables the robot, when controlled by such a program, to make inferences and to plan its own actions in a real environment. One should, first of all, supply the robot with an adequate world model. This extreme top-down approach puts little emphasis on integrating reasoning and planning with sensory-motor abilities. Witness the modest performance of the earliest AI-based robots like Shakey. Indeed, at about the same time, a less top-down approach produced a different family of robots, like Stanford Cart, described by Hans Moracev.[60] Nonetheless, we would have to wait until the early 1980s for a robot architecture in line with the bottom-up approaches that spread fairly independently, such as ALife, animats and animate vision.

The leading proponent of this new robotics was Rodney Brooks. His idea, also suggested to him by Moracev's investigations, was to abandon the top-down strategy of knowledge representation and the central control of reasoning and planning processes, which had been investigated by AI researchers in the higher levels of intelligence, and to deal with perception and motor processes. These low-level processes suffice to ensure adaptation to the environment in lower organisms such as, just to mention examples that are known to us, amoeba and *Stentor*, or simple animals such as *Limax* and *Aplysia*, which exhibit elementary forms of associative learning. In fact, these animals, as well as less simple ones, survive in their environments without performing very elaborate reasoning or using explicit knowledge regarding such environments. According to Brooks, it is not a good idea to construct a robot by trying to directly simulate higher cognitive processes, which we do not sufficiently understand yet. We do have a good knowledge of how simple forms of in-

[60] See Moracev's essays in Langton (1989) and in Minsky (1985), a volume that is also a good introduction to various aspects of robotics (including industrial robotics, a matter we do not touch on here).

telligence work, based as they are firstly on sensory-motor abilities. Thus, a good strategy might be to begin with the construction of artifacts which could exhibit these abilities.

Brooks' approach was ideally linked to Grey Walter's. But Brooks himself insightfully pointed out what separates his own robots from cybernetic robots. Firstly, the computational elements in the latter were vacuum tubes, and, secondly, there was a lack of mechanisms that could suggest how to implement levels below that of complete behavior, i.e. how to organize behavior functionally into simpler modules. As Brooks concluded, "the mechanisms of cybernetics and the mechanisms of computation were intimately interrelated in a deep and self-limiting way" (Brooks, 1995: 38). Moreover, as we saw, the power of digital computation, and its flexibility compared to analogical computation, were, generally speaking, undervalued by cyberneticians.

The robot architecture Brooks proposed is, therefore, an alternative to those of early AI robotics, while at the same time trying to identify a level of abstraction that allows it to overcome the limitations of cybernetic robotics. Brooks' "subsumption architecture" describes the agent as composed of distinct control levels, which act on the environment without the supervision of a single control and planning system based on a global world-model. In a subsumption architecture, low-level routines that operate by means of continuous feedback loops with the environment, thus controlling a reactive behavior, are coupled to high-level routines that control more complex behaviors. For example, Allen, the first of these new robots or "creatures," is capable of avoiding the various people and obstacles it encounters along its path (a low-level, essentially reactive, task) while it seeks a goal assigned to it by the operator (a higher-level task). Brooks called this approach "behavior decomposition," to distinguish it from the "functional decomposition" of early robotics, i.e. the separation of the roles of perception, planning and action. According to Brooks, it is not a world model that guides Allen's behavior; rather, the robot "used the world as its own model," constantly comparing each individual goal with real-time events (Brooks, 1991a: 148). Brooks' simple creatures might be seen, so to speak, as a sufficiency proof that in order to simulate the intelligent (adaptive) interaction of an agent with its environment it is not necessary to call upon world models, explicit representations of knowledge, or centralized planning.

Research in robotics has dealt with the problems Brooks' claims raised. Firstly, Brooks himself was aware of the difficulties of his original strategy. Integrating the elementary components of a behavior that has a certain level of complexity may, in the long run, turn out to be impracticable. Research in evolutionary robotics has tackled this problem by using genetic algorithms (Cliff et al., 1993).[61] One example is offered by experiments on the mobile robot Khepera (Nolfi and Parisi, 1995), which was trained to recognize and

[61] The line of research using genetic algorithms has a long tradition, beginning with John Holland. We left Holland in the days of his collaboration with Rochester, when they were simulating Hebb's learning theory on a computer (see p. 175). After moving to the University of Michigan, Holland brought his idea of genetic algorithms to maturity during the mid-1960s, influenced by, among others, a book by the evolutionary biologist, R.A. Fisher, *Genetic Theory of Natural Selection*. His ideas came together in the volume he published in 1975, *Adaptation in Natural and Artificial Systems*. From then on, for about a decade, genetic algorithms were the subject of a number of research projects that remained on the fringes of the AI community, above all doctoral theses by Holland's students and reports to informal gatherings, which were often not even published. Reawak-

grasp a target object. Secondly, as Wyeth and Browning (1998: 530) observe, behavioral models inspired by Brooks' robotics and exhibiting abilities at the reactive level (the lowest level of the subsumption architecture) now abound, but the performance of models exhibiting higher abilities varies enormously, depending on the kind of representations they implement. In fact, purely reactive agents always react in the same way to the same sensory pattern, whereas more evolved agents can modify how they react to the same sensory pattern through learning. We will return to the issue of representations in the next chapter. Meanwhile, let us see how Wyeth and Browning's observation is valid in a case-study, that of spatial navigation. The latter involves understanding how spatial patterns can be internally coded by an agent (either natural or artificial) and how it uses such patterns to move about, in real time, in a more or less complex environment.

In its interaction with the environment, the agent can exhibit primitive navigation behaviors (for example, wall-following) or simple obstacle-avoidance behaviors by making use of a merely reactive control. But it can also exhibit more complex behaviors, based on global planning strategies and map generation, which involve higher control-levels. In the latter case, can the agent limit itself to establishing an essentially qualitative map of the environment, one based on topological relationships between certain landmarks it detects in the environment, such as adjacency? Or does it actually need a fairly accurate world model, in the form of a cognitive map, one based on metric relationships between the landmarks, such as absolute angles and distances? In addition, can the internal spatial representations the agent uses be distributed rather than centralized? [62]

One of the behavior-based models that sheds light on some of these questions is the robot Toto, build by Maja Mataric (1990; 1995). At first, she proposed to use the robot as a biologically realistic model of how a rat's hippocampus works. [63] The robot includes a circular omni-directional three-wheeled base, which allows it to move along a continuous path in a closed real environment, like a room furnished with various objects. It can thus exhibit reactive behaviors, such as boundary-following (it moves by following the walls and object boundaries) and object avoidance (it avoids other robots or people moving about in the room). While so moving, the robot detects landmarks in the environment using sonar sensors and a compass. The robot is able to recognize a certain number of landmark types. One type is the corridor, which is stored by the robot as a combination of moving straight and receiving short lateral distance readings.

---

ened interest in them is certainly due to the spread of parallelism (in this regard, mention should be made of Hillis' connection machine) and the study of dynamic complex systems, but it was also due to more recent investigations on pre-biotic development. Genetic algorithms represent a highly idealized model of natural selection processes. They start by randomly generating a population of strings, corresponding to genotypes in natural evolution, each of which represents a possible solution to a given problem. The population is made to evolve by applying operators based on mutation and recombination criteria that simulate genetic processes in natural evolution. In this way, the "parent" strings generate other strings, which represent new solutions to the problem, perhaps better ones. After this, the genetic algorithms are used in classifier systems, genuine automatic learning systems. Holland points out that he incorporated into them some of the learning procedures of Samuel's checkers program (Holland, 1990). ·

[62] Insightful discussion of this issue can be found in Prescott (1994; 1996).

[63] The hippocampus has a crucial role in the construction of maps of the environment. See Redish (1999) for a critical review, developing J.A. O'Keefe and L. Nadel's classical approach.

As the robot moves about in the environment, following walls and object boundaries, it does not limit itself to exploratory activity, but gradually constructs, during that same exploratory activity, an internal graph-shaped representation of the environment. The nodes of the graph correspond to landmarks in the environment, and the arcs between the nodes correspond to adjacency relationships between landmarks. The *distributed* nature of this representation can be recognized in the way landmarks are stored, and its *qualitative* nature comes from the fact that the accuracy of the representation is rather low, based as it is on topological information. However, given the limited performance expected from the robot, this is precisely what characterizes its robustness compared to robots which use very precise sensors and accurate control of their position in the environment.

The map put together in this way is used by the robot to represent the general structure of the environment. In later explorations, the robot is thus able to reach previously visited places (actually, landmarks) in the environment that the operator chooses as the goal. The robot is also able to choose the shortest path to places that it has reached previously by longer or less direct paths. This kind of path planning is the robot's higher-level (not simply reactive) task. It is implemented in the robot using a variant of spreading activation of the graph nodes.[64] Given the goal and the robot's current location, the activation spreads from the goal in all directions throughout the graph. This makes it possible to compute the distances between known landmarks that produce alternative paths. In this way, the robot, at a given choice point, is able to take the shortest path to the goal.

According to Mataric, the robot does not use the apparatus of the earliest AI-based robots, i.e. an inference engine that generates a plane based on a pre-established world model. Nor does the robot make use of a metric map stored in a centralized data structure, a map which, to be successful, should be very accurate. Rather than maximizing the map's accuracy, the robot pays for the unavoidable uncertainty and even errors that it can accumulate while it is acquiring information about the environment. Anyway, its use of primarily topological information proves to be sufficient to make up for that weakness.

As Mataric acknowledges, this simplifies computation but also limits the robot's performance to a quite simple kind of path planning, that of detecting shortcuts along paths it has *already* traversed. The metric component, limited in the present robot to computing the length of the paths, would have to be "extended" to the construction of a true metric map, if the robot were to perform more complex path-finding tasks (Mataric, 1990: 173). For example, the task of finding new shortcuts that were not paths it had previously traversed would require the ability of "reasoning" or "making geometric inferences," as Mataric put it (Mataric, 1995: 177). This would also increase the biological plausibility of the model.

Investigations into biologically plausible models include the so-called "synthetic complete models," in the field of both simulated animats or real robots, and commonly studied simple organisms, ones even simpler that those considered by the connectionist modeling in the previous section. A case in point is the nematode *Caenorhabditis elegans*, an organism endowed with about three hundred neurons, whose DNA sequencing and expression pattern mapping biologists have been able to describe completely.

[64] Spreading activation was introduced by Quillian in the context of semantic networks (see above, p. 193), and is usually considered by new connectionists to be among the contributions that influenced their investigations.

An early project was to build a detailed simulation model of this organism. As the project's promoters explained, despite the completeness of much of the empirical data about *Caenorhabditis elegans*, the complexity of genetic and cellular interactions make full understanding and testing of biological hypotheses extremely difficult. The construction of a computer simulation model can help (Kitano et al., 1998: 142). However, these researchers distinguish their "synthetic method," based on a realistic simulation of the organism, from that of ALife, which is more concerned with abstract dynamic models, even if they are biologically inspired (p. 153). This modeling methodology can be placed in the tradition of experiments that have emerged in very different contexts in our investigation under the banner of the synthetic method. This methodology is also shared by a second modeling project for *Caenorhabditis elegans*. In the latter, hypotheses about the nerve connections responsible for controlling phototaxis in the organism are tested by building a nematode-like mobile robot that reproduces the essential features of the phenomenon (Morse et al., 1998).

This latter case can be placed among the models of spatial navigation in open environments, and it is here that the construction of mobile robots converges with research in cognitive ethology. Rudiger Wehner, together with various collaborators, has conducted numerous observations of a simple invertebrate, the Saharan desert ant of the genus *Cataglyphis*, creating ingenious experiments to discover how the ant finds its way back to its nest. In fact, once it has left the nest in search of food, *Cataglyphis* can go as far as two hundred meters, exploring the terrain along a very irregular and winding path. But as soon as it finds food, it returns straight to the nest, following an apparently goal-oriented path. Since the ant does not leave pheromone trails, and since the environment where it moves usually lacks any kind of reliable landmark cues, Wehner's explanation, based on behavioral evidence and neurophysiological hypotheses, is that *Cataglyphis* successfully performs its task because it is endowed with an authentic skylight compass. It thus continuously measures all angles steered and all distances covered and integrates them into a main home vector. In this way, it succeeds in always having a continually-updated vector pointing to its home. The main (egocentric) navigational methods used by the ant in its environment are therefore path-integration when it is outward bound and dead-reckoning when it is homeward bound.

According to Wehner, these methods provide "a striking example of how evolution has designed a particular neural mechanism to accomplish a particular task, rather than arrived at an all-purpose mental representation of the external world" (Wehner et al., 1996: 131). This interpretation is in line with the skepticism about representations that is typical of much new robotics. And indeed various hypotheses about the use of the compass by *Cataglyphis* have been tested by Wehner himself, who assisted in the construction of a mobile robot. The robot moves about freely in the same environment as *Cataglyphis*, the desert of North Africa, and it embodies the skylight compass mechanism (Lambrinos et al., 1997).

In the previous section we mentioned the persistent attention paid to models of conditioned learning by researchers in various fields, from animal behavior to neural nets to neurosciences. In robotics as well, lively attention has been paid to this subject. In Edelman's synthetic neural modeling, one version of Darwin III became the 'brain' of a mobile robot, NOMAD. It was endowed with a sensory apparatus consisting of a television camera and a kind of 'snout' that allowed it to grab small objects. Along with various collaborators, Edelman experimented with NOMAD's ability to learn by simple conditioning, embodying in it different hypotheses about synaptic plasticity. The goal was to build a biologically plausible model of value-dependent learning, i.e. learning based on adaptive values which the operator assumes are 'innate' in the organism. In this case the modeling method simultaneously takes into account the properties of the nervous system, the body (the phenotype) and the environment (Verschure et al., 1995).

If these behavior-based and synthetic modeling approaches are interested in fairly biologically plausible robots, other approaches are more concerned to achieve efficient performance in spatial navigation. This is the case of CUQEE III (Figure 6.5), the maze-solving robot rat built by Wyeth and Browning (1998). As they observe (p. 529), Mataric's robot, in the above-mentioned version, would find itself in difficulty if the goal were not connected to walls, because its most successful exploration strategy consists in boundary following. It would not be an efficient complex maze solver like a real rat, or even like CUQEE III. Actually, Wyeth and Browning are interested in a robot displaying efficient performance, i.e. learning a maze in the shortest possible time.[65] Precisely this aspect, however, leads them to take into account, on the one hand, the features of navigation in real animals (which are an excellent source of suggestions for any engineering approach as well) and, on the other hand, the kind and power of the representations the robot uses. CUQEE III is able to solve mazes of considerable complexity, but through a metric map, in which relations between the objects in its world, rather than the relations between the agent and the objects, are stored—precisely as suggested by Tolman's experiments on cognitive maps in rats.[66]

The maze used by Wyeth and Browning is a 16×16 cell grid, with each cell measuring 18×18 cm. The cells have walls that can be positioned in various ways, so as to obtain different corridors. They can even be in a zigzag, which can be crossed diagonally by the robot (which can thus go forward more quickly than it could by following the walls of the corridors). The goal is the center of the maze. The robot, a cart with two driving wheels as actuators, has sensors (two on the sides and one in front) that allow it to perceive its distance from the walls. It also has an odometric sensor (in the wheels) that detects the current velocity and the distance traveled. This robot differs from cybernetic maze-solving robots for the aforementioned reasons. In particular, the robot's architecture calls for three levels: (1) the lowest level of behavior, the "schema level," or a purely *reactive* control level; action is generated by means of simple interaction with the environment and without accessing memory; (2) behavior at the "cognitive level," which uses a map of the maze to plan action by selecting schemas; (3) a "motivational level," which generates goals and has available to it a set of "values" that the robot can use to evaluate the most suitable strategies.

[65] CUQEE III was designed to participate in international competitions where maze-solving robots competed to find the shortest path that would bring them to the center of an unknown maze, and afterwards to run the remembered path. For details, see http://www.engr.ucsb.edu/~ieee/mm.html.
[66] See Chapter 4, p. 136.

These three levels work in parallel, so that the robot moves and solves the maze at the same time. According to the authors, while the first level makes no reference to genuine internal representations, the second level does, and in a crucial way. It is on the latter level that the robot constructs a map, and it does so precisely by starting from the primitive perceptual "schemas" of the first level. These schemas communicate information about the maze (for example, the presence or absence of walls in a cell). The maze's representation is facilitated by its very structure: the 16×16 cell grid can be represented univocally and regularly. On the basis of the information provided by the perceptual level, while it is constructing its map, the robot uses an algorithm that computes the time it takes to run from each of its starting positions to the goal. In the end, it learns the most direct path to the goal (in effect, the path that allows it to reach the goal most quickly). Whether this approach could deal with more natural, and eventually changing, environments remains to be ascertained.

The different robots we have discussed so far crystallize, from different points of view, some of the main open problems in current research in robotics. As we saw, early robots relied on general representations of the world and centralized planning but were barely capable of acting fluidly in real time. Behavior-based robots are endowed with numerous feedback controls and scanty representational and planning abilities: they are robust and reactive to changes in the environment and can locally determine the best action to take, but presently are not capable of handling global strategies.

Several robot competitions, such as those sponsored by the AAAI (American Association for Artificial Intelligence) beginning in 1992, or the soccer competitions sponsored by the Robot World Cup (RoboCup) Federation beginning in 1997, have pointed out the limitations of both pure planning architectures à la Shakey and pure subsumption architectures.[67] Most practical autonomous systems, such as many soccer robots, tend to include reactivity and reasoning in multilayer architectures consisting of a low-level or reactive system, which functions on a short time-scale, and a high-level or deliberative system for planning and reasoning, which functions on a fairly long time-scale. In contrast to behavior-based robots such as Mataric's, these "hybrid" architectures separate the robot's control system into these communicating parts, arranged in a hierarchical fashion. The *Cognitive Robotics Manifesto* at the 1998 AAAI Symposium pointed out the principles of a trend in robotics which is equally distant from the disembodied knowledge representation and planning of early AI and from pure subsumption architectures.[68]

Methods from heuristic search, as well as from classical and fuzzy logic in knowledge representation and control, have been given a new impetus by soccer robots, and are currently being explored and applied. The result is that, in principle, one can build certain robots reacting in real time to a changing environment without sacrificing their planning and inferential abilities. Reasoning may supply incomplete information through inferences from available data, so deriving an executable plan.[69] As Bonasso and Dean

---

[67] For a general presentation of RoboCup see http://www.robocup.org/

[68] See for a review Carlucci Aiello et al. (2000).

[69] See Shen et al. (1998) and Nardi (2000). Carlucci Aiello et al. (2001) review R. Reiter's development of the logicist approach in the field of robotics.

Fig. 6.5. Robots from the 1990s. From top to bottom: a successor of Ross' and Shannon's maze-learners, G. Wyeth and B. Browning's CUQEE III (courtesy of G. Wyeth); the Italian ART (Azzurra Robot Team) in action, winning the second prize in RoboCup, Stockholm, 1999 (courtesy of D. Nardi).

(1997: 20) concluded in their retrospective review of the AAAI robot competitions, a major lesson is that a lot of everyday activities can be done by reactive or model-less robots, but global planning and reasoning capabilities are needed for tasks in which there is uncertainty and in which time "is important, although non supercritical." In many current robots control and sensing are distributed, and planning is centralized, although the representations used in planning are tailored to the robot's task.

Work on soccer robots provides a framework for investigating cooperative multi-agent systems.[70] The ambitious long-term aim of the RoboCup project, however, is to build humanoid soccer robots, which would replace the present car-shaped robots of different sizes (Figure 6.5). At the moment, work in humanoid robotics is still at the preliminary stages, but humanoid robots are also used as models for testing theories in psychology. For example, in Brooks' Cog Project, the robot Cog provides a biologically realistic model of infant learning of hand-eye coordination (see Adams et al., 2000).

In conclusion, research in robotics during the 1990s offers a wide spectrum of disparate methodological proposals and experimental results. These range from biological plausibility to engineering efficiency, and from realistic modeling to simplified modeling. Such diversity in methods and goals has emerged at other points in our investigation. In the next chapter we discuss it in the context of the host of issues raised by the discovery of the artificial.

---

[70] One of the numerous examples in this field is the study of mobile robots simulating ant behavior (Krieger et al., 2000). But see p. 161 above for earlier projects of reproducing social and game-playing behavior in group of mobile robots.

CHAPTER 7

THE MANY FORMS OF THE ARTIFICIAL

The public emergence of cybernetics can be dated rather sharply because of the nearly simultaneous appearance [in 1943] of three basic papers on the subject. Rosenblueth, Wiener and Bigelow showed how simple goals and purposes could be realized in feedback machines. McCulloch and Pitts pointed out how some other logical categories and mental concepts could be represented in 'neural' nets, and Craik suggested a variety of ways by which machines might use models and analogies. To be sure, all of these had their own intellectual ancestors, but here for the first time we see a sufficiently concrete (i.e. technical) foundation for the use of mentalistic language as a constructive and powerful tool for describing machines (M. Minsky).

1. Five theses on the artificial

Now the time has come to put some order into the threads running through our investigation. We will do so by trying to identify certain theses that have marked the various stages in the discovery of the artificial, both before and after the advent of cybernetics. We formulate them as follows:

(*i*) *Functionalism.* The processes of adaptation, learning, and intelligence can be studied without considering the specific features of the organic structure directly. There is a *functional organization* which is common to both organic and inorganic, or artificial, structures or realizations.

(*ii*) *Modeling Method.* The hypothesis that the processes of adaptation, learning and intelligence are 'physical' can be tested by the building of models that simulate those processes. This modeling method is concerned with the *constraints* to be imposed on the physical artifacts so that they can be used as explanatory tools. These artifacts, however, are meant as *sufficiency* proofs for those processes, which would allow one to dispense with non-naturalistic explanatory entities.

(*iii*) *Representationalism.* Knowledge of the external world on the part of organisms comes about through *representation*, just as in the case of artifacts that simulate their behavior.

(*iv*) *Mentalism.* The observer can legitimately describe an artifact by making use of a *mentalistic* and *teleological* vocabulary, to control and predict its behavior. This is the language of beliefs, purposes, and desires that is commonly used by humans to control and predict the behavior of other humans.

(*v*) *Identity of Explanatory Principles.* The explanatory principles for the simplest processes of adaptation, learning and intelligence are not qualitatively different from those for higher processes, such as insight, creativity and consciousness. Success in the artificial simulation of the former paves the way for the empirical hypothesis that, in principle, it is possible to simulate the latter, whose *complexity* can thus be dealt with through the ordinary criteria of scientific analysis.

The various approaches to simulative methodology that we discussed in previous chapters either share some or all of these theses or give them different interpretations. Therefore, these theses might enable us to identify points of convergence and divergence between those approaches, with the aim of getting a deeper understanding of the crucial issues dealt with in previous chapters.

Questions raised by these theses are currently the subject of controversy among philosophers, but we will not consider them in that context, unless occasionally (the technical, philosophical literature is enormous). Our aim is to discuss the questions raised mainly in relation to the experimental results on the modeling of mental life which have come to the fore during our investigation into the discovery of the artificial.

2. Some initial distinctions

Calling to mind the robot approach, certainly the most consistent project before the advent of cybernetics, Hull, in the period when he supported it, would have shared the theses listed above, with the possible exception of Thesis (*iv*), *Mentalism*. This thesis, as well as the others, was explicitly endorsed by Rashevsky during the years when he was concerned with the robot approach.

Even cyberneticians and the psychologists of the cybernetics age who were concerned with behavioral models would have agreed with all five theses. In particular, many of them would have interpreted Thesis (*iii*), *Representationalism*, in accordance with the argument shared by Hull and Craik: since representations are *physical* "imprints" or "replicas," they can in principle be realized in an artifact; and both in organisms and in artifacts they are *symbolic*, i.e. they are in a relationship of "parallelism" with the external world. For Hull, as for Craik, representations are coded in organisms as neural circuits or patterns in the nervous system, through mechanisms hypothesized by the connectionist and associationist tradition. These neural circuits or patterns are what represent concepts and object perceptions. Craik extended this notion of representation to artifacts like computing machines and various analog devices, where representations consisted of physical states. These should perform a function analogous to the states of the nervous system in organism, although the latter are much more flexible.

With the advent of cybernetics, representations of this sort were given a central role by MacKay, who introduced the notion of an "imitative mechanism" through which the agent, whether an organism or an artifact, interacts adaptively with the outside world. MacKay considered the agent's response to an incoming stimulus pattern to be based on an internal "act of replication" of such a pattern. Through this act certain parameters of disequilibrium or mismatch are minimized until there is a sufficient degree of resemblance between the incoming stimulus pattern and the inner replica. In perception, this physical matching procedure functions as "the internal representative or *symbolic correlate* of the corresponding percept" (MacKay, 1952: 73). In the case of a simple feedback mechanism such as a thermostat, the present temperature is compared with the goal temperature in order to reduce the discrepancy. MacKay believed that an imitative mechanism of this kind was the basis of more and less complex abilities in both organisms and machines, from stimulus classification and concept formation to consciousness.[1] We shall return to some aspects of this point later in this chapter.

One artifact explicitly designed to exhibit some of those abilities was Rosenblatt's Perceptron. However, the Perceptron was intended to simulate more closely the architecture of neural connections, which were considered the physical basis for object perception and concept formation. Thus it was necessary to state the neurological hypotheses in a more explicit and quantitative way than in approaches like those of Craik or MacKay. As we have seen, it was again the connectionist and associationist tradition that came to Rosenblatt's rescue, and this time through the mediation of Hull and Hebb. The philosophy that inspired Rosenblatt was the same: the representations he postulated, i.e. the internal code that allowed the system interacting with the environment to store information regarding the stimuli, consist of certain patterns of neural connections. As Rosenblatt (1958) said, new information means the "creation" of new connections, so that stimulus recognition or classification (in fact, the appropriate response) occurs through the automatic activation of these connections. Rosenblatt's very terminology, and his reference to Hull's anticipatory goal response and to Hebb's cell assemblies, made his intentions explicit.

By the time Rosenblatt was writing digital computers were a reality, and the notion of representation began to be a central issue in programming. Rosenblatt explicitly rejected what he dubbed the approach of "symbolic logic, digital computers and switching theory." He traced this approach back to the pioneering works by Rashevsky and by McCulloch and Pitts, and to theoretical investigations by Stephen Kleene and the early Minsky (to stick with the authors he mentions).[2] Rosenblatt emphasized that in this approach representations were considered coded images of sensory stimuli, which have a one-to-one mapping with the latter, according to the model of computer memories. Unlike the Perceptron approach, stimulus recognition or classification would thus take place through what he called the 'match' between two patterns, one of sensory input, and one coded as a representation, or internal image.[3] This is how Rosenblatt summarized the differences between the representations in the Perceptron and those in digital computers:

> The important feature of this [connectionist] approach is that there is never any simple mapping of the stimulus into memory, according to some code which would permit its later reconstruction. Whatever information is retained must somehow be stored as *a preference for a particular response*; i.e. the information is contained in *connections* or *associations* rather than topographic representations (Rosenblatt, 1958: 386-387).

---

[1] See Cordeschi et al. (1999).

[2] Note that Rosenblatt includes Rashevsky, McCulloch and Pitts as pioneers of an approach that he contrasted with his own, while, in popular accounts by contemporary connectionists, these authors always appear together as the pioneers of neural nets. Actually, McCulloch and Pitts' 1943 contribution was equally fundamental both in neural net research and in computer science. Among the theorists Rosenblatt considered as his own source of inspiration there were authors concerned in different degrees with neurological research, such as Hebb, P.M. Milner and John Eccles, and cyberneticians such as Ashby and Uttley. These hints suggest how the history of connectionism needs more accurate reconstruction (see Aizawa, 1992 for analogous considerations).

[3] MacKay, too, had distinguished his own approach from what he called the "passive template-fitting method" he attributed to McCulloch and Pitts among others (MacKay, 1951: 113). He later used the expression "implicit representations" to define the symbolic correlates which were at the core of the *active* matching procedure mentioned above.

Rosenblatt's criticism is directed at a notion of representation and memory that later became prevalent within AI and cognitive science. In the 1950s, the notion of a computer program began to suggest new versions both of Thesis (*i*), *Functionalism*, and of Thesis (*iii*), *Representationalism*. Regarding the latter, from its outset AI emphasized the role of representation as a symbol structure, as we saw in Chapter 5. Using this notion, a distinction is often made in cognitive science between physical symbols, which constitute the internal representations of a computational system, and the non-physical *content* of those representations, which constitute the interpretation of these symbols. This is, for example, the distinction between the "syntactic level" and the "semantic level" in computational systems that Pylyshyn proposed in *Computation and Cognition* (Pylyshyn, 1984). He took it from Newell's distinction between "symbol level" and "knowledge level" (Newell, 1982).[4] Both Newell and Pylyshyn postulated a lower level, underlying the syntactic level in the hierarchy, where the symbols are realized or instantiated: the "hardware level." So realized or instantiated, symbols play a causal role in determining the behavior of the computational system. In much of cognitive science, this notion of symbolic representation was assumed to be common both to computational systems and to human beings. In the latter case, the symbol structures, which are assumed to be instantiated in the brain, have as their content the content of beliefs, desires, expectations, and the like.

We will later see why it was deemed necessary to split the cognitive system into three levels (semantic, syntactic, and physical), and what problems are thereby engendered. In the meanwhile, let us look at how the above hypothesis became the pivotal point for a new representational theory of mind, of a computational kind, and what its impact was on Thesis (*i*), *Functionalism*.

In Hull's physicalism, which was consistent with the philosophy of Perceptrons, representations are "imprints" or "replicas" coded in neural patterns that are causally linked with the outside world. In the computational-representational theory of mind, symbol structures are assumed to be the indispensable medium for justifying the causal action of the system or agent on the world, especially in the course of complex actions. We have seen some instances of this claim in AI. For example, when the agent has to evaluate different alternatives or make a plan in a problem-solving task, the symbol structures that represent possible alternatives for that plan are manipulated according to rules before the agent makes its own decision. The "symbolic" activity of the nervous system, hypothesized by Craik, was interpreted in AI in terms of representations manipulated through explicit rules.[5]

[4] According to Newell, this hierarchy of levels, including the knowledge level, characterizes Physical Symbol System architectures (see p. 207 above). In particular, a system's adaptive or rational behavior at the knowledge level can be predicted on the basis of the *content* of representations plus its knowledge of its goals, whereas the symbol level is the level of the computer program, i.e. of the *actual* information-processing mechanisms that the adaptive or rational system uses in order to attain those goals. At the latter level the system can be viewed as the "administrative" (or bounded rationality) agent Simon described in the 1940s (see p. 178 above). As Newell (1982: 117) concluded, this notion of knowledge derived from work in AI as well as in psychology and in the social sciences, and it is to be seen "as a refinement of this existing view of adaptive systems, not as a new theory."

[5] Johnson-Laird (1983), in the framework of cognitive science, and before him Newell and Simon (1963), in the framework of Information Processing Psychology, referred to Craik's claim, developing it in a computational sense. Craik's starting point, however, was Hull's connectionism with his notion of "symbolism" or "paral-

It is within this computational-representational theory of mind that a hypothesis was proposed for solving some of the enigmas of the mind-body problem that have emerged at various points in our investigation, particularly in the context of behaviorism. For example, according to Pylyshyn, what causes behavior is not the *content* of the mental states (i.e. the content of certain desires or beliefs or expectations), but their physical *form*. This was assumed to consist of symbol structures, which are physically realized or instantiated in the brain. On the one hand, certain paradoxes we have already mentioned in the course of our investigation could thus be removed, for example those deriving from assuming non-physical 'ideas' as causes of physical behavior. On the other hand, some of the difficulties in behaviorist and physicalist explanations of purposeful behavior could be avoided, for example, the objection concerning *non-existent* things that can cause behavior, which we saw raised by Richard Taylor against Rosenblueth and Wiener (Chapter 4). Given that it is not the content of a representation but the symbol structure that causes behavior, Pylyshyn concludes that no problem ensues from the fact that such content might refer to a future event, as in the case of a purpose, or the fact that it does not even exist, as in the case of something which is part of a false belief (Pylyshyn, 1984: 25-28).

We have already pointed out that the origin of these problems goes back a long way, and it is not by chance that, once the possibility of a vitalist solution was discarded, Pylyshyn also rejected any physicalist approach of a behaviorist sort. In particular, he rejected Hull's solution, based on the anticipatory goal response, to the problem of the alleged causal role of mental states (of ideas) in behavior (p. 41). At the same time, he also rejected the reductionist-physicalist approach (p. 33), in which the study of the causal role of mental states was exhausted by studying the brain, and the solution of the mind-body problem was entrusted to neurology. In the course of our investigation we have seen some forewarnings of this thesis, but it was not until the 1950s and 1960s that it was made popular by materialist philosophers, like Herbert Feigl and D.M. Armstrong, in the form of the mind-brain identity theory. Briefly, according to such a theory, a type of mental state must be *identified* with a corresponding type of brain state.

Criticisms of this theory were raised, above all, after the publication of Putnam's seminal 1960 article, "Minds and Machines," which is usually seen as introducing the functionalist thesis into the philosophy of mind. In later articles, Putnam pointed out why he had introduced the notion of *functional description* by reference to Turing machines. He considered the machine table a normal form of functional description of those machines, one that grounded the notion of "functional isomorphism" between systems. Computers that are physically realized in different hardware are instances of functional-

---

lelism" in the nervous system (see below). C.R. Gallistel argues that Hull did not maintain a representational theory, because learning was for him explained by the selective reinforcement of certain connections. Representations are understood by Gallistel as a model of the world, and in this sense he refers to Tolman's cognitive map and to the latter's criticism of Hull (Gallistel, 1997: 7, and see also above, p. 136). Our thesis is that it is possible to speak of *representations* both for Hull and for Tolman: if those of Tolman (the central maps) are considered by Gallistel close to the computational conception, or symbol-processing, those of Hull (the imprints) can be considered close to the conception of new connectionism and behavior based robotics. Of course, this raises the question as to whether it is possible to consider the neural patterns of the connectionists as symbolic representations, as Vera and Simon (1993) do. We will deal with at least some aspects of this problem later on.

ly isomorphic systems, i.e. ones where a mapping exists between their various states that preserves functional relations. Although it is not possible to give a similar description in normal form for living organisms, this suggests that mental states too could be considered as realizable in different physical systems—not only in organic ones, like the brain, but also in inorganic ones, like given computer hardware. It made no sense, therefore, *to identify* types of mental states with types of brain states, as mind-brain identity theorists believed. Mental (or psychological) states should be studied by referring not to their physical realization or instantiation, which could differ from time to time, but to their common *functional organization*, i.e. to their interactions with each other and with sensory inputs and behavioral outputs.[6] Briefly, this was the "multiple realizability thesis," which was later developed especially by Fodor (1974), and was often closely tied to *Turing machine functionalism.*

Turing machine functionalism was consistent with what we called *machine functionalism* in Chapter 5. According to the latter, organisms and machines can be studied from the point of view of their common functional organization. This kind of functionalism, various forewarnings of which we have noticed in the early decades of the twentieth century, comes to the fore with the advent of cybernetics and computer science. Ashby had already spoken of "isomorphic machines," and with the advent of the 'intelligent' computer the functional comparison between minds and programs is put forward. At the beginning of AI, then, this idea took specific form in the claim that it is *precisely at the program level*, or that of symbol structure manipulation, that intelligence processes are properly analyzed, by abstracting from their realization at the physical level. Mind is viewed as intrinsically computational. Thesis (*i*), *Functionalism*, has become popular in this *computational* variant in much of AI and cognitive science. Before discussing the questions raised by this variant of functionalism, it will be useful to reconsider Thesis (*ii*), the *Modeling Method.*

3. The modeling method and functionalism

From the very beginnings of the discovery of the artificial, Thesis (*ii*), the *Modeling Method*, pointed to a strategy in the study of organism behavior which could support the traditional behavioral sciences, psychology and neurology. It was among such disciplines that Bent Russell aimed to put his "engineering profession" approach long ago, in 1913.

---

[6] See the essays collected in Putnam (1975). We are not concerned here with the later evolution of Putnam's thought, nor with the issue of disembodied minds and other technical philosophical problems of functionalism, such as that of *qualia*, which have been discussed by Ned Block, Donald Davidson, Fred Dretske, Jaegwon Kim, William Lycan and others. (See Bechtel, 1988, for a concise taxonomy of various forms of functionalism in the philosophy of mind.) Our aim is to discuss functionalism in relation to the modeling method in the empirical research on mental life, particularly with regard to several issues touched on in previous chapters. Functionalism, and multiple realizability too, are considered here as empirical hypotheses. For this very reason we will never resort to the popular slogan that as the computer software stands to the hardware, so the mind stands to the brain, which is considered a typical claim of functionalism. Although such a slogan has been often ventured within AI and cognitive science, we argue that it either entails too strong a version of the structure/function distinction or is based on a caricature of functionalism, at least as regards the epistemological issues we will discuss here.

The advantages and risks of the modeling method were pointed out by Craik when he proposed it in 1943 as the "synthetic" method, to distinguish it from the "analytic" method, that of neurology. Among its advantages is generality, which makes it possible to state explanatory principles that are "more fundamental," i.e. common to both organisms and machines. Among its risks is the possibility of making misleading analogies by invoking *ad hoc* principles (Craik, 1966: 9). The advantages and risks of the modeling method have become evident at different stages in our investigation, which was concerned with the strategy of mental life models in the most widely-ranging contexts throughout the twentieth century.

Put very generally, the strategy of building mental life models starts from a theory about a phenomenon in living organisms, such as adaptation or learning or the functioning of the nervous system. The theory is based on the behavior exhibited by organisms or, where available, on verbal reports or neurophysiological data. Then the theory is used as the basis for building a *functioning* artifact.[7] The artifact "embodies" the explanatory principles (or the hypotheses) of the theory, as behavioral scientists have put it at least since the days of Bent Russell. The artifact is thus taken as a *test* of the plausibility of the theory. If the artifact behaves, in one or more aspects, as the theory predicts, we have a more or less satisfactory proof of the sufficiency of the (physical) processes postulated by the theory.

This procedure, based on comparing the performance of artifact and organism, had already been defined as "synthetic" by Stephen, Hull, and Ross in the 1920s and 1930s, and was based on what we called machine functionalism: building a model of a behavior meant building a machine (usually an electro-mechanical device) that would show, as Ross put it, the "sufficient condition" for that behavior. The sufficient condition was provided by the functional relations between stimulus and response, without calling into play the specific underlying structure or substratum, whether organic or inorganic. And yet, as we saw in Chapter 3, it was precisely Ross' robot rat which, while learning a maze, did not behave as predicted by any theory of trial-and-error learning of the day, though it 'learned' just like a real rat, according to Ross test. Attempts to make artifacts more realistic from a psychological point of view, i.e. from that of the behavioral theory proposed to explain learning in organisms, were not lacking during those years. We have mentioned Ellson's model of Hull's simple trial-and-error learning theory, which, unlike other models, attempted to simulate not only the performance (the response) but also the reaction times and errors of the organism while learning. Another example was

[7] We would want to emphasize the point about the *realizability* of the models, because we have distinguished, above all in Chapter 2, between certain generic analogies, more or less important or seminal in the study of a mental life phenomenon, and working models of that phenomenon. As we have pointed out on various occasions, this does not prove that the principles used to build models are the same as those of living systems ("it only suggests that," as Needham put it: see above, p. 227). As Craik said, "we are [...] concerned not with a high probability that the *actual* mechanism is the same in the model and the reality, but with the probability that the *type* of mechanism is the same" (Craik, 1943: 109). This should at least save us from the impression Jennings had when considering von Uexküll's mechanical analogies, i.e. that "there are two systems [the organism and the analogy] to grasp in place of one" (see above, p. 73). For a more skeptical view on artificial models in behavioral sciences, see Negrotti (1999).

the mobile robot in which Bradner thought he would embody the goal gradient hypothesis, which Hull had introduced to explain trial-and-error learning in mazes. Craik did not appreciate Bradner's model of learning: he believed it was an *ad hoc* simulation, based on mechanisms that were implausible from the biological point of view. Craik, in proposing the synthetic method, relied on models that would not simply mimic the behavior of organisms but would embody "general principles," i.e. principles common to organisms and machines. These principles would make it possible to reproduce in machines at least some of the "essential features" of the phenomenon under investigation. This expression recurs in many of the authors we have discussed, and refers to those features which are suggested by the theoretical hypotheses appealed to in explaining that phenomenon.

Although in a rather confused way, these approaches raised the question of the *constraints* to be imposed on an artifact so that it would be a psychologically realistic model. Functional equivalence alone was not very relevant to this aim. In fact, functional equivalence concerns the sole constraint of equivalence with respect to stimulus-response behavior, but other constraints should be identified as regards the features of the phenomenon under investigation that are essential according to the theory. Just think of the increasing number of features which, according to Hull, his future "psychic" machine would have had to satisfy. Problem-solving and planning abilities, insight and all other high cognitive processes that had to be explained by his associationist theory could be considered sources of constraints. Because of the simplicity of the artifacts, however, none of these modeling approaches addressed one of the questions that would later become prominent: when the comparison between the overt behavior of the organism and that of the model succeeds only in part, it is necessary to start a *revision* process, which may involve both the theory and the model. In this case, the model assumes at least an important heuristic role: it can suggest new hypotheses to explore and relevant implications for the theory itself. As MacKay put it,

> We can think of [the model] as a kind of template which we construct on some hypothetical principle, and then hold up against the real thing in order that the discrepancies between the two may yield us fresh information. This in turn should enable us to modify the template in some respect, after which a fresh comparison may yield further information, and so on (MacKay, 1954: 404).

We have seen several examples of this methodology, which set different goals in just as many different contexts, from Wyckoff's hypothesis revision, based on the functioning of the model, to Rochester's theory-model cycle; from Newell and Simon's "revised models" to Johnson-Laird's "dialectical process" between theory and models; from models that embody Edelman's theory of neural Darwinism up to the various "complete synthetic models" of biological organisms in the 1990s. In all these cases, the model was seen as a *third* way to represent the theory, an alternative to the two more traditional ways, the verbal and the mathematical. In turn, the representation of the theory through a model is provided by a physical analog, usually an electronic device, or by a computer program.

When computer simulation was used, this could be done with different aims. For example, in Newell and Simon's Information Processing Psychology the program, besides being a way to represent the theory, was also itself a theory, in fact a simulative microtheory (the *general* theory consisted of a body of qualitative generalizations suggested by simulation).[8] The program thus sought to be an explanation of the behavior of one human agent in a given task environment: by introducing theoretical entities and hypotheses related to information processes, the program made it possible to predict and control the evolution of that behavior. In Edelman's synthetic neural modeling the program, as a simulation model, embodies the main hypotheses of the theory (in fact, the theory of neural Darwinism) and is a way of representing it, but it is not the theory. The program is used as a test of the theory.

In ALife, Harnad (1994) proposed a distinction between "virtual" ALife, which studies organisms in computer simulated environments, and "synthetic" ALife, which builds artifacts, such as mobile robots, in real environments. He maintained that virtual ALife systems are *ungrounded* systems no less than those of classical AI. Therefore, virtual ALife cannot tackle what he calls the "symbol grounding problem," while synthetic ALife can.[9] According to Harnad, in a simulated or virtual world, it is always the observer, or interpreter, who attributes meaning to the symbols. On the contrary, an artifact that interacts with the real world can become *grounded* to the extent that "the connection between its internal symbols and what they are about is direct and unmediated by external interpretation" (p. 298). We will come back to this kind of argument in the next section, when we take up the issue of representations again. Meanwhile, it should be noted that, although there is no consensus concerning the ontology of ALife (Olson, 1997), this distinction between *simulated* and *realized* agents is not new. It was used by Pattee (1989) in the same context of ALife, and Steels calls the strategy of realizing models such as mobile robots the "synthetic method." Such robots, being situated in the real world, do indeed mean that the synthetic method "goes further than a computer simulation" (Steels, 1995: 93). This is the path that could lead to a '*nouvelle* AI,' to use a now fashionable expression. Steels argues that the synthetic method consists of building artifacts with the aim of testing a theory. He compares the mental life modeling method with the traditional theory validation method, and emphasizes a theory-model revision cycle analogous to that proposed by various model builders we have mentioned in previous chapters.

Nevertheless, as our investigation into the discovery of the artificial has shown, it is not *per se* the fact that an artifact actually interacts with the real world, and is thus an instance of the synthetic method as Steels sees it, that gives it a theoretical import. A mobile robot can be relevant from the point of view of its performance without being so from the point of view of its biological or psychological plausibility. It could be the product of brilliant engineering applications, which do not as such embody any neurological or behavioral theory. In this regard, the only differences between certain engineering products

[8] See p. 182 above. In this case, one important problem regards the program-theory relationship. We cannot deal with this problem here, limiting ourselves to mentioning it in the form of Newell's question: "What aspects of a program actually make a psychological claim?" (Newell, 1990: 23). In fact, programs contain many mechanisms that make the simulation function, and are not always easily distinguishable from mechanisms that are theoretically relevant. The question is discussed by Cooper et al (1996), also as regards Newell's SOAR.

[9] The symbol grounding problem is the question of how artificial systems could manipulate intrinsically meaningful symbols (Harnad, 1990).

in the new robotics, which we saw in the previous chapter, and certain earlier robots, from those of Ross to many of the cybernetic robots, are ones of technology and architecture. Conversely, a computer simulation could be considered relevant for a theory in the very sense pointed out by Steels, and thereby it could be an instance of the synthetic method: for example, Edelman's simulated automata, or Hawkins' simulated model of *Aplysia*.

Therefore, if the synthetic method is a method for validating behavioral theories, as Steels, among others, points out, it is not simply the fact that it "goes further than" a simulation that makes it useful to that end. The question, instead, is this: what requirements must a model satisfy, either as a computer simulation or as a 'real' analog, in order to be worth considering in the context of the *explanation* of mental life?

This question brings us back to Thesis (*i*), *Functionalism*. Edelman rejects functionalism and accepts the synthetic method, which, in the form of his synthetic neural modeling, has gone from early computer simulations to later implementation in mobile robots, such as NOMAD. Generally speaking, Edelman's criticism of functionalism is aimed at Turing machine functionalism, which he believes to be at the basis of cognitive science. More recently, Edelman and co-workers have pointed out that the functionalist approach to organism behavior leaves an unsolved problem, namely, the fact that the models that such an approach proposes "are in principle undetermined" (Verschure et al., 1995: 247). The problem, as they summarize it, is the following. Just as different functionally equivalent or isomorphic machines *cannot be distinguished* from each other in terms of their response, so also, to the extent that functionalism is limited to identifying the relation between stimulus, internal states, and response, without considering how these relate to the actual mechanisms that generate the observed behavior, that relation can be described by *multiple* functional models. These are based on different assumptions, which give rise to the same response and satisfy the same predictions, with the result that "a selection between these alternative models cannot be made by sole reference to the observed response" (p. 248). We already know Edelman's proposal: build a model (now in the shape of a real robot) which embodies some constraints related to the components that influence the organism behavior at *several* levels (at least the phenotype, the nervous system and the properties of the environment). These biologically plausible constraints are supposed to guarantee that such a model is not undetermined, as a functional model is.

The problem of functional equivalence is not a novel one. Indeed, Edelman and co-workers exemplify the above difficulty of the indeterminacy of functional models by referring to Edward Moore's essay in *Automata Studies* in 1956 about isomorphic machines, a notion which recalls Ashby's claims mentioned earlier when discussing machine functionalism. Turing machine functionalism, in the form of Putnam's functional isomorphism, can be regarded as the more recent variant of this kind of functionalism. To this extent, Turing machine functionalism is exposed to the objection above regarding the alleged indeterminacy *in principle* of models. But in cognitive science Turing machine functionalism was questioned because the objection that *functional* models are undetermined had already been discussed, precisely for the reasons pointed out by Edelman and co-workers. The problem, in this case, was the choice of *constraints* to impose on programs so that they could be considered psychologically plausible models of cognitive processes rather than *ad hoc* simulations or mere mimicry.[10]

Now, as Pylyshyn said, "if the only constraint we place on the process is that it solve the problem in finite time, then the Turing-Church thesis states that if the problem is mechanistically solvable there exists a Turing machine (in fact infinitely many) which will fit the requirements" (Pylyshyn, 1979: 43). Clearly, this constraint alone is not strong enough to make programs relevant in explaining a cognitive phenomenon. And in fact, when the issue of constraints was raised in cognitive science, it was not limited to considering the performance of a program (as it is legitimate to do, say, in evaluating an expert system). On the contrary, once the functional relation between the incoming stimuli and the observed behavior was stated, the problem was raised of identifying the intermediate processes or actual mechanisms which generate that behavior.[11] To this end, additional constraints were considered. Pylyshyn pointed to various kinds of such constraints: some had already been identified in cognitive-modeling research, while little attention had been paid to others before the 1980s.

Among the first kind of contraints, Pylyshyn mentioned those already discussed in the days of Newell and Simon's human behavior simulation. By studying the thinking-aloud protocols, as we saw in Chapter 5, they had identified some constraints that would make a program a candidate explanation. Thinking-aloud protocols are a source of constraints which, in its original form, raises a lot of methodological questions, widely discussed by several authors. Nonetheless, thinking-aloud protocols explicitly suggested for the first time how the *grain* of the simulation was to be specified, beyond mere functional equivalence. In fact, Newell and Simon put forward a computational analysis not only of broad human behavior, but also of the actual mechanisms involved, an analysis that Simon and co-workers then pursued, as we saw in the previous chapter, in various task environments.[12] Among the second set of constraints, or sources of constraints, Pylyshyn included various forms of learning, development, neurophysiological evidence, and the properties of the architectur—all issues among the most controversial in current cognitive science. On that occasion Pylyshyn concluded that certain constraints suggested by neuroscience *could* be relevant in cognitive science: for example, the data regarding pathologies such as aphasia and agnosia, or those regarding the modularity of certain brain functions (Pylyshyn, 1978: 126).

Pylyshyn dealt extensively with the issue of constraints in *Computation and Cognition*, with the aim of better defining the natural kind of cognitive science and, according-

[10] In fact Turing machine functionalism is often a straw man for critics of functionalism in general, who argue that according to functionalism 'the brain is a Turing machine.' In the face of the empirical evidence from cognitive modeling, one wonders who *really* would defend such a sort of functionalism.

[11] Bechtel (1982) calls "vacuous functional explanation" an explanation which was limited to considering in models the functional stimulus-response relation alone, and in an enlightening way he discusses some instances taken from the history of science.

[12] On similar grounds Newell and Simon had already rejected the Turing test (see p. 182 above). Pylyshyn also rejects it, because he considers such a test to be based only on the property of plasticity or universality of Turing machines. This kind of "input-output, or 'Turing,' equivalence" (Pylyshyn, 1984: 54) between the computational model and the organism is not the right level for cognitive modeling (see below).

ly, of identifying the constraints to be imposed on computational models. He raised precisely the question of the *indeterminacy* of functional models, in the sense then emphasized by Edelman and co-workers. Pylyshyn calls the models based on mere functional equivalence, i.e. equivalence with respect to input-output behavior, "weakly equivalent." Weak equivalence is given by a *sufficiency* test. It exhibits a mechanical procedure which can generate a given behavior (for example, an instance of a certain cognitive ability), in fact a procedure whose results can be computed by a Turing machine (Pylyshyn, 1984: 75).[13] Such a sufficiency test, however, says nothing about the cognitive processes involved. Pylyshyn rejected the old expression "behavior simulation" used to describe the building of computational models in cognitive science. In fact, computational models have to be "strongly equivalent" to human behavior, i.e. they have to satisfy the criteria of explanatory adequacy, concerning suitable law-like generalizations, and to identify those constraints which indicate the "fine grain correspondence" between cognitive and computational processes. The constraints that Pylyshyn identified at the cognitive architecture level were meant to be a response to those who believed that, since the functional equivalence criterion is weak, and models remain actually undetermined, one must appeal to biological constraints: only these would identify the right grain of analysis for models (p. 121). With this last move, Pylyshyn touched on the issue of *biological* constraints, which would later be brought into prominence, by Edelman for example. However, at the time Pylyshyn's conclusions about the role of neuroscience in the discovery of functional features of the cognitive architecture were on the whole skeptical (he was perhaps theorizing too strong a structure/function distinction). Moreover, he excluded the possibility that consciousness or emotions should be studied as essential features of cognition (these are issues now at the foreground of much cognitive science research: see e.g. Picard, 1997).

The central role played by constraints is evident in other research programmes in cognitive science. For example, Johnson-Laird argued in *Mental Models* that functionalism (in fact, Turing machine functionalism) suggests a "weak constraint" on the *theory* of mental models, that according to which mental models are computable and the machinery for constructing and interpreting them is made up of algorithmic procedures (Johnson-Laird, 1983: 398). Additional constraints are to be used to specify the set and the types of mental models, and several sections of the book are devoted to this issue. But the general theory, or at least parts of it, should be embodied in computer programs, according to Johnson-Laird's methodological claim about theory testing. Programs should thus satisfy in turn a cluster of constraints regarding, for example, syllogistic reasoning, as this is explained by the theory of mental models. In fact, programs have to be able to simulate difficulties and errors in human performance, individual differences in inferential ability, or how children acquire such an ability, and so on.

Newell (1990) argued that the proposal of a unified architecture of cognition like SOAR means precisely moving in the direction of taking multiple constraints into ac-

[13] In Pylyshyn's view, this *constructivist* statement is something more than a mere *existence* proof, i.e. the proof, given by the existence of digital computers, that "certain types of semantically described processes are compatible with materialism" (see section 2 above, and Chapter 5 as regards analogous materialistic claims and sufficiency statements in early AI).

count. These constraints must reflect the fact that the mind "has been built up in response to many different requirements" (p. 18), all of them necessary for ensuring successful interaction with the environment. Among these requirements are flexibility, learning, operating in real time, development and being realizable as a nervous system. SOAR certainly does not satisfy all of these ("no individual science can deal with very many of these constraints," as Newell puts it); but the hope was that one could include as many of them as possible in SOAR's architecture. As for the latter constraints in the above list, those included in what Newell called the "biological band," it seemed to him that SOAR satisfied some of them (first of all, that of operating in real time). As for the rest, he stated a conclusion that clarifies, because it refers to the history, how the indifference towards neuroscience (and a strong structure/function distinction) attributed to 'classical' cognitive science no longer constitutes a distinctive feature of each of its research programmes:

Throughout the history of information-processing psychology, an important element of its rhetoric has been that it is not anchored to the structure of the brain. [...] It was, I think, an important stance and the right one for its time. [Nevertheless] information processing can no longer be divorced from brain structure. [...] The great gain [...] is that *many additional constraints can be brought to bear as we examine information processing more deeply.* But that puts it too abstractly. The great gain is that we finally *bridge the chasm between biology and psychology with a ten-lane freeway* (Newell, 1990: 483, my italics).

In a nutshell, the modeling method imposes a certain number of constraints on artifacts *beyond* that of functional equivalence. So modeling method is functionalism plus constraints. What about multiple realizability in different stuff?

William Bechtel and Jennifer Mundale claim that the multiple realizability thesis, supported since the days of Putnam's and Fodor's functionalism, cannot be maintained. In fact, the conclusion usually drawn from the multiple realizability thesis was that neuroscience is of little or no relevance for computational theories of the mind. Taking the example of visual perception, Bechtel and Mundale show how an understanding of the psychological function is based, instead, on brain decomposition (in this regard, they rehearse criticisms leveled by Ballard and others against Marr). Conversely, they hold that abandoning the multiple realizability thesis does not lead one to abandon functionalism, which they define as "the claim that psychological states are to be identified in terms of their functional roles" (Bechtel and Mundale, 1999: 204). They persuasively show how it is precisely an experimental practice of this sort, one based on functional characterization, that has always guided neurological research in the identification of brain areas.

The version of multiple realizability that was the subject of Bechtel and Mundale's criticism is the one where one mental state is realizable in different individuals, even of different species (this was the version Putnam himself had in mind when he spoke, for example, of 'fear' in mammals, in reptiles, etc., to show that there is no single type of brain state corresponding to 'fear' which is common to all species). As regards the version of multiple realizability in which mental states are realizable *in different stuff,* whether organic or inorganic, Bechtel and Mundale do not commit themselves very much, simply stating their skepticism about the possibility that mental states could be realized in current computers. Apart from computers (leading players in the multiple realizability considered by early functionalism), this is precisely the version of multiple realizability that is the core of the modeling method, which we have discussed above. In the modeling strategy, multiple realizability in different substrates can be maintained no less than functionalism, once the caveat about the constraints is made, a point which Bechtel and Mundale do not take up. In our view, constraints are what makes the life "more difficult" for functionalist, to use Dennett's expression (Dennett, 1996: 77). In particular, constraints from the "biological band" are what prevents the functionalist from accepting versions of multiple realizability divorced from neuroscience.

Note that functionalism and multiple realizability alike have been shared as a starting-point, so to speak, for identifying constraints on models both by computationalism, which characterizes the top-down approach commonly attributed to classical cognitive science, and by bottom-up approaches. Take the case of ALife, both in its "strong thesis" (the afore-mentioned "big claim" by Langton, in which simulated life is literally genuine life) and in its "weak thesis" (whose goal is to build simulative models of living organisms and their environment).[14] Both these theses accept the idea of *common functional organization*: the kind of stuff is irrelevant for the understanding of the phenomenon (it could be organic compounds or silicon and copper and so on). ALife takes into account, however, biological constraints concerning genotype, phenotype and environment. Precisely as in the case of classical cognitive models, such constraints *limit* the simulations one could accept as behavioral models in ALife. In this case too the usual caveat is valid: "simulations that are dependent on *ad hoc* or special-purpose rules and constraints for their mimicry cannot be used to support theories of life" (Pattee, 1989: 68). We can thus conclude that what ALife rejects is the *computational* version of functionalism: for this version, above all in the past, constraints concerned the cognitive or higher processes or mechanisms exclusively. In fact, anyone who supports the modeling method in the study of organism behavior, whether top-down or bottom-up, cannot help but agree with the claim that the constituents of the (inorganic) model have the same *functional role* as the constituents of the (organic) phenomenon one seeks to explain. And in both cases, one abstracts from the specific stuff of the physical realization. What distinguishes the different claims is which constraints and how many are to be imposed on models so that they are relevant for explanation.

Now, just as there is no unanimity concerning which top-down or cognitive constraints to impose on models, so there is no unanimity about bottom-up or biological constraints. Both PDP connectionist models and Hopfield net models are rejected by the proponents of so-called "realistic models of the brain" or Edelman's synthetic neural modeling. Instead, they consider an ever greater number of anatomical and physiological features of the nervous system and of the body (the phenotype) in their interaction with the environment. On the basis of empirical evidence, these features impose on models much stronger constraints than those pointed out by neo-connectionists from the 1980s onwards. After all, for Edelman neural net models would not be any less 'functionalist' than those of cognitive science. According to Edelman, connectionists delude themselves in thinking that they are proposing the right biological constraints, when instead they are us-

---

[14] On the computational side, the strong thesis of ALife can be compared to Pylyshyn's claim that cognition is *literally* computation. He carried to its extreme consequences the thesis that "strongly equivalent" models (or programs) are not simulations useful for the understanding of behavior, but *explanations* themselves.

ing principles and rules that are unacceptable *precisely* from the point of view of biological plausibility, such as the usual backpropagation algorithm (Reeke et al., 1989).

Our investigation suffices to show that, from Bent Russell's rudimentary models up to Perceptrons and the most advanced PDP and Hopfield models, the fact that one proposes a connectionist or neural net architecture does *not* in itself mean satisfying the requirement of biological plausibility. We could have models that were based on the functional organization of neural nets with suitable learning algorithms without such models being biologically plausible, or interesting as explanatory tools. The very question of model indeterminacy, raised by their functional equivalence at the symbol level, could be raised by their functional equivalence at the neural net level, if the appropriate constraints were not identified.[15] But note that the use of biologically not plausible principles at a certain level of the model may, under certain conditions, not conflict with biological constraints at another level. For example, Churchland and Sejnowski show the role of some neural net models in testing different neurophysiological hypotheses concerning the functioning of the vestibule-eye circuit, and also in evaluating experimental results apparently in conflict with each other.[16] This is so *despite* the fact that these models are based on the (biologically implausible) backpropagation algorithm as a global learning rule. In this case, the degree of realism of the model is ensured by the constraints on the simulated net that come from anatomo-physiological knowledge about real neural circuits.

The moral is that there is no generally or *a priori* valid decision criterion for establishing which constraints to take into consideration. Rather, they are suggested by the state of experimental knowledge, by rival psychological or neurological hypotheses and by the performance of the very models. Constraints, once identified, limit what we are prepared to consider plausible models for the sake of explanation, but every model, even if it is *realistic*, is so at a certain level of abstraction and simplification of reality. As Pylyshyn put it, a bit paradoxically, in the language of the top-down approach, "if we apply minimal constraints we will have a Turing machine. If we apply all the constraints there may be no place to stop short of producing a human" (Pylyshyn, 1979: 49). Of course, beyond the paradox, the issue of constraints cannot be posed simply in a cumulative way, as if it were a matter of their progressive *addition*, with the *a priori* certainty that this will not, sooner or later, question the model *architecture* itself. Note, however, that this is true whether one starts top-down (from cognitive constraints) or bottom-up (from biological constraints). In the first case, the issue of the additional constraints might be put too abstractly, to repeat Newell's words (in fact, the issue could be evaluated in different ways, depending on our propensity for a more or less *modular* view of the central nervous system). In the second case, one has little idea of how to reach the higher processes by cumulatively applying bottom-up constraints, because the (more or less 'realistic') bottom-up models currently stop at the simulation of simple perform-

---

[15] Propaganda is always possible, of course. Consider for example: "The mere constraint that operations be carried out by synaptically interconnected neurons is incomparably stronger than any constraint accepted by other approaches, notably in artificial intelligence" (Hanson and Olson, 1990: 2). See instead Montague and Dayan (1998) for a balanced review of neurophysiological models.

[16] Churchland and Sejnowski (1992, Chapter 6). The vestibule-eye circuit has the function of stabilizing the images arriving from the retina while the head is being moved.

ance. Designs for situated robots that handle fragments of language, such as the "Talking Heads experiments" by Steels (1999), are interesting because they explicitly try to tackle this limitation of bottom-up models.

In conclusion, Thesis (*ii*), the *Modeling Method*, always has as its starting-point Thesis (*i*), *Functionalism*. When raising the issue of the psychological or biological plausibility of the models, *all* model builders have to reckon with the various questions raised by functionalism, from model indeterminacy to common functional organization and multiple realizability. Where the researchers have disagreed was in the choice of which constraints to privilege in order to identify, through possible solutions of those questions, the natural kind of mental life science. In other words, they disagreed about the choice of the level (or levels) of abstraction or simplification that they believe useful for model building. Is the program (or symbol) level the right one, as upheld in classical cognitive science, or is it the neural net (or subsymbolic) level? And how dramatic is this distinction? Or should one consider other levels, such as those identified in Edelman's synthetic neural modeling, or in ALife's evolutionary processes? And in this case, is there a crucial difference between the computer *simulation* of these processes, or still others that are believed to be the essential features of organism behavior, and their *realization* in real agents, as claimed in situated robotics?

The answer to these questions concerns the usual procedures of scientific research, and the problems here are the same as those surfacing in other scientific disciplines. Sometimes these questions tend to be posed in terms of philosophical oppositions in cognitive science, but the final test in discriminating among different models (bottom-up or top-down, call them what you will) is in the range of the empirical phenomena regarding mind and behavior that can be explained through one model or another. Indeed, it does not seem possible to decide in advance which is the best modeling strategy in *all* cases regarding mental life. This is also true because, at present, the relations between the aforementioned levels of are not always easily identifiable. As suggested by the empirical evidence discussed in the previous chapter, one is able to take into account certain biological constraints when considering models of the lower abilities of living organisms, while in the case of higher abilities recourse must be made to models where cognitive constraints play their role at the symbol level. Furthermore, as Harnad perceptively put it, if, on one side, models based on simple functional equivalence are *undetermined*, on the other side, models that push themselves, say, up to the level where they synthetically reproduce neurons in the majority of their physico-chemical features risk being *overdetermined*. In order to be as realistic as possible, these models should include physical and functional properties that might be irrelevant or *non-essential* (Harnad, 1994: 299). In this case, the end result is that the models obscure those principles or hypotheses that they were supposed to clarify.

To be sure, our aim is to approximate more and more closely to the real phenomenon, and more constraints increase the probability that the model would enable us to grasp that phenomenon. But we must not delude ourselves that the best rule is always: the more constraints, the better. Unless we conclude that "the best [...] model for a cat is another, or preferably the same cat."[17]

---

[17] To quote the quip of Rosenblueth and Wiener (1945: 320).

4. Representations and mentalistic language

In recent times a debate has ignited over the nature and the role of representations in studying mental life. For ALife and for robotics *à la* Brooks or *à la* Edelman, and *a fortiori* for situated cognition theorists, the question of representations is one that concerns the top-down approach of AI. Thus Thesis (*iii*), *Representationalism*, has either been rejected or polemically ignored by them. Among neoconnectionists, and among philosophers of mind as well, there is no agreement about the very role of representations. They speak of distributed representations (Churchland, 1986), or of subsymbolic representations (Smolensky, 1988). These representations are still the subject of dispute. For various proponents of symbolic AI and cognitive science, for example, neural nets in fact do nothing but make associations, and they are not capable of processing symbolic representations, which are indispensable in order to recognize the working of a mind.[18] Here is the origin of the above-mentioned criticism by Pylyshyn of Hull's behaviorism: he and Fodor pointed to the roots of the 'errors' of neoconnectionists in the associationism of Hull and his successors, like Hebb (Fodor and Pylyshyn, 1988). Conversely, today neoconnectionists have been led to reevaluate the associationist inspiration behind behaviorism, reducing the strong criticism that both cognitivism and AI have always leveled at it, and bringing into the foreground of neural net research the issues of self-organization and learning. Dennett (1996: 87) calls the performance in which current neural nets excel "ABC learning," where the alphabetical order would suggest the historical order of the tendencies that have influenced their development: Associationism, Behaviorism, Connectionism (although our investigation into the discovery of the artificial shows that the order of these tendencies has not always been so linear).

One approach to cognition which refers to complex dynamical systems, of which the connectionist models are instances, is that supported by Tim van Gelder. This view of cognition is advertised as non-computational and non-representational, and reiterates the claim we have discussed several times, in which the agent and the environment are dynamic components of a single system. One of the claims of this approach is that the essentially denotational mechanism of representations, typical of computational models, is not able to grasp the complexity of the mutual relationship between those components. In order to achieve this, the decisive role is played by the mathematics that describes the evolution of complex systems. For van Gelder, an elementary prototype of a dynamic system is the most oft-mentioned historical antecedent of the cybernetic machine, Watt's governor, which deposes the Turing machine, in his opinion, as a prototype of cognition (van Gelder, 1995).[19]

At least one point unites all these positions, which are in various ways hostile to Thesis (*iii*), *Representationalism*: they all reject the notion of representation as symbol structure. The latter is usually considered as strictly related to a global or centralized world

---

[18] See Bechtel and Abrahamsen (1991) for a review of these claims.

[19] Ashsby's homeostat better represents, however, an elementary prototype of a dynamic system. A critical analysis of van Gelder's approach is given by Eliasmith (1997). Kejizer and Bem (1996) discuss it in the context of other non-representational claims, like that of Brooks. For an introduction to dynamic systems, see Serra and Zanarini (1994).

model, to the extent it deals with the explicit goals, beliefs and intentions of the agent, as this is described, for example, at Newell's knowledge level or Pylyshyn's semantic level. Representations and world model are not deemed to be necessary to produce intelligent behavior in creatures, to use Brooks' term, which are able to interact with the real world. Several authors, indeed, consider the 'being-in-the-world' of an agent as a precondition for representation manipulation.[20]

In fact, we have seen how representations were invoked in many senses throughout our investigation. Rosenblatt pointed out the difference between a representation as the internal code of incoming inputs in a neural net, such as a Perceptron, and a representation as a data structure, to be fully developed by AI. We have also seen that even cybernetic artifacts much simpler than a Perceptron—those considered to be *teleological,* beginning with Craik and Wiener—could be said to have representations. In this sense, a simple thermostat has at least a representation of the environment temperature, an 'imprint' consisting of a particular position of its bimetallic lamina. We mention the thermostat here because, in recent times, it has played a starring role in this kind of dispute.[21] MacKay emphasized that the thermostat could perhaps be considered the simplest case of an artificial system equipped with the "imitative mechanism" mentioned above (MacKay, 1951: 106). After him, Dennett made the thermostat his favorite example of an inorganic system where the representational mechanism is present in a form that is at least minimal (Dennett, 1978; 1996).

In a rather more interesting sense, even Grey Walter's mobile robots could be said to be artifacts that have local-level internal representations of the world, i.e. the real environment in which they go around. These representations are imprints (we continue to use Hull's term) or patterns which are coded as physical states in electronic circuits (they reproduce, for example, the variable sensitivity of the system to different light or sound stimuli). The same could be said of Brooks' creatures. Allen, the mobile robot mentioned in Chapter 6, was equipped with a sonar that played the role of a distance sensor, and the perception of an obstacle to avoid was coded as an 'internal representation.' Brooks himself used this very terminology (Brooks, 1991b: 231), but elsewhere he showed dissatisfaction with it ("we are not happy with calling such things a representation"): in fact, it evoked all the paraphernalia of symbolic AI, such as a centralized world model, explicit rules, variable instantiation, planning, and so forth (Brooks, 1991a: 139). In short, if those are representations, they are such in a very *trivial* sense, since the mutual relationship between the agent and the environment is so direct and immediate that it does not make much sense to say that the first *represents* the second. This idea is probably shared by all the aforementioned positions hostile to the computational version of Thesis (*iii*), *Representationalism.*

[20] Dreyfus (1992) has become the ritual reference point for this claim of Heideggerian ascendencies. As for Brooks (1991a), he did not see himself in a Heideggerian position. Dreyfus' claims have been taken up by other researchers, among them Winograd and Flores (1986) (but see Vera and Simon, 1993, for a criticism). Lakoff and Johnson (1999) use some of the authors and issues already introduced by Dreyfus as the pivot of their rebuttal of the "symbol manipulation metaphor" of AI and cognitive science. We will not dwell on these issues here.

[21] But one should remember that the thermostat was described in 1917 by Perry as an instance of a self-regulating artifact that could be described as teleological, although in a "broad sense," and in 1932 by Stanley Gray, although with different intent (see Chapter 4).

Representational talk, therefore, for Brooks and for many others, seems to boil down to a simple way of speaking of the outside observer, rather than being an explanatory tool. Brooks himself sometimes uses this mentalistic terminology when he speaks of Allen's "desire" to explore the world around it, of its "instinct" to avoid obstacles, and so forth. This is the same lexicon used, more or less neutrally, by Grey Walter with regard to his tortoises, or by Braitenberg for his vehicles.

In fact, when we ask ourselves whether or not representations have an *explanatory* role, we tend to involve Thesis (*iii*), *Representationalism*, in the question, raised by Thesis (*iv*), *Mentalism*, regarding the legitimacy of mentalistic language, or the role of the vocabulary of beliefs, desires and purpose used by folk psychology. Without delving into the many questions all this has raised among philosophers of mind, let us consider what our investigation into the discovery of the artificial could suggest on this matter.

The question of the legitimacy of mentalistic language has always been linked, in turn, to that of the conflicting relationships between psychology and neurology. To remain within the context of the authors we have discussed in previous chapters, we know that the opposing solutions to this tangle of problems, the eliminativist and the mentalist, were supported by Meyer and McDougall, respectively—not to mention Jennings, who, opposing Loeb, proposed a mentalistic approach, one that was nevertheless remote from that of vitalism. Furthermore, we know that in the years preceding the advent of cybernetics the question was raised of how to attribute scientific dignity to the folk vocabulary of teleology. From that time on, although the core of the dispute shifted to *intentionality*, primarily as taken in Franz Brentano's sense, basic distinctions do not seem to have changed much.[22] The roots of some issues concerning teleological language and intentionality can be traced back to those very years. These issues are still debated by philosophers of mind today. We are alluding at least to those problems we pointed out in Chapter 4, for example, the usefulness or pertinence of mentalistic language and the observer's role in attributing purposes.

The first problem can be formulated by translating Warren's question, mentioned in Chapter 4, into these terms: what do we gain, at the *explanatory* level, by interpreting in mentalistic or intentional terms phenomena in which the human mind is *not* involved? This question addresses the issue of the role played by the vocabulary of folk psychology in dealing with the 'non-human' world: the apparently intentional behavior of lower and higher animals, plants, artifacts of different kinds, and so forth. So why, in particular, use mentalistic language instead of causal or physical language to deal with the behavior of certain artifacts? This first problem is closely linked with the second, namely, that of the observer's role in attributing purpose to a system he interacts with. This is evident in the famous thesis about teleology proposed in 1943 by Rosenblueth, Wiener and Bigelow. These authors asserted the usefulness and plausibility of the vocabulary of what we call folk psychology in describing the non-human world of artifacts (those with neg-

---

[22] Usually, the reference point for these discussions is Brentano's claim about the autonomy of mental states (see for example Dennett, 1978). Intentionality is considered a property, that of 'being directed towards,' which is shared by certain mental states, such as beliefs or desires. See Albertazzi (forthcoming) for an introduction to the issue of intentionality in Brentano and the contemporary philosophy of mind.

ative feedback). At the same time, they stressed the observer's interest, in order to legitimize the attribution of purpose to any system, organic or artificial, capable of adaptively interacting with its environment.

Later philosophical reflection, running from MacKay to Dennett, owes much to that contribution. According to these authors as well, though from different points of view, the attribution of purpose to a system, whether organic or artificial, is an option for the observer, justifiable by the fact that such a system behaves as a rational agent. To control and predict its behavior, the observer *decides* to assume a "personal attitude" towards it, as MacKay (1962) put it, or an "intentional stance," to use the now better known terminology of Dennett (1978). In sum, the observer makes a pragmatic choice.[23]

But the origin of these claims seems to be rooted in earlier research. Jennings pointed out the usefulness of assuming a 'stance' of the above sort when the attribution of subjective states to non-human minds, even to lower animals, had to be justified. Lillie insisted on the role played by the outside observer in judging certain behaviors as purposeful, both in organisms and in artifacts equipped with automatic control. Rashevsky claimed the usefulness and necessity of mentalistic language in predicting and controlling the behavior of machines characterized by a certain complexity: in interacting with these machines, the observer is compelled to use that language to understand their 'purposes.'

On the opposite side, we have seen McDougall and Taylor tackle these very issues about the nature of purpose by introducing a markedly realist requirement with respect to pragmatic stances like those we have just mentioned. For McDougall, the purposive vocabulary is delegated to describing the behavior of all living organisms, and only them. For Taylor, when one properly speaks of purpose, one makes reference to the interest of the *system* or the agent (to the latter's beliefs and desires), not to that of the *observer*. For both, finally, the 'purpose' (in quotation marks) of an artifact is intrinsically different from the purpose (without quotation marks) of its designer. One must distinguish, McDougall insisted, between "derived" teleology, or "pseudo-teleology," which is concerned with artifacts, and "true" teleology, which is concerned with the designer of artifacts

In these disputes a clear distinction is made between a first-person criterion in the use of mentalistic vocabulary, legitimized by the direct experience the agent has of itself and of the outside world, and a third-person criterion, that of the observer who attributes knowledge and rationality to an agent in order to control and predict its behavior. In particular, McDougall's distinction between true and derived teleology is echoed in John Searle's well-known realist thesis on the alleged intentionality of artifacts—a thesis about which he has long argued with Dennett. Just as for McDougall I can "personify" my car by saying "she is behaving badly to-day" (McDougall, 1923a: 43), without thinking it *really* behaves that way, so for Searle I can use the same sentence, with regard to this same artifact, for the sake of a "metaphorical attribution of intentionality" (Searle, 1980: 419).[24] In Searle's view, the first-person aspect of intentionality characterizes what he calls "in-

---

[23] However, MacKay's claim should not be construed as a conventionalist one (see, for example, MacKay, 1962: 97-98). Dennett later defended his "stance" from the criticism of being a simply conventionalist stance (see, for example, Dennett, 1996).

[24] Of course, Searle's position is far from McDougall's spiritualism.

trinsic intentionality." There is no difference between attributing intentionality to a car, a thermostat or a program: the intentionality of any artifact is always "derived" from that, "intrinsic" or "original," of its designer. The designer, now in the guise of the programmer, is the one who attributes meaning to symbols. The program is bound to manipulate symbols at a purely *syntactic* level, following rules which are pre-established by the programmer.

Searle's conclusions are evident as regards the computational theories of mind. For example, in Searle's view, the alleged semantic or intentional level is not grasped by the program except in a "derived" way, and hence it is not an autonomous *explanatory* level. It is on this basis that Searle proposed his popular distinction between "strong" AI (which deludes itself into thinking it can propose theories of the mind through computational models) and "weak" AI (which legitimately designs programs that imitate, without thereby expecting to explain, human performance).

The Churchlands have objected that Searle's argument against the semantics of AI and classical cognitive science does not necessarily extend to neural net models (P.M. Churchland and P.S. Churchland, 1990). This claim, too, is strongly reminiscent of earlier ones, put forward by the connectionists of the 1950s. Samuel, in a little-known article in *Science*, anticipated criticisms like those of Searle. He mentioned the counter-objection of the connectionism of his day, and also the difficulties of the latter, in a sense not so different from those of current connectionism.[25]

> The 'intentions' which [the computer] seems to manifest are the intentions of the human programmer, as specified in advance, or they are subsidiary intentions derived from these, following rules specified by the programmer. [...] An apparent exception of these conclusions might be claimed for projected machines of the so-called 'neural net' type. [...] It is maintained by many serious workers that such nets can be made to exhibit purposeful activity by instruction and training with reward-and-punishment routines similar to those used with young animals. [...] At the present time, the largest nets that can be constructed are nearer in size to the nervous system of a flatworm than to the brain of man [...] (Samuel, 1960: 741).

The Churchlands' counter-objection to Searle refers to their specific criticism of symbolic AI, which in the 1980s reignited the debate between eliminativists and mentalists. In previous chapters we mentioned how mentalistic language had fluctuating fortunes, from the claim that it had an autonomous role in psychology to the claim that it could be reduced to neurological language. In the end, we saw that mentalistic language was legitimized among philosophers and psychologists with the advent of cybernetics and AI. Afterwards, various of the aforementioned theoretical proposals came to light, such as Fodor's theses about multiple realizability and the autonomy of psychology, Dennett's intentional stance and Pylyshyn's semantic level. And the Churchlands, also referring to the new neural net models, again stated the reductionist claim about the mind-body problem and the eliminativist claim as regards folk psychology. One aspect that often recurs in our investigation into the discovery of the artificial will not escape the reader's notice:

[25] The context of Samuel's article is to be found in the problem raised by Wiener in an earlier article, also in *Science*, about the threat that the new technology based on modern machines could represent in the future for humans, who could be dethroned by them. Samuel argued the opposite, and their disagreement seems to express for the first time the opposing evaluation of the future of information processing technology.

it is the advent of *new* artifacts—in the past, devices equipped with rudimentary asso-ciative capabilities and systems based on various kinds of automatic control, and today computer programs, new neural nets and new robots—that usually re-opens questions about the nature of mental representations, purpose, meaning and intentionality.

Thus, Thesis (*iii*), *Representationalism*, is involved in the issue of the explanatory role of mentalistic language, raised by Thesis (*iv*). Now we can better appreciate why, al-though for some authors that role is justified exclusively by the *actual* presence of rep-resentations in organisms and in machines, for others mentalistic language can legiti-mately be used only because to speak about organisms or machines in terms of beliefs, desires and purposes is more useful than to speak about them in terms of neural or ma-chine structure. Indeed, at least in certain cases, for the outside observer it is the *sole* way of speaking about them that actually works.[26]

As to living organisms, this issue is complicated by the controversy about whether some, or even all, non-human animals possess mental representations and use symbolic systems that share some significant properties with human language. In this case as well, we shall only touch on a few aspects of the controversy that bring us back to the central issues addressed in our investigation.

Let us take the *Paramecium* studied by Jennings. According to Jennings, this organ-ism has a very rudimentary "action system," and yet one is inclined to describe its be-havior in terms of choice, purposes, and so forth. A reduction of this talk to physical caus-es is of no use if one wants to control and predict its behavior. Dennett too would prob-ably not object to treating *Paramecium* as an intentional system, thereby endorsing a de-scription in the mentalistic vocabulary of folk psychology. According to Dennett, a sys-tem does not have to have representations in order to be described in terms of beliefs, purposes and desires; it is sufficient that it behave *as if* it were a rational agent. For Fodor, on the contrary, it is crucial to show "why *Paramecia* don't have mental representations," as it says in the title of one of his well-known articles, provoked by Dennett's earlier ob-jections (Fodor, 1986). Fodor took on the task of demonstrating that only systems that can respond selectively to non-nomic stimulus properties have representational mental states, and that simple systems as *Paramecium* cannot. Therefore, its description with mentalistic terms, no less than that of thermostat, is purely metaphorical. More general-ly, "the theory of representational mental states ought to qualify over mental representa-tions (roughly, over mental symbols, sentences in the language of thought)" (p. 21), and this would fully justify the use of mentalistic vocabulary. It would seem, however, that for Fodor, not just human beings (including children in the pre-linguistic phase), but at least *certain* animals have abilities that recall the presence of a language of thought.[27]

It was Pylyshyn who tried to justify in greater detail Fodor's realist claim about the

---

[26] The canonical example is that in Dennett (1978) of the computer with which one plays chess, with respect to which the "intentional stance" is unavoidable (see also MacKay, 1962, on the "personal attitude" that one decides to assume towards a chess-playing machine).

[27] For example, Fodor and Pylyshyn (1988) mention the possibility that even the minds of non-linguistic or-ganisms might be *systematic*, i.e. capable of making representations both of *aRb* and *bRa*, responding suitably to both. Sterelny (1990) is still a good introduction to Fodor's claims about the issues we are dealing with in the present chapter.

role of representations when mentalistic vocabulary is used. According to Pylyshyn, organisms and artifacts that need to be described at the *semantic* level, i.e. by attributing to them goals, beliefs and desires, are those whose representations are physically instantiated, in the brain or in a hardware, as codes, i.e. as symbol structures capable of causing behavior. To be able to *explain* the behavior of these agents, therefore, all three levels at which a genuinely cognitive system can be split up (semantic, symbolic and physical) are necessary. From Pylyshyn's point of view, systems of this kind include, among living systems, human minds and, among artifacts, programs. It is impossible, for example, not to invoke the symbol level to identify the *actual* decision processes or chains of inference in which the reasoning on the beliefs, desires and purposes of symbol systems, such as human minds and programs, is coded. Furthermore, it is impossible to draw out the common explanatory generalizations that concern decision processes and inference chains except by appeal to their semantic content, that is, by referring to the contents of those very beliefs, desires and purposes (Pylyshyn, 1984: 45-48).[28] Therefore, one cannot explain human minds, since they are symbol systems, without referring to the semantic level, that of the content of the representations.

As for non-human minds, those of animals, Pylyshyn acknowledges the need for the semantic level and the related representational and mentalistic lexicon *at least* in the case of primates (p. 132). It is not very clear, however, how much of the phenomenology of the animal world would, for him, remain excluded from the natural kind of cognitive science. It is very clear, instead, that what is valid for human minds is also valid for programs. Indeed, the latter offer an example of actually *existing* physical systems which have causal power at the syntactic level and intentional content at the semantic level. On the contrary, mentalistic language is not needed for describing the functioning of the thermostat: its description at the physical level captures all the relevant explanatory generalizations.[29] To say that the thermostat *represents* temperature is, rather, a way of connecting the operation of the device and the intentions of its designer: "what is crucial here is that we do not need the notion of representation to explain how a device works, only to explain how it performs the function intended by its designer" (p. 26).

We are referring again to Pylyshyn's radical claims in *Computation and Cognition* because these brought to the fore several problems which cognitive science has faced up to the present. For example, Pylyshyn's notion of semantic content is meant to weaken the conventional attitude in attributing intentionality to artificial systems such as pro-

---

[28] The following example, later much discussed by Stephen Stich and others, reveals Pylyshyn's anti-behaviorist stance. A desire or purpose of a human agent (say, to abandon a building on fire) can be provoked by a variety of different stimuli (seeing flames, hearing a fire alarm, and so forth), and it can be realized at the symbol level by a variety of decision processes or inference chains, which consist of a variety of purposeful actions or plans. Now one cannot think of *reducing* that desire or purpose of the agent to his disposition to behave in a certain way, because one cannot know which of the various actions or possible plans he will carry out to satisfy that desire or purpose. Without using suitable generalizations formulated in a mentalistic lexicon, without talk of the agent's *desires* and *purposes*, we are not be able to interpret his actions, nor, in general, to predict and control his behavior (see also the discussion by Pylyshyn, 1984, Chapter 1). Note that this point regarding agents desires and purposes was raised by Tailor against Rosenblueth, Wiener and Bigelow: see p. 131 above

[29] For a different evaluation in AI, see, for example, McCarthy (1979).

grams. Actually, Pylyshyn emphasizes the *system's* intentions rather than the *observer's* intentions.[30] This relevant shift of emphasis, no less than the recognition of the specific nature of programs in comparison with other artifacts, was meant to provide the basis for a reply to Searle's objection on the derived intentionality of programs. Pylyshyn admits that the intentionality of artifacts which do not have to be described at the semantic level is in fact relative to their designer, but in the case of computational systems he invokes "something stronger than derived semantics" (p. 39). This should be justified by the reduced "latitude" the observer or designer has in attributing intentionality to these artifacts. In particular, it would be possible to endow the computational system with transducers, which would let it interact with its environment. The latitude that the observer has in assigning a semantic interpretation would thus be reduced: the system—in this case a robot endowed with transducers—would be able to link symbols to states in the external world. However, Pylyshyn admits the difficulties in putting forward necessary and sufficient conditions for attributing intentionality, i.e. a kind of objective criterion for identifying representations endowed with content. While asserting the *explanatory* (and not simply *descriptive*) role of the semantic level, he still leaves the way open for a weaker solution, perhaps more in harmony with that of Dennett.[31]

Pylyshyn's proposal for shifting the emphasis from the observer's to the system's intentions, with the aim of countering Searle's objection on derived intentionality, leads us to say some more about some of the issues we touched on earlier. In fact, the proposal for endowing a program with transducers, in order to connect it with (and thus ground it to) the real world, was known to Searle as a variant of the 'robot reply' to his own objection. Searle had already observed that the connection between symbols and the world is, in this case, mediated by representations that still are *supplied* to the system by the programmer (Searle, 1980: 452). This rejoinder from Searle is commonly shared by situated cognition theorists and by many proponents of situated robotics. The latter, in turn, believe that situated robots, unlike the early 'program *plus* transducers' robots, could actually provide a basis for meeting Searle's objection.

This is the case, for example, with Steels (1995: 94) when he distinguishes, as we have seen above, between simulation and realization. A situated robot could be put into a condition to build representations of the world on its own, thus developing its own ontology. Paul Verschure holds that this might also be the way to tackle the symbol-grounding problem. Automata like NOMAD are not completely ungrounded as symbol systems, be-

[30] This move was also at the core of Newell's criticism of Dennett's intentional stance, usually, and perhaps not correctly, viewed as analogous to the knowledge level description of the rational agent (see Newell, 1993, p. 36). This move seems to be sensitive to the criticisms raised to AI's sloppy use of a mental jargon (i.e. terms like 'goal' or 'understand') to refer to programs and data structures (see McDermott, 1976; and recall Wilkes' remarks at the early days of computer programs, p. 173).

[31] "In cognitive science," Pylyshyn concluded, "the goal is not merely to describe the regularities of behavior but to relate these regularities to causal mechanisms in an organism. Thus generalizations of such a nature that no one has any idea (however sketchy) how they can possibly be realized by some mechanism are interpreted as *descriptions* of phenomena, not *explanations*" (Pylyshyn, 1984: 110). Earlier, however, he had acknowledged that the ascriptions of intentionality, even when used in an instrumental or heuristic way, may still be "crucial," because they may be the sole effective way to capture the relevant generalizations (p. 30 n.).

cause their interaction with the world is not mediated by representations assigned by the outside on the basis of the observer-relative ontology. Verschure recognizes, however, the obvious fact that even in this case, *to the extent that such robots are behavioral models*, the designer plays a role which, without being comparable to that of the designer of an AI system (such as an expert system), nevertheless exposes the model to the risk of receiving *too much* knowledge from its designer. This could happen when the designer attributes "values" to the model. Nonetheless, since values, for Edelman, are innate patterns that in nature are the equivalent of evolutionary processes, they are "less problematic," as Verschure put it, than the (arbitrary) assumptions regarding knowledge in an expert system. Unlike the latter, values impose constraints on the model that are suggested by disciplines like developmental biology and genetics, and as such they are "clearly definite and testable" hypothetical constructs (Verschure, 1993: 73).

This set of problems leads us again to Thesis (*ii*), *Modeling Method*, and to an issue that we had set aside, i.e. the observer's role in identifying and evaluating the constraints to be imposed on the model. Biological constraints, which had been called upon to resolve the problem of the model's *indeterminacy*, are now invoked to reduce to the minimum the *latitude* left to the observer or interpreter in attributing representations to the model, thus addressing the problems of symbol-grounding and observer-relativity. The idea is, in short, that one approaches something 'intrinsic' or 'original' as regards representations, in a sense very close to Searle's claim.

If one considers the observer as model builder, we can see that his third-person viewpoint is the current one in scientific practice, where one constructs theories and models by selecting the functions believed to be *essential* to the phenomenon under study. The observer's role cannot be sidestepped, any more than the process of identifying hypothetical constructs in theory-building. As we have seen, models that include biological constraints are *a priori* no better or worse than models that include different constraints. These models identify functions like any other model, and it seems unlikely that identifying *biological* functions is *per se* more secure, more testable and, above all, less observer-relative than identifying other functions. Note that for a radical proponent of situated cognition like William Clancey, situated robotics is very far from giving a satisfactory solution to the question of the designer-artifact relationship. In an analysis of Mataric's robot, which we described in Chapter 6, Clancey concludes that this is not a satisfactory example of situatedness: the robot, in constructing its world map, makes too much use of representations and categories which are *predefined* by its designer (in this case walls, obstacles etc.) (Clancey, 1993). Indeed, Clancey's criticism of representationalism is based on the claim of 'direct,' or non-mediated, knowledge of the outside world on the part of organisms, a claim akin to the one supported by Gibson (1979).

At this point we are puzzled in the face of opposing criteria regarding the nature of representations: the pragmatic and liberal criterion linked to the interests of the observer, the demarcating and restrictive criterion linked to language-like structures, and the eliminative criterion linked to the claim of direct perception. We wish to sketch a proposal for dealing with this puzzle, a proposal that should be far more developed than is possible here, but that at least touches on the issues in the discovery of the artificial.

Let us go back to Johnson-Laird's distinction between "Cartesian automata," whose responses are based on a causal interaction with the world, and "Craikian automata," whose responses are mediated by representations of the world.[32] To say that a Craikian automaton has representations of the world means, according to Johnson-Laird, that it is able to establish a correspondence between its internal states and the world's states: *reference* consists of this correspondence. Generally speaking, for Johnson-Laird, possessing representations does not entail a system's ability to deal with language-like structures: fairly simple animals, like flies and bees, are Craikian automata. They are organisms whose interaction with the world cannot be *explained* if one does not postulate that they have representations of the world and carry out computations on these representations, that are more or less complex in different cases.[33] Complex artifacts, including certain computer programs, are also Craikian automata, but so are much simpler artifacts, though in a highly incomplete form. Longuet-Higgins' automaton, which we mentioned in Chapter 4, is one of these artifacts. Clearly, artifacts such as this carry out computations, not on representations as language-like symbol patterns, but on representations as analog patterns.[34]

More explicitly, Simon and Alonso Vera stressed that there is no basic distinction between analog and discrete representations and computations: in both cases, it is always a matter of *symbols*, i.e. patterns that denote, and of computations on symbols. Given this definition of representation (and of symbol), both connectionist systems and Brooks' reactive creatures handle representations. Patterns of activations in an artificial neural net (and in a population of neurons as well) are representations, and Brooks' creatures have representations that are such not in the trivial sense we mentioned above, but in a much important sense: *they are representations of world states and of the functional role of these states*. According to Simon and Vera, the fact that these representations are temporary (i.e. information is not kept after being used in an action) and decentralized (i.e. not subjected to global control) does not mean that they are not *symbols*. Thus, situational feedback governing the reactive activity of Brooks' creatures consists of a minimal symbolic-representational apparatus. Both Brooks' creatures and other even more simple systems, such as thermostats, are instances of Physical Symbol Systems. In all cases, "sensory information is converted into symbols which are then processed and evaluated in order to determine the appropriate motor symbols that lead to behavior" (Vera and Simon, 1993: 34). Simon and Vera's claims suggest that we could usefully distinguish between representations of different levels of complexity, and our investigation into the discovery of the artificial seems to confirm this. Let us review briefly this point.

[32] See pp. 137-138.

[33] Human minds are *also* Craikian automata. Reference requires the existence of representations that correspond to states of the external world. However, Johnson-Laird points out that, in the human case, there is an *intentional* correspondence, linked to consciousness. Actually, our investigation into the discovery of the artificial has mainly focused not on the subjective phenomenology of *consciousness* (and emotion as well) but on forms of *awareness*, such as those involved in activities like focus of attention, selection, reporting and the like. Representations (and symbols) are a case in point—they are considered here as linked to awareness, not necessarily to conscious activity.

[34] This distinction should be made more precise than we can do here. It involves the distinction between digital computing and analog computing, which in turn refers to the problem of identifying symbols as discrete units. For a discussion of this point, see Trautteur (1999).

Automatic control, or feedback, devices, currently considered to be at the base of pure-reactive-agent behavior, were pointed out by the pioneers of cybernetics with the aim of analyzing the adaptive and goal-directed behavior of organisms and machines alike. They usually described both systems as representational. According to Craik, for example, these systems (such as an automatic anti-aircraft system) have inner states that represent events in a changing external environment through continuous, real-time feedback loops. The representational description of such a correlation between a system's inner states and the world is consonant with that given by Simon and Vera in terms of the minimal representational (feedback-based) apparatus, and probably with that given by Johnson-Laird in terms of Craikian automata. Both feedback mechanisms, such as thermostats, and old phototropic machines, such as Hammond Jr. and Miessner's automaton, or current, pure reactive robots, can thus be viewed as fairly simple Craikian automata, endowed with a minimal or *low-level representational apparatus*, in which inner states are linked to sensory information.[35]

We saw that it was probably Lotka who first stressed the role, in such simple self-controlling systems, of representations as symbols denoting world states. Rough and special-purpose as they may be, these representations are not so trivial: they constitute the apparatus whereby the system's action may be *mediately* determined by the state of the external world, as Lotka put it. The state of the system becomes in a certain suitable manner a function of the state of the external world. Lotka distinguished between those simple systems, that show an "automaton type," at bottom reactive, behavior, and systems that show an "elastic type" behavior, which can be observed in higher animals when they are planning an action, or in man when consciously choosing between different alternatives. Memory and also knowledge of previously experienced events must be present in these latter cases.

The adaptive value of these elastic type behaviors was pointed out by, among others, Hull, who maintained that the "transformation of mere action into thought" was revealed through them. Hull attempted a mechanistic explanation of a system's ability to acquire inner states in its interaction with the external world, states that the system can store in its memory as imprints or replicas of events in the outer world. Once acquired, this "subjective parallel" of the external world *can be manipulated by the system independently* of the sequence of those events, and have the causal role of guiding the system's reaction to an event that is, as Hull put it, "not here and not now." In this case, the system's action sequence is caused not by its continuous interaction with changing events in the world, as in the case of automaton type behavior, but by its possession of knowledge of events before they actually take place.[36]

This is however a "rudimentary form of thought," Hull concluded. As we saw in previous chapters, Hull, and Craik and cyberneticians after him, were investigating a mechanistic explanation of other, higher forms of thought. Hull's anticipatory goal reaction should have explained these latter forms, which are present in animals too—for example in the commonplace rat exploring a maze by vicarious trial-and-error, and so symbolically

[35] We described Hammond Jr. and Miessner's electric dog as a machine endowed with a single, invariable decision rule (see p. 20, and also p. 151).
[36] Think of a system endowed with distance receptors. See above, pp. 99-100.

sampling the consequences of one course of action as opposed to another.[37] What all these forms of thought or subjective parallelism have in common is that they give both the organism and the machine an enlarged range of behavior possibilities, and endow them with increasing "degrees of freedom," as Hull put it, with respect to the environment. Craik pointed out how these systems would not go far in processing the data of experience if they were not capable of those and other more complex interactions with the world that are mediated by dynamic patterns or mental models, as he called them. At the upper band of this representational continuum, we thus find very complex (human) Craikian automata, capable of manipulating representations of absent and non-existent objects, as in cases of high problem-solving, hypothesis formation and invention. We could call these *high-level representations*, in order to distinguish them from the above-mentioned low-level representations, determined by situational feedbacks, in fairly simple Craikian automata.

What do these different low-level and high-level representations have in common? Once again, Craik might suggest the answer. First, the "*material* of symbolism," as he would have called it, is always present: in both cases, there are symbols denoting events in the outside world and, above all, there is a well-defined apparatus for coding, processing and decoding symbols. Second, the system's activity seems in both cases to be directed by the *discrepancy* between the on-going situation and the goal.

Craik's intuition was perhaps best developed by MacKay during the cybernetic age. Consider again the case of planned actions that are directed towards non-existent objects. Taylor, when discussing Rosenblueth and Wiener's claim in 1955, denied the possibility of construing these purposeful actions in terms of the elimination of a discrepancy through negative feedbacks. But Craik had introduced inner models or patterns for representing goals, such as those mentioned above, which are not present in the world as physical objects, and might be non-existent. Craik was therefore suggesting that these goals are to be viewed, generally, as abstract states, not as physical objects. This is MacKay's own move when proposing his "imitative mechanism" for explaining purposeful behavior, the mechanism of reducing and eliminating discrepancy through cyclic or feedback action. In his opinion, discrepancy is between a *state* (the inner "symbolic correlate," as MacKay put it) representing the current situation and a *state* representing the goal; the feedback correlation abstractly concerns states. This feedback-based description applies thus equally well to pursuing a physically existent object and an abstract one, "to a self-guided missile chasing an aircraft, and a man chasing the solution to a crossword puzzle" (MacKay, 1956: 34).

We have seen, however, that cybernetic models proved not to be able to simulate this imitative mechanism in the case of cognitive activities such as solving crossword puzzles (or playing chess, and so on). These activities entail hierarchies of trial-and-error or selective procedures and the agent's knowledge and experience. It was early AI that dealt with those complex procedures underlying cognitive activity, which had not been realized through cybernetic artifacts. AI programs too were considered teleological systems, but goals were viewed as symbol structures holding information about desired objects. Other symbol structures were used to organize the behavior of the system, such as processes for creating sub-goals, selecting methods for attempting them, testing them,

[37] See p. 103 above, and the analysis of vicarious trial-and-error by Mowrer (1960b: 212 ff.)

and so on. On this basis Pylyshyn suggested the above-mentioned way of considering actions towards non-existent objects in terms of complex information-processing systems.

One would be tempted to conclude that certain main features of the imitative mechanism of pattern-matching underlying, according to MacKay, higher cognitive activities were realized through AI information-processing systems. In a sense, a feedback loop, which is at the core of MacKay's imitative mechanism and of Craik's parallel mechanism as well, is also present in AI problem-solving programs.[38] Heuristic procedures in automated problem solving are a case in point. Think of the matching procedure used by LT in theorem proving: at each step, feedback is obtained as the result of the substitution of a formula, and this feedback can be used to guide the next step. Thus, the feedback keeps the search on the correct path.[39]

This is not, however, the continuous feedback from the organism's own sensory receptors while action is in progress, i.e. the actual, sensory feedback from on-going behavior stressed by Wiener himself in the case of voluntary goal-directed movements, in which a standard is constantly being compared with actual performance. Such feedback takes account of the *immediate* or real-time effects of an action, and as such it is under the control of its own stimulus consequences. On the contrary, feedback in a problem-solving task usually consists properly of a cyclic loop working on long time intervals, and occurring only *after* a particular response is completed. This is the remote feedback, as it were, that yields the effect in any selective or trial-and-error procedure, in which the consequence of a response, whether successful or not, *acts back* upon that response. In this kind of comparatively slow cyclic action, there are forms of memory, learning and experience that we saw stressed from the time of Thorndike and Hull, and that Craik himself believed to be at the basis of the law of effect.[40]

We might conclude, in the spirit of Craik, that both transduction (perceptual-encoding and motor-decoding) processes and more-or-less high cognitive processes require some form of representation, minimal in the first case and complex or full-blown in the latter; further, both require some form of cyclic action, a real-time cyclic action in the first case and a long-time one in the latter. High-level representation is what characterizes a *complete* cognitive system, capable of a high degree of freedom with respect to the environment, which is greatest in the case of humans. But Simon and Vera, in describing the different levels of detail in which representations are processed by cognitive systems, persuasively show how such systems are able to properly use both minimal and elaborate representations, so reacting rapidly or planning actions. Furthermore, they observe that the description of Brooks' creatures and other 'situated' systems as maintain-

---

[38] We dare say this, notwithstanding the fact that MacKay always distinguished his own approach from that of symbolic AI. For an analysis of this point see Cordeschi et al. (1999).

[39] These heuristic procedures that tend to make the present state closer to some goal state, or "difference engines" as Minsky (1987) calls them, were fully investigated during the development of AI, as well as methods for representing the agent's knowledge and experience (see Chapters 5 and 6). Of course, there are cases in which goals are very vaguely defined, as in discovery programs. For example, the "goal criterion" of AM is given by heuristics that guide the search on the basis of certain priority ratings (Lenat, 1983a: 257).

[40] See above, pp. 147-148. A careful analysis of these kinds of feedback in several authors we discussed in previous chapters, from James and Thorndike up to the cyberneticians, can be found in Mowrer (1960b, Chapter 6).

ing certain causal relations with the world, thus ruling out any representational talk, "does not explain *how* such relations are maintained" (Vera and Simon, 1993: 40).

Other authors have stressed a more 'minimalist' stance, according to which transduction processes such as those in tropistic organisms or in simple reactive robots should not be viewed as representational. Clark (1997) distinguishes these systems, endowed with simple feedback loops or "adaptive hookups" as he puts it, from systems that have a mere causal correlation with the environment. He admits that the first systems, unlike the latter, have inner states that "are supposed (by evolution, design, or learning) to coordinate [their] behaviors with specific environmental conditions," but concludes that "we gain little by treating [these] inner state as representational" (p. 147). We could say that, for Clark, genuine representations are those that enlarge the range of behavior possibilities of a system, increasing its degree of freedom with respect to the environment: "adaptive hookup thus phases gradually into genuine internal representation as the hookup's complexity and systematicity increase" (*ibid*.). This means that there is a representational continuum that includes thinking about the distant, the absent and the non-existent, progressing to complex imagining and other abstract forms of thought that we discussed in the course of our investigation.

That a distinction should be made between abstract *representations* and, as it were, mere *presentations* of objects, directly linked to perception, is a claim that has already been stated. Mowrer, who developed several of Hull's representational-mediational concepts, shared the thesis that such a distinction lies in the fact that "perception does not give [the organism] a *representation* of the world, but a direct *presence* of the world himself." Present events are not to be viewed as re-presented perceptually, whereas events *not* present perceptually, such as non-existent ones, can be represented in the organism "via images, concepts, and symbols" (see Mowrer, 1960b: 258).

Clark rightly stresses that representations do not require the presence of classical language-like structures. But he perhaps believes that genuine representations are not perceptual-information processing. We saw, for example, in the previous chapter that in behavior based robotics they usually tend to consider as representations only those patterns, such as topological or, more properly, metric maps, "emerging," as Mataric puts it, from the purely perceptual-reactive level. This is the "schema level," as Wyeth and Browning call the lowest level of competence of an agent interacting with the world. Schemas are not considered representations by them, because schemas do not generate or access memory, and have no reference to the agent's knowledge or experience of the world. In the case of such claims, one might paraphrase what Marr and Poggio said about their work on computer vision: examine all the possible ways of "squeezing the last ounce of information" from situational feedback or, if you like, from the pure reactive level, before appealing to the influence of representations on intelligent action.[41]

---

[41] Marr and Poggio's claim was quoted by Fodor (1983: 73). Nolfi and Floreano (2000, Chapter 5) point out a similar strategy. They show how pure reactive robots are able to solve certain tasks without having resort to internal representations, such as the cognitive or metric maps invoked by Tolman and Gallistel (see below) in real rats solving those tasks (for example, to locate food without using external cues). Conversely, they show how pure reactive robots, when reducing the constraints present in the environment, i.e. the opportunities that such robots can exploit in order to find simple solutions, become less and less able to solve those tasks, which can only be solved by agents having internal representations.

We suspect that a disagreement might rise at this point as to the notions of symbol, of representation as an inner state *denoting* external events, and of semantic content, but we will not undertake a discussion of these issues here. On the basis of our reading of the discovery of the artificial, we would suggest that the continuum of representational possibilities mentioned by Clark includes at its lower end cases of fairly simple adaptive behavior. Once it is agreed that the system's inner states are denotational, a more liberal stance seems natural, that of also considering as representational inner states at a low level of competence of a system interacting with the world, i.e. a level that does not entail explicit maps and planning, but still entails a mapping between a symbol denoting the situation and a symbol denoting the appropriate response.

Actually, a lot of the organism's low-level activities seem to entail some non-trivial denotational-computational apparatus, which would be difficult to understand if we ruled out the representational talk. A case in point is perception. Gibson's claim that the agent has a direct perception of the world, i.e. perception without the mediation of some representation, had already been challenged by Marr. He agreed with Gibson that a large part of animal and human perceptual activity involves low-level or early-vision mechanisms, delegated, for example, to identify object surfaces or textures. Contrary to what Gibson believed, however, it is not because those mechanisms are low-level that it is possible to stop considering them as involving computations of representations, which are far from being trivial. A good example of such an activity could be the detection of physical invariants, such as an object surface, by invertebrates, an activity that involves computations of representations, as first shown in the classic results concerning the visual system of the fly obtained by Poggio and W. Reichardt (Marr, 1982: 29-34).[42]

Another case comes from cognitive ethology. In the previous chapter, we mentioned Wehner's skeptical conclusions about the idea that ants and bees use a global, all-purpose representation of the world to navigate in their environment. Nevertheless, Wehner himself, although stressing the *direct* interaction these simple animals have with their environment, has to admit that they are equipped with a very efficient computational apparatus, even though it is minimal and special-purpose. This apparatus processes representations of the environment that are rudimentary, low-level and not the object of central planning, but that are far from trivial. Note that Wehner's conclusions conflict with those of other researchers, like Gallistel. For the latter, it is impossible to explain certain behaviors of the same animals studied by Wehner without postulating computational abilities regarding explicit representations, including those of three-dimensional space. These fairly high-level representations would make reference to a true cognitive or metric map of the environment—precisely what Wehner excludes (see for example Gallis-

---

[42] Johnson-Laird mentioned such results when he attributed to the fly simple representational abilities, related to Marr's "primal sketch" (on this point, see also Boden, 1984). Vera and Simon (1993) give a criticism of Gibson's 'ecological' claims. From another point of view, criticism of such claims had been made by Fodor and Pylyshyn (see Pylyshyn, 1984: 180 ff.). But Pylyshyn calls into question whether the representations to which Marr referred (those involved in early vision, as the example of the fly suggests) were genuine representations, given that they have no reference to *content* (pp. 214-215). As we have seen, Pylyshyn's criterion for speaking of representations was very strong, since it necessarily implies an appeal to the semantic level (for a critique see Barsalou, 1999: 589).

tel, 1997). Disputes of this sort show how it is difficult to distinguish in certain cases between low and high-level representations, implicit and explicit representations, in the continuum of possibilities, even in front of behavioral evidence.

Some conclusions might be put forward at this point. First, representations are to be viewed not as language-like structures, but as a coding apparatus that the system crucially uses in its interaction with the world. Simple systems too can have access, while interacting with the world, to representations with a different, non language-like, nature, albeit a computational one. Such representations are usually such that they are the object of computations that are anything but simple. The famous example of Simon's ant, which navigates its zig-zag way home by interacting with its environment without any need for explicit representation and planning, was taken up enthusiastically by Brooks himself, by Langton, and by other critics of representationalist claims. But, as Simon himself says, this is an example that cannot be generalized:

> A complex task is much more difficult to accomplish when assisted only by direct feedback from the environment than when there is also a way of maintaining some sort of representation of the world. Of course, pure planning, with no situational feedback, is equally ineffective, but it is unfortunate that failures of pure planning schemas have motivated researchers to argue for the opposite extreme instead of a more sophisticated intermediate strategy (Vera and Simon, 1993: 15-16).

Furthermore, one can reject centralized world models, but a lot of empirical evidence suggests that the agent's interaction with the world cannot be successfully explained without the mediation of representations of very different degree of complexity. There is a rhetorical sound to the eliminativist claim that extends the skepticism about representations as constituting a centralized world model to skepticism about every kind of representation. Future developments in experimental research in AI and situated models, as well as in neuroscience and in cognitive ethology, will be able to suggest new hints for approaching this issue. But complete cognitive architectures do not seem to be possible without high-level representations and planning.

David Kirsh firstly stressed this point with regard to Brooks' original slogan "knowledge without representations." Kirsh pointed out that Brooks' claims were close to Gibson's. He argued convincingly that it would be difficult for, so to speak, Gibsonian creatures such as Brooks' reactive robots, which are assumed to extract information *directly* from the world, to achieve a performance of a complexity much higher than that of quite simple organisms: "only in a rhetorical sense [...] can moboticists [the proponents of new mobile robots] contend that they abjure representations" (Kirsh, 1991: 180). The very evidence from robotics in later years seems to confirm this conclusion. Brooks himself afterwards clarified his earlier radical skepticism about representations (Brooks, 1995). Nonetheless, he had, on various occasions, formulated a very strong claim, one which would point to his simple creatures as leading to the successful replication of human intelligence in a machine. Arguing that his early creatures showed how intelligent behaviors can be exhibited without knowledge, planning, world models and maps and so forth, he had concluded: "in our more radical moments we believe that this will hold true all the way through to human level intelligence" (Brooks, 1991b: 238). And yet, claims of this very sort often paved the way taken by AI during its brief history: every time new research areas were proposed, again Kirsh observed, it was easy to see "early results as compelling evidence for strong conclusions" (Kirsh, 1991: 173).

The discussion of the theses we proposed at the start of this chapter suggests some further conclusions. If one retrospectively thinks of the path taken by the discovery of the artificial, one can conclude that the opposition between the organic and the inorganic world has been much reduced over time. Machines of different complexity have, from time to time, suggested how to overcome such an opposition, or at least some of its aspects. Traditional dichotomies, like natural/artificial, causal/teleological, automatic/learned, have been radically re-stated when not side-stepped. Furthermore, certain claims, included in some of the above-mentioned theses, that sounded provocative now seem much less so. Think, for example, of the claim that building inorganic models constitutes a kind of therapy against vitalism, a claim on which Hull used to insist in the days of the robot approach. Even though this claim was openly maintained by various authors, even in recent times (from Newell and Simon in the early days of AI to Langton at the beginnings of ALife), it should be said that the evidence in neuroscience, and more generally in the biological sciences, broadly diminished its interest. The same empirical evidence makes it clear that certain forms of explanation that ignore the "biological band" can be put into question no less than certain forms of extreme reductionism, which obscure the autonomy of the different levels in experimental research on mental life. This was another re-occurrence of the oscillation between mentalism and functionalism on the one hand and physicalism and reductionism on the other, which has characterized the sciences of the mind throughout the twentieth century.

5. The discovery of the artificial: hopes, defeats and successes

So far we have said nothing explicit about the last of the theses listed at the beginning of this chapter, i.e. Thesis (v) *Identity of Explanatory Principles*. Many leading figures in the discovery of the artificial presented this as an empirical hypothesis, but it was also expressed as a hope. The hope was that, by *complicating* the behavioral models, by gradually integrating them over wider task domains and introducing suitable constraints, it would have become possible to integrate their performances in more complex artifacts. In the end, it would have become possible to obtain satisfactory models of features of mental life long held to be unfathomable or elusive, like insight, creative thinking, and the various aspects of conscious experience.

At the beginning of the 1930s, Hull thought about the future "psychic" machine in terms of this hope. Even at the beginning of cybernetics and AI, a hope of this sort was certainly felt by many pioneers, such as Minsky, Rosenblatt and Simon. For the latter, for example, there never was any qualitative difference between the processes of insight and scientific creativity, on the one hand, and those of ordinary problem solving, on the other. Therefore, both these processes could be analyzed using the same computational procedures, and in this respect Thesis (v) *Identity of Explanatory Principles* retains its validity.

Not all researchers concerned with reproducing mental activities in machines today subscribe to Thesis (v) in this especially strong version. Suppose they were shown the list of the abilities of human mind that Rashevsky indicated long ago, in 1931, as achievable by future machines.[43] Many researchers would maintain that some of these abilities have already been realized in machines or will be in whole or in part. They might put among these abilities that of understanding a natural language, or of carrying on a conversation. But many other researchers would believe that other abilities of human mind, like the one Rashevsky mentioned of lying intentionally or those more unfathomable or elusive abilities we mentioned above, would always be barred to machines. This would be so whatever the "tremendous expense and labor" that Rashevsky, in his days, predicted would be forthcoming.

Leaving aside the question—always a matter of opinion—of the *limit* of the performance that could be achieved by future machines, the hope implicit in Thesis (*v*) was as follows: progress in building artifacts (whatever they might be) capable of exhibiting various abilities or features of living organisms, such as learning, problem solving, phenotype, development and so forth, would come about by starting with a study of simple situations, in which some success had already been achieved, and then passing on to a study of more complex situations. The hope has always been the same, from the toy-problems and the microworlds of classical AI to the new robotics and Edelman's synthetic neural modeling.

Thesis (*v*) could thus exemplify the general modeling strategy of science, as Rosenblueth and Wiener described it: a hierarchy that goes "from relatively simple, highly abstract [models], to more complex, more concrete theoretical structures," i.e. structures closer to the *real* complexity of the original phenomenon (Rosenblueth and Wiener, 1945: 319). Nevertheless, Thesis (*v*) encounters difficulties that have led to great disappointments among researchers in the field of behavior modeling. Even if the evolution of the scientific enterprise might be described, though with varying degrees of success in different scientific domains, in the cumulative way suggested by Rosenblueth and Wiener, nothing of the sort could be expected in the case of the research based on mental life models, i.e. on the strategy summarized by Thesis (*ii*), whose projects and results we have discussed in this book.

Think of the fragmentary, and not infrequently occasional, nature of the pre-cybernetic projects which occupied a good part of our investigation. We do not even know exactly why Hull definitively abandoned the robot approach. We must make some conjectures, which we have not been able to offer as regards other researchers, such as Bent Russell. These researchers could have shared with Hull a hope similar to that implicit in Thesis (*v*), but one must suppose that they soon became aware of the impossibility of realizing such a hope through the mere *complication* or *broadening* of their models. Despite the fact that this impossibility appears evident in hindsight, due as it is to the primitive state of technology, it is striking that these pre-cybernetic projects were abandoned and forgotten so soon. After all, even if the results were modest, the modeling methodology that inspired them was in harmony with later theoretical results and technology.

One might be struck by a coincidence. At the time that Hull, around 1935, abandoned his robot approach, Turing defined the notion of the machine that bears his name. One could conjecture that the later interest of Turing's heirs in the approach inspired by his machine, then baptized as AI, and its rapid growth beginning in the mid-1950s, con-

[43] See above, p. 96.

tributed to obscuring the cybernetics of the Ashbys, Grey Walters and Rosenblatts, and was even more clearly responsible for the fall into obscurity of the pre-cybernetic approaches of Hull and others.

A conjecture of this sort would be misleading. There is no doubt that these pre-cybernetic modeling experiments share with cybernetics, and with many current research programmes that follow its ideals, numerous issues and goals. Think, for example, of the associationist and connectionist claims, the robotics of synthetic animals, the interest in the issue of learning, and also in specific forms of learning (an instance is classical conditioning, which was inherited from cybernetic modeling and later returned to favor at the crossroads of new connectionism, behavioral neuroscience and new robotics). Nevertheless, it was not with the advent of cybernetics that those earlier modeling experiments had the revenge one might imagine. On the one hand, Hull himself did not seem to see in cybernetics the conditions for a resumption of the robot approach, or for an attempt to restate it along the path he undertook after abandoning it about ten years earlier, i.e. the logical-deductive construction of psychological theories. On the other hand, the cyberneticians themselves were criticizing the earlier tradition of behavior modeling. It is true that their influential precursor, Craik, made explicit reference to the robot approach, but he did so to criticize the robotics of the 1930s, which he considered a by-product of the synthetic method. The outstanding exponent of such robotics was Ross, who had already used the expression "synthetic method" to describe his own method. He was always mentioned in the cybernetic literature on maze-solver robots. Nonetheless, we have seen that this kind of synthetic animals was not appreciated by cyberneticians whose main interest was theory construction, like Pask or Gabor. The latter, indeed, wrote off the pre-cybernetic models of conditioning as trivial when compared to the neural nets of his day.

Moreover, it should be stressed that, if Hull, from time to time, was popular during the cybernetics years, it was not because of the robot approach, but because of his experimental and quantitative investigations of learning, his approach to theory construction and the relevance of the hypothetical constructs he introduced. Hebb and Rosenblatt mentioned him because of the latter, as did Mowrer and George, a cybernetician for whom Hull's theories, no less than Tolman's, "could be restated in a manner making them suitable for a computer program" (George, 1961: 178). In all these references no mention ever is made of the simulative methodology that was at the core of the robot approach. One would have to wait for the book by Miller et al. (1960) for this to obtain real acknowledgement, but this acknowledgement, soon forgotten, does not go much beyond the role of the robot approach as an antivitalist therapy. Cybernetics, finally, because of the very complexity of its interdisciplinary programme, never presented itself as a homogeneous research programme, and the very term Wiener introduced, as Pask points out, was soon interpreted in different ways.[44]

All this leads to the conclusion that it is not possible to reconstruct the discovery of the artificial throughout the twentieth century as the development and fluctuating fortunes of two opposing trends: one that starts from behaviorist modeling and, passing through cybernetics, arrives at current developments in neural nets, ALife and new robotics, and

[44] See Pask (1961: 15), who mentions the various definitions of cybernetics, besides that of Wiener himself, given by Ashby, Stafford Beer, Couffignal (see also Chapter 5, n. 18).

the other, born with Turing and leading to symbolic AI. According to such a viewpoint, this second tendency prevailed for a long time, to the detriment of a different and homogeneous tradition, that of the so-to-speak *non-symbolic* artificial. It is instead true that, in the second half of the twentieth century, with the advent of cybernetics, the fragmentary, and not infrequently occasional, investigations of the artificial change radically, above all because of the advent of computer science and technology. Without the latter, literally none of the current experiments in the field of the sciences of the artificial could be imagined. As we saw in previous chapters, however, not even in this case have we witnessed a really cumulative evolution of these sciences. Certainly they have taken shape in a way that has no precedent, but the effect has been that of multiplying research paths, making them more ambitious, but also more tortuous and unpredictable.

It thus does not seem a good idea to describe the discovery of the artificial throughout the twentieth century in terms of the confrontation of rival 'paradigms' *à la* Kuhn.[45] Those who insisted on opposing their subsymbolic paradigm to the symbolic one of AI were the connectionists of the 1980s. At first, it seemed that one was witnessing the effect of some trauma. Rosenblatt was right, and Minsky and Papert's 1969 book on *Perceptrons* had wrongly erased neural nets from the world of research. Perhaps Minsky and Papert's role had been overvalued a good deal. It is true that, after the publications of *Perceptrons*, there was a reduction in the financing of neural net research (see also Papert, 1988, on this point). However, the problem is whether Minsky and Papert's book was the cause or rather a symptom, as Bechtel and Abrahamsen (1991: 15) point out. Indeed, a research project can hardly be brushed aside by one book, if such a project does not have its own limitations. At least two relevant facts are not taken sufficiently into account. Firstly, as Minsky himself stresses, "it was not until the 1980s that the new field of computational complexity had matured enough to supplement, with other techniques, the group-theoretic exploitations of pattern symmetries that [Papert and I] had developed [in *Perceptrons*]."[46] Secondly, James McClelland, a leading figure in neural net research, points out that, given that most research on neural nets involves simulating them on computers, "the world wasn't ready for neural networks [...] The computing power available in the early sixties was totally insufficient for this." He thus refuses to blame Minsky and Papert's book for the demise of neural nets in the 1960s.[47]

Though it is obvious, it still seems worthwhile to recall that this limitation in computer performance was also a contributory factor in the development of *symbolic* AI. Think how AI investigations into knowledge representation prevailed over the earlier investigations on heuristic search in toy-problem domains. This is a phenomenon that simply would not have been possible without the availability, from a certain time onwards,

---

[45] In *The Structure of Scientific Revolutions* Kuhn suggested that the proponents of rival paradigms raise different questions, adopt different solutions for those questions, and use different meanings for concepts. The analogy is that of Gestalt shift: the proponents of a rival paradigm see things in a totally different way.

[46] Minsky refers here to the development of the mathematical approach of *Perceptrons*, up to its culmination in the 1990s, due to the theoretical investigations of computational complexity by Kay-Yeung Siu and Vwani Roychowdury (Minsky, 1995: xvii).

[47] This judgment by McClelland and that by Simon, which we mention immediately afterward, have been collected by Crevier (1993: 309 and 146-147).

of computers with large memories and great computing power. Simon says that what initially oriented his and Newell's research group towards tasks where not much knowledge was needed was also the lack of such computers. It was known that knowledge was relevant for intelligence, but it was not possible to embody the necessary, vast amount of knowledge into machines. The fact remains that the actual computing power of early computers encouraged investigations into weak heuristics and toy problems, at the time considered the real *Drosophila* of AI. There it was possible to control combinatorial explosion, and there the first decisive successes occurred. Although, seen in retrospect, these successes, or some of them, could today appear limited, for their day they were undeniably such that they encouraged certain research projects, and even certain hopes, rather than others.

A very different case, but one which should nevertheless suggest some reflections, is that of machine translation. Research in this field soon entered a blind alley, and financing was interrupted in the mid-1960s. As we have seen, this research was resumed years later, when a more promising way to tackle it was found. This led to the connection of machine translation with research on natural language understanding and knowledge representation. Even here, computing power made these investigations of machine translation possible, and also made possible current developments, which are certainly more modest than the ambitious early projects.

Before the alleged opposition of symbolic paradigm and subsymbolic paradigm, other oppositions were claimed, this time in symbolic AI: the heuristic-search paradigm versus the knowledge paradigm, the logicist paradigm versus the antilogicist paradigm, the declarativist paradigm versus the proceduralist paradigm. But none of these could be seen as a paradigm in the *technical* sense above, i.e. *à la* Kuhn.[48] Rather, each of them is a watchword for different, and even competing, trends in research occurring in a history, like that of AI, where the most diverse paths were followed and then abandoned, only in some cases to be taken up again after time had passed; where failures in one path sometimes caused the choice of the opposite extreme, to repeat Simon and Vera's words; where there never was any unanimity, either about its own definition or about its own aims and subject matter (the *human* mind or the *artificial* one?).[49] This certainly is not a description of a 'mature' science, but that is what our investigation suggests.[50] It should

[48] See the seminal paper by Newell (1983), who argued that the notion of 'paradigm,' as well as that of 'research programme,' are too coarse-grained units of historical analysis in AI. He identified several "intellectual issues" (performance vs learning, search vs knowledge, procedural vs declarative representation, an so on) which have had some prominence at one time or another during the history of AI.

[49] Patrick Hayes concludes that "the attempts to define AI tend to offend people, for any definition is bound to exclude someone, and nobody likes that he is not working in the area he thinks he is working" (Hayes, 1984: 161). And recall that Newell and Simon's Information Processing Psychology was defined as "the field that uses methods alien to cognitive psychology to explore questions alien to AI" (Cohen and Feigenbaum, 1982: 7).

[50] Perhaps, one might call a "part-whole problem," as Pylyshyn puts it, the difficulty in accumulating or incrementally extending results in IA and cognitive science. This can be summarized by the fact that a computational system "which is able to encompass some domain of evidence A may bear very little resemblance to a system which is able to encompass both some domain of evidence A and some domain of evidence B" (Pylyshyn, 1979: 53). This "kind of incompleteness" might be seen as a not minor source of the disappointments of many researchers in AI and cognitive modeling.

be added that many of those alleged oppositions between paradigms have not always and everywhere been felt with the same harshness. The opposition between declarativists and proceduralists, McDermott (1976) observed, did not worry those at Carnegie-Mellon, who have not suffered at all.

Against this rather tumultuous background, the demise of neural nets and their revival in the climate of the new-connectionism euphoria in the 1980s, which has soon diminished, does not appear to be as disconcerting an event as it has sometimes been made out to be. Rather, it is against this background that one must view both the demise of cybernetic robotics and its current reevaluation, along with the investigations in new robotics in its many forms, including architectures à la Brooks and hybrid architectures, evolutionary robotics and synthetic neural modeling. And the fact that it is possible, in certain cases, to integrate symbolic AI and connectionist results seems to confirm this, making their representation as two opposed paradigms merely a rhetorical exercise.[51] Margaret Boden has insisted that such an opposition cannot be proposed. She claims that in both approaches, the symbolic and the connectionist, people are working on the same problems and are posing questions held in common. These questions for the most part have the same origin in the 1943 article by McCulloch and Pitts, which is equally fundamental for both AI and neural nets (Boden, 1993). In a sense, it would be more appropriate to speak of two different computational styles, a symbolic one and a 'brain style,' or subsymbolic one.

That the development of psychology in the twentieth century cannot be construed in terms of rival paradigms is pointed out by the historians of psychology.[52] As for the discovery of the artificial and its developments in the framework of the sciences of the mind, we argue that an analogous interpretative criterion is valid. Therefore, it might be useful to identify some theses (*at the very least* those indicated at the beginning of this chapter) which make it possible to individuate both convergences and divergences among various approaches, considered as research trends within a substantially shared methodology.

There is a question posed by, among others, Smolensky (1988) that goes beyond simple diversity in computational styles, and that would make the claim of opposition between symbolic and connectionist paradigms justifiable, if only because, in the light of connectionism, one might then see the intrinsic limitations of the symbolic AI research programme. Smolensky wondered whether models consisting of finite nets of artificial neurons, interpreted as *analog* computational devices based on *continuous physical*

---

[51] Some of Verschure's evaluations of Edelman's approach and that of SOAR in the development of future research led him to conclude that the two approaches "could be used to constrain each other" (Verschure, 1993: 74). Thornton (1997) points out a "hybrid" approach, where ALife requirements of evolution and AI requirements of an organism's representational abilities could integrate each other. Goodale and Humphrey (1998) argue a "duplex" approach to vision, in which Marrian and Gibsonian approaches are not seen as mutually exclusive, but as complementary in their emphasis on different aspects of visual function (thanks to Giuseppe Boccignone for drawing my attention on this point). Finally, we mentioned "hybrid" approaches for integrating, on the one hand, neural nets and symbolic systems (p. 214) and, on the other hand, different trends in current robotics (p. 239).

[52] See Mecacci (1992) for a discussion of the 'paradigm' and 'research programme' methodologies in the development of psychology in the twentieth century.

processes, might not yield to a "new (in fact connectionist) theory of analog parallel computation," capable of challenging a "strong construal" of Church's thesis (p. 3). In Church's thesis, which concerns the class of functions calculable by *discrete* mechanical procedures, Smolensky summarizes the theoretical assumptions of symbolic AI. The new connectionist computational theory would then support, according to Smolensky, the claim of an analog computer that would not be simulated by any Turing machine.[53] In the current state of knowledge, this is a mere hypothesis, one which, if it ever were realized, would lead to the *terra incognita* where connectionist theories really would be an alternative to symbolic ones.

The question posed by Smolensky about the symbolic versus connectionist debate could be posed whenever there is a proposal to provide models of cognition based on analog components. Can analog computation go beyond the limits of digital computation? The question might concern the alleged opposition between classical or symbolic AI and *nouvelle* AI. But whether approaches such as dynamic systems, ALife or new robotics will eventually scale up to the most evolved or human forms of intelligence, thus giving birth to the 'new paradigm' of *nouvelle* AI, is an empirical question, as Pfeifer and Vershure (1995) conclude. In the sciences of the artificial, the final test is always the range of empirical phenomena which are successfully dealt with. Presently, we cannot glimpse the substitution of one paradigm with another; rather, there are research trends that confront each other, or make an effort to integrate each other, or coexist separately in the realm of the many forms of the artificial. The research area of ALife is covered neither by symbolic AI nor by connectionism. But ALife usually misses out what is achieved by both these approaches individually. And to argue that ALife is the actual, successful alternative to the present symbolic and connectionist approaches, with their different limitations, would indeed be an instance of the aforementioned attitude that takes early results as compelling evidence for strong conclusions.

It is in this attitude that we might find the roots of the recurring euphorias and disappointments that have marked the discovery of the artificial and its developments in the twentieth century. Presently, the multiplicity of points of view, hypotheses and experimental approaches seems to be what best characterizes the sciences of the artificial. This may leave us disappointed or thrilled, but certainly not indifferent.

[53] An extensive discussion of this claim is given by Tamburrini (1997).

REFERENCES

Abraham, T. (forthcoming), (Physio)logical circuits: the intellectual origins of the McCulloch-Pitts neural networks, *Journal of the History of the Behavioral Sciences*.

Adams, B., Breazeal, C., Brooks, R.A. and Scassellati, B. (2000), Humanoid robots: a new kind of tool, *IEEE Intelligent Systems*, 15 (4): 25-31.

Aizawa, K. (1992), Connectionism and artificial intelligence: history and philosophical interpretation, *Journal of Experimental and Theoretical Artificial Intelligence*, 4: 295-313.

Aizawa K. (1996), Some neural network theorizing before McCulloch: Nicolas Rashevsky's mathematical biophysics, *Brain Processes, Theories, and Models. An International Conference in Honor of W.S. McCulloch 25 Years after his Death*, MIT Press, Cambridge, Mass.: 64-70.

Albertazzi, L. (forthcoming), *An Introduction to Brentano*, Kluwer Academic Publishers, Dordrecht.

Amit, D. (1995), The Hebbian paradigm reintegrated: local reverberations as internal representations, *Behavioral and Brain Sciences*, 18: 617-657.

Ammons, R.B. (1962), Psychology of the scientist: Clark L. Hull and his *Idea Books*, *Perceptual and Motor Skills*, 15: 800-802.

Anderson, J.A. and Rosenfeld, E. (eds.) (1988), *Neurocomputing*, MIT Press, Cambridge, Mass.

Anderson, J.A., Pellionisz, A. and Rosenfeld, E. (eds.) (1990), *Neurocomputing 2*, MIT Press, Cambridge, Mass.

Andrew, A.M. (1958), Machines which learn, *New Scientist*, n. 4: 1388-1391.

Angyan, A.J. (1959), *Machina reproducatrix*. An analogue model to demonstrate some aspects of neural adaptation, *Proceedings of the Teddington Symposium on Mechanisation of Thought Processes*, vol. 2, HMSO, London: 933-943.

Apter, M.J. (1970), *The Computer Simulation of Behaviour*, Hutchinson, London.

Ash, M.G (1995), *Gestalt Psychology in German Culture, 1890-1967: Holism and the Quest for Objectivity*, Cambridge University Press, Cambridge.

Ashby, W.R. (1940), Adaptiveness and equilibrium, *Journal of Mental Science*, 86: 478-483.

Ashby, W.R. (1945), The physical origin of adaptation by trial and error, *Journal of General Psychology*, 32: 13-25.

Ashby, W.R. (1948), Design for a brain, *Electronic Engineering*, 20: 379-383.

Ashby, W.R. (1950), A new mechanism which shows simple conditioning, *Journal of Psychology*, 29: 343-347.

Ashby, W.R. (1952/1960), *Design for a Brain*, Chapman and Hall, London (2nd edition: Wiley, New York, 1960).

Ashby, W.R. (1956), *An Introduction to Cybernetics*, Chapman and Hall, London.

Attneave, F. (1959), *Applications of Information Theory to Psychology*, Holt, Rinehart and Winston, New York.

Baernstein, H.D. and Hull, C.L. (1931), A mechanical model of the conditioned reflex, *Journal of General Psychology*, 5: 99-106.

Bain, A. (1873), *Mind and Body. The Theories of Their Relation*, Henry King, London (2nd edition).

Ballard, D.H. (1991), Animate vision, *Artificial Intelligence*, 48: 57-86.

Ballard, D.H. (1993), Sub-symbolic modelling of hand-eye co-ordination, in D. Broadbent (ed.), *The Simulation of Human Intelligence*, Blackwell, Oxford: 71-102.

Bancroft, W.D. (1911), An universal law, *Journal of the American Chemical Society*, 33: 91-120.

Bar-Hillell, Y. (1960), The present status of automatic translation of languages, *Advances in Computers 1*, Academic Press, New York: 91-163.

Barnden, J.A. and Pollack, J.B. (eds.) (1991), *High-Level Connectionism Models*, Ablex, Norwood, N.J.

Barsalau, L.W. (1999), Perceptual symbol systems, *Behavioral and Brain Sciences*, 22: 577-660.

Bechtel, W. (1982), Two common errors in explaining biological and psychological phenomena, *Philosophy of Science*, 49: 549-574.

Bechtel, W. (1988), *Philosophy of Mind*, Erlbaum, Hillsdale, N.J.

Bechtel, W. and Abrahamsen, A. (1991), *Connectionism and the Mind*, Blackwell, Oxford.

Bechtel, W., Abrahamsen, A. and Graham, G. (1998), The life of cognitive science, in W. Bechtel and G. Graham (eds.), *A Companion to Cognitive Science*, Blackwell, Oxford: 2-104.

Bechtel, W. and Mundale, J. (1999), Multiple realizability revisited: linking cognitive and neural states, *Philosophy of Science*, 66: 175-207.

Beer, R. (1995), A dynamical systems perspective on agent-environment interaction, *Artificial Intelligence*, 72: 173-215.

Bennett, G.K., and Ward, L.B. (1933), A model of the synthesis of conditioned reflexes, *American Journal of Psychology*, 45: 339-342.

Berkeley, E.C. (1949), *Giant Brains or Machines that Think*, Wiley, New York.

Berkeley, E.C. (1951), Light sensitive electronic beast, *Radio Electronics*, December: 47-58.

Berkeley, E.C. (1952), Algebra in electronic design, *Radio Electronics*, February: 55-58.

Berkeley, E.C. (1959), *Symbolic Logic and Intelligent Machines*, Reinhold, New York.

Berkeley, E.C. and Jensen, R.A. (1950), World's smallest electric brain, *Radio Electronics*, October: 29-30.

Bernard, C. (1865), *Introduction à l'Etude de la Médicine Expérimentale*, Garnier-Flammarion, Paris.

Bernstein, J. (1978), *Science Observed*, Basic Books, New York.

Bertalanffy, L. von (1968), *General System Theory*, Braziller, New York.

Blanzieri, E., Grandi, F. and Maio, D. (1996), High-order behaviour in learning gate networks with lateral inhibition, *Biological Cybernetics*, 74: 73-83.

Bledsoe, W.W. (1977), Non-resolution theorem proving, *Artificial Intelligence*, 9: 1-35.

Bledsoe, W.W. and Loveland, D.W. (eds.) (1984), *Automated Theorem Proving. After 25 Years*, American Mathematical Society, Providence.

Boakes, R. (1984), *From Darwin to Behaviorism. Psychology and the Mind of Animals*, Cambridge University Press, Cambridge.

Bobrow, D.G. (ed.) (1980), Special issue on non-monotonic logic, *Artificial Intelligence*, 13, n. 1-2.

Boden, M.A. (1972), *Purposive Explanation in Psychology*, Harvard University Press.

Boden, M.A. (1984), Animal perception from an Artificial Intelligence viewpoint, in C. Hookway (ed.), *Minds, Machines and Evolution*, Cambridge University Press, Cambridge: 153-174.

Boden, M.A. (1993), The impact on philosophy, in D. Broadbent (ed.), *The Simulation of Human Intelligence*, Blackwell, Oxford: 178-197.

Bonasso, P. and Dean, T. (1997), A retrospective of the AAAI robot competitions, *AI Magazine*, 18 (1): 11-23.

Boring, E.G. (1946), Mind and mechanism, *American Journal of Psychology*, 59: 173-192.

Bouquet, P. and Cimatti, A. (1995), Mechanizing local reasoning with contexts, *Working Notes of the IJCAI-95 Workshop on Modelling Context in Knowledge Representation and Reasoning*, LAFORIA n. 96/11: 13-23.

Bowden, B.V. (ed.) (1953), *Faster than Thought*, Pitman, London.

Bradner, H. (1937), A new mechanical 'learner', *Journal of General Psychology*, 17: 414-419.

Braitenberg, V. (1984), *Vehicles. Experiments in Synthetic Psychology*, MIT Press, Cambridge, Mass.

Broadbent, D.E. (1956), The concept of capacity and the theory of behaviour, in C. Cherry (ed.), *Information Theory*, Butterworths, London: 354-360.

Broadbent, D.E. (1957), A mechanical model for human attention and immediate memory, *Psychological Review*, 64: 205-215.

Broadbent, D.E. (1958), *Perception and Communication*, Pergamon, Elmsford, N.J.

Broadbent, D.E. (1961), *Behavior*, Methuen, London.

Broadbent, D.E. (1984), The Maltese cross: a new simplistic model for memory, *Behavioral and Brain Sciences*, 7: 55-94.

Brooks, R.A. (1991a), Intelligence without representation, *Artificial Intelligence*, 47: 139-159.

Brooks, R.A. (1991b), How to build complete creatures rather than isolated cognitive simulators, in K. VanLehn (ed.), *Architecture for Intelligence*, Erlbaum, Hillsdale, N.J.: 225-239.

Brooks, R.A. (1995), Intelligence without reason, in L. Steels and R. Brooks (eds.), *The Artificial Life Route to Artificial Intelligence: Building Embodied, Situated Agents*, Erlbaum, Hillsdale, N.J.: 23-81.

Buckley, K.W. (1989), *Mechanical Man. John Broadus Watson and the Beginning of Behaviorism*, Guilford, New York.

Burattini, E. and Marciano, F. (1969), DIANA: un simulatore di rete neurale, Technical Report 12-69, Istituto di Cibernetica, Naples.

Burattini, E., De Gregorio, M. and Tamburrini, G. (2002), Hybrid expert systems: an approach to combining neural computation and rule-based reasoning, in C.T. Leondes (ed.), *Fuzzy Logic and Expert Systems Applications*, Academic Press, Boston: 1315-1354.

Bush, V. (1945), That man may think, *Atlantic Monthly*, 176: 105-108.

Caianiello, E.R. (ed.) (1968), *Neural Networks*, Springer, Berlin.

Carlucci Aiello, L., Nardi, D. and Pirri, F. (2001), Case studies in cognitive robotics, in V. Cantoni, V. Di Gesù, A. Setti and D. Tegolo (eds.), *Human and Machine Perception 3: Thinking, Deciding, and Acting*, Kluwer Academic Publishers, Dordrecht.

Ceccato, S. (1958), La machine qui pense et qui parle, *Actes du 1er Congrès International de Cybernétique*, Gauthier-Villars, Paris: 288-299.

Chomsky, N. (1957), *Syntactic Structures*, Mouton, The Hague.

Churchland, P.M. and Churchland P.S. (1990), Could a machine think? Recent arguments and new prospects, *Scientific American*, 262 (1): 32-37.

Churchland, P.S. (1986), *Neurophilosophy. Toward a Unified Science of the Mind-Brain*, MIT Press, Cambridge, Mass.

Churchland, P.S. and Sejnowski, T.J. (1992), *The Computational Brain*, MIT Press, Cambridge, Mass.

Churchman, C.W. and Ackoff, R.L. (1950), Purposive behavior and cybernetics, *Social Forces*, 29: 32-39.

Churchman, C.W., Ackoff, R.L. and Arnoff, E.L. (1957), *Introduction to Operation Research*, Wiley, New York.

Clancey, W. J. (1993), Situated action, *Cognitive Science*, 17: 87-116.

Clark, A. (1997), *Being there. Putting Brain, Body, and World Together Again*, MIT Press, Cambridge, Mass.

Cliff, D., Harvey, I. and Husbands, P. (1993), Explorations in evolutionary robotics, *Adaptive Behavior*, 2: 73-110.

Coburn, H.E. (1951), The Brain Analogy, *Psychological Review*, 58: 155-

Coburn, H.E. (1952), The Brain Analogy: a discussion, *Psychological Review*, 59: 453-460.

Coburn, H.E. (1953), The Brain Analogy: association tracts, *Psychological Review*, 60: 197-206.

Cohen, P.R. and Feigenbaum, E.A. (1882), *The Handbook of Artificial Intelligence*, vol. 3, Pitman, London.

Colton, S. (1999), Refactorable numbers, *Journal of Integer Sequences*, 2, Article 99.1.2. Electronic Journal, http://www.research.att.com/~njas/sequences/JIS/

Cooper, R., Fox, J., Farringdon, J. and Shallice, T. (1996), A systematic methodology for cognitive modelling, *Artificial Intelligence*, 85: 3-44.

Cordeschi, R. (1988), Purpose, feedback and homeostasis: dimension of a controversy in psychological theory, in S. Bem, H. Rappard and W. van Horn (eds.), *Studies in the History of Psychology and the Social Sciences*, Psychologisch Instituut, Leiden: 119-129.

Cordeschi, R. (1991), The discovery of the artificial. Some protocybernetic developments 1930-1940, *Artificial Intelligence and Society*, 5: 218-238.

Cordeschi, R. (1996), The role of heuristics in automated theorem proving. J.A. Robinson's resolution principle, *Mathware and Soft Computing*, 3: 281-293.

Cordeschi, R., Tamburrini, G. and Trautteur, G. (1999), The notion of loop in the study of consciousness, in C. Taddei-Ferretti and C. Musio (eds.), *Neuronal Bases and Psychological Aspects of Consciousness*, World Scientific, Singapore: 524-540.

Corsi, P. (ed.) (1994), *The Enchanted Loom. Chapters in the History of Neuroscience*, Oxford University Press, New York and Oxford.

Craik, K.J.W. (1943), *The Nature of Explanation*, Cambridge University Press, Cambridge.

Craik, K.J.W. (1945), The present position of psychological research in Britain, *British Medical Bulletin*, 3: 24-26.

Craik, K.J.W. (1947), Theory of the human operator in control systems. I. The operator as an engineering system, *British Journal of Psychology*, 38: 56-61.

Craik, K.J.W. (1948), Theory of the human operator in control systems. II. Man as an element in a control system, *British Journal of Psychology*, 38: 142-148.

Craik, K.J.W. (1966), *The Nature of Psychology*, ed. by S.L. Sherwood, Cambridge University Press, Cambridge.

Crevier, D. (1993), *AI. The Tumultuous History of the Search for Artificial Intelligence*, Basic Books, New York.

Crile, G.W. (1921), A suggestion as to the mechanism of memory, *Journal of Comparative Psychology*, 1: 201-211.

Crovitz, H.F. (1990), Association, cognition, and neural networks, in M.G. Johnson and T.B. Henley (eds.), *Reflections on* The Principles of Psychology. *William James after a Century*, Erlbaum, Hillsdale, N.J., 1990: 167-182.

Crozier, W.J. (1928), Tropisms, *Journal of General Psychology*, 1: 213-328.

Dartnall, T. (ed.) (1994), *Artificial Intelligence and Creativity, An Interdisciplinary Approach*, Kluwer Academic Publishers, Dordrecht.

de Latil, P. (1953), *Introduction à la Cybernétique*, Gallimard, Paris.

Dennett, D.C. (1978), *Brainstorms: Philosophical Essays on Mind and Psychology*, Bradford Books, Montgomery.

Dennett, D.C. (1996), *Kinds of Minds*, Basic Books, New York.

Deutsch, J.A. (1953), A new type of behaviour theory, *British Journal of Psychology*, 44: 304-317.

Deutsch, J.A. (1954), A machine with insight, *Quarterly Journal of Experimental Psychology*, 6 (part I): 6-11.

Deutsch, J.A. (1960), *The Structural Basis of Behavior*, Cambridge University Press, Cambridge.

Deutsch, K.W. (1951-52), Mechanism, teleology, and mind, *Philosophy and Phenomenological Research*, 12: 185-223.

Dodge, R. (1926), Theories of inhibition, *Psychological Review*, 33: 106-122.

Dreyfus, H. (1992),*What Computers still can't do*, MIT Press, Cambridge, Mass.

Driesch, H. (1909), *Philosophie des Organischen*, Engellmann, Leipzig.

Dunlap, K. (1928), A revision of the fundamental law of habit formation, *Science*, 67: 360-362.

Dupuy, J.-P., Heims, S.J. and Lévy, P. (1985), *Histoires de Cibernétique*, Cahiers du CREA, Paris.

Eames, C. and Eames, R. (eds.) (1990), *A Computer Perspective. Background Of Computer Age*, Harvard University Press, Cambridge, Mass.

Eier, R. and Zemanek, H. (1960), Automatische Orientierung im Labyrinth, *Elektronische Rechenanlagen*, 2: 23.

Eliasmith, C. (1997), Computation and dynamical models of mind, *Minds and Machines*, 7: 531-541.

Ellson, D.G. (1935), A mechanical synthesis of trial-and-error learning, *Journal of General Psychology*, 13: 212-218.

Ericsson, K.A. and Simon, H.A. (1981), Sources of evidence on cognition. A Historical Overview, in T. Merluzzi, C. Glass and M. Genest (eds.), *Cognitive Assessment*, Guilford, New York: 16-51.

Ernst, G. and Newell, A. (1969), *GPS: A Case Study in Generality and Problem Solving*, Academic Press, New York.

Esper, E.A. (1966), Max Meyer: the making of a scientific isolate, *Journal for the History of the Behavioral Sciences*, 2:107-131.

Esper, E.A. (1967), Max Meyer in America, *Journal for the History of the Behavioral Sciences*, 3:107-131.

Fearing, F. (1930), *Reflex Action. A Study in the History of Physiological Explanation*, MIT Press, Cambridge, Mass.

Feigenbaum, E.A. (1969), Artificial Intelligence: themes in the second decade, *Proceedings of Information Processing 68*, North Holland, Amsterdam: 1008-1024.

Feigenbaum, E.A., Buchanan, B.G. and Lederberg, J. (1971), On generality and problem solving: a case study using DENDRAL program, *Machine Intelligence 6*, Edinburgh University Press, Edinburgh: 165-190.

Feigenbaum, E.A. and Feldman, J. (eds.) (1963), *Computers and thought*, McGraw-Hill, New York.

Fodor, J.A. (1974), Special sciences (or: the disunity of science as a working hypothesis), *Synthese*, 28: 97-115.

Fodor J.A. (1983), *The Modularity of Mind*, MIT Press, Cambridge, Mass.

Fodor, J.A. (1986), Why Paramecia don't have mental representations, *Midwest Studies in Philosophy*, 10: 3-23.

Fodor, J.A. and Pylyshyn, Z.W. (1988), Connectionism and cognitive architecture: a critical analysis, *Cognition*, 28: 3-71.

Ford, K.M. and Hayes, P.J. (1998), On computational wings: rethinking the goals of Artificial Intelligence, *Scientific American*, Special Issue, Winter:

Frank, L.K., Wiener, N., Hutchinson, G.E., Livingston, W.K. and McCulloch, W.S. (1948), Teleological mechanisms, *Annals of the New York Academy of Sciences*, 50: 189-277.

Frost, E.P. (1912), Can biology and physiology dispense with consciousness?, *Psychological Review*, 19: 246-252.

Gabor, D. (1956), Models in cybernetics, in *I Modelli nella Tecnica*, Accademia Nazionale dei Lincei, Rome.

Gallistel, C.R. (1997), Symbolic processes in the brain: the case of insect navigation, in D. Scarborough, D.N. Osherson and S. Sternberg (eds.), *An Invitation to Cognitive Science*, vol. 4, MIT Press, Cambridge, Mass.: 1-51.

Gallistel, C.R. (2000), The replacement of general-purpose learning models with adaptively specialized learning models, in M.S. Gazzaniga, *The New Cognitive Neurosciences*, MIT Press, Cambridge, Mass.: 1179-1191.

Gamba, A., Gamberini, L, Palmieri, G. and Sanna, R. (1961), Further experiments with PAPA, *Nuovo Cimento*, Suppl., 20: 221-231.

Gardner, H. (1985), *The Mind's New Science. A history of Cognitive Revolution*, Basic Books, New York.

Gardner, M. (1982), *Logic Machines and Diagrams*, Harvester, Brighton (2nd edition).

Gazzaniga, M.S. (1998), *The Mind's Past*, University of California Press, Berkeley

Gelernter, H. (1959), Realization of a geometry-theorem machine, *Proceedings of an International Conference on Information Processing*, UNESCO, Paris: 273-282.

Gelernter, H., Hansen, J.R. and Loveland, D.W. (1960), Empirical explorations of the geometry-theorem proving machine, *Proceedings of the Western Joint Computer Conference*, 17: 143-147. Reprinted in E.A. Feigenbaum and J. Feldman (1963).

Gelperin, A., Hopfield, J.J. and Tank D.W. (1985), The logic of *Limax* learning, in A. Selverston (ed.), *Model Neural Networks and Behavior*, Plenum, New York: 237-261.

George, F.H. (1961), *The Brain as a Computer*, Pergamon, Oxford.

Gibson, J.J. (1979), *An Ecological Approach to Visual Perception*, Houghton Mifflin, Boston.

Giunchiglia, F. (1995), An epistemological science of common sense, *Artificial Intelligence*, 77: 371-392.

Goodale, M.A. and Humphrey, G.K. (1998), The objects of action and perception, *Cognition*, 67: 181-207.

Goldstine, H.H. (1972), *The Computer from Pascal to von Neumann*, Princeton University Press, Princeton, N.J.

Gray, G.W. (1935-1936a), Machines which imitate life, *Harper's Monthly Magazine*, 172: 341-352.

Gray, G.W. (1935-1936b), Thinking machines, *Harper's Monthly Magazine*, 172: 416-425

Gray, J.S. (1932), A behavioristic interpretation of intelligence, *Psychological Review*, 39: 271-278.

Green, C. (1969), Theorem-proving by resolution as a basis for question-answering systems, *Machine Intelligence 4*, Elsevier, New York: 183-205.

Greenberger, M. (ed.) (1962), *Management and the Computer of the Future*, Wiley, New York.

Gregory, R.L. (1983), Forty years on: Kenneth Craik's *The nature of explanation*, *Perception*, 12: 233-238.

Griffin, D.R. (1976), *The Question of Animal Consciousness*, The Rockefeller University Press, New York.

Grossberg, S. (1982), A psychophysiological theory of reinforcement, drive, motivation, and attention, *Journal of Theoretical Neurobiology*, 1: 286-369.

Gutknecht, M. and Pfeifer, R. (1990), An approach to integrating expert systems with connectionistic networks, *AICOM*, 3: 116-127.

Hanson, S.J. and Olson, C.R. (1990), Introduction: connectionism and neuroscience, in S.J. Hanson and C.R. Olson (eds.), *Connectionist Modeling and Brain Function*, MIT Press, Cambridge, Mass.: 1-4.

Harnad, S. (1990), The symbol grounding problem, *Physica D*, 42: 335-346.

Harnad, S. (1994), Levels of functional equivalence in reverse bioengineering, *Artificial Life*, 1: 293-301.

Harrington, A. (1989), A feeling for the 'whole': the holistic reaction in neurology from the fin-de-siècle to the interwar years, in R. Porter and M. Teich (eds.), *The Fin-de-Siècle and its Legacy*, Cambridge University Press, Cambridge.

Hassenstein, B. (1970), *Biologische Kybernetik*, Quelle & Meyer, Heidelberg. English translation: *Information and Control in the Living Organism*, Chapman and Hall, London, 1971.

Hawkins, J.K. (1961), Self-organizing systems. A review and commentary, *Proceedings of the IRE*, 49: 31-48.

Hawkins, R.D. (1989), A biologically realistic neural network for higher-order features of classical conditioning, in R.G.M. Morris (ed.), *Parallel Distributed Processing. Implications for Psychology and Neurobiology*, Clarendon, Oxford: 214-247.

Hawkins, R.D., Abrams, T.W., Carew, T.J. and Kandel, E.R. (1983), A cellular mechanism of classical conditioning in *Aplysia*: activity-dependent amplification of presynaptic facilitation, *Science*, 219: 400-405.

Hayes P.J. (1979), The logic of frames, in D. Metzing (ed.), *Frame Conceptions and Text Understanding*, De Gruyter, Berlin.

Hayes P.J. (1984), On the difference between psychology and AI, in M. Yazdani and A. Natayanan (eds.), *Artificial Intelligence: Human Effects*, Horwood, Chichester.

Hebb, D.O. (1949), *The Organization of Behavior*, Wiley and Chapman, New York and London.

Hebb, D.O. (1951-52), The role of neurological ideas in psychology, *Journal of Personality*, 20: 39-55.

Heims, S.J. (1991), *The Cybernetics Group*, MIT Press, Cambridge, Mass.

Herrick, C.J. (1929), *The Thinking Machine*, University of Chicago Press, Chicago.

Hewitt, C. (1991), Open information systems: semantics for distributed artificial intelligence, *Artificial Intelligence*, 47: 79-106.

Hilario, M.(1995), An overview of strategies for neurosymbolic integration, *Connectionist-Symbolic Integration: from Unified to Hybrid approaches*, Working Notes, IJCAI '95, Montreal, August 19-20: 1-6.

Hilgard, E.R. (1936), The nature of the conditioned response. II, *Psychological Review*, 43: 547-564.

Hilgard, E.R. (1956), *Theories of Learning*, Appleton, New York.

Hilgard, E.R. and Marquis, D.G. (1940), *Conditioning and Learning*, Appleton, New York.

Hinde, R.A. (1960), Energy models of motivation, Models and analogues in biology, *Symposia of the Society of Experimental Biology*, n. 14, Cambridge University Press, Cambridge: 199-212

Hobhouse, L.T. (1901), *Mind in Evolution*, Macmillan, London.

Hobhouse, L.T. (1913), *Development and Purpose*, Macmillan, London.

Hodges, A. (1983), *Alan Turing: the Enigma*, Simon and Schuster, New York.

Hofstadter, D.R. and the Fluid Analogies Research Group (1995), *Fluid Concepts and Creative Analogies. Computer Models of the Fundamental Mechanisms of Thought*, Basic Books, New York.

Holland, J.H. (1990), Concerning the emergence of tag-mediated lookahead in classifier systems, *Physica D*, 42: 188-201

Hopfield, J.J. (1982), Neural networks and physical systems with emergent collective computational abilities, *Proceedings of the National Academy of Sciences of U.S.A*, 79: 2554-2558. Reprinted in J.A. Anderson and E. Rosenfeld (1988).

Howard, I.P. (1953), A note on the design of an electro-mechanical maze runner, *Durham Research Review*, n. 4: 54-61.

Hull, C.L. (1929), A functional interpretation of the conditioned reflex, *Psychological Review*, 36: 498-511.

Hull, C.L. (1930a), Simple trial-and-error learning: a study in psychological theory, *Psychological Review*, 37: 241-256.

Hull, C.L. (1930b), Knowledge and purpose as habit mechanisms, *Psychological Review*, 37: 511-525.

Hull, C.L. (1931), Goal attraction and directing ideas conceived as habit phenomena, *Psychological Review*, 38: 487-506.

Hull, C.L. (1932), The goal gradient hypothesis and maze learning, *Psychological Review*, 39: 25-43.

Hull, C.L. (1934), The concept of habit-family hierarchy and maze learning, *Psychological Review*, 41: 33-54 (Part I); 134-152 (Part II).

Hull, C.L. (1935a), Thorndike's *Fundamental of learning*, *Psychological Bulletin*, 32: 807-823.

Hull, C.L. (1935b), The mechanism of the assembly of behavior segments in novel combinations suitable for problem solution, *Psychological Review*, 42: 219-245.

Hull, C.L. (1937), Mind, mechanism, and adaptive behavior, *Psychological Review*, 44: 1-32.

Hull, C.L. (1942), Conditioning: outline of a systematic theory of learning, *Yearb. Nat. Soc. Stud. Educ.*, 41: 61-95.

Hull, C.L. (1943), *The Principles of Behavior*, Appleton-Century, New York.

Hull, C.L. (1952), Clark L. Hull, in G. Boring et al. (eds.), *A History of Psychology in Autobiography*, vol. 4, Clark University Press, Worcester, Mass.: 143-162.

Hull, C.L. (1962), Psychology of the scientist: IV. Passages from the *Idea books* of Clark L. Hull, *Perceptual and Motor Skills*, 15: 814-882.

Hull, C.L. and Baernstein, H.D. (1929), A mechanical parallel to the conditioned reflex, *Science*, 70: 14-15.

Hutchins, W.J. (1986), *Machine Translation. Past, Present and Future*, Horwood, Chichester.

Huxley, J. (1927), Mind considered from the point of view of biology, *Journal of Philosophical Studies*, 2: 328-348.

Huxley, T.H. (1874), On the hypothesis that animals are automata, *Forthnightly Review*, 22: 558-580. Reprinted in T.H. Huxley, *Collected Essays*, vol. 1, Macmillan, London 1893: 199-250.

James, W. (1878), Remarks on Spencer's definition of mind as correspondence, *Journal of Speculative Philosophy*, 12, 1-18. Reprinted in W. James, *Collected Essays and Reviews*, ed. by R.B. Perry, Longmans, London 1920: 43-68.

James, W. (1879), Are we automata?, *Mind*, 4: 1-22.

James, W. (1890), *The Principles of Psychology*, Holt, New York. Dover Edition, New York, 1950, 2 vols.

Jennings, H.S. (1902), Artificial imitations of protoplasmatic activities, and methods for demonstrating them, *Journal of Applied Microscopy and Laboratory Methods*, 5: 1597-1602.

Jennings, H.S. (1904), Physical imitations of the activities of Amoeba, *American Naturalist*, 38: 625-642.

Jennings, H.S. (1906), *Behavior of the Lower Organisms*, Columbia University Press, New York. New edition, with an Introduction by D.D Jensen, Indiana University Press, Bloomington, 1962.

Jennings, H.S. (1908), The interpretation of the behavior of the lower organisms, *Science*, 27: 698-710.

Jennings, H.S. (1909a), The work of J. von Uexküll on the physiology of movements and behavior, *Journal of Comparative Neurology and Psychology*, 19: 313-336.

Jennings, H.S. (1909b), Tropisms, *Rapports du VIme Congrès International de Psychologie*, Genève: 307-324. Kraus-Thomson Edition, Nendeln, Liechtenstein, 1974.

Jennings, H.S. (1910), Diverse ideals and divergent conclusions in the study of behavior in lower organisms, *American Journal of Psychology*, 21: 349-370.

Jennings, H.S. (1927), Diverse doctrines of evolution, their relation to the practice of science and of life, *Science*, 65: 19-25.

Johnson, M.G. and Henley, T.B. (eds.) (1990), *Reflections on* The principles of psychology. *William James after a Century*, Erlbaum, Hillsdale, N.J.

Johnson-Laird, P.N. (1983), *Mental Models*, Cambridge University Press, Cambridge.

Jonçich, J. (1968), *The Sane Positivist. A Biography of Edward L. Thorndike*, Wesleyan University Press, Middletown, Connecticut.

Kejizer, F.A., and Bem, S. (1996), Behavioral systems interpreted as autonomous agents and as coupled dynamical systems: a criticism, *Philosophical Psychology*, 9: 323-346.

Kirsh, D. (1991), Today the earwig, tomorrow man?, *Artificial Intelligence*, 47: 161-184.

Kitano, H., Hamahashi, S. and Luke, S. (1998), The perfect *C. elegans* project: an initial report, *Artificial Life*, 4: 141-156.

Kosslyn, S.M. (1994), *Image and the Brain. The Resolution of the Imagery debate*, MIT Press, Cambridge, Mass.

Krieger, M.J.B., Billeter, J.-B. and Keller, L. (2000), Ant-like allocation and recruitment in cooperative robots, *Nature*, 406: 992-995.

Krim, N.B. (1934), *Electrical circuits illustrating mammalian behavior and their possible engineering value*, Thesis presented for the Degree of Bachelor of Science, Yale Library, Massachusetts Institute of Technology.

Krueger, R.G. and Hull, C.L. (1931), An electro-chemical parallel to the conditioned reflex, *Journal of General Psychology*, 5: 262-269.

Kubanoff, J.H. (1953), Timothy: a robot electronic turtle, *Radio and Television News*, 49, n. 4: 35-38 and 150-154.

Lakoff, G. and Johnson, M. (1999), *Philosophy in the Flesh. The Embodied Mind and its Challenge to Western Thought*, Basic Books, New York.

Lambrinos, D., Maris, M., Kobayashi, H., Labhart, T., Pfeifer, R. and Wehner, R. (1997), An autonomous agent with a polarized light compass, *Adaptive Behavior*, 6: 131-161.

Langley, P., Simon, H.A., Bradshaw, G.L. and Zytkow, J.M. (1987), *Scientific Discovery. Computational Exploration of the Creative Processes*, MIT Press, Cambridge, Mass.

Langton, C.G. (ed.) (1989), *Artificial Life*, Addison-Wesley, Reading, Mass.

Lashley, K.S. (1924), Studies of cerebral function in learning. VI, *Psychological Review*, 31: 369-375.

Lenat, D.B. (1979), On automated scientific theory formation: a case study using the AM program, *Machine Intelligence 9*, Halsted, New York: 251-286.

Lenat, D.B. (1983a), Learning by discovery: three case studies in natural and artificial systems, in R.S. Michalski, J.G. Carbonell and T.M. Mitchell (eds.) (1983), *Machine Learning. An Artificial Intelligence Approach*, Tioga, Palo Alto: 243-306.

Lenat, D.B. (1983b), EURISKO: a program that learns new heuristics and domain concepts, *Artificial Intelligence*, 21: 61-98.

Lenat, D.B. and Brown, J.S. (1984), Why AM and EURISKO appear to work, *Artificial Intelligence*, 23: 269-294.

Lenat, D.B. and Feigenbaum, E.A. (1991), On the thresholds of knowledge, *Artificial Intelligence*, 47: 185-250.

Lillie, R.S. (1915), What is purposive and intelligent behavior from the physiological point of view?, *Journal of Philosophy, Psychology and Scientific Methods*, 12: 589-610.

Lillie, R.S. (1922), Growth in living and non-living systems, *Scientific Monthly*, 14: 113-130.

Lillie, R.S. (1928), Analogies between physiological rhythms and the rhythmical reactions in inorganic systems, *Science*, 67 (1746): 593-598.

Loeb, J. (1900), *Comparative Physiology of the Brain and Comparative Psychology*, Putnam, New York. Italian translation: *Fisiologia Comparata del Cervello e Psicologia Comparata*, with an Introduction by the Author, Sandron, Milan, 1907.

Loeb, J. (1905), *Studies in General Physiology*, University of Chicago Press, Chicago.

Loeb, J. (1906), *The Dynamics of Living Matter*, Macmillan, New York.

Loeb, J. (1912), *The Mechanistic Conception of Life*, University of Chicago Press, Chicago.

Loeb, J. (1915), *Mechanistic science and metaphysical romance*, Yale Review, 4: 766-785.

Loeb, J. (1918), *Forced Movements, Tropisms, and Animal Conduct*, Lippincott, Philadelphia and London.

Lotka, A.J. (1925/1956), *Elements of Physical Biology*, William and Wilkins, Baltimore (2nd edition, with the title *Elements of Mathematical Biology*, Dover, New York, 1956).

MacKay, D.M. (1951), Mindlike behaviour in artefacts, *British Journal for the Philosophy of Science*, 2:105-121.

MacKay, D.M. (1952), Mentality in machines, *Proceedings of the Aristotelian Society*, Supplements, 26: 61-86.

MacKay, D.M. (1954), On comparing the brain with machines, *Advancement of Science*, 10: 402-406.

MacKay, D.M. (1956), Towards an information-flow model of human behavior, *British Journal of Psychology*, 47: 30-43.

MacKay, D.M. (1962), The use of the behavioural language to refer to mechanical processes, *British Journal for the Philosophy of Science*, 13: 89-103.

Maes, P. and Nardi, D. (eds.) (1988), *Meta-level Architectures and Reflection*, Amsterdam, North Holland.

Maretti, E. (1957), Modello meccanico di operazioni mentali, *Atti del Convegno sui Problemi dell' Automatismo*, C.N.R., Rome: 6-14.

Margalef, R. (1968), *Perspectives in Ecological Theory*, University of Chicago Press, Chicago.

Marr, D. (1982), *Vision*, Freeman, New York.

Mataric, M.J. (1990), Navigating with a rat brain: a neurobiologically-inspired model for robot spatial representation, *From Animals to Animats*, MIT Press, Cambridge, Mass.: 169-175.

Mataric, M.J. (1995), Integration of representation into goal-driven behavior-based robots, in L. Steels and R. Brooks (eds.), *The Artificial Life Route to Artificial Intelligence: Building Embodied, Situated Agents*, Erlbaum, Hillsdale, N.J.: 165-181.

Mayr, O. (1970), *The Origins of Feedback Control*, MIT Press, Cambridge, Mass.

McCarthy, J. (1959), Computers with common sense, *Proceedings of the Symposium on Mechanisation of Thought Processes*, vol. 1, H.M. Stationery Office, London, 75-84.

McCarthy, J. (1977) Epistemological problems of Artificial Intelligence, *Proceedings of the Fifth International Joint Conference on Artificial Intelligence*: 1038-1044.

McCarthy, J. (1979), Ascribing mental qualities to machines, in M. Ringle (ed.), *Philosophical Perspectives in Artificial Intelligence*, Harverster, Brighton: 161-195.

McCarthy, J. (1988), Mathematical Logic and Artificial Intelligence, *Daedalus*, 117: 297-311.

McCarthy, J. and Hayes, P.J. (1969), Some philosophical problems from the standpoint of artificial intelligence, *Machine Intelligence 4*, Edinburgh University Press, Edinburgh: 463-502.

McCorduck, P. (1979), *Machines who Think*, Freeman, San Francisco.

McCulloch, W.S. (1953), Summary of the point of agreement reached in the previous nine conferences on cybernetics, in H. von Foerster, M. Mead and H.L. Teuber (ed.), *Cybernetics. Circular Causal Feedback Mechanisms in Biological and Social Systems. Transactions of the Tenth Conference*, Josiah Macy, Jr. Foundation, New York: 69-80.

McCulloch, W.S., Oettinger, A.G., Rochester, N. and O. Schmitt (1956), The design of machines to simulate the behavior of the human brain, *IRE Transactions on Electronic Computers*, EC-5: 240-255.

McCulloch, W.S. and Pitts, W. (1943), A logical calculus of the ideas immanent in nervous activity, *Bulletin of Mathematical Biophysics*, 5: 115-137. Reprinted in J.A. Anderson and E. Rosenfeld (1988).

McDermott, D. (1976), Artificial Intelligence meets natural stupidity, *Sigart Newsletter*, 57: 4-9.

McDermott, D. (1988), A critique of pure reason, *Computational Intelligence*, 3: 155-160.

McDougall, W. (1898), A contribution towards an improvement in psychological method. I, II, III, *Mind*, 7: 15-33, 159-178, 364-387.

McDougall, W. (1901), On the seat of psycho-physical processes, *Brain*, 24, 577-630.

McDougall, W. (1902), The physiological factors of the attention-process. I, *Mind*, 11: 316-351.

McDougall, W. (1903), The physiological factors of the attention-process. II, *Mind*, 12: 289-302.

McDougall, W. (1905), *Primer of Physiological Psychology*, Dent, London.

McDougall, W. (1906), The physiological factors of the attention-process. IV, *Mind*, 15: 329-359.

McDougall, W. (1911), *Body and Mind. A History and a Defense of Animism*, Methuen, London.

McDougall, W. (1923a), *An Outline of Psychology*, Methuen, London.

McDougall, W. (1923b), Purposive or mechanical psychology?, *Psychological Review*, 30: 273-288.

McDougall, W. (1926), Men or robots?, in C. Murchison (ed.), *Psychologies of 1925*, Clark University Press, Worcester, Mass.: 273-305.

McDougall, W. (1929), *Modern Materialism and Emergent Evolution*, Methuen, London.

Mecacci, L. (1979), *Brain and History*, Brunner-Mazel, New York.

Mecacci, L. (1992), *Storia della Psicologia del Novecento*, Laterza, Rome.

Messadié, G. (1961), Une extraordinaire société scientifique, *Science et Vie*, n. 520.

Metropolis, N., Howlett, J. and Rota, G.C. (eds.) (1980), *A History of Computing in Twentieth Century*, Academic Press, New York.

Meyer, J.-A. and Guillot, A. (1994), Four years of animat research, *From Animals to Animats 3*, MIT Press, Cambridge, Mass.: 2-11.

Meyer, M. (1908a), The nervous correlate of pleasantness and unpleasantness, *Psychological Review*, 15: 292-322.

Meyer, M. (1908b), The nervous correlate of attention, *Psychological Review*, 15: 358-372.

Meyer, M. (1909), The nervous correlate of attention. II, *Psychological Review*, 16: 36-47.

Meyer, M. (1911), *The Fundamental Laws of Human Behavior*, Badger, Boston.

Meyer, M. (1912), The present status of the problem of the relation between mind and body, *Journal of Philosophy*, 9: 365-371.

Meyer, M. (1913), The comparative value of various conceptions of nervous function based on mechanical analogies, *American Journal of Psychology*, 24: 555-563.

Meyer, M. (1925), Some nonsense about the 'common path', *Psychological Review*, 32: 431-442.

Meyer, M. (1934), Frequency, duration and recency vs. double stimulation, *Psychological Review*, 41: 177-183.

Michalski, R.S., Carbonell, J.G. and Mitchell, T.M. (eds.) (1983), *Machine Learning. An Artificial Intelligence Approach*, Tioga, Palo Alto.

Miessner, B.F. (1912), The wirelessly directed torpedo. Some new experiments in an old field, *Scientific American*, June: 53.

Miessner, B.F. (1916), *Radiodynamics: The Wireless Control of Torpedoes and Other Mechanisms*, Van Nostrand, New York.

Miessner, B.F. (1964), *On the Early History of Radio Guidance*, San Francisco Press, San Francisco.

Mignault, A. and Marley, A.A. (1997), A real-time neuronal model of classical conditioning, *Adaptive Behavior*, 6: 3-61.

Miller, G.A., Galanter, E. and Pribram, K.H. (1960), *Plans and the Structure of Behavior*, Holt, Rinehart and Winston, London.

Milner, P.M. (1993), The mind and Donald O. Hebb, *Scientific American*, 268 (1): 104-109.

Minsky, M.L. (1959), Some methods of heuristic programming and artificial intelligence, *Proceedings of the Teddington Symposium on Mechanisation of Thought Processes*, vol. 1, H.M. Stationery Office, London: 3-27.

Minsky, M.L. (ed.) (1968), *Semantic Information Processing*, MIT Press, Cambridge, Mass.

Minsky, M.L. (1975), A framework for representing knowledge, in P. Winston (ed.), *The Psychology of Computer Vision*, McGraw-Hill, New York: 211-277.

Minsky, M.L. (ed.) (1985), *Robotics*, Omni Publications International.

Minsky, M.L. (1987), *The Society of Mind*, Simon and Schuster, New York.

Minsky, M.L. (1995), Foreword to Siu, K.-Y., Roychowddhury, V. and Kailath, T., *Discrete Neural Computation. A Theoretical Foundation*, Prentice Hall, Englewood Cliffs, N.J.: xiii-xvii.

Minsky, M.L. and Papert, S. (1969), *Perceptrons*, MIT Press, Cambridge, Mass. Reprinted in 1988, with the Authors' Preface and Postfaction.

Montague, P.R. and Dayan, P. (1998), Neurobiological modeling, in W. Bechtel and G. Graham (eds.), *A Companion to Cognitive Science*, Blackwell, Oxford: 526-541.

Moore, O.K. and Lewis, D.J. (1953), Purpose and learning theory, *Psychological Review*, 60: 149-156.

Morgan, C.L. (1896), Animal automatism and consciousness, *Monist*, 7: 1-18.

Morgan, C.L. (1900), *Animal Behaviour*, Edward Arnold, London.

Morse, T.M., Ferrée, T.C. and Lockery, S.R. (1998), Robust spatial navigation in a robot inspired by chemotaxis in *Caenorhabditis elegans*, *Adaptive Behavior*, 6: 393-410.

Mowrer, O.H. (1960a), *Learning Theory and Behavior*, Wiley, New York.

Mowrer, O.H. (1960b), *Learning Theory and the Symbolic Processes*, Wiley, New York.

Nardi, D. (2000), Artificial Intelligence in Robocup, *ECAI 2000*, Springer, Berlin.

Needham, J. (1928), Recent developments in the philosophy of biology, *Quarterly Review of Biology*, 3: 77-91.

Needham, J. (1929), *The Skeptical Biologist (Ten Essays)*, Chatto and Windus, London.

Negrotti, M. (1999), *The Theory of the Artificial*, Intellect Books, Exeter.

Nemes, T.N. (1969), *Cybernetic Machines*, Iliffe Books and Akadémiai Kiadó, Budapest.

Newell, A. (1973), Artificial Intelligence and the concept of mind, in R.C. Schank and K.M. Kolby (eds.), *Computer Models of Thought and Language*, Freeman, San Francisco.

Newell, A. (1982), The knowledge level, *Artificial Intelligence*, 18: 87-127.

Newell, A (1983), Intellectual issues in the history of Artificial Intelligence, in F. Machlup and U. Mansfield (eds.), *The Study of Information. Interdisciplinary messages*, Wiley, New York: 187-227.

Newell, A. (1990), *Unified Theories of Cognition*, Harvard University Press, Cambridge, Mass.

Newell, A. (1993), Reflections on the knowledge level, *Artificial Intelligence*, 59: 31-38.

Newell, A., Shaw, J.C. and Simon, H.A. (1958), Elements of a theory of human problem-solving, *Psychological Review*, 65: 151-166.

Newell, A., Shaw, J.C. and Simon, H.A. (1962), The processes of creative thinking, in H.E. Gruber, G. Tirrel and H. Wertheimer (eds.), *Contemporary Approaches to Creative Thinking*, Atherton, New York.

Newell, A. and Simon, H.A. (1959), The simulation of human thought, Paper presented at a Program on current Trends in Psychology (P-1734), The University of Pittsburgh, Pittsburgh.

Newell, A. and Simon, H.A. (1963), Computers in psychology, in R.D. Luce, R.R. Bush and E. Galanter (eds.), *Handbook of Mathematical Psychology*, vol. 1, Wiley, New York: 361-428.

Newell, A. and Simon, H.A. (1972), *Human Problem Solving*, Prentice-Hall, Englewood Cliffs, N.J.

Newell, A. and Simon, H.A. (1976), Computer Science as empirical inquiry: symbols and search, *Communications of the ACM*, 19: 113-126.

Newquist, H.P. (1994), *The Brain Makers*, Sams, Indianapolis, Indiana.

Nilsson, N.J. (1971), *Problem Solving Methods in Artificial Intelligence*, McGraw-Hill, New York.

Nolfi, S. and Floreano, D. (2000), *Evolutionary Robotics*, MIT Press, Cambridge, Mass.

Nolfi, S. and Parisi, D. (1995), Evolving non-trivial behaviors on real robots: an autonomous robot that picks up objects, in M. Gori and G. Soda (eds.), *Topics in Artificial Intelligence*, Springer, Berlin.

O'Donnell, J.M. (1985), *The Origins of Behaviorism. American Psychology, 1870-1920*, New York University Press, New York.

Oettinger, A.G. (1952) Programming a digital computer to learn, *Philosophical Magazine*, 43: 1243-1263.

Okada, T. and Simon, H.A. (1997), Collaborative discovery in a scientific domain, *Cognitive Science*, 21: 109-146.

Olson, E.T. (1997), The ontological basis of strong Artificial Life, *Artificial Life*, 3, 29-39.

Papert, S. (1968), McCulloch et la naissance de la cybernétique, in C. Cellérier, S. Papert and G. Voyant, *Cybernétique et Épistémologie*, PUF, Paris.

Papert, S. (1988), One AI or many?, *Daedalus*, 117: 1-14.

Pask, G. (1961), *An Approach to Cybernetics*, Hutchinson, London.

Pattee, H.H. (1989), Simulations, realizations, and theories of life, in C.G. Langton (ed.), *Artificial Life*, Addison-Wesley, Reading, Mass: 63-75.

Pauly, P.J. (1987), *Controlling Life. Jacques Loeb and the Engineering Ideal in Biology*, Oxford University Press, Oxford.

Pavlov, I.P. (1927), *Conditioned Reflexes: An Investigation of the Physiological Activity of the Cerebral Cortex*, English translation, Oxford University Press, Oxford.

Perry, R.B. (1917a), Purpose as systematic unity, *Monist*, 27: 352-375.

Perry, R.B. (1917b), Purpose as tendency and adaptation, *Philosophical Review*, 26: 477-495.

Perry, R.B. (1918), Docility and purposiveness, *Psychological Review*, 25: 1-20.

Perry, R.B. (1935), *The Thought and Character of William James*, vol. 2, Milford, London.

Pfeifer, R. and Verschure, P. (1995), The challenge of autonomous agents: pitfalls and how to avoid them, in L. Steels and R. Brooks (eds.), *The Artificial Life Route to Artificial Intelligence: Building Embodied, Situated Agents*, Erlbaum, Hillsdale, N.J.: 237-263.

Piaget, J. (1941), Le méchanism du développment mental et les lois du groupement des opérations. Esquisse d'une théorie opératoire de l'intelligence, *Archives de Psychologie*, 28: 215-285.

Picard, R.W. (1997), *Affective Computing*, MIT Press, Cambridge, Mass.

Pillsbury, W.B. (1911), *The Essentials of Psychology*, Macmillan, New York.

Poggi, S. (1994), *Gestalt Psychology: Its Origins, Foundations and Influence*, Olschki, Florence.

Postman, L. (1947), The history and present status of the law of effect, *Psychological Bulletin*, 44: 489-563.

Pratt, V. (1987), *Thinking Machines*, Blackwell, Oxford.

Prescott, T.J. (1994), Spatial learning and representation in animats, *From Animals to Animats 3*, MIT Press, Cambridge, Mass.: 164-173.

Prescott, T.J. (1996), Spatial representation for navigation in animats, *Adaptive Behavior*, 4: 85-123.

Putnam, H. (1975), *Mind, Language and Reality. Philosophical Papers*, vol. 2, Cambridge University Press, Cambridge.

Pylyshyn Z.W. (ed.) (1987), *The Robot's Dilemma: the Frame Problem in Artificial Intelligence*, Ablex, Norwood, N.J.

Pylyshyn, Z.W. (1978), Computational models and empirical constraints, *Behavioral and Brain Sciences*, 1: 93-127.

Pylyshyn, Z.W. (1979), Complexity and the study of artificial and human intelligence, in M. Ringle (ed.), *Philosophical Perspectives in Artificial Intelligence*, Harvester, Brighton.

Pylyshyn, Z.W. (1984), *Computation and Cognition. Toward a Foundation for Cognitive Science*, MIT Press, Cambridge, Mass.

Qin, Y. and Simon, H.A. (1990), Laboratory replication of scientific discovery processes, *Cognitive Science*, 14: 281-312.

Randell, B. (ed.) (1975), *The Origins of Digital Computers*, Springer, Berlin.

Raphael, B. (1976), *The Thinking Computer. Mind Inside Matter*, Freeman, San Francisco.

Rashevsky, N. (1931a), Learning as a property of physical systems, *Journal of General Psychology*, 5: 207-229.

Rashevsky, N. (1931b), Possible brain mechanisms and their physical models, *Journal of General Psychology*, 5: 368-406.

Rashevsky, N. (1935), Outline of a physico-mathematical theory of the brain, *Journal of General Psychology*, 13: 82-112.

Rashevsky, N. (1938/1960), *Mathematical Biophysics. Physico-Mathematical Foundations of Biology*, University of Chicago Press, Chicago (2nd edition: Dover, New York, 1960, 2 vols.).

Redish, A.D. (1999), *Beyond the Cognitive Map*, MIT Press, Cambridge, Mass.

Reeke, G.N., Sporns, O. and Edelman, G.M. (1989), Synthetic neural modelling: comparisons of population and connectionist approaches, in R. Pfeifer, Z. Schreter, F. Fogelman-Soulié and L. Steels (eds.), *Connectionism in Perspective*, North Holland, Amsterdam: 113-139.

Richardson, L.F. (1930), The analogy between mental images and sparks, *Psychological Review*, 37: 214-227.

Richman, H.B. and Simon, H.A. (1989), Context effects in letter perception: comparison of two theories, *Psychological Review*, 96: 417-432.

Richman, H.B., Staszewski, J.J. and Simon, H.A. (1995), Simulation of Expert Memory using EPAM IV, *Psychological Review*, 102: 305-330.

Rochester, N., Holland, J.H., Haibt, L.H. and Duda, W.L. (1956), Test on a cell assembly theory of the action of the brain, using a large digital computer, *IRE Transactions on Information Theory*, IT-2: 80-93. Reprinted in J.A. Anderson and E. Rosenfeld (1988).

Rosenblatt, F. (1958), The Perceptron: a probabilistic model for information storage and organization in the brain, *Psychological Review*, 65: 386-408. Reprinted in J.A Anderson and E. Rosenfeld (1988).

Rosenblatt, F. (1959), Two theorems of statistical separability in the Perceptron, *Proceedings of the Teddington Symposium on Mechanisation of Thought Processes*, vol. 1, HMSO, London: 421-450.

Rosenblueth, A. and Wiener, N. (1945), The role of models in science, *Philosophy of Science*, 12: 316-321.

Rosenblueth, A. and Wiener, N. (1950), Purposeful and non-purposeful behavior, *Philosophy of Science*, 17: 318-326.

Rosenblueth, A., Wiener, N. and Bigelow, J. (1943), Behavior, purpose and teleology, *Philosophy of Science*, 10: 18-24.

Rosenfield, I. (1992), *The Strange, Familiar, Forgotten. An Anatomy of Consciousness*, Alfred Knopf, New York.

Ross, T. (1933), Machines that think, *Scientific American*, 148: 206-208.

Ross, T. (1935), Machines that think. A further statement, *Psychological Review*, 42: 387-393.

Ross, T. (1938), The synthesis of intelligence. Its implications, *Psychological Review*, 45: 185-189.

Rossi, P. (1970), *Philosophy, Technology and the Arts in the Earlier Modern Era*, Harper and Row, New York.

Rumelhart, D.E., McClelland, J.L. and the PDP Research Group (1986), *Parallel Distributed Processing: Explorations in the Microstructure of Cognition*, 2 vols., MIT Press, Cambridge, Mass.

Russell, S.B. (1913), A practical device to simulate the working of nervous discharges, *Journal of Animal Behavior*, 3: 15-35.

Russell, S.B. (1915), The function of incipient motor processes, *Psychological Review*, 22: 163-166.

Russell, S.B. (1916), The effect of high resistance in common nerve paths, *Psychological Review*, 23: 231-236.

Russell, S.B. (1917a), Compound substitution in behavior, *Psychological Review*, 24: 62-73.

Russell, S.B. (1917b), Advance adaptation in behavior, *Psychological Review*, 24: 413-425.

Russell, S.B. (1918), Communication, correspondence and consciousness, *Psychological Review*, 25: 341-358.

Russell, S.B. (1920), Brain mechanisms and mental images, *Psychological Review*, 27: 234-245.

Russell, S.B. (1921), The evolution of nerve muscle mechanisms, *Journal of Comparative Psychology*, 1: 395-412.

Samuel, A.L. (1959), Machine learning, *The Technology Review*, 62 (1): 42-45.

Samuel, A.L. (1960), Some moral and technical consequences of automaton—a refutation, *Science*, 132 (3429): 741-742.

Savage, T. and Cowie, R. (1992), Are artificial neural nets as smart as a rat?, *Network*, 3: 47-59.

Schank, R.C. (1972), Conceptual dependency: a theory of natural language understanding, *Cognitive Psychology*, 3: 552-631.

Schank, R.C. and Abelson, R.P. (1977), *Scripts, Plans, Goals and Understanding*, Erlbaum, Hillsdale, N.J.

Schank, R.C. and Nash-Webber, B.L. (eds.) (1975), *Theoretical Issues in Natural Language Processing*, Bolt, Beranek and Newman, Cambridge, Mass.

Searle, J.R. (1980), Minds, brains, and programs, *Behavioral and Brain Sciences*, 3: 417-424.

Sejnowski, T.J., Koch, C. and Churchland, P.S. (1990), Computational neuroscience, in S.J. Hanson and C.R. Olson (eds.), *Connectionist Modeling and Brain Function*, MIT Press, Cambridge, Mass.: 5-35.

Selfridge, O.G. (1959), Pandemonium: a paradigm for learning, *Proceedings of the Teddington Symposium on Mechanisation of Thought Processes*, vol. 1, H.M. Stationery Office, London: 513-526. Reprinted in J.A. Anderson and E. Rosenfeld (1988).

Serra, R. and Zanarini, G. (1994), *Complex Systems and Cognitive Processes*, Springer, Berlin.

Shannon, C.E. (1938), A symbolic analysis of relay and switching circuits, *Transactions of the American Institute of Electrical Engineers*, 57: 713-723.

Shannon, C.E. (1950), Programming a computer for playing chess, *Philosophical Magazine*, 41: 256–275.

Shannon, C.E. (1951), Presentation of a maze-solving machine, in H. von Foerster (ed.), *Cybernetics. Circular Causal Feedback Mechanisms in Biological and Social Systems. Transactions of the Tenth Conference*, Josiah Macy, Jr. Foundation, New York: 173-180.

Shannon, C.E. (1953), Computers and automata, *Proceedings of the IRE*, 41: 1234-1241.

Shen, W.-M., Adibi, J., Adobbati, R., Cho, B., Erdem, A., Moradi, H., Salemi, B. and Tejada, S. (1998), Toward integrated soccer robots, *AI Magazine*, 19 (3): 79-85

Sherrington, C.S. (1906), *The Integrative Action of the Nervous System*, Constable, London.

Siekmann, J. and Wrightson, G. (eds.), (1983), *Automation of Reasoning. Classical papers on Computational Logic*, Springer, Berlin.

Simon, H.A. (1947), *Administrative Behavior*, Macmillan, New York.

Simon, H.A. (1961), The control of mind by reality: human cognition and problem solving, in S.M. Farber and R.H.L. Wilson (eds.), *Man and Civilization*, McGraw-Hill, New York.

Simon, H.A. (1969/1981), *The Sciences of the Artificial*, MIT Press, Cambridge, Mass. (2nd edition: MIT Press, Cambridge, Mass., 1981).

Simon, H.A. (1972), The theory of problem solving, *Proceedings of Information Processing 71*, North Holland, Amsterdam: 261-277.

Simon, H.A. (1973), The structure of ill structured problems, *Artificial Intelligence*, 4: 181-201.

Simon, H.A. (1979), *Models of Thought*, Yale University Press, New Haven and London.

Simon, H.A. (1980), Cognitive science: the newest science of the artificial, *Cognitive Science*, 4: 33-46.

Simon, H.A. (1989), *Models of Thought II*, Yale University Press, New Haven and London.

Simon, H.A. (1991), *Models of My Life*, Basic Books, New York.

Simon, H.A. and Newell, A. (1956), Models: their uses and limitations, in L.D. White (ed.), *The State of the Social Sciences*, Chicago University Press, Chicago: 66-83.

Simon, H.A. and Siklóssy, L. (eds.), *Representation and Meaning*, Prentice-Hall, Englewood Cliffs, N.J.

Sinaiko, H.W. (ed.) (1961), *Selected Papers on Human Factors in the Design and Use of Control Systems*, Dover, New York.

Sluckin, W. (1954), *Minds and Machines*, Penguin Books, Harmondsworth, Middlesex

Smith, F.V. (1960), *Explanation of Human Behaviour*, Constable, London.

Smith, L.D. (1986), *Behaviorism and Logical Positivism. A Reassessment of the Alliance*, Stanford University Press, Stanford, 1986.

Smith, L.D. (1990), Models, mechanism, and explanation in behavior theory: the case of Hull versus Spencer, *Behavior and Philosophy*, 18: 1-18.

Smith, S. (1914), Regulation in behavior, *Journal of Philosophy*, 12: 320-326.

Smith, S. and Guthrie, E.R. (1921), *General Psychology in Terms of Behavior*, Appleton, New York.

Smolensky, P. (1988), On the proper treatment of connectionism, *Behavioral and Brain Sciences*, 11: 1-74.

Somenzi, V. (1956), Can induction be mechanized?, in C. Cherry (ed.), *Information Theory*, Butterworths, London: 226-230.

Somenzi, V. (1987), The 'Italian Operative School', *Methodologia*, 1: 59-66.

Spence, K.W. (1951), Theoretical interpretation of learning, in C.P. Stone (ed.), *Comparative Psychology*, Prentice Hall, New York (3rd edition).

Spencer, H. (1855/1890), *The Principles of Psychology*, Longman, London (3rd edition: William and Norgate, London and Edinburgh, 1890, 2 vols.).

Stanley-Jones, D. and Stanley-Jones, K. (1960), *The kybernetics of natural systems*, Pergamon, Oxford.

Steels, L. (1995), Building agents out of autonomous systems, in L. Steels and R. Brooks (eds.), *The Artificial Life Route to Artificial Intelligence: Building Embodied, Situated Agents*, Erlbaum, Hillsdale, N.J.: 83-121.

Steels, L. (1999), *The Talking Heads Experiment*, vol. 1, Laboratorium, Antwerpen (pre-edition).

Stephens, J.M. (1929), A mechanical explanation of the law of effect, *American Journal of Psychology*, 41, 1929: 422-431.

Stephens, J.M. (1931), Some weaknesses in the explanation of habit fixation as conditioning, *Psychological Review*, 38: 137-152.

Stephens, J.M. (1967), *The Process of Schooling. A Psychological Examination*, Holt, Rinehart and Winston, New York.

Sterelny, K. (1990), *The Representational Theory of Mind*, Blackwell, Oxford.

Sun, R. and Bookman, L.A. (eds.) (1995), *Computational Architectures Integrating Neural and Symbolic Processes*, Kluwer Academic Publishers, Dordrecht.

Sutherland, W.R., Mugglin, M.G. and Sutherland, I. (1958), An electro-mechanical model of simple animals, *Computers and Automation*, 7 (2): 6-8, 23-25, 32.

Thagard, P. (1988), *Computational Philosophy of Science*, MIT Press, Cambridge, Mass.

Tamburrini, G. (1997), Mechanistic theories in cognitive science: the import of Turing's thesis, in ML. Dalla Chiara, K. Doets, D. Mundici and J. van Bentham (eds.), *Logic and Scientific Method*, Kluwer Academic Publishers, Dordrecht: 239-257.

Taube, M. (1961), *Computers and Common Sense. The Myth of Thinking Machines*, Columbia University Press, New York.

Taylor, R. (1950a), Comments on a mechanistic conception of purposefulness, *Philosophy of Science*, 17: 310-317.

Taylor, R. (1950b), Purposeful and non-purposeful behaviour: a rejoinder, *Philosophy of Science*, 17: 327-332.

Taylor, R. (1966), *Action and Purpose*, Prentice-Hall, Englewood Cliffs, N.J.

Taylor, W.K. (1956), Electrical simulation of some nervous system functional activities, in C. Cherry (ed.), *Information Theory*, Butterworths, London: 314-328.

Tesauro, G. (1986), Simple neural models of classical conditioning, *Biological Cybernetics*, 55: 187-200.

Tesauro, G. (1990), Neural models of classical conditioning: a theoretical viewpoint, in S.J. Hanson and C.R. Olson (eds.), *Connectionist Modeling and Brain Function*, MIT Press, Cambridge, Mass.: 74-104.

Thorndike, E.L. (1898), Animal intelligence. An experimental study of the associative processes in animals, *Psychological Review*, Series of Monograph Supplements, 2, n.4.

Thorndike, E.L. (1908), A pragmatic substitute for free will, in *Essays Philosophical and Psychological*, Longmans, Green and Co., New York.

Thorndike, E.L. (1911), *Animal Intelligence*, Macmillan, New York.

Thorndike, E.L. (1914), *Educational Psychology. Briefer Course*, Teacher College, Columbia University Press, New York.

Thorndike, E.L. (1915), Watson's *Behavior*, *Journal of Animal Behavior*, 5: 462-467.

Thorndike, E.L. (1919), *The Elements of Psychology*, Seiler, New York (2nd edition).

Thorndike, E.L. (1931), *Human Learning*, Macmillan, New York.

Thorndike, E.L. (1932), *The Fundamentals of Learning*, Teacher College, Columbia University Press, New York.

Thornton, C. (1997), Brave mobots use representation: emergence of representation in fight-or-flight learning, *Minds and Machines*, 7: 475-494.

Tolman, E.C. (1925), Behaviorism and purpose, *Journal of Philosophy*, 22: 36-41. Reprinted in E.C. Tolman (1958).

Tolman, E.C. (1939), Prediction of vicarious trial and error by means of the schematic sowbug, *Psychological Review*, 46: 318-336. Reprinted in E.C. Tolman (1958).

Tolman, E.C. (1948), Cognitive maps in rats and men, *Psychological Review*, 55:189-208. Reprinted in E.C. Tolman (1958).

Tolman, E.C. (1958), *Behavior and Psychological Man*, University of California Press, Berkeley and Los Angeles.

Trautteur, G. (ed.) (1995), *Consciousness: Distinction and Reflection*, Bibliopolis, Naples.

Trautteur, G. (1999), Analog computation and the continuum-discrete conundrum, in R. Lupacchini and G. Tamburrini (eds.), *Grounding the Effective Processes in Empirical Laws. Reflections on the Notion of Algorithm*, Bulzoni, Rome: 23-42.

Troland, L.T. (1928), *The Fundamentals of Human Motivation*, Van Nostrand, New York.

Turing, A.M. (1936-37), On computable numbers, with an application to the *Entscheidungsproblem*, *Proceeding of the London Mathematical Society* (2nd series), 42: 230-265; 43: 544.

Turing, A.M. (1950), Computing machinery and intelligence, *Mind*, 59: 433-460

Tustin, A. (1953), Do modern mechanisms help us to understand the mind?, *British Journal of Psychology*, 44: 24-37.

Uexküll, J. von (1903), Studien über den Tonus. I, *Zeitschrift für Biologie*, 44: 269-243.

Uexküll, J. von (1908), Die Neuen Fragen in der Experimentallen Biologie, *Rivista di Scienza-Scientia*, 3: 72-86.

Uexküll, J. von (1920), *Theoretische Biologie*, Springer, Berlin. English translation: *Theoretical Biology*, Kegan Paul, London, 1926.

Uttley, A.M. (1954), The classification of signals in the nervous system, *EEG Clinical Neurophysiology*, 6: 479-484.

Uttley, A.M. (1959), The design of conditional probability computers, *Information and Control*, 2: 1-24.

van de Vijver, G. (ed.) (1992), *New Perspectives on Cybernetics. Self-Organization, Autonomy and Connectionism*, Kluwer Academic Publishers, Dordrecht.

van Gelder, T. (1995), What might cognition be, if not computation, *Journal of Philosophy*, 91: 345-381.

Vera, A.H. and Simon, H.A. (1993), Situated action: a symbolic interpretation, *Cognitive Science*, 17: 7-48.

Verschure, P.F.M.J. (1993), Formal minds and biological brains, *IEEE Expert*, 8 (5): 66-75.

Verschure, P.F.M.J., Wray, J., Sporns, O., Tononi, T. and Edelman, G.M. (1995), Multilevel analysis of classical conditioning in a behaving real world artifact, *Robotics and Autonomous Systems*, 16: 247-265.

von Foester, H. and Zopf, G.W. (eds.) (1961), *Principles of Self-Organization*, Pergamon, Oxford.

Walker, S.F. (1990), A brief history of connectionism and its psychological implications, *Artificial Intelligence and Society*, 4: 17-38.

Wallace, R.A. (1952), The maze-solving computer, *Proceedings of the ACM*, Rimbach, Pittsburgh: 119-125.

Walter, W. G. (1950), An imitation of life, *Scientific American*, 182: 42-45.

Walter, W. G. (1951), A machine that learns, *Scientific American*, 185: 60-63.

Walter, W. G. (1953), *The Living Brain*, Duckworth, London.

Walter, W. G. (1956), 'Thinking machines', *Process Control and Automation*, 3 (12): 428-434.

Walton, A. (1930), Conditioning illustrated by an automatic mechanical device, *American Journal of Psychology*, 42: 110-111.

Warren, H.C. (1914), The mental and the physical, *Psychological Review*, 21: 79-100.

Warren, H.C. (1916), A study of purpose. I, II, III, *Journal of Philosophy, Psychology and Scientific Methods*, 13: 5-26; 29-49; 57-72.

Waters, R.H. (1948), Mechanomorphism: new term for an old mode of thought, *Psychological Review*, 55: 139-142.

Watson, J.B. (1913), Psychology as the behaviorist views it, *Psychological Review*, 20: 158-177.

Watson, J.B. (1914), *Behavior: an Introduction to Comparative Psychology*, Holt, New York.

Watson, J.B. (1919), *Psychology from the Standpoint of a Behaviorist*, Lippincott, Philadelphia.

Wehner, R., Michel, B. and Antonsen, P. (1996), Visual navigation in insects: coupling of egocentric and geocentric information, *Journal of Experimental Biology*, 199: 129-140.

Weizenbaum, J. (1976), *Computer Power and Human Reason*, Freeman: San Francisco.

Wiener, N. (1948/1961), *Cybernetics, or Control and Communication in the Animal and the Machine*, MIT Press, Cambridge, Mass. (2nd edition: MIT Press, Cambridge, Mass., 1961).

Wiener, N. (1950), *The Human Use of Human Beings*, Houghton Mifflin, Boston.

Wilkes, M.V. (1951), Can machines think?, *Spectator*, n. 6424: 177-178.

Wilkes, M.V. (1953), Can machines think?, *Proceedings of the IRE*, 41: 1230-1234.

Wilson, S.W. (1990), The animat path to AI, *From Animals to Animat*, MIT Press, Cambridge, Mass: 15-21.

Winograd, T. (1972), *Understanding Natural Language*. Academic Press: New York.

Winograd, T. and Flores, F. (1986), *Understanding Computers and Cognition: A New Foundation for Design*, Ablex, Norwood, N.J.

Wyckoff, Jr., L.B. (1954), A mathematical model and an electronic model for learning, *Psychological Review*, 61: 89-97.

Wyeth, G. and Browning, B. (1998), Cognitive models of spatial navigation from a robot builder's perspective, *Adaptive Behavior*, 6: 509-534.

Yerkes, R.M. (1906), Objective nomenclature, comparative psychology and animal behavior, *Journal of Comparative Neurology and Psychology*, 16: 380-390.

Yovits, M.C. and Cameron, S. (eds.) (1960), *Self-Organizing Systems*, Pergamon, Oxford.

Yovits, M.C., Jacobi, G.T. and Goldstein, G.D. (eds.) (1962), *Self-Organizing Systems 1962*, Spartan Books, Washington.

Zangwill, O.L. (1980), Kenneth Craik: the man and his work, *British Journal of Psychology*, 71: 1-16.

Zeleny, M., Klir, G.J. and Huddorf, K.D. (1989), Precipitation membranes. Osmotic growths and synthetic biology, in C.G. Langton (ed.), *Artificial Life*, Addison-Wesley, Reading, Mass: 125-139.

Zemanek, H. (1958), La tortue de Vienne et les autres travaux cybernétique, *Actes du 1er Congrès International de Cybernétique*, Gauthier-Villars, Paris: 770-780.

Zemanek, H., Kretz, H. and Angyan, A.J. (1961), A model for neurophysiological function, in C. Cherry (ed.), *Information Theory*, Butterworths, London: 270-284.

Zuriff, G.E. (1985), *Behaviorism: a Conceptual Reconstruction*, Columbia University Press, New York.

LIST OF MACHINES

The list includes all machines mentioned or described in the text and in the Plates up to the early developments of AI. The year is usually that of the publication of the machine's description. When the original description has not been found, the author of the description is mentioned.

1912   Chess playing machine by L. Torres y Quevedo, built in 1912 and described by C. Eames and R. Eames

1913   Models of learning by S. Bent Russell

1914   Phototropic automaton ("electric dog") Seleno by J.H. Hammond Jr. and B.F. Miessner

1920   Automatic correlation calculating machine by C.L. Hull, described by C. Eames and R. Eames "Protozoon" by F. Lux, described by T.N. Nemes

1925   Mechanical "beetle", described by A.J. Lotka

1929   Trail-and-error learning model by J.M. Stephens
        Phototropic automaton Philidog, described by P. de Latil

1930   Model of learning by L.F. Richardson
        Model of conditioning by A. Walton

1931   Model of conditioning by H.D. Baernstein and C.L. Hull
        Model of conditioning by Krueger and C.L. Hull
        Models of learning by N. Rashevsky

1933   Trial-and-error learning model by G.K. Bennett and L.B. Ward
        Maze-solver machine ("arm") by T. Ross

1934   Models of learning by N.B. Krim

1935   Trial-and-error learning model by D.G. Ellson
        Maze-solver machine ("robot rat") by T. Ross, in collaboration with B. Sullivan, W.A Dillman and S. Smith

1936   Universal machine by A.M. Turing

1937   Maze-solver robot by H. Bradner

1938   Models of memory by T. Ross

1939 Phototropic automaton, described by P. de Latil
   Design for a hypothetical robot ("schematic sowbug") by E.C. Tolman

1941 Z3 computer by K. Zuse

1943 Different feedback devices by K.J.W. Craik
   COLOSSUS computer by T.H. Flowers and W.W. Chandler

1944 Mark I computer by H. Aiken

1946 Homeostat by W. Ross Ashby
   ENIAC computer by J.P. Eckert and J.W. Mauchley

1949 EDSAC computer by M. Wilkes, W. Renwick, D.J. Wheeler and coworkers
   MADM computer by F. Williams, T. Kilburn and M.H.A. Newman
   (with A.M. Turing working on the software side of the machine)

1950 ACE computer by G.G. Alway, D. Davies, J.H. Wilkinson
   and M. Woodger (design by A.M. Turing)
   Model of simple conditioned reflex by W. Ross Ashby
   Small "electric brain" by E.C Berkeley and R.A. Jensen
   Szeged phototropic robot, described by T.N. Nemes
   Design for chess-playing computer programs by C. Shannon
   Phototropic robot by H. Singleton, described by N. Wiener
   Machina speculatrix by W. Grey Walter

1951 Phototropic robot Squee by E.C. Berkeley
   Brain Analogy model by H.E. Coburn
   NIMROD computer, built by the Ferranti
   Snarc learning machine by M. Minsky
   Maze-solver machine ("finger") by C. Shannon
   EDVAC computer built by R.L. Snyder, S.E. Gluck and W.H. Boghosian
   (early design by J. von .Neumann)
   Machina docilis by W. Grey Walter
   Early experiments in machine translation by Y. Bar-Hillell,
   followed by A.G. Oettinger, M. Masterman and S. Ceccato

1952 Learning computer programs by A.G. Oettinger
   Checkers program by A.L. Samuel
   Maze-solver machine ("mouse") by C.E. Shannon
   Checkers program by C.S Strackey
   Maze-solver machine by R.A. Wallace

1953   DEUCE computer, built by the Teddington National Physical Laboratory
        and the English Electric Company
        Maze-solver machine by I.P. Howard
        Phototropic robot Timothy by J.H. Kubanoff

1954   Maze-solver machine by J.A. Deutsch
        Early work on chess-playing programs by A. Newell and H.A. Simon
        Neural net models by A.M. Uttley
        Model of learning by L.B. Wyckoff

1955   Computer simulation of Hebb's learning theory by N. Rochester, J.H. Holland,
        L.H. Haibt and W.L. Duda
        Checkers learning program by A.L. Samuel
        Exemplar of a *Machina speculatrix* , described by H. Zemanek

1956   Model of some mental operations Adamo II by S. Ceccato and E. Maretti
        Associative-memory nets by W. K. Taylor
        Exemplar of a Homeostat, described by H. Zemanek
        Logic Theorist (Logic Theory Machine) by A. Newell, J.C. Shaw
        and H.A. Simon

1958   *Mechano trolley*, described by A.M. Andrew
        General Problem Solver by A. Newell, J.C. Shaw and H.A. Simon
        Perceptron by F. Rosenblatt

1959   *Machina reproducatrix* by A.J. Angyan
        Geometry Theorem Machine by H. Gelernter and coworkers
        Advice Taker by J. McCarthy
        Pandemonium by O.G. Selfridge
        Machina versatilis by W.R. Sutherland, M.G. Mugglin and I. Sutherland

1960   *Machina combinatrix* by A.J. Angyan, described by H. Zemanek and H. Kretz
        Maze-solver machine by R. Eier and H. Zemanek
        Adaline neural net by B. Widrow and M.E. Hoff

1961   E. Caianiello's mathematical learning theory, later implemented
        in the electronic neural-net simulator DIANA by E. Burattini and F. Marciano
        Perceptron PAPA by A. Gamba, L. Gamberini, G. Palmieri and R. Sanna
        Early experiments with a scene-analysis program by L. Roberts
        Machina combinatrix (modified version) by H. Zemanek, H. Kretz
        and A.J. Angyan

NAME INDEX

Abelson, R.P. 203
Abraham, T. 94 n.
Abrahamsen, A. 214 n., 215, 257 n., 276
Ackoff, R.L. 150 n.
Adams, B. 240
Aiken, H. 154, 173
Aizawa, K. 94 n., 218 n., 243 n.
Albertazzi, L. 259 n.
Amit, D. 216 n.
Ammons, R.B. 112
Anderson, J.A. 212-214, 216-218
Andrew, A.M. 164
Angyan, A.J. 162-164, 187
Apter, M.J. 151 n., 229-230
Aristotle, 218
Armstrong, D.M. 245
Ash, M.G. 105 n.
Ashby, W.R. xv, xviii, 18, 25-27, 77, 119-120, 151-153, 158, 163, 170, 172, 174 n., 176, 186-187, 189, 226 n., 231, 243 n., 246, 250, 257 n., 275
Attneave, F. 168 n.

Babbage, C. 171
Backus, J. 181, 187
Baernstein, H.D. xv, 85-86, 88-89, 90, 92, 94, 96-97, 106, 110-111, 114, 144, 223
Bain, A. 34-35, 39, 42, 44, 54 n., 65, 217
Baldwin, M.J. 18-19, 21, 52
Ballard, D.H. 232, 253
Bancroft, W.D. 125-126
Barenfeld, M. 208
Bar-Hillel, Y. 192-194, 201 n., 203 n.
Barnden, J.A. 214-215
Barsalou, L.W. 215 n., 271 n.
Bartlett, F.C. 143 n., 168 n.
Baylor, G. 208 n.
Bechtel, W. 211 n., 214 n., 215, 246 n., 251 n., 253-254, 257 n., 276
Beer, R. 231 n.

Beer, S. 174 n., 231 n., 275 n.
Beer, T. 71 n., 231 n.
Bem, S. 257 n.
Bennett, G.K. 92, 111
Berkeley, E.C. 160-161, 164
Bernard, C. 17 n., 21
Bernstein, J. 189 n.
Bethe, A. 10 n., 71 n.
Bigelow, J. xii-xiii, 117-118, 119 n., 120-121, 128, 130, 139, 141, 144 n., 150 n., 153, 165-166, 173, 241, 259, 263 n.
Binet, A. 9
Black, F. 198
Blanzieri, E. 219, 224
Bledsoe, W.W. 200
Block, N. 246 n.
Boakes, R. 9 n., 11 n., 37 n., 122 n.
Bobrow, D.G. 194-195, 202 n.
Boccignone, G. 278 n.
Boden, M.A. 116 n., 136, 186, 271 n., 278
Böhm, C. 181
Bonasso, P. 238
Bookman, L.A. 214 n.
Boring, E.G. xix, 105, 112-113, 137, 150 n., 230
Borsellino, A. xix
Bouquet, P. 202 n.
Bowden, B.V. 177 n.
Bower, G.H. 215 n.
Bradner, H. xv, 108-110, 146, 162-163, 230, 248
Braitenberg, V. xii, xix, 213, 230, 259
Brentano, F. 259
Broadbent, D.E. 168-169, 179, 183
Brooks, R. 232-234, 238, 240, 257-259, 266, 269, 272, 278
Brown, J.S. 210
Browning, B. 234, 237-239, 270
Buckley, K.W. 63

Pitts, W. 94 n., 114, 153-154, 165, 174-
    175, 187-188, 241, 243, 278
Poggi, S. 105 n.
Poggio, T. 206, 270-271
Pollack, J.B. 214-215
Polya, G. 178
Postman, L. 54 n., 75 n., 82 n.
Pratt, V. 171 n.
Prawitz, D. 199
Prescott, T.J. 234 n.
Pribram, K.H. 76 n., 114, 117
Putnam, H. 199, 245, 246 n., 250, 253,
Pylyshyn, Z.W. 202 n., 211-212, 244-
    245, 251-252, 254 n., 255, 257-
    258, 261-264, 269, 271 n., 277 n.

Qin, Y. 209
Quillian, M.R. 193-194, 196, 202-203,
    235 n.

Raphael, B. 194, 200
Rashevsky, N. xiii, xv, 94-98, 101, 112,
    116, 187, 228-229, 242-243, 260,
    274
Redish, A.D. 234 n.
Reeke, G.N. 226, 255
Reichardt, W. 271
Reiter, R. 238 n.
Richardson, L.F. 162 n.
Richman, H.B. 208, 215
Roberts, L. 205
Robinson, J.A. 199, 200 n.
Rochester, N. 174-176, 180, 183, 191,
    212, 233 n., 248
Romanes, G. 9
Rosenblatt, F. 187-189, 212, 213 n., 216,
    218, 243-244, 258, 273, 275-276
Rosenbloom, P. 207
Rosenblueth, A. xii-xiii,,114, 117, 119-
    121, 128, 130-131, 132 n., 139,
    141, 144 n., 145 n., 150 n., 153,
    165-166, 173, 228 n., 241, 245,
    256 n., 259, 263 n., 268, 274

Rosenfeld, E. 213 n., 214, 216-217
Rosenfield, I. xix, 226 n.
Ross, T. xv-xv, 106-109, 111, 157-158,
    160, 162, 172, 239, 247, 250, 275
Rossi, P. 7 n., 12 n.
Roychowdury, V. 276 n.
Rumelhart, D. 213, 215
Russell, B. 180
Russell, S.B. xii-xiii, xv, 31-33, 56-63,
    66-72, 74-75, 76 n., 80-81, 86,
    126, 246-247, 255, 274
Rutishauser, H. 181

Sachs, J. 1
Samuel, A.L. xv, 173, 176-178, 180, 190,
    234 n., 261
Savage, T. 218 n., 219 n.
Schank, R.C. 202-203, 206, 211
Schmitt, O. 174-176, 189
Searle, J.R. 260-261, 264-265
Sejnowski, T.J. 224, 255
Selfridge, O.G. 178, 180, 187-188
Serra, R. 257 n.
Shannon, C.E. 153, 158-160, 162-163,
    165, 171, 173-174, 176-178, 239
Shaw, J.C. 178-183, 184 n., 186, 190,
    199, 202
Shen, W.-M. 238 n.
Sherrington, C.S. 42, 44, 67 n.
Sherwood, S. 140 n.
Siekmann, J. 191 n., 200 n.
Siklóssy, L. 191,195-196
Simmons P.L. xvii, xix
Simmons R.F. xvii, xix
Simon, H.A. xvi-xvii, xx, 142 n., 155,
    178-187, 190-197, 199-200, 202,
    205-211, 215, 226 n., 227, 230,
    244 n., 245 n., 248, 251, 258 n.,
    266-267, 269-270, 271 n., 272-
    273, 276 n., 277
Sinaiko, H.W. 143 n.
Singleton, H. 166
Siu, K.-Y., 276 n.

Ward, L.B. 92, 111
Warren, H.C. 104 n., 123-130, 133-135,
    142, 144, 259
Watson, J.B. 30, 33, 46 n., 47 n., 58, 63-67,
    75 n., 80, 82, 84, 101-102, 105 n.,
    112
Watt, J. 118, 257
Weaver, W. 192
Wehner, R. 236, 271
Weizenbaum, J. 196
Wells, O.D. 174 n.
Weyhrauch, R. 210
Whitehead, A.N. 180
Widrow, B. 212
Wiener, N. xi-xiii, xv, xvii, 6-7, 113-115,
    117-121, 125, 128, 130-131, 132 n.,
    139, 141-143, 144 n., 145 n., 149 n.,
    153, 158, 163, 166, 173, 174 n.,
    178, 227, 228 n., 241, 245, 256 n.,
    258-259, 261 n., 263 n., 268-269,
    274-275
Wilkes, M.V. 154, 171-173, 264 n.
Wilson, S. 231
Winograd, T. 204, 206, 211, 258 n.
Winston, P. 205
Wöhler, F. 228
Wrightson, G. 191 n., 200 n.
Wyckoff, L.B., Jr. 169-170, 183, 248
Wyeth, G. 234, 237-239, 270

Yerkes, R.M. 30, 82 n.
Yovits, M.C. 212 n.

Zadeh, L. 202
Zanarini, G. 257 n.
Zangwill, O.L. 137 n., 144 n.
Zeleny, M. 230
Zemanek, H. 160, 162 n., 163
Zopf, G.W. 212 n.
Zuriff, G.E. 116 n.
Zuse, K. 154

SUBJECT INDEX

ACE, 154

Action system, 1-2, 17-21, 23-28, 53, 77 n., 172 n., 228 n., 262

Adaline, 212

Adamo II, 162 n.

Adaptation, 11, 13, 18, 23, 28, 54 n., 83, 88, 114-115, 119-122, 126, 129, 133, 145, 151-152, 158, 184 n., 189, 231-232, 241, 247

Advice Taker, 198-201

AI (Artificial Intelligence), xi, xiv, xvii-xviii, 132 n., 142, 143 n., 155, 170, 174, 176, 178 ff., 185, 187 ff., 244 ff.

distributed, 229 n.; *see also* Multi-agent systems

nouvelle, xviii, 249, 279

strong vs weak, 261

ALife (Artificial Life), xi, xviii, 190, 226, 229-232, 236, 249, 254, 256-257, 273, 275, 278 n., 279

Allen, 233, 258-259

AM, 209-210, 214, 269 n.

ANALOGY, 194

Analytic method, 2, 17, 20, 25, 28-29, 144, 146, 247; *see also* Synthetic approach; Synthetic method

Animat, 231-232, 235

Anticipation, 102, 104, 116, 123-125, 128, 135, 145, 148; *see also* Teleology

Anticipatory goal reaction, 103-104, 116, 216, 243, 245, 267

Aplysia, 219-220, 222-224, 232, 250

Artificial

amoeba, 227-228

as algorithmic/computational, xiii, 276

as inorganic/non-symbolic, xiii, 276

cell, 230

eye, 100

discovery of, xi ff., 33, 72, 84, 94, 116, 138, 145, 151, 153, 162, 190, 193, 217-218, 226-227, 240, 241 ff.

Intelligence, *see* AI

Life, 229-230; *see also* ALife

living system, 229

membrane, 228

muscle, 229

neural nets, *see* Neural nets

vision, *see* Vision, computer

ARTORGA, 174 n.

Associationism, 32-33, 44, 52, 54, 82-84, 91, 105, 136 n., 171, 175, 183, 193, 214, 216-218, 219 n., 242-243, 248, 257, 275

Attraction of nervous impulse, law of, 40-41, 44-45, 47, 57

Automaton, xii, 30, 37 n.

Cartesian, 137, 266

clockwork, xiii, 7

Craikian, 137-138, 142, 145, 266-268

Edelman's, 226, 264

Longuet-Higgins', 137, 266

negative-feedback, xiii, 7, 20

phototropic, xii, 7-9, 26, 122, 155, 160, 230

selfacting (teleautomaton), 5

Theories, 32, 48-49, 68, 96, 116, 123 n.; *see also* Gost Theories

Autonomics, 229

BACON, 209

Behaviorism, xiii, 30, 63, 68-69, 101, 112, 133 n., 136, 168 n., 184, 218, 245, 257

Block worlds, 205

Boolean algebra, 153, 160-161, 187

Bounded rationality, 178, 181, 244 n.

Caenorhabditis Elegans, 235-236

Cataglyphis, 236

Cell assemblies, 216, 243

Checkers, xv, 173-174, 176-177, 190, 234 n.

STUDIES IN COGNITIVE SYSTEMS

1. J.H. Fetzer (ed.): *Aspects of Artificial Intelligence*. 1988
ISBN 1-55608-037-9; Pb 1-55608-038-7
2. J. Kulas, J.H. Fetzer and T.L. Rankin (eds.): *Philosophy, Language, and Artificial Intelligence.*
Resources for Processing Natural Language. 1988 ISBN 1-55608-073-5
3. D.J. Cole, J.H. Fetzer and T.L. Rankin (eds.): *Philosophy, Mind and Cognitive Inquiry.*
Resources for Understanding Mental Processes. 1990 ISBN 0-7923-0427-6
4. J.H. Fetzer: *Artificial Intelligence: Its Scope and Limits*. 1990
ISBN 0-7923-0505-1; Pb 0-7923-0548-5
5. H.E. Kyburg, Jr., R.P. Loui and G.N. Carlson (eds.): *Knowledge Representation and Defeasible
Reasoning*. 1990 ISBN 0-7923-0677-5
6. J.H. Fetzer (ed.): *pistemology and Cognition*. 1991 ISBN 0-7923-0892-1
7. E.C. Way: *Knowledge Representation and Metaphor*. 1991 ISBN 0-7923-1005-5
8. J. Dinsmore: *Partitioned Representations*. A Study in Mental Representation, Language Understanding and Linguistic Structure. 1991 ISBN 0-7923-1348-8
9. T. Horgan and J. Tienson (eds.): *Connectionism and the Philosophy of Mind*. 1991
ISBN 0-7923-1482-4
10. J.A. Michon and A. Akyürek (eds.): *Soar: A Cognitive Architecture in Perspective*. 1992
ISBN 0-7923-1660-6
11. S.C. Coval and P.G. Campbell: *Agency in Action*. The Practical Rational Agency Machine.
1992 ISBN 0-7923-1661-4
12. S. Bringsjord: *What Robots Can and Can't Be*. 1992 ISBN 0-7923-1662-2
13. B. Indurkhya: *Metaphor and Cognition*. An Interactionist Approach. 1992
ISBN 0-7923-1687-8
14. T.R. Colburn, J.H. Fetzer and T.L. Rankin (eds.): *Program Verification*. Fundamental Issues in
Computer Science. 1993 ISBN 0-7923-1965-6
15. M. Kamppinen (ed.): *Consciousness, Cognitive Schemata, and Relativism*. Multidisciplinary
Explorations in Cognitive Science. 1993 ISBN 0-7923-2275-4
16. T.L. Smith: *Behavior and its Causes*. Philosophical Foundations of Operant Psychology. 1994
ISBN 0-7923-2815-9
17. T. Dartnall (ed.): *Artificial Intelligence and Creativity*. An Interdisciplinary Approach. 1994
ISBN 0-7923-3061-7
18. P. Naur: *Knowing and the Mystique of Logic and Rules*. 1995 ISBN 0-7923-3680-1
19. P. Novak: *Mental Symbols*. A Defence of the Classical Theory of Mind. 1997
ISBN 0-7923-4370-0
20. G.R. Mulhauser: *Mind Out of Matter*. Topics in the Physical Foundations of Consciousness
and Cognition. 1998 ISBN 0-7923-5103-7
21. K.L. Butler: *Internal Affairs*. Making Room for Psychosemantic Internalism. 1998
ISBN 0-7923-5261-0
22. B.A. Thyer (ed.): *The Philosophical Legacy of Behaviorism*. 1999 ISBN 0-7923-5736-1
23. D. Livingstone Smith. *Freud's Philosophy of the Unconscious*. 1999 ISBN 0-7923-5882-1
24. M. Perlman: *Conceptual Flux*. Mental Representation, Misrepresentation, and Concept Change.
2000 ISBN 0-7923-6215-2
25. J.H. Fetzer: *Computers and Cognition: Why Minds are Not Machines*. 2001
ISBN 0-7923-6615-8

STUDIES IN COGNITIVE SYSTEMS

KLUWER ACADEMIC PUBLISHERS – DORDRECHT / BOSTON / LONDON